Democratizing Capital

Democratizing Capital

The History, Law, and Reform of the Community Reinvestment Act

Richard D. Marsico
Professor of Law
New York Law School

Carolina Academic Press
Durham, North Carolina

Library of Congress Cataloging-in-Publication Data

Marsico, Richard, 1960–
Democratizing capital / by Richard Marsico.
p. cm.
Includes index.
ISBN 0-89089-329-2 (alk. paper)
1. United States. Community Reinvestment Act of 1977. 2. Bank loans--Law and legislation--United States. 3. Community development--Law and legislation--United States. I. Title.

KF1035.M37 2004
346.73'0821753--dc22

2004019515

Carolina Academic Press
700 Kent Street
Durham, North Carolina 27701
Telephone (919) 489-7486
Fax (919) 493-5668
www.cap-press.com

Printed in the United States of America

To my wife, whose support, encouragement, and enthusiasm through countless hours made this book possible.

To my parents, thank you for everything.

To my children, in the hope that they will live in a society in which the spirit of laws like the Community Reinvestment Act has reached its full potential.

ACKNOWLEDGMENTS

This book would not have been possible without the help of several people and organizations; I thank them here at the risk of leaving some out.

I thank the many clients, students, organizations, and colleagues with whom I have worked on CRA challenges and issues, including Asian Americans for Equality, Center for Community Change, Community Coalition for Fair Banking, Ecumenical Community Development Organization, Fifth Avenue Committee, Inner City Press/Community on the Move, Interfaith Center for Corporate Responsibility, National Community Reinvestment Coalition, Neighborhood Economic Development Advocacy Project, New York State Division of Human Rights, South Brooklyn Legal Services, David Berenbaum, Ray Brescia, Carol Buckler, Michelle Cotton, Allen Fishbein, Debbie Goldberg, Larry Grosberg, Jasmine Hopper, Donna Katzin, Lori Keitz, Richard Krulik, Chris Kui, Brad Lander, Matthew Lee, Sarah Ludwig, Josh Silver, John Taylor, April Tyler, and Jean Vernet.

I thank Professor Roberto Unger, whose law school seminar taught me that social reform and economic development are not necessarily in conflict.

I thank my research assistants, especially In-Yu Woo, Scott Lustig, Anna Shusterman, Megan Eiss-Proctor, and Robert Whalen.

I thank my assistants Susan Demaio and Cathy Jenkins.

For their comments on earlier drafts, I thank Jean Marie Brescia, Steve Ellmann, Josh Silver, Michael Sinclair, and the participants in several New York Law School Tuesday Faculty Lunches.

Finally, I thank New York Law School for its generous financial support of my research.

Contents

Democratizing Capital

Introduction

The term "democratizing capital" in this book's title has two related meanings, and the Community Reinvestment Act ("CRA") democratizes capital in both ways.[1] The first may be analogized to voting. The CRA has democratized decisions about the distribution of capital by extending at least part of the decision-making "franchise" to previously "disenfranchised" people, in particular low-income and minority persons.[2] Second, the CRA has played a role in distributing loans to people—particularly low-income and minority individuals—who previously did not receive loans, thus including them in the economic mainstream and giving them the same economic opportunity as others.[3] The CRA has done this by influencing banks to make loans to low-income and minority individuals to purchase, refinance, or improve a home; to open or expand a small business; or to support a small farm.[4]

The seeds for democratizing capital are contained in the statute that enacted the CRA. The CRA imposes on banks a "continuing and affirmative obligation to help meet the credit needs of the local communities in which they are chartered,"[5] including low- and moderate-income ("LMI") neighborhoods.[6] The CRA places enforcement of this obligation in the hands of four federal administrative agencies that regulate banks (the "federal banking agencies" or the "agencies").[7] The CRA requires these agencies to examine each bank periodically to determine whether it is helping to meet community credit needs, to issue a written public report—including a rating—evaluating the bank's CRA performance, and to take the bank's CRA record into account when considering certain bank expansion applications.[8] When a bank files one of these expansion applications, any member of the public may file comments with the federal banking agency that regulates the bank opposing the application on the basis that the bank has failed to meet its CRA obligations. Members of the public, and in particular community-based organizations operating in LMI, predominantly minority, and inner-city neighborhoods (collectively "redlined neighborhoods") have used this opportunity to file comments opposing bank merger applications.

The seeds for democratizing capital have borne fruit. The opportunity for disenfranchised members of redlined neighborhoods to comment on a bank's CRA record when it files an expansion application has given them a powerful voice in decisions about the distribution of loans.[9] Banks, which are generally sensitive to bad publicity and risk-averse in their expansion applications, are anxious to have good CRA records both as good public relations and to ensure approval of their expansion applications. Public comments, and the delay and risk they cause to bank expansion plans, have brought banks to the bargaining table with community groups, resulting in bank pledges to lend more than one trillion dollars to LMI and predominantly minority neighborhoods nationwide.[10] Even if banks do not have expansion plans in the immediate future, their desire for good public relations, their discovery that CRA-related lending can be profitable, and their desire to prevent comments opposing future expansion applications have motivated them to change their lending practices, introduce new loan products, and partner with community groups to make lending to LMI and minority persons and neighborhoods part of their business strategies.

Despite its success in democratizing capital, the CRA has not reached its full potential. There remains a disproportionate distribution of costly subprime lending in LMI and predominantly minority neighborhoods and a disproportionate percentage of low-income persons who do not participate in the banking system.

4 reasons The thesis of this book has four parts. First, one of the main reasons the CRA has not reached its full potential for democratizing capital is that the federal banking agencies utilize subjective standards for evaluating the CRA performance of banks. Such standards limit the power of the franchise the CRA extends to LMI and minority persons and the amount of capital they receive because subjective standards make it difficult to hold a bank accountable for a poor CRA record or to know how much lending a bank should be doing.

Second, in contrast to subjective standards for evaluating CRA performance, a fixed set of criteria composed of quantitative measures of bank lending, quantitative measures of community credit needs, and objective standards for evaluating bank lending would maximize the CRA's potential for democratizing capital. Such criteria would make it easier to hold a bank accountable for a poor CRA record and would more clearly define how much lending a bank should be doing.

Third, a major reason the agencies have failed to adopt quantitative measures and objective standards for evaluating CRA performance is the agencies' fear that such standards would "allocate credit." The CRA's legislative history makes clear that Congress did not intend the CRA to allocate credit, and the agencies fear credit allocation could lead to unsafe and unsound banking practices.

The fourth part of the thesis is that it is possible to establish criteria for evaluating CRA performance that are composed of quantitative measures and objective standards that maximize the CRA's potential for democratizing capital without allocating credit. The CRA performance evaluation criteria this book proposes in chapter eight have been developed based on the notion that while the CRA is not intended to allocate credit, it is intended to influence banks to lend more money in redlined neighborhoods, and it is permissible under the CRA to influence banks to lend in such areas up to the point of allocating credit.

Specifically, the CRA evaluative criteria this book proposes are composed of three characteristics that will maximize the CRA's potential for democratizing capital: quantitative measures of bank lending; quantitative benchmarks of community credit needs; and objective standards for determining whether bank lending meets credit needs. Such criteria would make it possible for community groups to hold banks accountable for poor CRA records and would help ensure that banks are distributing sufficient capital to meet community credit needs.

The reason the CRA has not met its potential for democratizing capital and exploring how it might do so is the story this book tries to tell. The story begins in chapter one, with the legislative history of the CRA. Congress passed the CRA to influence banks to make loans to redlined neighborhoods. Congress intended the CRA to eliminate the banking practice known as "redlining," which is the refusal to lend in low-income, predominantly minority, or inner-city neighborhoods, regardless of credit risk,[11] and to increase bank lending in these neighborhoods. When Congress amended the CRA and other banking laws with CRA-related provisions on six separate occasions, it took a number of steps to strengthen the CRA's extension of the franchise over decisions about the distribution of capital, primarily through expanding the amount and quality of information about bank lending records that is available to the public. While Congress intended the CRA to influence banks to make more loans to redlined neighborhoods, Congress also stated that it did not intend the CRA to allocate credit, another way of stating that the CRA was not to be used to create lending quotas. Congress did not ban quotas, but the legislative history indicates that quotas are not permissible under the CRA.

Based on this legislative history, the federal banking agencies may adopt criteria for evaluating CRA performance that influence banks to lend up to the point of setting quotas.

Chapter two describes the structure of the CRA. Reflecting its legislative history, the CRA is designed to influence banks to lend more money in underserved neighborhoods without allocating credit. The CRA places an obligation on banks to help meet community credit needs. It creates an enforcement mechanism that influences banks to make loans to satisfy this obligation. Enforcement comes in the form of periodic evaluations of a bank's CRA record by the federal banking agency that regulates it, public disclosure of information about a bank's CRA record, and scrutiny of a bank's CRA record by the agency that regulates it when the bank submits an expansion application. The CRA does not, however, contain enforcement provisions that might lead to credit allocation, such as mandatory penalties for a bank that fails to satisfy its CRA obligations or the right of individuals to sue in court for CRA violations.

The story then moves, in chapter three, to the first CRA enforcement regime, which lasted from 1978 through mid-1997. In enforcing the CRA, the federal banking agencies—all of which had opposed the CRA—did not emphasize the portion of the CRA or its legislative history that focused on increasing lending to redlined neighborhoods. Instead, they focused on the portion of the legislative history that prohibited credit allocation. The agencies treated the CRA as a law that was intended to correct an information failure in the market. According to this theory, banks redlined because they decided it was not worth the expense or time to seek creditworthy borrowers in particular neighborhoods, especially LMI, inner-city, or predominantly minority communities. The agencies' perspective was that the CRA requires banks to seek information about lending opportunities in redlined neighborhoods and market loans there. The first set of CRA regulations, which were in force from 1978 through mid-1997, reflected this position. The criteria for evaluating CRA performance in the regulations and the agencies' enforcement of the CRA emphasized the efforts a bank undertook to make loans in its local community.[12] A bank's actual lending was of secondary importance to its efforts to lend. When the agencies evaluated bank lending, they used vague and inconsistent criteria and subjective standards that made it impossible for members of the public to know what a bank's CRA obligations were, let alone hold a bank to them.

Over time, the first CRA enforcement regime generated great dissatisfaction. The regime had the unfortunate distinction of generating dissension among the banks it regulated, the residents of redlined neighborhoods that it was intended to benefit, and the law's enforcers, the federal banking agencies themselves.[13] They all agreed that the CRA was enforced in an arbitrary and inconsistent manner. Bankers complained that it generated unnecessary burden and paperwork and subjected bank expansion plans to undue delay and expense. Community groups asserted that the federal banking agencies did not fulfill their responsibility to enforce the CRA and that the standards for evaluating bank lending were too vague and subjective to allow them to hold a bank accountable for a poor record of meeting community credit needs.

In response to the many criticisms of the first CRA enforcement regime, the federal banking agencies began a rule-making process in July 1993 that culminated in new CRA regulations in April 1995 that were fully phased in by July 1997. Chapter four describes the efforts to reform the CRA regulations. The new regulations made some improvements and some progress towards implementing criteria for evaluating CRA performance that consist of quantitative measures of bank lending, quantitative benchmarks of community credit needs, and objective terms for evaluating bank performance. Specifically, the second set of CRA regulations eliminated the criteria that evaluated bank efforts to lend and replaced them with criteria that evaluated a bank's lending, investment, and service performance. The regulations require the federal banking agencies to consider the extent of the bank's lending in its community, the geographic distribution of its loans, and its lending to persons of different income levels. However, the regulations do not spell out clearly and unambiguously how to measure bank lending, how to measure community credit needs, or how to evaluate whether the lending meets credit needs. Thus, despite the improvement, the new regulations fall short of fulfilling the capital-democratizing promise of the CRA.

The first proposed draft of the new regulations, however, came very close to utilizing quantitative measures and benchmarks and objective standards for evaluating CRA performance. It had a "market share" test, which would have evaluated a bank's record of meeting community credit needs by comparing a bank's market share of loans in LMI neighborhoods (quantitative measure of bank lending) with its overall market share of loans (quantitative benchmark of the bank's ability to meet overall community credit needs). If the bank's market share in LMI neighborhoods was "comparable" to its overall market share, it presumably was meeting community credit needs. There was also a loan-to-deposit ratio ("LDR") test, pursuant to which the percentage of a bank's deposits that it returned to the community in the form of loans (quantitative measure) would be compared with a 65% LDR (quantitative benchmark). An LDR of 65% was presumably reasonable (a quasi-objective standard). Finally, the proposed regulations evaluated the percentage of a bank's loans in its community (quantitative measure). If a majority of loans were in the bank's community (quantitative benchmark), this was "appropriate." The banking industry criticized the market share and LDR tests as allocating credit, and the federal banking agencies dropped them from the final regulations.

The failure of the federal banking agencies to adopt CRA regulations that use criteria for evaluating CRA performance composed of quantitative measures and objective standards means the CRA still has a long way to go before reaching its potential for democratizing capital. This is borne out in chapter five, which investigates how the federal banking agencies have implemented the second set of CRA regulations. Chapter five examines CRA performance evaluations, agency decisions on bank expansion applications, and the agencies' CRA examination manuals and other regulatory materials. Despite improvements in the second set of CRA regulations, the agencies continue to enforce the CRA in a way that makes it nearly impossible for community groups to hold a bank accountable for a poor lending record. The agencies did not use a fixed set of CRA evaluative criteria, frequently employed criteria consisting of a quantitative measure of bank lending and a quantitative benchmark of community credit needs but used subjective standards to compare bank lending with the benchmark, did not define the level of performance required to meet a particular subjective standard, used the subjective evaluative standards inconsistently and almost always in a way that favored banks, and did not define the weight each criterion had. The agencies' decisions on expansion applications similarly did not use a fixed set of criteria and used subjective standards for evaluating bank lending. The decisions generally listed facts about the bank's lending, emphasized strengths and excused weaknesses, and did not describe the reasoning the agency employed in reaching the decision. Finally, the compliance manuals do not require banking agency examiners to use a fixed set of criteria when evaluating a bank's CRA performance.

The story next moves to chapter six, which examines the impact the CRA has had on distributing loans to LMI and minority persons and neighborhoods. There is substantial evidence consistent with the conclusion that the CRA has encouraged banks to lend more money to LMI and minority persons and neighborhoods than they would have without the CRA. Nevertheless, there is evidence that the CRA has not realized its potential. LMI and minority neighborhoods receive a disproportionate share of costly subprime and predatory loans; many residents of such neighborhoods who received subprime loans could have received a prime loan; and a large percentage of the LMI persons do not even have a bank account.

The book then moves to its final two chapters, which examine whether it is possible to create CRA evaluative criteria that do not allocate credit and are composed of quantitative measures of bank lending, quantitative benchmarks of community credit needs, and objective standards for evaluating whether bank lending meets community credit needs. Chapter seven examines other federal government interventions in the credit markets in order to define credit allocation more specifically and to distinguish governmental credit allocation from governmental efforts to influence bank lending decisions. Several examples show this difference, including the Department of Justice's enforcement of the fair-lending laws, laws and regulations governing Fannie Mae and Freddie Mac, laws establishing lending requirements for banks with interstate branches, and home mortgage-lending disclosure laws.

Finally, chapter eight proposes CRA evaluative criteria that maximize the CRA's potential for democratizing capital. The criteria are composed of quantitative measures of bank lending, quantitative benchmarks of community credit needs, and objective standards for evaluating whether bank lending meets community credit needs. Chapter eight demonstrates that the proposed criteria will strengthen the franchise over lending decisions that the CRA extends to previously disenfranchised community members, will influence banks to lend more money to LMI and minority persons previously excluded from the economic system, and will not allocate credit.

CHAPTER ONE

The Legislative History of the CRA

Introduction

The legislative history of the Community Reinvestment Act ("CRA") shows that the purpose of the CRA was to end the bank practice known as redlining—refusing to lend in certain neighborhoods, especially low-income, predominantly minority, and inner-city neighborhoods—due to perceived credit risks, and to increase the amount of money banks lend in their local communities in general and in redlined neighborhoods in particular.[1] The CRA expresses a congressional preference for banks to make loans in their local communities and in LMI neighborhoods and threatens sanctions for banks that do not comply. In using the CRA to express a preference and threaten sanctions, Congress intended to influence banks to lend more money in redlined neighborhoods.

The legislative history of the CRA also shows that in passing the CRA, Congress did not intend to create a system of government-imposed credit allocation, and equated credit allocation with lending quotas. Congress did not establish lending quotas, require banks to lend to particular persons or organizations, or create mandatory sanctions for failing to lend.

Based on the legislative history, the four federal agencies that regulate banks[2] (the "federal banking agencies" or the "agencies") may promulgate CRA regulations that contain criteria for evaluating the CRA performance of a bank that consist of quantitative measures of bank lending, quantitative benchmarks of community credit needs, and objective standards for evaluating whether bank lending meets community credit needs.[3]

The difference between allocating credit and influencing bank lending decisions is not just semantic. It is the difference between setting mandatory quotas—which Congress did not do in passing the CRA—and setting up a system intended to end redlining and increase lending in redlined communities, which Congress did in passing the CRA. Former Federal Reserve Governor Lawrence Lindsey made a statement that makes this distinction between influencing banks to lend and allocating credit through quotas: "The CRA established a national goal and put considerable power in both supervisory agencies and the public to enforce it but left the details of how the goal should be accomplished to local communities and depository institutions."[4] The CRA influences banks to lend in redlined neighborhoods but does not specify amounts, types, terms, or recipients of loans. As Lindsey continued, "No one in Washington has yet been employed to decide how much or what type of CRA lending should be made in the individual communities... [banks] represent."[5]

Congress passed six significant amendments to the CRA and three CRA-related amendments to other banking laws on six separate occasions. The provisions and legislative histories of the amendments on the first five occasions indicate they were congressional attempts to clarify and strengthen the CRA's influence over bank lending decisions. They helped democratize capital by requiring the federal banking agencies to disclose more information to the public about bank lending records and the standards the agencies use to evaluate them. The purpose of the amendments Congress passed on the sixth occasion it amended the CRA and related laws is mixed. On the one hand, the amendments strengthened the CRA by prohibiting banks from going into the insurance or securities businesses unless they have at least a satisfactory CRA record. On the other hand, they weakened the CRA by limiting the frequency of CRA exams for small banks with satisfactory or better CRA records. The amendments also included a provision requiring community groups and banks to disclose certain CRA-related agreements they enter. While the purpose of this amendment might have been to create a chilling effect on groups' efforts to comment on bank applications, it is not clear the amendment will have this effect.

The Purpose of the CRA

Congress passed the CRA in light of evidence that banks were engaged in two interrelated practices—redlining and capital export—which, CRA's supporters argued, contributed to the deterioration of inner-city neighborhoods.[6] Redlining is the practice by which a bank draws a red line around a neighborhood on a map and refuses to lend there because of perceived credit risks associated with the neighborhood.[7] Capital export is the practice by which a bank exports the deposits of one neighborhood's residents to other communities and makes loans in those other communities despite local lending opportunities. Congress identified several different types of neighborhoods as being victimized by these practices, including LMI,[8] minority,[9] urban and inner-city,[10] older,[11] and rural and small towns (collectively "redlined neighborhoods").[12] Senator William Proxmire, the CRA's primary sponsor, described these related practices:

> [B]anks and savings and loans will take deposits and instead of reinvesting them in that community, they will invest them elsewhere, and they will actually or figuratively draw a red line on a map around areas of their city, sometimes in the older neighborhoods, sometimes ethnic, and sometimes black, but often encompassing a great area of their neighborhood.[13]

The legislative history contains several examples of redlining. Senator Proxmire stated, "The data provided by that act [the Home Mortgage Disclosure Act] remove any doubt that redlining indeed exists, that many creditworthy areas are denied loans."[14] Senator Proxmire cited several examples: banks in Brooklyn invested only 11% of their deposits in Brooklyn; banks in Washington, D.C. invested 90% of their deposits outside of the city; Los Angeles, Chicago, Cleveland, and St. Louis suffered from disinvestment.[15] According to a survey of Washington, D.C. banks conducted by the Senate Committee on Banking, Housing, and Urban Affairs, one bank had a policy of making no home mortgage loans and a savings and loan made 99% of its home mortgage loans in the suburbs.[16]

According to CRA's supporters, when banks export capital, they fail to meet local credit needs for housing, small businesses, and farms, to the detriment of these communities.[17] "We also know that small town banks sometimes ship their funds to the major money markets in search of higher interest rates, to the detriment of local housing, to the detriment of small business, and farm credit needs."[18] Senator Proxmire stated, "This denial of credit, while it is certainly not the sole cause of our urban problems, undoubtedly aggravates urban decline."[19]

Senator Proxmire seemed to take moral offense at redlining and capital export: "[T]he banking industry must be encouraged to reinvest in local needs rather than continuing to favor speculative loans to shaky foreign regimes, to REITS [Real Estate Investment Trusts], to unnecessary supertanker fleets, to bank insiders, and all of the other questionable ventures that have managed to get credit while our local communities starve."[20] He asserted that many of the banks that defend their poor lending records on the ground of lack of demand or the need to protect deposits "are often the same banks that have squandered money on speculative real estate loans or credits to shaky foreign regimes."[21] Similarly, critical of a banker who sent him a letter defending Third World lending because of a "soft" domestic loan market, Senator Proxmire stated:

> What does he mean by a soft loan market at home? Has he talked to young families in Brooklyn and small businessmen in Milwaukee who cannot get loans? What does he mean by urgent financing needs in the developing countries? What about urgent economic development needs in Detroit, Philadelphia, Baltimore, and Boston?[22]

Proxmire criticized another bank that made no home mortgage loans in Washington D.C. because it made a "great volume of loans to the outside real estate interests of its own board."[23] Senator Paul Sarbanes, another CRA supporter, also reflected this moral umbrage: "Why should not a banking institution have a responsibility to meet the credit needs of the local communities in which they are located, in the very communities from which they are drawing their sustenance? Why should they not have a responsibility to respond to that community?"[24]

Responding to the evidence of redlining and disinvestment, Congress intended that the CRA have both a prohibitive effect and an affirmative impact. The prohibitive effect was to end redlining.[25] Senator Proxmire stated, "The provision is intended to eliminate the practice of redlining by lending institutions."[26] The affirmative impact was that banks would increase their lending in redlined neighborhoods so their credit needs would be met.[27] The CRA clearly expresses a congressional preference for banks to lend in their local communities. In the hearings on the CRA held by the Senate Committee on Banking, Housing, and Urban Affairs ("Senate Hearings"), Senator Proxmire stated, "If you have competing banks, one bank has a good record of making loans, the other has not, in the local community, then preference would be given under this legislation to the bank that has the better record...."[28]

The legislative history of the CRA contains several references to the CRA's goal of increasing bank lending in redlined communities. Senator Proxmire was clear about this: "[B]anks and thrifts are indeed chartered to serve the convenience and needs of their communities, and as the bill makes clear, convenience and needs does not just mean drive-in teller windows and Christmas Club accounts. It means loans."[29] Similarly, he stated, the CRA "would provide that a bank charter is indeed a franchise to serve local convenience and needs, including credit needs."[30] Senator Proxmire characterized the CRA as "the best opportunity we have to provide effective investment buildup in our cities on a sound basis...."[31] He also stated that the CRA was designed to "provide as much incentive as we could for local investment in local communities."[32] It would "encourage" bankers to "get out of the office" and find the market for loans in their local community.[33] Under the CRA, the federal banking agencies would encourage bankers to give "priority" to meeting local credit needs. [34]

CRA's public opponents, including Senators Jake Garn, Richard Lugar, Robert Morgan, Harrison Schmitt, and John Tower, recognized and supported the CRA's purpose. In the Senate Hearings, Senator Tower said, "I don't quarrel with the ends of the proposal and that is providing mortgage credit to creditworthy purchasers in the inner-city areas."[35] Senator Morgan stated, "I support wholeheartedly the ultimate intent of this bill, which is to assure that the credit needs of the inner city are adequately met."[36] In the report on the CRA by the Senate Committee on Banking, Housing, and Urban Affairs ("Senate Report"), the opponents on the Committee stated, "[W]e support the intent of the bill to insure greater credit availability for the inner cities...."[37]

As part of this affirmative purpose to increase bank lending in redlined neighborhoods, CRA's supporters also envisioned the CRA as a means to leverage billions of private loan dollars from banks to enable government redevelopment programs to be effective. The CRA was passed as part of the Housing and Community Development Act of 1977.[38] In passing the CRA, Congress recognized the "vital interconnection between successful community and housing development and local private investment activities."[39] According to the House Conference Report, the CRA is "designed to encourage more coordinated efforts between private investment and federal grants and insurance in order to increase the viability of our urban communities."[40]

Senator Proxmire was explicit that private money was necessary to help rebuild urban communities. In his opening remarks at the Senate Hearings, Proxmire stated, "Government through tax revenues and public debt cannot and should not provide more than a limited part of the capital required for local housing and economic development needs. Financial institutions in our free economic system must play the leading role."[41] When Senator Proxmire introduced the CRA, he stated that the public sector did not have sufficient funds to finance all domestic capital needs, and that private financial institutions were the main source of capital for economic development.[42] He later stated, "If we are going to rebuild our cities, it will have to be done with the private institutions. The banks and savings and loans have the funds."[43]

Similarly, Congress indicated that the success of federal development programs "depends in large part upon the availability of private capital, particularly as made available through local lending and financial institutions."[44] As Senator Proxmire stated, "[I]t is possible that the Federal Government may put in a few billion dollars this year or over the next few years to help rebuild our cities. But it will be peanuts compared to what the financial institutions can put in, if they have the will to do it."[45]

When he introduced the CRA, Senator Proxmire justified the effort to influence banks to lend in redlined neighborhoods as a *quid pro quo*.[46] He stated that the public charter that banks receive justifies imposing public obligations on banks.[47] "[A] public charter conveys numerous economic benefits and in return it is legitimate for public policy and regulatory practice to require some public purpose...."[48] He listed several benefits of a bank charter. Banks enjoy protection against competition from other businesses. Banks hold a "semi-exclusive franchise."[49] Senator proxmire elaborated, "The Government limits the entry of other potential competitors into that area if such entry would unduly jeopardize existing financial institutions."[50] The government also restricted "competition [among banks] by limiting the rate of interest payable on savings deposits and prohibiting any interest on demand deposits."[51] The government provides low-cost deposit insurance.[52] Finally, the government provides low-cost credit through the Federal Reserve Banks and the Federal Home Loan Banks.[53]

CRA Enforcement

Criteria for Evaluating a Bank's Record of Meeting Community Credit Needs

The legislative history contains a discussion about how to evaluate a bank's record of meeting the credit needs of the community. This discussion sheds light on the difference between allocating credit and influencing banks to lend more in redlined neighborhoods, further supports the proposition that Congress intended the CRA to influence banks to lend in redlined neighborhoods, and provides some guidance regarding criteria for evaluating CRA performance that influence banks to lend in redlined neighborhoods but do not allocate credit.

As initially introduced, the CRA included a mandatory loan-to-deposit ratio for evaluating a bank's record at meeting local credit needs. The CRA would have required banks to indicate, subject to regulatory approval, the percentage of their deposits that they would lend in their local communities.[54] However, Senator Proxmire dropped this provision in light of strong opposition that this mandatory loan-to-deposit ratio would have constituted credit allocation.[55]

The CRA's subsequent legislative history contains suggestions of the sorts of criteria the agencies could utilize in evaluating the CRA performance of a bank. Although not explicit, the discussions imply that it would be appropriate to adopt criteria for evaluating CRA performance composed of quantitative measures of bank lending, quantitative benchmarks of community credit needs, and objective standards for evaluating bank lending. For example, there is a suggestion that a bank's lending could be evaluated by comparing its performance to demand, measured by all loan applications received by all banks in the community and the number of loans banks make in the community.[56] The legislative history also suggests a quasi-objective standard for evaluating whether a bank's lending meets community credit needs: whether the bank is lending a "disproportionate" amount of credit outside the community.[57] Although the term "disproportionate" is not precise and is open to interpretation, the legislative history contains some guidance about its meaning. The Senate Report states that although Congress "rejected the course of setting percentage targets for reinvestment, it should be self-evident that an institution exporting 99 percent of its dollars outside of the city in which it is chartered is not serving community convenience and needs."[58] The Report continues that, in contrast, some savings and loans had been able to lend 80% of their deposits locally with no adverse effects on bank safety and soundness.[59] The report cited one bank that had gone from making 1% of its loans within its city to 20%.[60] In the Senate debates on the CRA, Senator Proxmire stated that Brooklyn and Washington, D.C. were suffering from disinvestment; banks in those areas were lending 89% and 90% of their deposits, respectively, elsewhere.[61] Finally, a colloquy between Senator Proxmire and Vincent J. Quinn, president and chairman of the board of the Brooklyn Savings Bank, suggests that "disproportionate" might be defined by comparing a bank's performance with other banks' performances based on their relative sizes. According to Senator Proxmire, Brooklyn Savings Bank, with $1.1 billion in assets, made 52 loans in Brooklyn in 1975, compared with the smaller GreenPoint Bank, which made 722 loans.[62] Quinn defended Brooklyn Savings Bank by asserting that there was not sufficient demand for loans in Brooklyn for all banks to originate the same percentage of their assets in loans in Brooklyn as GreenPoint Bank.[63] Proxmire responded by stating, "[W]hen you compare these, it looks as if this bank [GreenPoint] was more aggressive and active and serviced its community more effectively than your large bank did."[64]

Arthur Burns, former chairman of the Federal Reserve, outlined similar criteria the federal banking agencies would have to utilize if the CRA were enacted.[65] The federal banking agencies would have to identify the credit needs of the community, determine the extent to which they were being met, and determine whether a particular bank was doing its share. Burns opposed the CRA on the grounds that this would be unduly burdensome.[66]

Sanctions for Failing to Meet Community Credit Needs

Another way the legislative history of the CRA sheds light on the difference between allocating credit and influencing bank lending decisions and further indicates that Congress did not intend to allocate credit but did intend to influence banks to lend in underserved neighborhoods is Congress' consideration of sanctions for banks that do not satisfy their CRA obligations. Instead of imposing the sort of mandatory lending orders on a bank for failing to satisfy its CRA obligations that would accompany credit allocation, the sanction was "relatively weak."[67] Senator Proxmire stated, "You're not going to put a bank out of business if they don't loan locally."[68] Congress intended the federal banking agencies to use their authority to "encourage financial institutions to help meet local credit needs."[69]

Despite the fact that there were no mandatory sanctions, the agencies' encouragement was to be strong. The CRA required the federal banking agencies to "use the full extent of their authority...to encourage all regulated depository institutions' responsiveness to community needs."[70] Representative Ashley, a CRA supporter in the House, stated that the CRA "reaffirms and strengthens the powers of the federal financial supervisory agencies to assure that federally regulated financial institutions meet the credit needs of their communities."[71]

The legislative history indicates that this regulatory encouragement was to be both formal and informal. As to formal encouragement, the federal banking agencies would use their authority when examining banks and considering bank expansion applications to encourage them to lend in their communities.[72] According to Senator Proxmire, a poor CRA record would be grounds for denying an application, but this remedy was not mandatory. "We provided that when a bank wanted to open a branch the regulating agencies would have to take into account how much they invested locally, and they might have this as a decisive consideration under some circumstances."[73] An example from the legislative history of a formal effort was a state banking regulator that required city banks that wanted to open a branch in the suburbs to "emphasize lending to their inner city areas as a precondition for approval of the new suburban branch."[74]

As to informal encouragement, Senator Proxmire stated, "the record shows we have to do something to nudge them, influence them, persuade them to invest in their community."[75] The legislative history cites examples of instances in which regulatory persuasion resulted in increased lending.[76] In one case, the Federal Home Loan Bank Board, responding to complaints that a savings and loan in Washington, D.C. made 99% of its mortgage loans outside the District, urged the savings and loan to take affirmative steps to increase lending there.[77] As a result, the savings and loan increased its proportion of lending in the District to 20%.[78] According to the Senate Report, other branches in the District were able to make 80% of their loans there with no "adverse effect," thus the "Bank Board's suggestion that the [savings and loan] take affirmative steps to publicize the availability of credit to city residents was appropriate under the circumstances...."[79]

Opposition to the CRA

The opponents of the CRA, including the heads of three of the four federal banking regulatory agencies,[80] had several objections to the CRA. Primarily, they argued that the CRA was or would lead to credit allocation, and they equated credit allocation with credit quotas. During the Senate Hearings, Senator Tower stated, "This proposal would, as I read it, provide for a scheme of credit allocation...."[81] According to the opposition statement in the Senate Report, "The enactment of this Section would have adverse effects upon the free flow of capital within our economy, and 'a rose by any other name' is still 'credit allocation.' "[82] According to Senator Morgan, the CRA:

> is a significant step in the direction of credit allocation by the Congress of the United States. If bills of this nature are pushed to their ultimate conclusion, then the day will come when a financial institution may be forced to make an unsound loan in a specific location in order to meet its quota of loans in a given locality.[83]

Senator Lugar stated, "This perennial attempt to provide credit allocation, to provide by law some reason why loans must be made at the penalty of losing the business, is simply a gesture in futility."[84] Senator Tower stated, "I do not think that we should indulge in the authorization or, indeed, the mandate of a system of credit allocation. . . ."[85] Senator Schmitt argued that the CRA "is a step in the direction of credit allocation by Government agencies."[86]

According to the CRA's opponents, credit allocation was undesirable because it unduly interfered with the free market and could force banks to make unsound loans. Credit allocation "creat[ed] barriers to the free flow of funds to places they are needed."[87] The CRA's opponents described the United States as a constantly shifting "patchwork of capital short and capital surplus localities" that had been overcome, in large part, by the standardization of mortgage documents, the secondary mortgage market, and the weakening of geographic lending limits.[88] The free flow of funds ensured that money would go to the areas where it would get the highest return, guaranteed that the supply of mortgage funds would be constant where needed, and reduced the cost of mortgages by guaranteeing mortgage money would be available even in areas where the demand for mortgage loans was greater than the supply of money to make mortgages.[89] The CRA, opponents argued, by "[o]veremphasizing the need to meet local credit needs will discourage the free flow of funds and disrupt the flow of credit from capital surplus areas to capital short areas."[90] The CRA "would be a step backward, encouraging the creation of barriers to the free flow of funds to places they are needed."[91] Senator Tower argued, "Nothing could militate more strongly against the vitality of a market-regulated economy than a growing system of credit allocation."[92] Finally, credit allocation would force banks to make risky loans, and rather than doing this, banks would leave the neighborhoods the CRA intended them to serve.[93]

Similar arguments were made two years earlier when Congress considered the Home Mortgage Disclosure Act ("HMDA"), which required lenders to disclose the location of their real estate-related loans.[94] Opponents of HMDA argued that it would allocate credit. HMDA's opponents characterized credit allocation as a quota.[95] They argued that credit allocation would have the same negative effect: "Quota systems are a form of credit rationing. This means we would be taking from someone, the small business or the suburban homeowner, and giving to someone else, in this case the inner city homeowner."[96]

The opponents of the CRA made other arguments as well. They argued that the bill did not define key terms, did not contain standards for evaluating a bank's lending record, and that it would therefore be impossible to issue regulations.[97] The CRA, they argued, would require "bank examiners to assess the institution's record of meeting the credit needs of its primary service area; yet, the bill sets out no criteria or guidelines upon which this assessment is to be based."[98] Opponents argued that it would be impossible to define a proper reinvestment ratio.[99] They also argued that the law would burden banks with additional paperwork.[100] They believed that voluntary efforts to increase lending were preferable and already underway.[101] Opponents argued that the CRA was unnecessary because other federal laws, such as the Home Mortgage Disclosure Act, the Equal Credit Opportunity Act, and the various provisions of the federal banking laws that required banks to meet the convenience and needs of their communities, prohibited redlining.[102]

Finally, recognizing that one purpose of the CRA was to increase lending in redlined neighborhoods, the CRA's opponents claimed it would have the opposite effect.[103] It "would... have the adverse effect of causing a reduction in credit availability in these areas which we are trying so desperately to revitalize."[104] They argued that the CRA would deter banks from entering areas in need of revitalization for fear of the obligation to meet local credit needs.[105] In a letter to Senator Morgan, former Federal Reserve Chairman Arthur Burns stated, "to the extent that this or any other sanction should prove effective in causing credit to flow substantially into an area on the basis of non-market forces, entry by depository institutions into other similar areas would likely be discouraged."[106] Similarly, Senator Schmitt stated:

> The requirement that financial regulatory agencies allocate credit under this or any other scheme can have adverse effects. By forcing financial institutions to make loans of dubious quality, the Congress would easily convince financial institutions to close branches in decaying neighborhoods and thus, lead to further economic and social decline in these areas.[107]

Finally, opponents argued that the CRA's additional paperwork and bureaucracy would further discourage banks from opening branches in redlined areas.[108]

Response to the CRA's Opponents

CRA supporters denied that it allocated credit, and in making this denial confirmed that the CRA would influence banks to lend more in redlined neighborhoods. The Senate Report states:

> Charters have never constituted licenses to ignore local credit needs. Therefore, the Committee rejects the assertion that this Title allocates credit. It simply underscores the long-standing obligation to an institution's local service area implicit in existing law.[109]

Senator Proxmire also denied that the CRA allocated credit. In the Senate Hearings, he stated, "It does not provide for credit allocation. The worst thing we could do, in my opinion, would be to empower Dr. Burns or anyone else to allocate so much credit to this sector and so much credit to that one."[110] In introducing the CRA, Senator Proxmire stated that the CRA would not require "mandatory quotas, or a bureaucratic credit allocation scheme."[111] But it would influence banks to lend in redlined neighborhoods: "it is legitimate for public policy and regulatory practice to require some public purposes, without the need for costly subsidies...."[112]

Senators Sarbanes and Proxmire also implicitly denied that the CRA allocated credit when they stated that nothing in the CRA would require a bank to do anything that was contrary to the safe and sound operation of the bank.[113] The CRA itself would not permit this. Senator Sarbanes stated, "The bill is very, very careful in making it clear that, in meeting this responsibility, the safe and sound operation of the institution has paramount consideration."[114] Senator Proxmire, in introducing the CRA, stated, "The bill also does not substitute the judgment of the regulator for the judgment of a banker on individual loans. Each bank or savings association will be free to exercise its best judgment on individual loan applications."[115] Mandatory quotas could not be imposed on banks because they would always be overridden by safety and soundness concerns.[116] Supporters of the CRA also did not believe that loans in redlined communities were inherently riskier than other loans. "Moreover, there is no reason to assume that a higher degree of community reinvestment is incompatible with bank safety."[117] In fact, CRA supporters argued that it was riskier to lend outside of a bank's local community:

> Finally, there is no evidence that banks or thrift institutions have gotten into financial difficulty by overinvesting in their local communities. On the contrary, most of the recent financial difficulties suffered by banks arose from making insider loans to affiliated persons and speculative loans outside the community in which the bank was chartered.[118]

When introducing the CRA, Senator Proxmire summarized these beliefs: "investment by financial institutions in their communities need not involve risks greater than those normally taken by prudent lenders, and often involves less risk because of the lender's firsthand knowledge of his community."[119] Senator Proxmire cited a program in Philadelphia to make mortgages in previously redlined areas that had a default rate of 0.6%, similar to the default rate elsewhere.[120]

Amendments to the CRA

Congress made nine significant amendments to the CRA or other banking laws on six different occasions. Congress intended the first five amendments to refine and strengthen the CRA's influence over bank lending decisions. Three of these five amendments influence banks to lend more in redlined neighborhoods by expanding CRA-related public disclosure requirements. The sixth and seventh amendments strengthened the CRA by expanding it to cover the formation of financial conglomerates. The eighth and ninth amendments were adopted to weaken the CRA's influence. The eighth amendment requires banks and community groups to disclose CRA agreements they make and the ninth reduces the frequency of CRA examinations of small banks with satisfactory or better CRA records.

FIRREA Amendment

In the Financial Institutions Reform, Recovery, and Enforcement Act of 1989 ("FIRREA"),[121] Congress amended the CRA to require that the federal banking agencies disclose to the public their written CRA performance evaluations of banks, the CRA ratings they assigned to banks, and the facts upon which the ratings were based.[122] Prior to this, the written evaluation and rating were confidential. Congress intended public disclosure of the CRA performance evaluation reports to strengthen CRA enforcement "by allowing the public to know both what regulatory agencies are telling depository institutions and what the community reinvestment records of particular depository institutions are."[123] Congress intended this amendment to reiterate the purposes of the CRA, tighten CRA standards, and influence banks to make more housing, small business, and small farm loans.[124] The amendment "will help to ensure that financial institutions in communities across our Nation will remain viable and active members of the very communities they serve."[125]

FIRREA's legislative history also provides guidance about the types of credit Congress was especially interested in influencing banks to make available.[126] Congress indicated that CRA performance evaluations should place special emphasis on a bank's record "of serving the housing credit needs of low- and moderate-income persons, small business credit needs, small farm credit needs, and rural economic development."[127] Thus, FIRREA's amendments to the CRA, among other FIRREA provisions, "return[ed] savings and loans to their original purpose, mortgage lending, including for low- and moderate-income people."[128]

FDICIA Amendment

In the Federal Deposit Insurance Corporation Improvement Act of 1991 ("FDICIA"),[129] Congress amended the CRA once again in an attempt to strengthen its ability to influence bank lending decisions.[130] FDICIA expanded on FIRREA's disclosure requirements by requiring the federal banking agencies to disclose the data that support their conclusions about the bank's CRA rating.[131] Combined with FIRREA's disclosure requirements and its support for more housing, small business, and small farm loans, FDICIA's provision requiring disclosure of the data about a bank's CRA record represented another strengthening of CRA's influence over bank lending decisions. It does so by helping to define and disclose the standards the federal banking agencies use to evaluate a bank's record at meeting community credit needs. As the Senate Report on the amendment stated:

> Disclosure will make it possible for interested parties (e.g. Congress, community organizations, depository institutions, state and local officials) to determine the underlying standards and criteria regulators use to evaluate and rate CRA performance. Such parties will then be better able to determine how much credibility and weight they should assign to a particular CRA evaluation or rating. The Committee intends that, over time, implementation of the amendment should bring greater uniformity and consistency to the CRA process.[132]

HCDA and RTCA Amendments

Congress amended the CRA as part of the Resolution Trust Corporation Refinancing, Restructuring, and Improvement Act of 1991 ("RTCA")[133] and the Housing and Community Development Act of 1992 ("1992 HCDA").[134] The 1992 HCDA amendment stated that in assessing a bank's CRA record, the federal banking agencies could consider lending and investment activities undertaken by banks in cooperation with minority- and woman-owned banks or low-income credit unions as long as such activities help meet the credit needs of the bank's community.[135] Under the RTCA and 1992 HCDA amendments, when evaluating a bank's CRA record, the federal banking agencies may consider as a positive factor a bank's providing a branch located in a predominantly minority community or to a minority- or woman-owned bank.[136] Taken together, these provisions can be seen as an attempt to use the CRA to influence banks to assist minority- and woman-owned banks and low-income credit unions, presumably because these financial institutions, in turn, could be counted on to help meet the credit needs of redlined neighborhoods.

Riegle-Neal Amendment

As part of the Riegle-Neal Interstate Banking and Branching Efficiency Act of 1994, which allowed banks to open branches in more than one state, Congress amended the CRA to require the federal banking agencies to prepare a separate CRA performance evaluation for each state in which a bank with interstate branches has at least one branch.[137] Congress passed this amendment to alleviate concerns that banks would use interstate banking to siphon deposits from new states in which they opened branches to make loans in their home states.[138] Congress stated that this provision ensures that the principles of the CRA would be followed in interstate banking.[139] "[C]ommunities need not fear that increasing geographic opportunities for banks will deprive them of needed capital.... These provisions are designed to ensure that banks will not just vacuum up deposits in some States and reinvest them in other States."[140]

GLBA Amendments

The Gramm-Leach-Bliley Act of 1999 ("GLBA"), which repealed the Glass-Steagall Act and certain provisions of the Banking Act of 1933,[141] and amended the Bank Holding Company Act of 1956 and other federal banking laws that had prohibited banks from engaging in the securities and insurance businesses,[142] also amended the CRA and other related laws.[143] Three CRA-related amendments prohibit banks from engaging in the insurance or securities businesses unless they received at least a satisfactory rating on their most recent CRA examinations, require banks and community groups to disclose the terms of CRA agreements they enter, and limit the frequency of CRA examinations of small banks.[144] These CRA-related provisions of the GLBA reflect a compromise between supporters of the CRA, who hoped to extend it to the new businesses in which banks could engage,[145] and Senator Phil Gramm, who hoped to limit the CRA's influence.[146] As such, the GLBA's effect on the CRA's ability to influence banks to lend in redlined neighborhoods is mixed.

Under the GLBA, a bank holding company ("BHC") must become a financial holding company ("FHC") to engage in the securities or insurance businesses, but a BHC is not permitted to form an FHC unless all of the BHC's bank subsidiaries received at least satisfactory ratings on their most recent

CRA examinations.[147] Once formed, an FHC cannot engage in the securities or insurance businesses or purchase any company engaged in any of these businesses if any of the FHC's bank subsidiaries had less than a satisfactory rating on its last CRA exam.[148] A national bank must create a "financial subsidiary" to engage in the securities or insurance businesses, but the financial subsidiary is not eligible to engage in a newly permitted business unless the financial subsidiary and any of its affiliate banks received at least a satisfactory rating on their most recent CRA exams.[149]

These provisions of the GLBA are likely to have a mixed impact on the CRA's ability to influence banks to lend in redlined neighborhoods. On the one hand, these provisions provide FHCs and financial subsidiaries a strong incentive to achieve satisfactory CRA ratings for their subsidiary and affiliate banks. On the other hand, the incentive is limited because the banks do not need to maintain satisfactory CRA ratings in order for the FHC or financial subsidiary to engage in the new businesses.[150] Furthermore, the vast majority of banks already receive satisfactory or higher CRA ratings, so it is unclear whether this provision will have any real influence on banks.[151] Additionally, the fact that CRA obligations were not extended to the insurance or securities operations of FHCs or financial subsidiaries means that FHCs might shift assets out of banks and into these other businesses.[152] Finally, the fact that a BHC does not have to apply to the agency that regulates it for permission to create an FHC and a national bank does not have to apply to the Comptroller of the Currency to create a financial subsidiary deprives community advocates of the chance to oppose such applications on CRA grounds, undermining the CRA's influence on bank lending decisions.[153]

The second amendment, section 711 of the GLBA, also known as the CRA "Sunshine" provision, requires banks and community groups to disclose the terms of certain CRA-related agreements they reach.[154] In order to trigger the disclosure obligations, there are three requirements. First, the community group must have commented on, testified about, discussed, or otherwise contacted the bank concerning the CRA.[155] Second, the agreement must provide for cash payments, grants, or other consideration of more than $10,000, or loans amounting to more than $50,000 annually.[156] Third, the agreement must be in fulfillment of the bank's CRA obligations, which is defined as having an impact on a federal banking agency's decision to approve the bank's expansion applications or to assign a CRA rating to the bank.[157] There are different reporting requirements for banks and community groups. A bank must file an annual report with the federal banking agency that regulates it that shows information about payments, fees, or loans made to any party to the agreement or received from any party to the agreement, and aggregate data on loans, investments, and services provided by parties to the agreement.[158] There is no penalty for a bank that fails to report and the relevant federal banking regulatory agency cannot require a bank to comply with a reported agreement.[159] A community group must make an annual report to the relevant federal banking agency that contains an accounting of the funds received pursuant to the agreement, including a detailed, itemized list of the uses for which the funds were made, including compensation, administrative expenses, travel, and entertainment.[160] If a community group fails to report, the agreement is unenforceable.[161] If a person or community group uses funds received under an agreement for personal purposes, the federal banking agency that regulates the bank that entered into the agreement can require disgorgement of the funds from the offending individual or group and prohibit the offending individual or group from being party to a CRA agreement for ten years.[162]

The CRA Sunshine provision recognizes and regulates one of the primary ways that community groups have used the CRA to influence banks to lend in redlined neighborhoods: by filing comments opposing bank merger applications and negotiating lending agreements.[163] However, the CRA Sunshine provision creates at least two disincentives for a community group to file comments. First, if the group does so, the bank may not want to reach a lending agreement with it for fear of having to comply with the reporting requirements. Second, a group might not want to file comments because it might not want to be subject to disclosure requirements if it reaches a lending agreement with the bank. If these disincentives prove strong, the CRA Sunshine provision will undermine the CRA's potential for democratizing capital by creating a disincentive for members of the public to file comments on applications.[164] In fact, limiting the ability of community groups to participate in the CRA enforcement process by filing comments opposing bank mergers appears to have been the desire of Senator Gramm, who sponsored the CRA Sunshine provision, and who likened the challenge process to extortion.[165] Senator Gramm has stated, "We now have banks being extorted and being forced to make cash payments which are little more than bribes."[166]

Finally, the GLBA amended the CRA to prohibit the federal banking agencies from conducting CRA examinations of banks with $250 million or less in assets and an outstanding CRA rating more than once every five years, and more than once every four years for a bank with a satisfactory CRA rating.[167] While this reward may motivate small banks to achieve a high CRA rating in order to avoid CRA examinations, the long time between examinations limits the incentive to maintain a good CRA record between examinations.[168]

Conclusion

The legislative history of the CRA shows that in passing the CRA, Congress intended to influence banks to lend more in LMI, minority, and inner-city neighborhoods. Congress passed the CRA in light of evidence that banks had redlined these neighborhoods and exported their capital elsewhere. In light of this, the CRA has a dual purpose—to end redlining and to increase lending in redlined neighborhoods. Supporters of the CRA made clear, however, that while it was intended to influence banks to lend more in such neighborhoods, the CRA was not intended to create a system of government-imposed credit allocation. With two exceptions, amendments to the CRA and related banking laws generally strengthened the CRA's influence, primarily through increasing the amount of information available about bank lending and requiring the federal banking agencies to focus on home mortgage, small business, and small farm lending when evaluating banks for CRA compliance.

CHAPTER TWO

The Legal Structure of the CRA

Introduction

Reflecting congressional intent as expressed in its legislative history, the CRA is structured in a way that influences banks to lend in their local communities and in low- and moderate-income ("LMI"), predominantly minority, and inner-city neighborhoods (collectively "redlined" neighborhoods), but does not set quotas or force them to allocate credit. However, while the CRA explicitly states that banks have an obligation to meet credit needs, it does not explicitly ban credit allocation. This suggests that the federal banking agencies[1] may enforce the CRA in a way that broadly defines the affirmative obligation on banks to meet credit needs but narrowly defines credit allocation.

The CRA states that banks have an affirmative obligation to help meet the credit needs of their local communities, including LMI neighborhoods, without specifying how much a bank must lend. The CRA requires the federal banking agencies to examine individual banks periodically to assess their records of helping to meet credit needs, to publish an evaluation report—including a rating—for each bank, and to take the bank's record into account when considering an application by the bank to expand. Members of the public can file comment with the agencies on these applications. The agencies can deny an application because the bank has not met its CRA obligations. The CRA thus democratizes capital by influencing banks to lend more to redlined communities and by giving these communities a voice in bank lending decisions. But the CRA does not do this by allocating credit. The CRA does not impose specific lending targets on banks. It does not set lending quotas or specify the amount of credit banks are to make available, to whom, for what purpose, or on what terms. The CRA does not contain mandatory penalties for a bank that fails to meet community credit needs.

Several courts have issued decisions construing the CRA. These decisions are important because they help define the CRA's balance between influencing banks to lend and not allocating credit. The decisions, however, have tipped the balance too far in the direction of avoiding credit allocation, and in doing so, have undermined the CRA's potential for democratizing capital.

The Language of the Statute

This section examines the language and structure of the CRA as codified. In particular, it describes the standards the CRA suggests for evaluating a bank's CRA performance and the mechanism the CRA establishes for ensuring compliance with these standards. Both the standards and the enforcement mechanisms are designed to influence banks to lend in redlined neighborhoods.

CRA Performance Standards

The CRA does not contain specific criteria to evaluate a bank's record of helping to meet the credit needs of its local community. Nevertheless, the language of the CRA provides some guidance regarding the process for evaluating a bank's CRA performance and the criteria that the federal banking agencies should employ when evaluating a bank's data and record.

The CRA begins by reciting Congress' three findings in passing the law. These findings provide crucial guidance for developing a process for evaluating bank lending and adopting evaluative criteria. First, according to Section 2901(a)(1), banks are required to serve the "convenience and needs of the communities in which they are chartered to do business."[2] Second, "the convenience and needs of communities include the need for credit services."[3] Finally, banks "have continuing and affirmative obligation[s] to help meet the credit needs of the local communities in which they are chartered."[4] "Local communities" include "low- and moderate-income neighborhoods."[5]

These congressional findings suggest a three-step process for evaluating a bank's CRA performance. Since banks are required to serve the "convenience and needs" of their local communities, including LMI neighborhoods, and convenience and needs includes "credit," the first step of the process for evaluating a bank's CRA performance should be to determine the credit needs of its local community and LMI neighborhoods in that community. Second, since the bank's lending record is at issue, the bank's lending in its local community, and in LMI neighborhoods in that community, should be measured. Finally, the bank's lending should be compared with community credit needs to determine whether it is meeting its continuing and affirmative obligation to help meet the credit needs of its local community. This three-step process for evaluating a bank's CRA performance is reminiscent of the discussion of the process for evaluating a bank's CRA record that was suggested in the CRA's legislative history.[6] The Senate Report suggested that a bank's CRA record could be evaluated by counting the number of loan applications filed in the bank's community, determining the number and location of the bank's loans, and based on this, determining whether the bank's lending outside its community was disproportionate to its lending in the community.

Finally, Section 2901(b) of the CRA states that the federal banking agencies are to encourage banks to lend in their local communities "consistent with the safe and sound operation of such institutions."[7] This is reminiscent of the argument that CRA supporters made in the CRA's legislative history that the CRA would not allocate credit because it would not require banks to do anything that was not a safe and sound banking practice.[8]

CRA Enforcement Mechanisms

The CRA enforcement mechanisms are designed to influence bank decisions to lend in their local communities, but they do not allocate credit. The agencies' only enforcement authority is to examine banks for CRA performance and to take account of these evaluations in considering whether to grant certain bank expansion applications. Members of the public can participate in this enforcement process by submitting information to the federal banking agencies in connection with their CRA examinations of banks and by filing comments in connection with bank expansion applications.[9] The CRA does not create strict enforcement mechanisms common in other anti-discrimination laws that could lead to credit allocation.

CRA Performance Evaluations and Expansion Applications

Each federal banking agency is to use its supervisory authority over the banks it regulates to "encourage" them to "help meet the credit needs of the local communities in which they are chartered."[10] The CRA gives the federal banking agencies the supervisory authority to "encourage" banks to comply with the CRA on two occasions: when conducting a periodic examination of a bank's CRA record and when considering an application for a deposit facility.[11]

CRA Performance Evaluations

The first opportunity for the federal banking agencies to encourage banks to help meet the credit needs of their communities comes when an agency conducts a CRA performance evaluation ("PE") of the lending record of a bank it regulates.[12] The statutory description of what the federal banking agencies are to evaluate when conducting a PE provides additional guidance about the criteria for evaluating a bank's CRA performance. In addition, the content of the examination reports, their public availability, and their uses are designed to influence banks to make loans in their communities.

Section 2903(a)(1) of the CRA requires that, when examining a bank, the appropriate federal financial supervisory agency "shall assess the institution's record of meeting the credit needs of its entire community, including low- and moderate-income neighborhoods, consistent with the safe and sound operation of such institution...."[13] This language is different in a significant way from the statutory language describing the CRA's purpose. That language, in Section 2901(a)(3), states that a bank has an obligation to "help" meet the credit needs of its community. In contrast, Section 2901(a)(1) does not use the word "help" to modify a bank's obligations to meet community credit needs. Instead, banks are to be evaluated according to how well they meet credit needs. While the language of Section 2901(a)(3) requires banks to *help* meet the credit needs of local communities, the language of Section 2903(a)(1) indicates that banks will be evaluated for CRA compliance according to how well they *meet* the credit needs of their communities.

The language of Section 2903(a)(1), in turn, places a heavier burden on the federal banking agencies to evaluate a bank's CRA record. In contrast to evaluating whether a bank is *helping* to meet credit needs, which invites a subjective and open-ended analysis, evaluating whether a bank is *meeting* credit needs is a much more rigorous undertaking. In order to satisfy their obligation, the federal banking agencies must evaluate community credit needs, measure bank lending, and judge the bank's CRA performance by comparing its lending performance with community credit needs. Despite the fact that evaluating whether a bank is meeting credit needs requires a fairly rigorous and objective evaluation, the CRA does not state what a bank must do to meet community credit needs. But clearly a bank must do something.

Upon concluding a PE, the statute requires the federal banking agency to prepare a written evaluation of the bank's record of "meeting the credit needs of its entire community, including low- and moderate-income neighborhoods."[14] The PE must contain findings, conclusions, and one of four CRA ratings:[15] "outstanding"; "satisfactory"; "needs to improve"; or "substantial noncompliance."[16] The PE must state the federal banking agency's conclusions about each CRA performance assessment criterion identified in the federal banking agencies' CRA regulations, discuss the facts and data supporting the conclusions, and contain the bank's CRA rating and a statement describing the basis for the rating.[17] The report must present this information—except for the rating—separately for each metropolitan area in which the bank has at least one branch.[18] If the bank has branches in two or more states, the federal banking agency is to prepare a written report of the entire bank's CRA performance and a separate written report for each state in which the bank has at least one branch.[19] For each state in which the bank has a branch, the relevant federal banking agency must prepare a report for each metropolitan area in that state in which the bank has at least one branch, and a separate report for the non-metropolitan area of the state if the bank has at least one branch in a non-metropolitan area.[20]

The PEs are to be written and public, thus holding banks accountable. By requiring the agencies to prepare separate PEs for each metropolitan area in which the bank has a branch, for each state in which the bank has a branch, and for the non-metropolitan area of each state in which the bank has a branch, the CRA influences banks to lend throughout their service areas.

Bank Expansion Applications

The second opportunity the federal banking agencies have to enforce the CRA comes when they are considering a bank's application for a "deposit facility."[21] A bank must apply to the federal banking agency that regulates it before it can expand or engage in new lines of business, among other activities.[22] When considering such an application for a "deposit facility" (also referred to as an "expansion application"), the relevant federal banking agency is also to take the bank's CRA record into account.[23] This evaluation process influences banks to lend to redlined areas.

The applications that are included in the definition of "application for a deposit facility" are few in number but important. Six applications are covered, including applications for a charter for a national bank or federal savings and loan association, for deposit insurance, to establish a branch, to relocate a home office or branch, to merge with another bank, and to obtain the assets or assume the liabilities of another bank.[24] Since not all types of applications are covered, this enforcement mechanism is not as strong as it could be. However, the six applications that are covered are significant and relate directly to lending, creating a strong motive for banks that are planning to expand to lend in redlined neighborhoods.

The CRA does not explicitly give the federal banking agencies the authority to do anything other than consider the bank's CRA record in connection with an expansion application. Nevertheless, in their regulations, the federal banking agencies have given themselves the authority to deny an application based on a poor CRA record.[25] Although this authority is not in the statute, it appears to be a reasonable assumption of power.[26] It is consistent with Congress' intent that the agencies could deny an expansion application from a bank with a poor CRA record.[27] The federal banking agencies also have independent statutory authority to deny the applications that are covered by the CRA.[28] Thus, implicit in the agencies' authority under the CRA to take account of a bank's CRA record when deciding an application covered by the CRA is the authority to deny the application on CRA grounds.[29] Finally, the federal banking agencies have a separate statutory obligation to take the convenience and needs of the community into account when considering the applications that are covered by the CRA.[30] The CRA makes clear that convenience and needs include the need for credit services.[31] Thus, the CRA makes a bank's obligation to meet community credit needs part of the agencies' independent statutory evaluation of whether the convenience and needs of the community will be served by granting an application that is covered by the CRA.[32]

Another motive for banks to improve their lending records in redlined areas is that members of the public can file comments with the federal banking agencies opposing expansion applications on the grounds that the banks have not met their CRA obligations.[33] Banks' desire to avoid public comments, and the added public scrutiny and risk they bring to expansion applications, create a powerful motive for banks to improve their lending records prior to filing expansion applications.[34]

Limited Enforcement Mechanisms

These enforcement mechanisms are not so onerous that they allocate credit. First, although the federal banking agencies have the authority to deny a bank's expansion application on the grounds that the bank has a poor CRA record, there is only one time denial is mandatory. The mandatory denial does not come in connection with an application, but in connection with an election to become a financial holding company ("FHC"). Under the Gramm-Leach-Bliley Act, a bank holding company ("BHC") can elect to become an FHC, and therefore be permitted to engage in the securities and insurance businesses.[35] In order to make such an election, the BHC must file a notice containing certain information and representations, including a certificate that all its subsidiary banks have at least a satisfactory CRA rating.[36] If a BHC's subsidiaries do not all have a satisfactory CRA rating, the BHC cannot become an FHC. Second, a denial of an expansion application is not final. The bank can renew an application that has been denied on CRA grounds once it improves its record.[37]

The CRA also avoids allocating credit by staying away from stronger enforcement mechanisms common to other anti-discrimination statutes.[38] The CRA does not create civil or criminal sanctions for violations. It does not create a private cause of action.[39] It does not give the federal banking agencies the authority to enforce the law through administrative proceedings.[40] It does not require a bank to make loans as a remedy for a poor CRA record.[41] Finally, it does not require a bank to make any particular loan or to develop a specific type of lending program.[42]

Judicial Interpretation of the CRA

Judicial interpretation of the CRA has undermined CRA's potential for democratizing capital. The courts have mediated the CRA's tension between influencing banks to lend and not allocating credit in favor of ensuring that the CRA does not allocate credit at the expense of influencing banks to lend. The courts have appropriately given wide latitude to the federal banking agencies to enforce the CRA. However, they have inappropriately made it virtually impossible for individuals or community groups to go to court to challenge agency decisions approving bank expansion applications. The resulting virtual absence of judicial involvement in CRA enforcement cuts off an important avenue for members of the public to enforce the CRA.[43] Additionally, the public's voice in the application process is weakened because the agencies know they will not be held accountable by a court for their decisions on expansion applications.[44]

There are four key principles behind the limited role of the courts in enforcing the CRA. The first is that the CRA does not create a "private right of action." This means that a private citizen or a community group cannot file a lawsuit against a bank alleging that the bank has violated the CRA and seeking damages or an order from the court requiring the bank to comply with the CRA. Such a private right of action is common to other anti-discrimination laws such as the Fair Housing Act ("FHA")[45] and the Equal Credit

Opportunity Act ("ECOA").[46] Under these laws, an individual who feels that a bank denied a home mortgage loan application on account of the individual's race can sue the bank in court. This, in turn, leads to extensive involvement by the courts in interpreting and enforcing the FHA and the ECOA. Since the CRA does not create a private right of action, however, the potential for this type of extensive involvement by the courts in CRA interpretation and enforcement does not exist.

The second principle is that, as a result of the lack of a private right of action under the CRA, generally the only way for a court to get involved in a legal dispute regarding the CRA is in a lawsuit challenging a federal banking agency's decision on a bank's expansion application. Once a federal banking regulatory agency makes a decision on a bank expansion application, certain parties may have the right to challenge the decision in federal court.[47] The court can then review the agency's decision and uphold, reverse, or remand it to the agency for further consideration. This is a very limited role for the courts to play in enforcing the CRA.

Third, it is hard for a community group to participate in even this limited process because of a doctrine known as standing. In order to challenge an agency's decision in court, a community group must show it has standing to do so. Another way of saying this is that the community group must show it has suffered tangible harm as a result of the agency granting the application and that a decision by the court overturning the grant would redress the harm. The courts have made it nearly impossible for a community group to show that is has standing to challenge a federal banking agency's decision in court.[48] The courts have made it very difficult for a community group to prove that it satisfies the requirements for standing: that the injury it suffered is a result of the agency's action on the application and that this injury would be remedied by a decision overturning the grant of the application.[49] Courts have placed this limit on standing even if the community group filed comments opposing the bank's expansion application.[50]

Finally, the courts give broad discretion to the federal banking agencies in making decisions on bank expansion applications. As long as there is a "rational basis" for the agency's decision, the courts will uphold the decision.[51] In other words, as long as the agency's decision is not "arbitrary and capricious" or an "abuse of discretion," the decision will stand.[52] As long as there is a rational connection between the facts in the record and the agency's decision, the courts will not overturn the agency's decision.[53]

There are very few reported cases involving the CRA, and a community group has never successfully challenged a federal banking agency's approval of a bank expansion application on CRA grounds in court.[54] The leading case on the CRA is *Lee v. Board of Governors of the Federal Reserve System* ("*Lee I*").[55] *Lee I* involved two bank expansions involving four separate applications to two different federal banking agencies. The first expansion was a complex business arrangement between Chase Manhattan Corporation ("Chase") and United States Trust Corporation's ("UST") securities processing business, and included two applications by Chase to the Board of Governors of the Federal Reserve System (the "Federal Reserve") and an application by UST to the Office of Thrift Supervision ("OTS"). The second expansion was Chase's merger with Chemical Banking Corporation ("Chemical"); Chase applied to the Federal Reserve for permission to merge.[56] A community-based organization from the South Bronx, Inner City Press/Community on the Move ("ICP"), filed comments with the Federal Reserve and the OTS opposing the applications on the grounds that the banks had not met their CRA obligations.[57]

In its comments, ICP alleged several deficiencies in all three banks' CRA records. Among the charges, ICP alleged that Chase's Direct Banking Program was discriminatory because it required a minimum balance of $6,000 to waive electronic banking fees, disproportionately excluding LMI persons from the benefits of the program.[58] ICP argued that, based on data collected under the Home Mortgage Disclosure Act ("HMDA"), Chase engaged in discriminatory lending practices. ICP also alleged that Chase illegally "pre-screened" loan applicants from the South Bronx prior to receiving their loan applications, thus discouraging them from applying. ICP made similar allegations against Chemical. As to UST, ICP alleged that it failed to collect information about the race of home mortgage loan applicants in violation of HMDA, therefore making it impossible to evaluate UST's CRA record. ICP also alleged that UST excluded virtually all LMI neighborhoods from its CRA service community.

The Federal Reserve, after holding a public meeting on the Chase-Chemical merger application at which it heard testimony and received evidence, approved all three applications before it in three separate orders.[59] It found that each bank had earned either a satisfactory or outstanding CRA rating on its most recent CRA performance evaluation and it listed the efforts each bank was making to meet the credit needs of LMI areas, including Chase's pledge to lend and invest $18.1 billion over five years in LMI neighborhoods within its community.[60] The Federal Reserve also found that the HMDA data ICP used to support its claim of discriminatory lending was not sufficiently detailed to support such a claim. The Federal Reserve found no evidence that the Chase Direct Program had a discriminatory effect on LMI persons and noted that relevant regulations explicitly permit such programs. The Federal Reserve also found that UST did not violate HMDA by failing to gather the race and income of home mortgage loan applicants because it took the applications over the telephone and such applications were exempt from the regulatory reporting requirements.

The Federal Reserve and the OTS both approved the transactions at issue, and ICP challenged these approvals in court, before the United States Court of Appeals for the Second Circuit.[61] The court ruled that ICP lacked standing to pursue the litigation.[62] It also ruled that even if ICP did have standing, its challenge to the approvals was without merit.[63]

ICP made three arguments in support of its standing to challenge the Federal Reserve's and OTS' decisions. ICP argued first that it had standing because it had submitted comments opposing the application. Second, it alleged that members of ICP had been denied credit by "banks in their community" and "are likely to seek credit from banks in their community."[64] Because the Board and the OTS had ignored the poor CRA record of Chase, Chemical, and UST, ICP argued, these individuals were less likely to receive credit in the future. Finally, ICP alleged that, as a customer of Chemical, it would suffer from the anti-competitive effects of the merger of Chase and Chemical.[65]

The court rejected these grounds for standing. First, it ruled that mere participation in the administrative process does not alone confer standing.[66] While participation in the administrative process was a necessary aspect of standing, it was not sufficient to create standing. ICP still had to show an injury-in-fact from the agencies' decisions. The court noted the absence of any allegation that ICP's members had been denied credit by or planned to apply for credit from Chase, Chemical, or UST. The court also stated that ICP's claim that, as a customer of Chemical, it would suffer harm from Chase's increased market presence, was too speculative to create injury. Second, the court ruled that ICP had failed to establish that the Federal Reserve's action caused ICP's injury and that an order overturning the Federal Reserve's approval of the transaction would redress the injury. The court stated that the CRA is an "amorphous statute" and not a "directive to undertake any particular program or to provide credit to any particular individual."[67] The court also stated that the CRA was precatory and "sets no standards for the evaluation of a bank's contribution to the needs of its community."[68]

Even though the court determined that ICP did not have standing, the court considered the merits of ICP's claims. The court began its analysis of the merits by describing its "deferential standard of review" of Federal Reserve decisions.[69] The court stated that the Federal Reserve's findings are "conclusive so long as they are supported by substantial evidence."[70] The court referred to this as a specific application of the "arbitrary and capricious" standard of review of agency decisions.[71] The court reserved to itself the "ultimate say" on legal issues involved in the case, but stated that "the Board is the agency responsible for federal regulation of the national banking system, and its interpretation of pertinent federal statutes is entitled to substantial deference."[72]

The court stated, quoting from the CRA, that the Federal Reserve's responsibility under the CRA is to assess a bank's record of meeting the credit needs of its community and to take that record into account when evaluating an expansion application. The court found "no doubt that this mandate was carried out in these cases."[73] As a general matter, the court stated that "[e]ach of the Board orders at issue clearly addresses the relevant institutions' CRA records in its analysis of the convenience and needs of the communities to be served...," and cited the Board's seventy-two page decision approving the application, forty-five pages of which were dedicated to an analysis of the banks' CRA records.[74] In particular, the court stated that the Federal Reserve had properly resolved each issue. The court upheld the Federal Reserve's conclusion that HMDA data is not sufficiently detailed to determine conclusively whether a bank is engaging in lending discrimination.[75] The court stated, "[B]ecause the Board is one of the regulatory agencies charged with the responsibility for administering the CRA, its decisions on such matters are entitled to substantial deference, and we find no error in its conclusion."[76] Next, the court deferred "to the Board's interpretation of... [HMDA] regulations as applied to the particular facts" since it found that UST's failure to record the race and income of loan applicants did not violate HMDA.[77] Finally, the court affirmed the Board's decision that Chase's and Chemical's no-fee bank account product for high-balance accounts did not disproportionately discriminate against LMI borrowers.

Following *Lee I*, the United States District Court for the Southern District of New York issued another key decision that further limited the ability of community groups to establish standing to challenge a federal banking agency's decision approving an expansion application. In *Lee v. Federal Deposit Insurance Corp.* (*Lee II*),[78] ICP challenged four orders of the Federal Deposit Insurance Corp. ("FDIC") and the Office of the Comptroller of the Currency ("OCC"); three of them related to the UST-Chase merger and one order by the FDIC approving GreenPoint Bank's application to purchase sixty branches of Home Savings of America.[79]

In *Lee II*, ICP attempted to satisfy the Second Circuit's articulation of the standards for establishing standing in *Lee I* by alleging that the banks had denied credit to ICP members and that ICP members had concrete plans to apply for credit. ICP alleged that it could identify "individual members of ICP who have sought from, and have been denied mortgage, small business, or other lines of credit by Chase and who have concrete plans to reapply for such types of credit from that bank."[80] The court in *Lee II* ruled that the Second Circuit's decision in *Lee I* indicated that specific denials of credit are important to establish standing. However, the court in *Lee II* ruled that ICP did not allege the credit denials in specific detail as required by the Second Circuit. The district court also found the allegation of "concrete plans" to apply for credit was not sufficiently detailed to create standing. Instead, ICP had to allege that its members had pending applications the banks were likely to deny.

Second, ICP alleged that its members lived in buildings whose owners have "sought from, and have been denied loans, grants and community development investments by wholesale investment institutions, like UST, and who continue to endure the deterioration and unsafe conditions caused by the owners' inability to obtain refinancing or capital."[81] ICP also alleged that it had identified members of ICP who would apply for credit from UST if it served the Bronx. The court ruled that these allegations of injury-in-fact were too vague to create standing. As to past harm from the denial of loan applications, the court ruled that the owners of the building, not the tenants, were the parties who were injured. As to future harm—UST's possible denials of future loan applications submitted by Bronx individuals—the court ruled that future possible denials were too tenuous to create standing.

Third, ICP made several allegations of injury relating to GreenPoint. It alleged that it could identify ICP members who had been denied credit by other banks and who had plans to apply to GreenPoint. ICP also alleged that GreenPoint's lending practices have the potential for "adversely impacting the physical environs of all the residents of the South Bronx. . . ."[82] The court ruled that these allegations did not create standing because they did not allege injury-in-fact. The court ruled that credit denials by other banks did not create standing, that plans to apply for credit were too speculative, and that ICP's allegation that GreenPoint's injury to the physical environs of the South Bronx was too vague to create standing.

The court also ruled that ICP could not establish that the FDIC's and OCC's decisions caused these alleged injuries or that a decision by the court overturning the agency's decisions approving the applications would redress these injuries. As to causation, the court ruled that ICP failed to allege that the individual denials of credit could be traced to the FDIC's or the OCC's failures to regulate the banks properly under the CRA or that the loan denials would have been loan approvals if the FDIC and OCC had denied the banks' expansion applications. As to redressability, the district court echoed the Second Circuit's decision in *Lee I* by stating that the CRA was an amorphous statute that only required the federal banking agencies to take a bank's CRA record into account when considering an expansion application and did not establish standards for evaluating a bank's compliance with meeting community credit needs. Thus, an order by the court overturning the decision would not mean that ICP members would more likely obtain credit in the future.

The decisions in *Lee I* and *Lee II* have made it nearly impossible for a community group to establish standing. In doing so, the decisions showed a fundamental misunderstanding of the CRA and undermined the CRA's potential for democratizing capital. The courts made it impossible to allege injury-in-fact successfully. In *Lee II*, ICP seemed to satisfy *Lee I's* requirement that it show past denial of credit or future plans to apply. Nevertheless, the court in *Lee II* said ICP's allegation was insufficient. The courts also made it impossible for a community group to show that a decision overturning an agency's decision could redress an injury. The rationale was that the CRA was an amorphous statute that did not clearly identify the terms for evaluating bank performance. However, had the courts examined congressional intent in passing the CRA and the CRA's structure carefully, they would have seen that Congress intended the federal banking agencies to enforce the CRA in a way that ended redlining and capital export and influenced banks to lend in underserved neighborhoods.[83] If the agencies fail to enforce the CRA, redlined neighborhoods will be injured by continued redlining, capital export, and lack of reinvestment. Federal banking agencies can enforce the CRA effectively by denying a bank expansion application if the bank has a poor CRA record. If an agency's decision on an expansion application does not properly implement the agency's responsibility to enforce the CRA, the residents of the neighborhoods involved will suffer harm because the banks involved and other banks will continue to fail to meet community credit needs. A court order overturning an agency decision granting an application of a bank that is not meeting community credit needs would redress this harm.

Conclusion

The CRA is designed to exert a strong influence on banks to lend in redlined areas, thus democratizing capital. The CRA places an obligation on banks to meet community credit needs. The CRA performance evaluation influences banks to lend to redlined neighborhoods. The required contents of the evaluation provide details about a bank's lending record in its local community in all metropolitan and non-metropolitan areas in which it has a branch. Public disclosure of the reports and the ratings are designed to hold banks open to public scrutiny. The opportunity for regulatory and public scrutiny of a bank's CRA record in connection with an expansion application also creates a strong motive for banks to lend. The applications at stake are important to banks. The CRA has this powerful influence on bank lending decisions without setting loan quotas or mandating particular loans on particular terms to a particular person or group of persons. It does not include mandatory penalties or create a private cause of action. Despite the CRA's intent and structure, courts construing the CRA have made it virtually impossible for a community group to challenge an agency's decision approving a bank expansion application, undermining the CRA's influence on banks and its potential for democratizing capital.

CHAPTER THREE

The First CRA Enforcement Regime: 1977–97

Introduction

After Congress passed the CRA in 1977, the four federal administrative agencies that regulate banks were responsible for enforcing it. These agencies—the Board of Governors of the Federal Reserve System, the Office of the Comptroller of the Currency, the Federal Deposit Insurance Corporation, and the Federal Home Loan Bank Board (currently the Office of Thrift Supervision)(collectively the "federal banking agencies" or the "agencies")—promulgated regulations enforcing the CRA that remained in effect until mid-1997, when the agencies replaced them with new regulations. The controlling principle underlying the federal banking agencies' approach to enforcing the CRA from 1977 through mid-1997 (the "first CRA enforcement regime") was that Congress did not intend the CRA to allocate credit. The federal banking agencies were so careful to avoid allocating credit that they did so at the expense of the CRA's main goal—ending redlining and increasing lending in low-and moderate-income ("LMI"), predominantly minority, and inner-city neighborhoods (collectively "redlined neighborhoods"). The federal banking agencies avoided allocating credit by taking an efforts-oriented approach to CRA enforcement. They took the position that the CRA was a mechanism to correct an information failure in the market. Redlining was the result of banks' failure to gather information about viable lending opportunities in redlined neighborhoods based on negative assumptions about those neighborhoods, and the CRA was intended to require banks to gather this information. Once banks had information about viable lending opportunities in these neighborhoods, loans would presumably follow.

Based on the federal banking agencies' fear of allocating credit and their view of the CRA as a tool to correct an information failure in the market, the first CRA enforcement regime had three key characteristics. First, when evaluating a bank's lending record, the federal banking agencies overemphasized the efforts the bank undertook to lend over its lending record. Second, the federal banking agencies did not adopt a fixed set of CRA evaluative criteria composed of quantitative measures of bank lending, quantitative benchmarks of community credit needs, and objective standards for evaluating whether a bank's lending met community credit needs. They frequently cited quantitative measures of bank lending, but did not use a fixed set of such measures. Additionally, they used wholly subjective standards to evaluate whether a bank's lending record met community credit needs, such as whether the lending was "reasonable." The third characteristic of the first CRA enforcement regime was that the federal banking agencies did not strictly enforce the CRA. They gave banks high CRA ratings, rarely denied bank expansion applications on CRA grounds, and when they used their authority to commence administrative enforcement proceedings against banks with poor CRA records, generally focused on bank lending procedures instead of lending records.

The three key characteristics of the first CRA enforcement regime undermined the CRA's potential for democratizing capital. The efforts-oriented approach and the subjective standards for evaluating a bank's CRA performance made it difficult for community groups to enforce the CRA, limiting the franchise over lending decisions the CRA extended to previously disenfranchised groups. The agencies' focus on efforts rather than results also limited the extent to which the CRA encouraged banks to distribute loans to underserved individuals, limiting their participation in the economic mainstream.

The agencies' approach to enforcing the CRA in the first CRA enforcement regime had several consequences. Enforcement was arbitrary and inconsistent, banks complained that they were required to do too much paperwork to document their efforts, and community groups claimed that they could not hold banks accountable for poor lending records. These complaints about the first CRA enforcement regime ultimately led to its downfall and replacement.

The Federal Banking Agencies' Perspective on the CRA and Credit Allocation

The federal banking agencies were fond of repeating that the CRA was not intended to and did not allocate credit. In passing the CRA, "Congress did not support nonmarket methods of credit allocation, such as quotas, to meet the credit needs of the local community."[1] The CRA was "not intended to establish a regulatory allocation of credit."[2] Congress did not require a bank to "make any specific number of loans in any targeted geographic area."[3]

Federal Reserve economist Glenn Canner cited the CRA's legislative history to support the argument that Congress did not intend the CRA to allocate credit. Canner cited several explicit statements by Senator Proxmire during Senate hearings on the CRA that Congress did not intend the CRA to allocate credit and that it would not set reinvestment targets.[4] Canner also cited Senator Proxmire's removal of a loan-to-deposit-ratio requirement from the initial version of the CRA as further evidence that Congress did not intend the CRA to allocate credit.[5] Canner wrote, "Although CRA is directed at the problem of meeting sound community credit needs, it was not intended to establish regulatory influence on the allocation of credit."[6] Canner, however, acknowledged that supporters of the CRA saw it as a way to increase bank reinvestment in low-income communities.[7]

Reflecting Canner's position, the federal banking agencies took the correct position that, in implementing the CRA, they could not allocate credit. However, they tried so hard to avoid allocating credit that they failed to carry out congressional intent that the CRA influence banks to lend more money in redlined neighborhoods. Thus, the federal banking agencies correctly stated that they could not dictate the proportion of credit that a bank should devote to a product, customer, or neighborhood,[8] or establish fixed ratios of loans to deposits in particular neighborhoods.[9] The Federal Reserve correctly stated that it was not authorized "to dictate what proportion or amount of an institution's funds must, or even should, be allocated to any particular credit need, borrower or neighborhood, or on what specific terms credit should be extended."[10] On the other hand, the federal banking agencies were incorrect when they said that they could not influence bank lending decisions.[11]

The federal banking agencies believed Congress was right not to allocate credit. "Congress wisely chose to avoid even the appearance of prescribing the allocation of credit."[12] Former Comptroller of the Currency Eugene Ludwig stated that a bank should not be required to "make any particular loan or lend to any particular borrower or class of borrowers."[13] Former Federal Reserve Governor Lawrence Lindsey stated, "The lesson of history is that moving in a purely political direction of banking, or heavy handed credit allocation, is not only bad for banking, it is harmful to society as a whole."[14] Lindsey stated that credit allocation could not work: "one may suspect whether any nationally imposed set of formulas on performance, no matter how sophisticated, could ever be made to work."[15]

The federal banking agencies were so concerned not to allocate credit that they took pains to avoid even influencing banks to lend in LMI neighborhoods. Instead, they approached the CRA as an effort to correct an information deficit in the market. Redlining was the result of banks lacking adequate information about credit opportunities in redlined neighborhoods and failing to look for them. The purpose of the CRA was to ensure that bankers sought this information. Federal Reserve economist Glenn Canner stated, "A basic goal of the CRA is to sensitize lenders to the credit needs of low- and moderate-income neighborhoods and small businesses located in these communities."[16] The federal banking agencies understood their CRA enforcement responsibilities as fixing this information failure. Once they did, banks would obtain information about creditworthy borrowers in redlined neighborhoods and loans would presumably follow. Robert Clarke, former Comptroller of the Currency, reflected this view when he stated, "In all communities there are opportunities for extension of credit to a variety of borrowers, including low- and moderate-income persons, and bankers will find these opportunities if they take the time to look for them."[17]

Three Federal Reserve economists, William C. Gruben, Jonathan A. Neuberger, and Ronald H. Schmidt, in an article entitled, *Imperfect Information and the Community Reinvestment Act*, described this perspective on the CRA.[18] They wrote that information about lending opportunities enables banks to distinguish among borrowers and projects and helps banks determine the risk of lending.[19] As a bank gathers more information, its ability to make safe and sound loans increases.[20] Information, however, is not without cost.[21] In order to collect adequate information, banks must incur significant costs, including opening a branch or loan origination office, conducting surveys regarding the value of neighborhood properties, and soliciting and evaluating loan applications from neighborhood residents.[22] In determining whether to do business in a particular neighborhood, bankers do a cost-benefit analysis. If they perceive that the cost of information-gathering will be high and the return on their investment will be low, they will not invest in information-gathering in a neighborhood. Bankers may perceive the potential costs and rates of return to be different among different neighborhoods.[23] Bankers may use factors such as high minority population, low average income, or average age of property as proxies for evaluating costs and rates of return.[24] Bankers will be unwilling to incur the cost of gathering information in neighborhoods with these characteristics because they believe the return on their investment in gathering information will not be sufficient.[25] This is, in effect, redlining. If, however, banks choose or are induced to invest in information-gathering in redlined neighborhoods, they may find worthwhile lending opportunities.[26] The CRA represents an inducement to do such information-gathering.[27] The authors concluded that one approach to enforcing the CRA based on this theory is an "efforts-oriented" approach, in which a bank's efforts to obtain information and make loans in redlined neighborhoods is the basis for evaluating its CRA record.[28] Under this approach, a CRA examination would evaluate a bank's efforts to ascertain the credit needs of its local community and its efforts to market its loans.[29] This is how the federal banking agencies enforced the CRA during the first CRA enforcement regime.[30]

The Three Key Characteristics of the First CRA Enforcement Regime

In exercising their responsibilities to enforce the CRA, the federal banking agencies correctly took the position that the CRA did not permit them to allocate credit by establishing lending quotas. In their zeal to avoid allocating credit, however, the agencies unduly limited their influence over bank lending decisions. Instead, they understood their responsibilities to be one step removed from influencing banks to lend in redlined neighborhoods; they worked to make sure that banks undertook efforts to learn about credit opportunities in their local communities. The federal banking agencies' failure to embrace the purpose of the CRA resulted in the three key characteristics of the first CRA regime—the overemphasis on efforts, the absence of objective standards, and the limited use of enforcement authority—which led to great dissatisfaction with the first CRA enforcement regime and ultimately its downfall.

The Overemphasis on Efforts

The first CRA enforcement regime overemphasized the efforts a bank undertook to help meet community credit needs. Federal Reserve economist Glenn Canner stated, "In assessing an institution's CRA record, a premium is placed on evidence of affirmative action taken by lenders to determine and meet community credit needs."[31] According to former Federal Reserve Governor Lawrence Lindsey, "the focus on process is a natural outgrowth of leaving the definition of an appropriate level of performance up to the needs of the community and the capacity of its institutions."[32] The federal banking agencies' emphasis on efforts was criticized. The Subcommittee on Housing of the Senate Committee on Banking, Housing, and Urban Affairs stated in a report (the "Senate CRA Report") that the agencies "overemphasize[d] the process of CRA at the expense of the substance of CRA—reinvestment by financial institutions in the communities in which they are chartered."[33] According to the Report, more important to the federal banking agencies than the number of loans a bank made to low-income and minority borrowers was "the number of contacts the bank's CRA officer initiated, the extensiveness of phone logs, attendance by banking officials at CRA-related meetings and seminars, and the frequency with which the CRA was discussed at board meetings."[34]

The overemphasis on efforts was a consequence of the federal banking agencies' desire to avoid allocating credit, combined with their vision of the CRA's role as correcting an information failure. Because the CRA does not allocate credit, "there will always be considerable focus on having an adequate process in place which, in fact, delivers product."[35] The emphasis on efforts "steered clear of any semblance of credit allocation, it created a different problem by placing an undue emphasis on documentation [i.e. written reports of lending efforts]."[36] Bankers spoke about documentation of lending efforts as the key to CRA success.[37] Banking consultants advised banks to document their efforts to satisfy the CRA.[38] Banking regulators gave similar advice.[39] Banks complained that they received poor CRA ratings solely because of lack of documentation.[40] One study concluded that large banks had higher CRA ratings than small banks because a large bank could afford a staff to document its CRA efforts.[41]

The four federal banking agencies each promulgated separate CRA regulations that were substantially identical.[42] They also adopted several joint regulatory statements, memoranda, and examination instructions that described and elaborated how they would apply the regulations. The emphasis on efforts was apparent in all these documents.

The CRA Regulations

The CRA regulations established twelve assessment criteria to evaluate a bank's CRA performance.[43] The first three CRA assessment criteria dealt with bank efforts to lend: (a) the bank's efforts to ascertain community credit needs; (b) the extent of the bank's marketing efforts; and (c) the extent to which the bank's board of directors and senior management were involved with the CRA.[44] The federal banking agencies placed disproportionately high emphasis on these three criteria, expecting that strong efforts would result in loans.[45] "[T]he regulation encourages institutions to become aware of the full range of credit needs of their communities and to offer the types of credit and credit-related services that will help to meet those needs."[46] Former Comptroller of the Currency Robert Clarke stated, "The CRA calls for process. Process that results in product. It is up to the senior management of an institution to create and maintain the process that delivers the product."[47] The regulations "placed emphasis on the need for a managed CRA program: Were procedures in place at the institution to promote community dialogue? How did the institution take its assessment of community needs into account in product design and marketing? If it analyzed its geographic distribution of credit on an ongoing basis, what were the institution's own goals for lending distribution and had they been met?"[48]

The only actual requirements the CRA regulations imposed on banks were related to notices, information, and procedures, not lending. The regulations required a bank to delineate the local lending community in which it would have its CRA obligations; post in the lobby of its branches and offices a notice that described its CRA obligations, how to obtain information about its CRA record, and how to file comments about its CRA performance; adopt a CRA statement that included a map of its local community, a list of the types of credit it made available, and a copy of its CRA notice; and maintain a public file containing comments about its CRA record, a copy of its most recent CRA performance evaluation, and its CRA statement.[49]

Other Regulatory Materials

In addition to the CRA regulations, the federal banking agencies jointly promulgated several regulatory materials that elaborated on their CRA enforcement policy. These materials, including the "Joint Statement," the "Policy Statement on the Analysis of the Geographic Distribution of Lending," and the "CRA Q & A," clearly reflected the agencies' overemphasis on efforts.

The Joint Statement

The Statement of the Federal Financial Supervisory Agencies Regarding the Community Reinvestment Act[50] (the "Joint Statement") is perhaps the clearest statement of the federal banking agencies' efforts-oriented approach to evaluating CRA compliance.[51] Promulgated in 1989, the Joint Statement was intended to describe the agencies' approach to enforcing the CRA. The Joint Statement did not "establish specific lending requirements or programs for financial institutions subject to the CRA."[52] Rather, it described the "policies and procedures that the Agencies believe financial institutions should have in place in order to fulfill their responsibilities under the CRA on an ongoing basis...."[53]

The most important statement of policy in the Joint Statement was that banks should treat their CRA obligations as part of their regular business.[54] There were three steps a bank should take: involve the board of directors and senior management in CRA activities and in developing a CRA plan; assign responsibility for CRA performance to a senior officer; and institute a system to monitor the CRA plan to make sure it was being followed.[55]

The Joint Statement described the factors the federal banking agencies would consider when evaluating a bank's CRA record. These included "the process by which a financial institution defines the community it serves, determines its credit needs, including its low-and moderate-income areas, and takes steps to help meet those needs through appropriate and prudent lending."[56] The Joint Statement recommended that a bank establish a CRA plan that included procedures for incorporating findings about community credit needs into the creation and marketing of loan products, appoint a senior officer to oversee implementation of the plan, establish an employee training program, and review its CRA statement at least annually.[57]

The Joint Statement made clear that the federal banking agencies would examine a bank's CRA record according to how well it followed its procedures. According to former Comptroller of the Currency Robert Clarke, "[D]uring the examinations, we monitor whether the bank's own systems are working, and require changes when necessary."[58] In order to enable them to evaluate a bank's procedures, the federal banking agencies expected "financial institutions to maintain reasonable documentation of the activities, such as those outlined in this Statement, that have been undertaken by the institution to implement the institution's CRA policies."[59]

The Joint Statement's emphasis on procedures was further demonstrated when it discussed what would happen if a bank examiner found that, contrary to the CRA, a bank's loans were concentrated outside of its community or in wealthy areas. In that instance, rather than examining bank lending policies and products in an effort to influence the bank to change its lending policies and adopt products that meet the credit needs of its local community, the examiner would investigate the bank's efforts to ascertain credit needs, communicate with all segments of its community, and advertise and market its services throughout its delineated community, to determine whether the bank was in compliance with the CRA.[60]

The Policy Statement on Analysis of Geographic Distribution of Lending

The Policy Statement on Analysis of Geographic Distribution of Lending (the "Policy Statement"), also focused on lending procedures. In the Policy Statement, the federal banking agencies stated that they expected banks to conduct, at least annually, an analysis of the disposition of the bank's loan applications to "ensure that potential borrowers are treated in a fair and nondiscriminatory manner and that all segments of the delineated community are appropriately served."[61] Banks should "document this analysis and make the documentation readily available to their examiners."[62] The federal banking agencies viewed banks favorably if they performed this analysis.[63]

The geographic analysis was to ensure that "policy and program goals and objectives are achieved and indicate whether any adjustments are necessary" and to allow a bank to "recognize and avoid the problems that may result from having unexplained geographic skewing of its lending distribution."[64] According to the Policy Statement, there is some lending distribution that is "appropriate," the distribution might be "skewed," and "adjustments" may be "necessary," but the Policy Statement offered no guidance about how to evaluate whether the level of lending was appropriate, whether lending distribution was skewed, or whether adjustments were necessary. Instead, the Policy Statement focused on procedures; banks had to do an analysis, document it, provide the documentation to the federal banking agency that regulates it, and determine whether its lending was consistent with policy objectives.

The CRA Q & A

The CRA Interagency Questions and Answers (the "CRA Q & A") contained thirty-one questions and answers about the CRA, most of which dealt with technical compliance and coverage issues such as which financial institutions are covered by the CRA (Question 1) and the documents that were to be placed in the bank's public CRA file (Question 10).[65]

Question 23, which was added in 1993, asked whether the process by which a bank attempted to meet its CRA obligations or its actual performance at making loans was more important in evaluating the bank's CRA record.[66] The answer: "The principal focus of the financial supervisory agencies and the activity most encouraged through an examination continues to be lending and other activities within the community that result in extensions of credit that help meet identified credit needs."[67]

The sincerity of the CRA Q & A's statement that lending performance was the most important part of CRA compliance is questionable in light of the CRA Q & A's failure to offer meaningful guidance about how to evaluate a bank's lending performance. The CRA Q & A also made clear that the remedy for poor performance was improved procedures. According to the CRA Q & A, a satisfactory or better CRA rating generally required that a bank's lending record was "consistent" with institutional capacity and the needs of the community, and that its lending activity reflected a "reasonable" penetration of all segments of the community.[68] "Consistent" and "reasonable" are vague and subjective terms that do not provide much guidance about appropriate lending levels. A bank's unsatisfactory lending performance was most likely the result of inadequate CRA procedures.[69] Effective procedures included oversight by the board of directors, the establishment of goals and objectives, community outreach and marketing, management and employee training, and regular monitoring of the bank's progress and performance.[70] Thus, "Process-oriented corrective measures should be implemented to make the institution more responsive to local credit needs."[71]

CRA Performance Evaluation Procedures

Procedures adopted by the federal banking agencies for conducting CRA performance evaluations reflect the overemphasis on efforts to lend rather than lending.[72] The examination procedures were not highly defined, but the most detailed procedures related to evaluating a bank's efforts to ascertain community credit needs and to advertise and market its products.[73] Former Comptroller of the Currency Robert Clarke described the emphasis on procedures during CRA evaluations: "the focus of supervisory activity is to ensure that the bank… has the procedures and accountability necessary to ensure a high level of performance."[74]

Lack of a Fixed Set of Quantitative and Objective CRA Evaluative Criteria

The second key characteristic of the first CRA enforcement regime was the federal banking agencies' failure to adopt a fixed set of CRA evaluative criteria composed of quantitative measures of bank lending, quantitative benchmarks of community credit needs, and objective standards for evaluating whether a bank was meeting community credit needs. Neither the CRA regulations, the federal banking agencies' instructions for applying them, nor other CRA regulatory materials contained such criteria for evaluating a bank's record.[75]

Of the twelve CRA assessment criteria in the regulations, only four dealt with the extent of a bank's lending in its local community. The following criteria are labeled with the same letters as they were in the regulations:

(e) the geographic distribution of the bank's loans, applications, and denials;
(h) the bank's participation in community development programs;
(i) the bank's origination of loans in its community; and
(j) the bank's participation in governmental loan programs.[76]

The instructions for applying these criteria used subjective standards.

Assessment Criterion (e): The geographic distribution of the bank's loans, applications, and denials

A bank's evaluation under this criterion depended on whether the geographic distribution of its loans, applications, and denials was "reasonable," "unjustified," or "disproportionate."[77] The CRA examination manual instructed bank examiners to determine "whether there is any indication of a geographic distribution of credit extensions, applications for credit, and credit denials which would signify failure to serve selected areas of local communities, particularly low- and moderate-income neighborhoods."[78] Revisions to the CRA examination manual in 1990 instructed examiners to review the geographic distribution of the bank's loans to determine whether the bank was extending credit throughout its community.[79]

Assessment Criterion (h): The bank's community development lending and activities

A bank's evaluation under assessment criterion (h) was based on whether the bank "affirmatively," "took some steps to," "sometimes," or "rarely" participated in community development lending and activities.[80] The CRA examination manual instructed bank examiners to determine whether the bank was involved in, or had considered becoming involved in, community development activities.[81] Revisions to the CRA examination manual in 1990 told examiners to determine the extent and nature of the bank's efforts to become aware of and involved in community development programs.[82]

Assessment Criterion (i): The origination of loans in the bank's community

A bank's evaluation under assessment criterion (i) was based on whether the bank made a "substantial majority" of loans inside its community, a "significant volume" of loans inside its community, a "significant volume" of loans outside its community, or a "substantial majority of loans outside its community."[83] There were no guidelines for defining "substantial" or "significant." The manual provisions for criterion (i) instructed bank examiners to determine "whether the institution has originated or purchased such loans or has plans to do so."[84] Revisions to the CRA examination manual in 1990 instructed bank examiners to determine the percentage of loans the bank made outside its community but did not include any criteria for evaluating the percentage.[85]

Assessment Criterion (j): The bank's participation in governmental loan programs

A bank's evaluation under this criterion was based on whether the bank's level of participation in governmental loan programs was "high," "periodic," "rare," or "little or no[ne]."[86] The CRA examination manual instructed bank examiners to determine whether the bank is involved in such programs.[87] Revisions to the manual in 1990 instructed bank examiners to determine the extent to which the bank participated in government loan programs.[88]

It was impossible to apply the standards for evaluating a bank's lending performance under CRA assessment criteria (e), (h), (i), and (j) consistently or objectively.[89] What, for example, was a "high level" of participation in community development loan programs and how was that distinguished from "periodic" participation? How was "periodic" participation, in turn, distinguished from "rare" participation, as distinct from "little or no" participation? What was a "reasonable" penetration of lending in all segments of the community, and how was it measured?[90] Was it making loans in the same percentage of LMI census tracts as in upper-income census tracts? Was it based on a bank's overall market share in low-income tracts compared with its market share in upper-income tracts? How was "reasonable" penetration distinguished from "unreasonable" penetration, and how was an "unreasonable" lending pattern different from a "substantially unjustified" pattern? What was a "substantial majority" of loans in the bank's community and how was that distinguished from a "significant volume" of loans?

Weak Enforcement

The third key characteristic of the first CRA enforcement regime was that the agencies rarely used the full extent of their authority to enforce the CRA. According to the Senate CRA Report, the agencies "have yet to fulfill their obligation to ensure that CRA is properly and completely implemented. The supervisory agencies' record of inconsistent and lax enforcement has engendered indifference and disinterest by the financial institutions."[91] Senator Alan Cranston, the chairperson of the subcommittee that issued the report, stated that the agencies' enforcement of the CRA had been "lax and grossly inconsistent," and accused the agencies of acting "as protectors of the banks rather than as regulators...."[92] The federal banking agencies were generally lenient with banks when conducting CRA performance evaluations, when considering bank expansion applications, and in administrative proceedings to enforce the banking laws and regulations. In each of these instances, the federal banking agencies also emphasized efforts and failed to use quantitative and objective criteria for evaluating CRA performance.

CRA Performance Evaluations

Inflated Ratings

The federal banking agencies' policy was to give banks high CRA ratings. According to former Comptroller of the Currency Robert Clarke, "We do not believe that a large number of banks should necessarily fall into the...[unsatisfactory] rating categories."[93] Table 3.1, showing the percentage of banks that received at least a satisfactory CRA rating, demonstrates this high curve.[94]

Kenneth Thomas' research indicates these high ratings may have been the result of grade inflation.[95] Thomas compared CRA ratings prior to and immediately following public disclosure of CRA ratings in 1990. He found that immediately following disclosure of CRA ratings, outstanding ratings declined from 11.8% to 8.7%, satisfactory ratings dropped from 84.9% to 80.3%, and unsatisfactory ratings increased from 3.3% to 11.0%.[96] He wrote, "It is possible to interpret the predisclosure distribution as being indicative of grade inflation because of the high proportion of above average ratings...and the lower proportion of above average ones."[97]

The Senate CRA Report analyzed the content of written CRA performance evaluation reports ("PEs") during the first CRA enforcement regime. Accord-

Table 3.1

PERCENTAGE OF BANKS RECEIVING AT LEAST A SATISFACTORY CRA RATING

Year(s)	Percentage
Pre-1990	98
1990–92	89
1993	93
1994	94.3
1995	96.3
1996	98.1
1997	98

ing to the Report, the PEs generally did not employ objective standards for evaluating whether a bank was meeting community credit needs, frequently contained little detail about bank lending records other than conclusory and subjective terms, and emphasized bank lending efforts over lending records. As a result, it was very difficult to discern the standards the federal banking agencies were applying, making it easier for the federal banking agencies to be lenient in evaluating and rating banks.[98] The following analysis is based on the Senate CRA Report.

Contents of the Evaluations

The PEs did not use a fixed set of CRA evaluative criteria composed of quantitative benchmarks of community credit needs or objective standards for evaluating whether a bank had met community credit needs.[99] They employed quantitative measures of bank lending, but without quantitative benchmarks of community credit needs or objective standards for evaluating whether bank lending met community credit needs, it was difficult to discern the meaning of the numbers. The PEs generally did not contain enough data or analysis of the data from which to infer the standards the federal banking agencies were applying to evaluate whether a bank was meeting the credit needs of the community.[100] The PEs sometimes did not state the number of loans a bank made.[101] When a PE did state the number of loans a bank made, it generally contained no comparative data to help determine whether the number of loans was sufficient to meet community credit needs.[102] The PEs used subjective terms such as a "very good volume" of loans or a "sufficient volume" of loans, and frequently simply listed the government-insured loan programs in which the bank was involved.[103]

In evaluating the geographic distribution of a bank's loans under assessment criterion (e), the PEs used vague and subjective terms such as "lending throughout" the community, a "reasonable penetration" of loans in all segments of the community, a "substantial majority" of loans in the bank's delineated community, and "most" loans within the delineated community.[104] The federal banking agencies occasionally used more specific measures of bank lending, but did not describe why the measures merited a satisfactory or unsatisfactory rating. For example, the federal banking agencies reported a bank's percentage of applications and loans within its community, a bank's rejection rate for loans in LMI census tracts compared with other census tracts, a bank's percentage of minority applicants compared with other banks, and a bank's market share of applications in LMI census tracts compared with its market share in tracts at higher income levels without further elaboration.[105]

The PEs rarely gave any details regarding community development activities under assessment criterion (h).[106] The reports used terms such as "willing" to participate, funded "some" projects, "various loans," and a "leadership" role to describe a bank's performance under this criterion.[107]

The PEs used vague terms such as "a handful," "numerous," "some," "limited," "adequate," or "low" to describe the level of a bank's lending under assessment criterion (i), the bank's origination of loans in its community.[108] As usual, none of these terms are defined. On other occasions, the PEs simply noted that the bank made loans, was generally responsive to community credit needs, or that it had loan penetration in its local community.[109] Occasionally, the PEs listed the total number and dollar amount of loans the bank made in its community without further elaboration.[110] To the extent the PEs used quantitative measures of bank lending, the measures included the bank's loan-to-asset ratio, loan-to-deposit-ratio, percentage of loans in its community, or changes in total lending activity, but the PEs did not use these measures consistently or offer any reasoning to explain how the measures justified their conclusions about the bank's compliance with the CRA.[111]

The PEs were also vague regarding the bank's participation in government loan programs under assessment criterion (j). Some PEs simply stated that the bank participated in government loan programs, other reports used vague terms such as "several," "limited," or "used."[112] In one PE the agency listed the number and dollar amount of loans the bank made without further analysis.[113]

The PEs also demonstrated the federal banking agencies' emphasis on efforts over lending.[114] For example, Bank of America and Wells Fargo received outstanding ratings even though they made relatively few home mortgage loans to African-Americans.[115] A Chicago bank received an outstanding rating even though it defined its local CRA lending community to exclude adjacent minority communities.[116] In contrast, another Chicago bank that made many multi-family housing loans in low-income neighborhoods received a less than satisfactory rating because it did not advertise its low-income mortgage products in wealthy neighborhoods.[117] Another bank received a high CRA rating based on its procedures, documentation, and participation in several governmental small business loan funds, even though there was no indication it had made any loans through these programs.

Bank Expansion Applications

The federal banking agencies' approach to enforcing the CRA when considering bank expansion applications was similar to their performance when examining banks for CRA compliance. They were lenient with banks, rarely denying an expansion application due to a poor CRA record. In their written decisions on applications, they did not use a fixed set of CRA evaluative criteria composed of quantitative measures of bank lending, quantitative benchmarks of community credit needs, or objective standards for evaluating whether a bank was meeting community credit needs. They emphasized bank lending efforts over actual lending. In the decisions, the agencies did not reason from facts about bank lending to conclusions about why the facts led to a particular result. Instead, they generally listed facts and then stated a conclusion.

Record of Denying Applications

The CRA requires the federal banking agencies to take a bank's CRA record into account when considering several types of bank expansion applications.[119] The agencies have given themselves the authority to deny banking applications on the grounds that the bank has a poor CRA record.[120] Despite this authority, the federal banking agencies generally preferred not to deny applications on CRA grounds, but to seek voluntary CRA compliance through obtaining commitments to improve CRA performance, conditioning application approvals on a bank's commitment to improve its CRA record, and suggesting that a bank withdraw its application until it improved its CRA record.[121] The federal banking agencies denied applications only when "no agreement can be reached in the short term or when the bank is uncooperative."[122] The agencies preferred conditioning an approval on improved CRA performance because this committed a bank to improving its record as monitored by the agency, as opposed to an outright denial, in response to which a bank might take no action.[123]

Consistent with their policy of encouraging voluntary CRA compliance in connection with bank expansion applications, the federal banking agencies rarely denied applications on CRA or any other grounds during the first CRA enforcement regime. It is difficult to get an exact count of the number of applications the agencies denied on CRA grounds during the first CRA enforcement regime. The best estimate is that through 1996, the agencies had denied only 31 of 105,000 applications on CRA grounds.[124]

Lack of Quantitative and Objective Evaluative Criteria

When analyzing the four CRA assessment criteria relating to bank lending in their decisions on bank expansion applications, the federal banking agencies did not use a fixed set of quantitative and objective evaluative criteria and did not employ reasoning to justify the conclusions they reached about a bank's CRA lending record. As a result, it was difficult to determine the standards the agencies applied and why a bank's record justified approval or denial of the application, and it was easy for the federal banking agencies to excuse what appeared to be a poor CRA record and grant an application.[125]

When evaluating assessment criterion (e), the geographic distribution of a bank's loans, in connection with considering a bank expansion application, the Board of Governors of the Federal Reserve System (the "Federal Reserve") employed several evaluative criteria composed of quantitative measures of bank lending and quantitative benchmarks of community credit needs, although never all in the same decision, without a discernible pattern, without objective standards for determining whether the bank's lending met the credit needs of the community, and with no analysis of why the results merited a denial or a grant of the application. The criteria they used included:

- total number of loans in LMI/predominantly minority census tracts;
- percentage of loans in LMI/predominantly minority census tracts compared with percentage of loans in affluent/predominantly white census tracts;
- percentage of loans in LMI/predominantly minority census tracts compared with the percentage of such loans for similar banks;

- percentage of loans in LMI/predominantly minority census tracts compared with percentage of LMI/predominantly minority census tracts in the community;
- loans per thousand owner-occupied housing units in LMI census tracts compared with other census tracts;
- percentage of LMI census tracts that received a loan;
- percentage of loans to minorities compared with the percentage of minorities in the community;
- market share of loans in LMI census tracts compared with market share in other census tracts;
- percentage of LMI census tracts from which the bank received an application;
- percentage of a bank's loans in LMI/predominantly minority census tracts compared with the percentage of the population living in such census tracts.[126]

Despite frequently finding that these measures showed that a bank was doing a better job at meeting the credit needs of affluent or predominantly white neighborhoods than LMI or predominantly minority neighborhoods, the Federal Reserve almost always excused such differences by indicating that the data that showed the differences were not sufficiently detailed to prove redlining or excused the bank by stating that it was making efforts to lend.[127] On the other hand, the Federal Reserve did not ignore blatant cases of redlining. In one case, the Federal Reserve denied an application in part because the bank had made small business and home mortgage loans in one part of its community but did not do so on a nearby Native American Indian reservation.[128] In another case, the Federal Reserve denied an application because the bank made only two loans in two years in LMI communities.[129]

The approach of the Office of the Comptroller of the Currency (the "OCC") to considering the geographic distribution of a bank's loans in connection with an application was similar to the Federal Reserve's. In one case, the OCC found that the geographic distribution of the bank's loans was "not reasonable," but nevertheless conditionally approved the bank's application.[130] In another case, the OCC conditioned its approval of an application on the bank's achieving a "reasonable" loan penetration in all segments of its community.[131]

When considering assessment criterion (h), the bank's participation in community development programs, the Federal Reserve and the OCC generally used quantitative measures of bank lending, but without any reasoning that linked the measures to their conclusions about the bank's CRA record.

The Federal Reserve frequently cited the number and dollar amount of community development loans the bank made without identifying the standards it used to evaluate the totals.[132] The OCC occasionally cited a bank's poor community development record as a basis for conditionally approving an application, but did not use quantitative measures of the performance.[133] In one case, the OCC stated that the bank was an "inactive" participant in community development activities.[134] In another case, the OCC found that the bank had "limited involvement" in community development programs.[135]

In evaluating assessment criterion (i), origination of loans in the bank's community, the Federal Reserve frequently cited the total number and dollar amount of loans the bank made in its community, but did not use objective standards for evaluating the sufficiency of that lending or any reasoning to support its conclusions.[136] The Federal Reserve also frequently considered a bank's loan-to-deposit ratio ("LDR") when evaluating the bank's lending, but did not apply objective terms for evaluating the LDR and was somewhat inconsistent in its analysis because it discounted the importance of a poor ratio while praising a good one.[137] The Federal Reserve also indicated that a low LDR was not *prima facie* evidence of redlining and not helpful in the case of a commercial bank with a diversified loan portfolio.[138] On the other hand, the Federal Reserve praised the CRA records of banks with "good," "improved," "reasonable," or "satisfactory" LDRs, while not offering a definition of "good," "reasonable," or "satisfactory."[139]

The Federal Reserve occasionally cited specific data about a bank's lending level in its local community and in LMI neighborhoods, but did not use objective standards to compare the lending with quantitative benchmarks of credit needs. For example, the Federal Reserve approved the application of one bank, which, over a two-year period, made 76% and 80% of its loans in its delineated community, and 28% of all loans one year in LMI communities.[140] The Federal Reserve also granted an application in which the bank made 53% of the total value of its loans in its delineated community.[141] The Federal Reserve did not offer any reasoning to justify its conclusions.

In several cases, the Federal Reserve considered claims that a bank made too many loans outside its local community. In these cases, the Federal Reserve examined the percentage of loans the bank made outside its community, the record of similar banks, and whether the extent of the bank's lending outside its community impaired its ability to meet local credit needs.[142] The Federal Reserve granted two applications in which one bank made a "substantial portion" and another bank more than half its loans outside its community, stating that these records were not inconsistent with the banks' CRA obligations.[143] On the other hand, the Federal Reserve denied four applications in which one bank made a "nominal" amount, another made 28%, the third made less than half, and the fourth made a "low" percentage of its loans in their local communities.[144] It is hard to distinguish among these six applications or to see the reason the Federal Reserve denied four of the applications and granted two.

Like the Federal Reserve, the OCC used vague and subjective terms to describe bank lending in its community, including a "substantial volume" of loans in the banks' community, "general responsiveness" to community credit needs, a "large volume" of loans outside its community, a "reasonable" loan penetration in all segments of its community, a "large concentration" of loans outside its community, "marginal responsiveness" to the needs of its community, a "majority" of loans outside its community, a "significant volume" of loans outside its community, or a "significant commitment" to residential mortgage lending in its community.[145]

In two cases, the OCC based the denial of a bank's expansion application on the bank's low percentage of loans in its community. In one case, the OCC denied an application in part because only 11% of the bank's loans were within its community.[146] In another case, the OCC denied an application because, among other reasons, 50% of the bank's total number and 90% of the dollar volume of the bank's loans were outside its community.[147] But the OCC backed away from using these numbers as objective standards by stating, "This is not to suggest that community credit needs are not being met, but this is a significant concern absent any significant activity by the bank to determine the community's credit needs."[148]

In evaluating a bank's participation in government loan programs under assessment criterion (j), the Federal Reserve frequently cited the total number and dollar amount of government-related loans the bank made.[149] The OCC occasionally cited a bank's "minimal" participation in governmental loan programs as a basis for conditionally approving an application.[150]

The Emphasis on Efforts

The federal banking agencies' emphasis on the efforts a bank undertook to meet the credit needs of its community was evident in their written decisions on bank expansion applications. On the rare occasions that the Federal Reserve denied an application on CRA grounds, a major reason was that the bank lacked appropriate procedures to implement its CRA obligations. The Federal Reserve took the position that prior to submitting an application, a bank had to have a CRA program in place that satisfied the Board's standards.[151] The most important parts of the CRA program were implementing adequate procedures to ascertain community credit needs, adequately advertising loan products, incorporating the CRA into the bank's management structure, and offering credit products suited to the community's credit needs.[152]

Poor CRA compliance procedures were also an important factor when the OCC denied bank expansion applications on CRA grounds. The OCC denied one application because the bank's advertising and its credit products were inadequate, and it had a low level of lending in its community.[153] The OCC denied another application because the bank needed to improve its efforts to ascertain community credit needs, its marketing, and its review of the geographic distribution of its loans.[154] In a third case, the OCC denied an application because the bank's record was less than satisfactory in assessing community credit needs, marketing credit products, types of credit offered and extended, geographic distribution of loans, discrimination and other illegal credit practices, and community development activities.[155] In another case, the OCC denied an application because the bank had not ascertained community credit needs, its board of directors was not involved in CRA activities, and it made 50% of the total number and 90% of the total dollar volume of its loans outside its community.[156] In one case, the OCC suggested that adequate procedures could have been a defense to the bank's poor lending record within its community. "This is not to suggest that community credit needs are not being met, but this is a significant concern, absent any significant activity by the bank to determine the community's credit needs."[157]

The OCC occasionally ordered conditional approval of applications because a bank had poor procedures to implement its CRA obligations. In one case, the OCC found that although the bank had made a substantial volume of loans in its service area and that its lending levels reflected a general responsiveness to its community's ascertained needs, it conditionally approved the bank's application because it had poor CRA procedures.[158] In other instances, the OCC conditioned its approval of applications on improved CRA programs when it found that the bank did not adequately ascertain community credit needs, advertise its products, analyze the geographic distribution of its loans, or involve its board of directors or senior management in the CRA process; failed to analyze its community delineation or to improve the documentation of its CRA activities; or had a poor record of involvement in community development activities.[159] When the OCC did include a poor lending record as a basis for conditionally approving an application, the OCC simply referred to the poor lending record without elaboration.[160]

When the OCC imposed conditions on granting an application or required commitments to improve a bank's CRA record, the conditions and commitments more frequently related to improving the bank's efforts than its lending record. Conditions and commitments included, for example, increasing advertising and credit needs ascertainment efforts, improving employee CRA training, designating a CRA officer, offering credit counseling, establishing a community advisory board, revising the bank's CRA statement, reconsidering the bank's CRA community delineation, analyzing the geographic distribution of the bank's loans, involving the bank's board of directors and senior management in the bank's CRA activities, and improving the bank's documentation of its CRA activities.[161] Conditions and commitments relating to lending generally did not establish lending targets. They included agreeing to participate in special lending programs, considering offering home mortgage loans, agreeing to make loans to purchase 3–4 unit residential properties, offering long-term low-downpayment mortgages, and increasing lending in LMI neighborhoods.[162] However, in a few cases, the OCC ordered banks to reach vague lending targets, such as a "reasonable" loan penetration in all segments of the bank's community.[163]

Administrative Enforcement Proceedings

During most of the first CRA enforcement regime, the federal banking agencies occasionally used their authority to enforce the banking laws and regulations in administrative proceedings[164] to enforce a bank's CRA obligations.[165] The administrative enforcement proceedings generally did not concern bank lending records under the four CRA assessment criteria that related to lending. Instead, they almost always dealt with the assessment criteria relating to lending procedures, with occasional reference to lending performance. In the consent orders resolving these proceedings, remedies included adopting a CRA statement, posting a public CRA notice, appointing a CRA officer, adopting a written CRA plan with goals and timetables, involving the board of directors more actively in the bank's CRA efforts, documenting the bank's CRA efforts, developing procedures to track the geographic distribution of the bank's loans, providing CRA training to bank employees, instituting CRA self-assessment procedures, adopting a new CRA community service area, expanding advertising efforts, ascertaining community credit needs, developing a comprehensive CRA self-assessment plan that quantifies the bank's CRA performance, issuing an expanded CRA statement, adopting CRA guidelines showing how the bank would address identified community credit needs and its desired geographic distribution of lending, and participating in community development programs.[166]

In two cases, however, the agencies did include clauses relating to lending. The OCC ordered a bank to adopt a written CRA program that included "goals and objectives to meet any identified credit needs, particularly those of low- to moderate-income residents."[167] Similarly, the Federal Reserve entered into an agreement with a bank that required the bank to define CRA goals and objectives, review its actual performance compared with its goals, and establish the desired geographic distribution of lending throughout its community.[168]

An example of a typical enforcement agreement is the Agreement By and Between South Branch Valley National Bank and The Office of the Comptroller of the Currency.[169] It contained at least twenty-seven separate requirements relating to CRA compliance, none of which involved making a loan. In some ways, this agreement epitomizes the agencies' approach to enforcing the CRA during the first CRA enforcement regime. The agreement required the bank to:

1) adopt a written CRA program;
2) establish board and management CRA committees;
3) appoint a CRA officer;
4) define and assign CRA responsibilities;
5) ensure that the CRA officer assesses the bank's CRA performance on a periodic basis;
6) ensure that all necessary personnel receive CRA training;
7) develop a written process to ascertain community credit needs;
8) establish documentation standards;
9) assign responsibility for ascertaining community credit needs;
10) establish meaningful contact with community representatives;
11) analyze demographic data;
12) formalize the product development process;
13) establish ascertainment goals and objectives;
14) assign responsibility for technical compliance to the CRA officer;
15) evaluate and consider advertising all credit products;
16) evaluate and consider advertising in media that reach the entire community;
17) develop a process to review the effectiveness of marketing efforts;
18) consider participating in governmental loan programs;
19) delineate a new CRA community;

20) review the CRA community delineation periodically;
21) periodically assess the geographic distribution of the bank's lending activities and the racial composition of applicants compared with the racial composition of the community;
22) determine whether there are disparities in lending and application patterns and take corrective steps if necessary;
23) adopt a branch closing policy that requires input from the community;
24) conduct tests for evidence of lending discrimination;
25) address the bank's community development lending activities;
26) develop formal contacts with representatives of community development programs; and
27) periodically assess whether the community contacts are promoting the bank's community development objectives.

Dissatisfaction with the First CRA Enforcement Regime

The federal banking agencies' approach to enforcing the CRA created dissatisfaction with the first CRA enforcement regime among bankers, community activists, and the federal banking agencies themselves. The banking industry cited the CRA regulations as the most costly and troublesome of all banking regulations.[170] Representatives of the banking industry complained that the CRA created unnecessary costs, regulatory burden, and unnecessary paperwork; that it was vague, subjective, and arbitrarily and inconsistently enforced; and that it allowed community groups to delay bank expansion applications unless banks met their demands for increased lending in their communities.[171] They also complained that the CRA emphasized a bank's lending procedures rather than its record of performance.[172] Legislation that would have addressed these concerns was frequently introduced into Congress, but was never passed.[173] Proposals included exempting small banks from the CRA and prohibiting members of the public from filing administrative challenges to a bank expansion application if the bank had a satisfactory or higher CRA rating.

Community activists and organizations supported the CRA, asserting that it was responsible for billions of dollars of loans in their communities.[174] Nevertheless, they argued that the law had not reached its full potential.[175]

They criticized and blamed the federal banking agencies for not enforcing the law sufficiently.[176] Community activists asserted that the absence of performance-based CRA evaluative criteria and the vague criteria and subjective standards the federal banking agencies used made it difficult for the community to hold a bank accountable for a poor CRA record.[177] Activists also asserted that the federal banking agencies' criteria for evaluating a bank's CRA record relied too heavily on a bank's efforts rather than a bank's lending record and that the government was too lenient in applying the criteria and enforcing compliance.[178] Community activists asserted that the CRA ratings the agencies gave banks were too high, particularly given continued evidence of redlining and disinvestment, and that the agencies too readily approved bank expansion applications even when a bank had a poor CRA record.[179]

The federal banking agencies agreed with many of these criticisms. Former Comptroller of the Currency Eugene Ludwig stated that CRA performance standards were unclear and subjective and that they were applied inconsistently.[180] He stated that the agencies relied too heavily on the process a bank followed to comply with the CRA rather than its lending results.[181] This, in turn, led to excessive documentation of efforts that did not necessarily result in loans.[182] Ludwig stated that enforcement of the CRA was uneven and limited because it relied too heavily on the bank expansion application process, and that banks that were actively expanding were held to a higher standard than others.[183] Ludwig stated that inconsistent CRA examination results were unfair to banks and made it difficult for members of the public to understand what the ratings meant.[184]

Former Federal Reserve Governor Lawrence Lindsey stated that the criticism that the CRA had failed to meet its objective was not without basis. "Inner cities still suffer from disinvestment. Large sections of the population do not have ready access to a bank branch. Statistical studies indicate that racially based differences in mortgage approval rates do exist, even after taking economic variables into consideration."[185] Lindsey also conceded that the agencies' absence of objective measures came at a price. "Living with the current uncertainty makes bankers nervous, community groups dissatisfied with their ability to hold institutions accountable, and everyone involved concerned about ensuring fair and consistent evaluations by the agencies."[186]

The Subcommittee on Housing of the Senate Committee on Banking, Housing, and Urban Affairs agreed with many of the criticisms of the CRA. In its investigation of CRA enforcement efforts, it found that the complaints about the CRA were for the most part justified. The Subcommittee found lax and inconsistent enforcement, excessive paperwork, emphasis on process over performance, and a tendency to protect banks rather than regulate them.[187] Senator Alan Cranston, the Chair of the Subcommittee, stated, "Large banks have excelled in creating extensive, expensive paper trails that do not necessarily translate into loans for the communities."[188] The Subcommittee also found evidence of grade inflation in the PEs. Banks received satisfactory or higher CRA ratings even in situations where an examiner found the bank's CRA community was not reasonable, the bank had no CRA programs in place, the bank repeatedly violated technical requirements of the Equal Credit Opportunity Act, the bank participated in government-guaranteed loan programs but had not yet originated a loan, and the bank's rejection rate for minorities was twice as high as for whites.[189]

CHAPTER FOUR

The Second Set of CRA Regulations and the Process of Adopting Them, 1993–95

Introduction

The criticism of the first CRA enforcement regime led to its ultimate downfall. By 1995, the federal banking agencies had adopted new CRA regulations that shifted the CRA enforcement paradigm from an emphasis on a bank's efforts to lend to an emphasis on lending. The second set of CRA regulations eliminates the efforts-oriented criteria of the first set of CRA regulations and adopts several quantitative measures of bank lending. The new regulations do not, however, contain quantitative benchmarks of community credit needs or objective standards for measuring a bank's performance at meeting community credit needs. The second set of CRA regulations thus represents an advance toward maximizing the CRA's influence over bank lending decisions and fulfilling the CRA's potential for democratizing capital both in terms of holding banks accountable for poor lending records and encouraging banks to lend to redlined neighborhoods, but does not do as much as it may to influence banks to lend in redlined neighborhoods or to democratize capital.

On July 15, 1993, responding to the criticisms of the first CRA enforcement regime, President Clinton called on the federal banking agencies to reform the CRA regulations.[1] The goal of the reform was to adopt CRA regulations that emphasized lending performance over process, were more objective, less subject to arbitrary interpretation, and reduced unnecessary paperwork.[2] The federal banking agencies issued two sets of proposed regulations, the first in 1993 (the "1993 proposal") and a revised proposal in 1994 (the "1994 proposal").[3] On May 5, 1995, the federal banking agencies published the final CRA regulations (the "second set of CRA regulations").[4] The second set of CRA regulations was phased in gradually, and completely replaced the first set of CRA regulations as of July 1, 1997.[5]

The 1993 proposal came the closest to adopting CRA evaluative criteria composed of quantitative measures of bank lending, quantitative benchmarks of community credit needs, and objective standards for evaluating bank lending. The 1993 proposal eliminated all the efforts-oriented criteria of the old CRA regulations and replaced them with criteria composed of quantitative measures and benchmarks and quasi-objective standards. In addition, the 1993 proposal contained strict enforcement mechanisms, established clear standards for invoking them, and imposed extensive data collection and reporting requirements.

There was significant opposition to the 1993 proposal, primarily from the banking industry, on the grounds that it "allocated credit." In response to these objections, the federal banking agencies promulgated the 1994 proposal, which removed the quantitative measures and quasi-objective standards of the 1993 proposal. Like the 1993 proposal, the 1994 proposal eliminated efforts-oriented criteria. However, unlike the 1993 proposal, it did not include quantitative benchmarks of community credit needs and diluted the quantitative measures of bank lending in the 1993 proposal by adding several non-quantitative measures. The standards for evaluating whether a bank's lending met the credit needs of the community were subjective.

The final set of CRA regulations, promulgated in 1995, was similar to the 1994 proposal. This second set of CRA regulations eliminates the efforts-oriented criteria of the old regulations, contains a mix of quantitative and non-quantitative measures of bank lending, and does not adopt quantitative benchmarks of community credit needs or objective standards for evaluating whether a bank's lending meets community credit needs.

Even though the second set of CRA regulations does not include quantitative benchmarks or objective standards, it does represent a significant shift in the perspective of the federal banking agencies on CRA enforcement. The fact that the agencies dropped the efforts-oriented criteria and adopted some quantitative measures of bank lending shows they no longer see the CRA as primarily a mechanism to correct an information failure in the lending market but recognize that the CRA's main purpose is to end redlining and influence banks to lend more in previously redlined neighborhoods. However, the federal banking agencies, in failing to adopt quantitative benchmarks of community credit needs and objective standards for evaluating bank lending for fear of allocating credit, did not maximize the CRA's influence over lending decisions or its potential for democratizing capital.

This chapter will review the 1993 proposal and the banking industry's opposition to it, examine the 1994 proposal, focusing on how it changed in response to the criticism of the 1993 proposal, and describe the final version of the second set of CRA regulations.

The 1993 Proposal

The 1993 proposal included quantitative measures of bank lending and quantitative benchmarks of community credit needs. Its standards for evaluating whether a bank's lending met community credit needs were quasi-objective: even though they allowed agency CRA examiners a range of discretion to evaluate bank lending, they were more specific and less subject to open-ended interpretation than the evaluative standards employed during the first CRA enforcement regime. The banking industry strongly opposed the 1993 proposal on the grounds that it allocated credit, and in response the federal banking agencies amended the proposal dramatically.

Description of the 1993 Proposal

The 1993 proposal contained different CRA evaluative criteria for large retail banks, small retail banks, and wholesale banks. Large retail banks with assets of $250 million or more were to be evaluated according to three tests: the lending test; the investment test; and the service test.[6] The lending test contained three criteria. The first criterion was the "market share test," under which a bank's market share of loans in low- and moderate-income ("LMI") neighborhoods was compared with its market share of loans in the rest of its service area.[7] The theory behind this test was that in order to meet the credit needs of LMI neighborhoods, a bank's record of meeting the needs of LMI neighborhoods—measured by its market share in such neighborhoods—should be roughly equal to its market share in other neighborhoods. The second criterion of the lending test was the percentage of LMI census tracts in the bank's service area in which the bank made a loan, and the total number and dollar volume of those loans.[8] Finally, the third criterion of the lending test was the percentage of the bank's loans that were in LMI census tracts.[9] As shown in Table 4.1, the standards for evaluating the bank's record

Table 4.1

Rating	Market share in LMI neighborhoods compared with other neighborhoods	Percentage of LMI tracts in which bank made a loan and total number and dollar volume of loans	Percentage of loans in LMI neighborhoods
Outstanding	Significantly exceeds	Significant in vast majority	Substantial
High satisfactory	Roughly comparable	Significant in most	Very significant
Low satisfactory	Roughly comparable	Significant in many	Significant
Needs to improve	Less than	Few	Insignificant
Substantial non-compliance	Significantly less than	Very few, if any	N/A

under these components were quasi-objective; they were more specific and less open to interpretation than the standards used in the first enforcement regime, but nevertheless not fully objective. The bank's examiner was to assign one of five ratings to the bank's performance on each of the three criteria of the lending test as shown in Table 4.1.[10]

The second and third tests for large retail banks—the service and investment tests—also featured criteria composed of quantitative measures of the bank's record and quasi-objective standards for evaluating the bank's performance. Under the service test, a large retail bank would be evaluated according to whether the percentage of its branches in LMI census tracts was substantial, very significant, significant, insignificant, or very small.[11] The investment test would evaluate a bank's community development investments based on the ratio of the value of its investments to its total assets.[12] A bank's rating on the investment test would be based on whether its investment/asset ratio was substantial, very significant, significant, insignificant, or very low.[13]

The 1993 proposal contained six evaluative criteria for small retail banks with assets of less than $250 million.[14] Two of the six criteria included quantitative measures of bank lending and quantitative benchmarks of community credit needs. The criteria involved the bank's loan-to-deposit-ratio ("LDR") and the percentage of the bank's loans within its service area.[15] According to the LDR criterion, if a bank's LDR (quantitative measure of bank lending) was at least 60% (quantitative benchmark of community credit needs), there was a presumption that the bank's LDR was reasonable.[16] As for the criteria relating to the percentage of loans, if a "majority" of the bank's loans (quantitative measure of bank lending) was in its service area, this was "appropriate."[17]

Finally, the 1993 proposal included two tests for evaluating the CRA record of wholesale banks not primarily engaged in retail banking. The first test—the investment test—measured the bank's community development loan-to-asset-ratio.[18] The bank's ratio was evaluated based on whether it was substantial, very significant, significant, insignificant, or very low.[19] The second test was the community development banking services test, which evaluated the wholesale bank's record of providing services to support community economic development.[20]

The 1993 proposal also contained several other provisions that were important in influencing banks to lend in redlined neighborhoods. First, it imposed on banks additional substantial reporting requirements for all small business and consumer loans, including the number of applications, denials, and approvals and the location by census tract of all loan applicants.[21] Second, a bank that received a "substantial noncompliance" CRA rating would automatically be subject to an administrative enforcement proceeding.[22] Third, a bank that received its third consecutive "needs to improve" CRA rating would have its rating automatically downgraded to a substantial noncompliance rating.[23] Finally, the 1993 proposal indicated that a bank expansion application would likely be granted if a bank had a CRA rating of satisfactory or higher, and likely rejected if the bank had a CRA rating of needs to improve or lower.[24]

Banking Industry Opposition to the 1993 Proposal

One of the banking industry's primary criticisms of the 1993 proposal was that it allocated credit, the main culprits being the market share and LDR criteria.[25] Opponents of the proposal argued that these two criteria would lead to unhealthy, weakened credit standards, and unsafe and unsound banking practices. The federal banking agencies argued that these tests did not allocate credit. They took the position that the market share test employed subjective standards and thus allowed for examiner discretion, while the 60% LDR benchmark was a screening mechanism and not dispositive.

The banking industry criticized the 1993 proposal on the grounds that the market share and LDR criteria allocated credit.[26] James M. Culberson, Chairman of the First National Bank and Trust Company, testifying on behalf of the American Bankers Association before the Subcommittee on Financial Institutions and Consumer Credit of the Senate Committee on Banking and Financial Services, stated, "The first proposal from the regulators raised additional concerns about credit allocation because of the inclusion of 'market share' tests."[27] An Indiana banker stated, "If these proposals go through, we'd never be able to fulfill these requirements without quotas."[28] Bankers predicted that the proposed regulations would force them to compete for market share in LMI neighborhoods, and thus would allocate credit.[29] As Culberson testified, "If a bank wants to earn an outstanding rating, its market share in low/moderate income markets must exceed the share in other markets. In effect, then, the market share test will lead to credit allocation."[30]

The reasons bankers gave for opposing credit allocation were similar to the arguments CRA's congressional opponents made against the CRA when it was passed. They argued that it would undermine bank safety and soundness and would fail to account for differences in loan demand across different regions of the country. Bankers warned that in order to ensure a favorable rating on the market share test, bankers would compete for market share in LMI neighborhoods by loosening their underwriting standards to the detriment of bank safety and soundness.[31] Mark Willis, chairperson of Chase Manhattan Community Development Corporation, testifying on behalf of the Consumer Bankers Association before the Subcommittee on General Oversight, Investigations, and the Resolution of Failed Financial Institutions of the House Committee on Banking, Finance, and Urban Affairs, stated, "Competing institutions will be tempted to 'buy' market share through aggressively low lending standards, thereby potentially undermining safety and soundness and jeopardizing the very neighborhoods and people we seek to serve."[32] Donald A. Mullane, the Executive Vice-President of Bank of America, echoed a similar sentiment: "Institutions may be tempted to sacrifice their lending standards and profitability to 'buy' greater volume than others, and this creates the pressure for every lender in the market to do the same."[33] James M. Culberson, on behalf of the American Bankers Association, stated that, "A system which drives banks to 'purchase' market share to meet some preconceived government notion of 'proper' market percentages would certainly be credit allocation, and it would also undermine safety and soundness."[34]

Bankers warned that not only would the market share test drive unhealthy competition, it would also likely do nothing more than redistribute a fixed pie of loans in LMI neighborhoods. Many who commented on the proposed regulations were "concerned that if one bank increased its market share, another would necessarily lose market share."[35] According to Mark Willis, "Whether a lender obtains adequate market share in low-to-moderate income loans is likely to have more to do with competition among lenders in the market area than with true CRA performance."[36]

Bankers also argued that there was not sufficient loan demand to meet the 60% LDR benchmark. James Lauffer, the president of the Independent Bankers Association, stated, "Many areas lack sufficient loan demand, making it impossible to meet an arbitrary 60% test. In addition, many markets experience significant seasonal variations. Half the banks do not meet the 60% test. It makes no sense for examiners to impose it on them, requiring thousands of banks to demonstrate that a lower rate is reasonable."[37]

The federal banking agencies denied that the 1993 proposal allocated credit. They asserted that since the standards for evaluating a bank's performance under the criteria were based on words rather than numbers, the market share and LDR criteria would not allocate credit.[38] Federal Reserve Governor Lawrence Lindsey stated, "Moreover, the terms used to describe different levels of performance include 'roughly comparable,' 'significant amount,' and similar words that are anything but precise. These general standards have been proposed, in part, to avoid giving specific numbers which would risk resulting in the specific allocation of the amount, type, or terms of credit institutions must provide."[39]

Comptroller of the Currency Eugene A. Ludwig defended the market share and 60% LDR criteria against charges of credit allocation. He stated that the 60% LDR test was not a bright line test but a reasonableness test, and the market share test was a screen and not a test.[40] Ludwig stated that the tests were "rebuttable presumptions" that an institution could answer based on its own situation.[41] Andrew Hove, acting director of the FDIC, agreed with this, stating that the proposal allows "examiners to make exceptions when the performance measures do not allow for unique circumstances."[42]

The 1994 Proposal

Despite their defense of the 1993 proposal against charges that it allocated credit, the federal banking agencies removed the market share and the 60% LDR criteria from the 1994 proposal. The agencies explained that many banks feared that the quantitative measures in the 1993 proposal would lead to credit allocation, and that "is an outcome we want to avoid. We will not set forth a regulation that would require any institution, in any community, to make any particular loan or to engage in any activity inconsistent with safety and soundness."[43] As a result, the "1994 proposal eliminated the features that gave rise to those concerns, such as the market share screen in the lending test."[44] The 1994 proposal also eliminated the 60% LDR criterion because many commenters perceived it as requiring small banks to achieve a 60% LDR, a result not intended.[45] The agencies also diluted the quantitative measures of bank lending by adding non-quantifiable measures, and restored significant subjectivity to the process of evaluating a bank's CRA record. As a result, although the 1994 proposal eliminated all the efforts-oriented criteria of the first set of CRA regulations, it mirrored the subjectivity in evaluating lending from the first CRA regulations.

Description of the 1994 Proposal

Instead of the quantitative benchmarks of community credit needs in the 1993 proposal, the 1994 proposal introduced the "performance context" as its measure of community credit needs against which to compare bank lending.[46] The federal banking agencies would consider community demographics and other relevant characteristics when determining whether a bank was meeting the credit needs of the community.[47]

Under the 1994 proposal, large retail banks would continue to be evaluated according to the lending, investment, and service tests as in the 1993 proposal. The lending test continued to employ quantitative measures of bank lending such as the percentage of the bank's lending within its service area and the number and dollar volume of home mortgage and small business loans according to borrower income, but included other, non-quantifiable criteria as well, such as the bank's use of innovative or flexible lending criteria.[48] The federal banking agencies also eliminated the quasi-objective standards for evaluating banks under the lending test criteria in the 1993 proposal and replaced them with purely subjective terms such as "excellent," "good," and "adequate."[49] Similarly, the 1994 proposal removed the community development loan/asset ratio test and replaced it with one quantitative measure of bank investments—the dollar value of community development investments—and added non-quantitative measures such as the bank's use of innovative investments and responsiveness to community economic development needs.[50] Finally, the 1994 proposal replaced the quantitative service test measures of the 1993 proposal with criteria such as the distribution of the bank's branches and the bank's record of opening and closing branches.[51]

For small banks, the 1994 proposal continued to include quantitative measures of bank lending, such as the bank's LDR and the percentage of loans in the bank's community, but it dropped the presumptions that a 60% LDR was reasonable and that a majority of loans in the bank's community was appropriate.[52] Instead, the sufficiency of a small bank's lending record would be based on whether its record was "reasonable."[53] For wholesale banks, the change in the 1994 proposal was similar: while the 1994 proposal continued to employ quantitative measures of wholesale bank community development lending and investments, such as the total number and dollar volume of such loans, it added non-quantifiable standards such as use of innovative investments and responsiveness to community credit needs.

Finally, the 1994 proposal changed the data disclosure requirements of the 1993 proposal, generally reducing them. Most importantly, instead of requiring banks to disclose the number of small business and consumer loan applications they received, their decisions on the applications, and the census tract of the loan applicant, the 1994 proposal required banks to report only the total number and dollar value of their small business loans according to the race and income of the borrowers.

The Second Set of CRA Regulations

In 1995, the federal banking agencies promulgated the final set of new CRA regulations. The regulations eliminate all the efforts-oriented criteria of the first set of regulations. The regulations replace them with both quantitative and non-quantitative measures of bank lending, investments, and services. The second set of regulations does not contain quantitative benchmarks of community credit needs or objective standards for evaluating a bank's record of meeting community credit needs.[54] Gone are the market share criteria for large retail banks and the 60% LDR criteria for small banks that were contained in the 1993 proposal.[55] This section will describe the four main components of the new CRA regulations: the performance context; the performance tests and evaluative criteria; enforcement; and data disclosure.

Performance Context

The new CRA regulations require the federal banking agencies to evaluate a bank's CRA record in light of several different factors, known as the "performance context."[56] Among the factors that the federal banking agencies must consider are demographic data such as median household income, the nature of the housing stock, and housing cost.[57] The federal banking agencies also consider other factors that could affect a bank's ability to lend, including the economic climate, the size and condition of the bank, and the bank's product lines and credit offerings.[58]

Performance Tests and Evaluative Criteria

The regulations recognize three types of banks and establish different criteria for evaluating their CRA performance.[59] Retail banks with $250 million or more in assets ("large banks") are evaluated according to the lending, investment, and service tests.[60] Wholesale and limited purpose banks are evaluated according to the community development test.[61] Retail banks with less than $250 million in assets ("small banks") are subject to the small bank performance test.[62] The new CRA regulations also offer an entirely new performance standard that any bank can adopt: the strategic plan option.[63]

Large Retail Bank

A large retail bank will receive one of five ratings on each of the three tests that apply to it and then, based on a combination of these ratings, one of four overall CRA ratings.

The Lending Test

The lending test covers a large bank's home mortgage, small business, small farm, and community development lending.[64] There are five components of the lending test, several of them contain evaluative criteria that rely on quantitative measures of bank lending:[65]

1. Lending activity: the total number and dollar amount of the bank's loans within the bank's service area.
2. Geographic distribution: the geographic distribution of the bank's loans, including:
    a. Proportion of the bank's loans in its service area;
    b. Dispersion of the bank's loans in its service area; and
    c. Total number and dollar amount of the bank's loans in LMI, middle income, and upper income census tracts within its service area.

3. Borrower characteristics: the distribution of the bank's loans based on borrower characteristics, including the total number and dollar amount of:
   a. Home mortgage loans to LMI, middle-income, and upper-income individuals;
   b. Small business and small farm loans to businesses and farms with gross annual revenue of $1 million or less; and
   c. Small business and small farm loans by loan amount at origination.
4. Community development lending: including the total number and dollar amount of community development loans and their innovativeness and complexity.
5. Innovative or flexible lending practices designed to address the needs of LMI individuals or neighborhoods.

Based on the bank's performance on these criteria, the examiner will assign one of five ratings to a bank's overall performance on the lending test: outstanding; high satisfactory; low satisfactory; needs to improve; or substantial noncompliance.[66] The regulations contain standards for evaluating a bank's performance and assigning a rating that are entirely subjective, including terms such as "excellent," "good," "adequate," and "poor," as Table 4.2 shows. [67]

The Investment Test

The second test for large retail banks is the investment test, which evaluates the bank's community development investments.[68] There are four evaluative criteria under the investment test; one is quantitative and the remaining three are not. The criteria are total number and dollar amount of investments, their innovativeness or complexity, the bank's responsiveness to community development needs, and the degree to which the investments are not provided by other private investors.[69] The bank's examiner assigns one of five ratings to the bank on the investment test: outstanding; high satisfactory; low satisfactory; needs to improve; and substantial noncompliance. The new CRA regulations contain subjective standards to evaluate a bank's investment performance under the criteria and assign a rating, as Table 4.3 demonstrates.[70]

The Service Test

The final test for large retail banks is the service test.[71] Under the service test, the bank's examiner will evaluate the bank's retail and community development banking services.[72] The evaluative criteria include the bank's branch distribu-

Table 4.2

Rating	Responsiveness to credit needs	Percentage of loans in assessment area	Geographic distribution of loans	Lending to borrowers at different income levels	Record of serving credit needs of under-served areas and individuals	Flexible or innovative lending practices	Community development lending
Outstanding	Excellent	Substantial majority	Excellent	Excellent	Excellent	Extensive	Leader
High satisfactory	Good	High	Good	Good	Good	Uses	Relatively high
Low satisfactory	Adequate	Adequate	Adequate	Adequate	Adequate	Limited	Adequate
Needs to improve	Poor	Small	Poor	Poor	Poor	Little	Low
Substantial non-compliance	Very poor	Very small	Very poor	Very poor	Very poor	No use	Few, if any

Table 4.3

Rating	Level of qualified investments	Use of innovative or complex investments	Responsiveness to community development needs
Outstanding	Excellent	Extensive	Excellent
High satisfactory	Significant	Significant	Good
Low satisfactory	Adequate	Occasional	Adequate
Needs to improve	Poor	Rare	Poor
Substantial non-compliance	Few	None	Very poor

tion by neighborhood income level, record of opening and closing branches by neighborhood income level, use of alternative systems for providing banking services such as ATMs, range of services provided, and extent of community development services.[73] The bank's examiner will assign one of five ratings to the bank on the service test based on the subjective standards shown in Table 4.4.[74]

Assigning the Overall CRA Rating to Large Retail Banks

Under the regulations, a bank receives a numerical score on each of the three tests based on the bank's rating on the tests. As shown in Table 4.5, the numerical scores are weighted so that the lending test is worth at least twice as much as the investment and service tests.[75] These scores are combined to generate a CRA rating for the bank as shown in Table 4.6.[76] In addition, the ratings must be adjusted based on the following guidelines: a large retail bank that receives a lending test score of outstanding must receive at least a satisfactory overall CRA rating; a large retail bank that receives outstanding ratings on the investment and services tests must receive at least a satisfactory CRA rating; and a large retail bank that does not receive at least a low satisfactory on the lending test cannot get a satisfactory CRA rating.[77]

Small Retail Banks

The new CRA regulations use five criteria to evaluate a small bank's lending record: LDR; percentage of loans in assessment area; record of lending to borrowers at different income levels and small businesses and small farms; geographic distribution of loans; and responsiveness to complaints.[78] There is one objective standard for evaluating the bank's performance; the rest are sub-

Table 4.4

Rating	Access to services by individuals and neighborhoods of different incomes	Effect of branch opening and closing record on accessibility of services to LMI individuals and neighborhoods	Service level to LMI individuals and neighborhoods	Level of community development services
Outstanding	Readily accessible	Improved accessibility	Tailored to needs of LMI individuals and neighborhoods	Leadership role
High satisfactory	Accessible	Did not adversely affect accessibility	Service level does not vary	Relatively high
Low satisfactory	Reasonably accessible	Did not adversely affect accessibility	Service level does not vary	Adequate
Needs to improve	Unreasonably inaccessible to portions of service area	Adversely affected accessibility	Services vary in a way that inconveniences LMI individuals and neighborhoods	Limited
Substantial non-compliance	Unreasonably inaccessible to significant portions of service area	Significantly adversely affected accessibility	Services vary in a way that significantly inconveniences LMI individuals and neighborhoods	Few, if any

Table 4.5

Component test rating	Lending	Investment	Service
Outstanding	12	6	6
High satisfactory	9	4	4
Low satisfactory	6	3	3
Needs to improve	3	1	1
Substantial non-compliance	0	0	0

Table 4.6

CRA Rating	Points
Outstanding	20 or more
Satisfactory	11–19
Needs to improve	5–10
Substantial non-compliance	0–4

jective. A small bank is eligible for a satisfactory CRA rating if its LDR is reasonable, a majority of loans are in its service area, its distribution of loans among individuals and neighborhoods of different income levels is reasonable, and it is generally responsive to complaints from the community.[79] A small bank is eligible for an outstanding CRA rating if it meets all of these standards and exceeds some.[80] Finally, a small bank will receive a needs to improve or substantial noncompliance rating depending on the degree to which it fails to meet these standards.[81]

Wholesale and Limited Purpose Banks

The second set of CRA regulations evaluates wholesale and limited purpose banks according to their community development lending, investments, and services.[82] The CRA regulations apply three tests to the bank's performance in these areas, one of which is quantitative: the total number and dollar amount of the bank's community development loans, investments, or services; their innovativeness, complexity, and unique nature; and the bank's responsiveness to community development needs.[83] The new CRA regulations do not contain objective standards for evaluating a wholesale bank's record under these criteria. Instead, as Table 4.7 shows, the new CRA regulations employ subjective standards.[84]

Table 4.7

Rating	Level of community development loans, investments, and services	Use of innovative or complex investments, loans, and services	Responsiveness to community development credit needs
Outstanding	High	Extensive	Excellent
Satisfactory	Adequate	Occasional	Adequate
Needs to improve	Poor	Rare	Poor
Substantial non-compliance	Few	None	Very poor

The Strategic Plan Option

The fourth type of performance evaluation under the new regulations is the strategic plan option, an alternative available to any bank.[85] This option allows a bank to define, in consultation with community groups, and as approved by its regulator, what constitutes a satisfactory CRA performance. A strategic plan must be in writing, contain measurable goals that specify what constitutes a satisfactory performance, and address lending, investment, and services.[86]

A bank that wishes to be evaluated according to the strategic plan option must submit its plan to the federal banking agency that regulates it for approval prior to adoption.[87] Before the bank submits its plan to the federal banking agency that regulates it, it must seek public comment on the plan; first informally by seeking suggestions from members of the public, and then formally by soliciting public comment through a newspaper notice.[88]

A plan may be for no more than five years, and any multi-year plan must have annual interim measurable goals under which the bank's CRA performance can be evaluated.[89] The plan must contain measurable goals for helping meet the credit needs of LMI communities and individuals through lending, investments, and services.[90] The goals must be sufficiently specific to enable the bank's federal banking agency to judge the merits of the plan.[91] The plan must specify the performance levels that constitute a satisfactory performance and may specify the performance levels that constitute an outstanding performance.[92] The bank may also elect in its plan to be evaluated according to the appropriate CRA performance evaluation (i.e. large bank, small bank, or wholesale bank evaluation) if it does not satisfy its goals for a satisfactory performance.[93]

In considering whether to approve a plan, the appropriate federal banking agency will consider several factors relating to the bank's proposed lending, investments, and services. First, it will consider the extent and breadth of the bank's proposed lending; the proposed distribution of loans among different neighborhoods, businesses and farms of different sizes, and individuals of different income levels; and the bank's proposed use of innovative and flexible lending criteria and programs.[94] Second, the federal banking agency will consider the amount and innovativeness of the bank's proposed investments.[95] Finally, the federal banking agency will consider the extent and innovativeness of the bank's plan for delivering retail banking and community development services.[96]

In determining whether to approve a bank's measurable lending, investment, and service goals, the federal banking agencies use subjective standards. The relevant federal banking agency will approve a plan if the plan's measurable goals for satisfactory performance adequately meet community credit needs and will approve measurable goals for outstanding performance if those goals substantially exceed the goals for satisfactory performance.[97] To assign a rating to a bank under the strategic plan option, the agencies employ subjective standards. The federal banking agency will award a satisfactory rating if the bank substantially achieves its goals for a satisfactory rating, outstanding if the bank exceeds its goals for a satisfactory rating and substantially achieves its goals for an outstanding rating, and needs to improve or substantial noncompliance depending on the extent to which the bank fails to meet substantially its goals for satisfactory performance.[98]

Enforcement

The new CRA regulations contain several enforcement provisions, including the effect discriminatory lending practices will have on a CRA rating and the effect a bank's CRA rating will have on an expansion application. In general, the enforcement provisions are more specific than in the first set of CRA regulations, but they are not as strict as they were under either the 1993 or 1994 proposals.

Assigning a CRA Rating

Evidence that a bank is engaged in discriminatory or illegal credit practices will have an adverse impact on the bank's CRA rating.[99] The degree of adversity depends on the extent and nature of the evidence and corrective action the bank has taken.[100]

Under the 1993 proposal, once a bank was about to receive its third consecutive overall CRA rating of needs to improve, the rating would be reduced to substantial noncompliance. The final regulations do not mandate this. In addition, under both the 1993 and 1994 proposals, a bank that received a substantial noncompliance CRA rating was automatically subject to an administrative enforcement action. This meant that the federal banking agency that regulated the bank was required to initiate an administrative enforcement action against it for violating the CRA. This could result in sanctions, including a fine and an order that the bank take specific steps to improve its record. The federal banking agencies dropped this mandatory enforcement provision from the final regulations.[101] This provision had been strongly opposed by the banking industry, and the Justice Department issued an opinion that the CRA did not authorize enforcement actions against banks with failing grades, thus dooming this provision.[102]

The Effect of a Bank's CRA Record on its Expansion Applications

The new CRA regulations state that the federal banking agencies will take a bank's CRA record and public comments about that record into account when considering a bank's application to establish a branch, relocate a branch, merge or consolidate with another bank, or acquire the assets or assume the liabilities of another bank.[103] Unlike the old regulations, however, the new regulations explicitly state that when considering an application, a bank's CRA performance may be the basis for denying or conditionally approving an application.[104] Although the banking industry urged the federal banking agencies to implement a "safe harbor" from CRA challenges to banks that achieve a satisfactory or higher CRA rating, the agencies declined to provide one in the new regulations.[105]

CRA Assessment Area

Under the first set of CRA regulations, a bank was required to delineate the geographic area in which it would have CRA obligations, and the appropriateness of the delineation was itself a separate assessment criterion for evaluating the bank's compliance with the CRA.[106] Under the second set of CRA regulations, a bank is still required to delineate the area in which it has its CRA obligations, but the delineation is not a separate assessment criterion.[107] Instead, the agency that regulates the bank evaluates the delineated CRA assessment area to make sure it is consistent with the regulations.[108] If the CRA assessment area is not appropriate, the agency designates a service area on its own.[109]

The new CRA regulations contain two guidelines for delineating an assessment area, one for wholesale banks and the other for all other banks. The delineated assessment area for a wholesale or limited purpose bank must consist of one or more Metropolitan Statistical Areas ("MSAs") or one or more contiguous political subdivisions such as a county, city, or town in which the bank has its home or branch office.[110] The delineated service area for other banks must consist generally of an MSA or contiguous political subdivision such as a county, city, or town; and the census tracts in which the bank has its main office, branches, or ATMs, and in which the bank has made a substantial portion of its loans.[111] The bank's delineated service area cannot reflect illegal discrimination and cannot arbitrarily exclude LMI neighborhoods.[112]

Data Disclosure Requirements

The second set of CRA regulations expands bank data disclosure requirements, but the requirements are more limited in scope than those contained in the 1993 or 1994 proposals. The CRA regulations require large banks to report the number of small business and small farm loans they made according to the income level of the census tract in which the business is located.[113] The provisions of the 1993 and 1994 proposals that would have required more detailed reporting about all loan applications filed or the race of borrowers were dropped from the final set of regulations. In addition to small business and small farm lending data, the regulations require banks to report the total number and dollar volume of their community development loans, information about home mortgage loans outside the MSAs in which the bank has a home or branch office or outside an MSA altogether, and a list of all branches opened and closed during the two previous years.[114]

Conclusion

The second set of CRA regulations improves the first set of regulations in that it eliminates the efforts-oriented evaluative criteria from the old CRA regulations and employs some quantitative measures of bank lending. However, the new CRA regulations do not sufficiently influence banks to lend in redlined neighborhoods and they do not maximize the CRA's potential for democratizing capital. They do not contain quantitative benchmarks of community credit needs or objective standards for evaluating whether a bank's lending meets those needs. The first set of proposed CRA regulations, issued in 1993, would have influenced banks more strongly to lend in redlined areas. It included criteria composed of quantitative measures of bank lending, quantitative benchmarks of community credit needs, and quasi-objective standards for evaluating a bank's record at meeting those needs. These provisions were dropped from the final CRA regulations after strong opposition from the banking industry, in part on the grounds that such criteria would constitute credit allocation. Despite the fact that the second set of CRA regulations does not utilize performance criteria that maximize the CRA's potential for influencing banks to lend in redlined neighborhoods or for democratizing capital, by dropping the efforts-oriented evaluative criteria from the old CRA regulations and establishing quantitative measures of bank lending, the second set of CRA regulations does take an important step toward fulfilling the CRA's potential.

CHAPTER FIVE

The Second CRA Enforcement Regime: 1997–2004

Introduction

This chapter examines the policies and practices the federal banking agencies employed in the second CRA enforcement regime from mid-1997 to 2004.[1] As described in previous chapters, the CRA democratizes capital by extending the "franchise" over bank lending decisions to those who previously did not have a vote and by including more people in the economic mainstream by encouraging banks to make loans to them. During the second CRA enforcement regime, the federal banking agencies have continued to enforce the CRA in a way that undermines the CRA's potential for democratizing capital. The federal banking agencies have not established CRA evaluative criteria composed of quantitative measures of bank lending, quantitative benchmarks of community credit needs, and objective standards for evaluating whether bank lending meets community credit needs. Without such criteria, it is difficult to hold a bank accountable for a poor lending record, thus limiting the power of the public's franchise over bank lending decisions. In addition, when the agencies apply the criteria they have adopted, they generally excuse banks from meeting the credit needs benchmarks the agencies themselves have established. This means that based on the agencies' own assessment of credit needs, creditworthy individuals are not receiving loans.

The first section of this chapter examines how the federal banking agencies evaluated bank lending when conducting CRA performance evaluations ("PEs") under the second set of CRA regulations. In the PEs studied in this chapter, the agencies did not use a fixed set of criteria for evaluating bank lending performance, used subjective and imprecise standards to compare bank lending with community credit needs, made misleading statements about poor performance, were inconsistent, and overrated banks.[2]

The second section examines how the agencies evaluated the lending performance of banks when considering expansion applications. The agencies did not use a fixed set of evaluative criteria, described bank lending in subjective terms, highlighted good performance, and ignored or excused weak performance. Their decisions lacked reasoning; generally the decisions just listed selected facts and granted the application. Finally, the agencies also did not explain in their decisions why poor lending records described in community comments were not sufficient to deny applications, even though the agencies frequently acknowledged the accuracy of such comments.

The third section examines CRA compliance manuals agency bank examiners use to evaluate banks for CRA compliance and other CRA regulatory materials the agencies issued. These materials do not require examiners to apply a fixed set of criteria and instruct examiners to use subjective standards to evaluate bank lending.

CRA Performance Evaluations

As described more fully in chapter four, the CRA regulations create the large bank PE for banks with $250 million or more in assets and the small bank PE for banks with less than $250 million in assets. The large bank PE consists of the lending, investment, and service tests. A large bank receives a separate rating on each test and each of these separate ratings is combined to give the bank an overall CRA rating. Five components of a large bank's lending are evaluated under the lending test. These include the bank's lending inside its CRA assessment area compared with outside, geographic distribution of loans, lending to borrowers at different income levels, and community development lending.[3] Based on the bank's performance on each of these components of the lending test, the bank receives one of five ratings on the lending test: outstanding; high satisfactory; low satisfactory; needs to improve; or substantial noncompliance. The small bank PE examines five factors: the bank's loan-to-deposit ratio; concentration of loans in its CRA assessment area; lending to borrowers at different income levels; geographic distribution of loans; and response to complaints. A small bank receives an overall CRA rating based on its performance on these criteria.[4]

This section analyzes a sample of sixteen large bank and sixteen small bank PEs in an attempt to discern the criteria the federal banking agencies use when they evaluate a bank's lending record in low- and moderate-income ("LMI") neighborhoods.[5] There are several conclusions that can be drawn from this analysis. First, the federal banking agencies did not use a fixed set of criteria to evaluate bank lending; they did not even come close.[6] Instead, each PE stands as a testament to the discretion the federal banking agencies have in conducting the PEs. Each PE is unique, using different evaluative criteria. No single evaluative criterion appeared in all of the PEs, and the criteria the agencies used generally appeared in only one or a few PEs. Second, many of the criteria included a comparison of a quantitative measure of the bank's lending with a quantitative benchmark of community credit needs. For example, a criterion might compare the percentage of the bank's home mortgage loans to LMI persons (a quantitative measure of lending) with the percentage of loans to LMI persons by all lenders combined (a quantitative benchmark of community credit needs). Third, even though the criteria included comparisons of quantitative measures of bank lending with quantitative benchmarks of community credit needs, the agencies used subjective and imprecise standards to make these comparisons and did not define the level of performance necessary to meet a particular standard. Fourth, the agencies often applied the subjective standards in the bank's favor, making misleadingly favorable statements about bank lending performance.[7] Fifth, the agencies often found that similar performances on these criteria met different standards.[8] Sixth, the agencies did not define the weight each criterion had. Frequently, a bank that performed poorly on one or more criterion nevertheless received a favorable evaluation on the relevant component of the lending test. Seventh, the federal banking agencies used subjective standards for evaluating bank performance on the four components of the lending test for large banks relating to retail lending. It was impossible to discern the level of performance necessary to meet a particular standard, the agencies frequently characterized banks with similar performances differently, and the agencies frequently overrated bank performance. Eighth, when evaluating small banks for CRA compliance, the agencies did not clearly distinguish the level of performance required to get a particular rating, rated similar performances differently, and frequently overrated banks.[9]

Lack of a Fixed Set of Evaluative Criteria

In the 32 PEs evaluated, the agencies used 82 criteria to evaluate large bank lending and 45 criteria to evaluate small bank lending.[10] The agencies rarely used a particular criterion in more than three PEs, and used very few criteria in more than two PEs.[11] The agencies used more than half the criteria in only one PE each.[12] They used twenty criteria in only two PEs each and four in three PEs each. The agencies used only seven criteria in ten or more PEs.

The criteria the federal banking agencies used most frequently to evaluate large bank lending are shown in Table 5.1 (All tables in this chapter appear a the the end of the chapter. The abbreviations in Table 5.1 and throughout the rest of this chapter are defined in endnote 1 to this chapter). The most popular criteria the federal banking agencies used to evaluate small bank lending are shown in Table 5.2.

Quantitative Measures of Lending and Quantitative Benchmarks of Community Credit Needs

All of the criteria described above employed quantitative measures of bank lending. Many of the criteria also used a quantitative benchmark of community credit needs against which to compare and evaluate the lending. The primary quantitative measures of bank lending the federal banking agencies used are shown in Table 5.3. The agencies used several quantitative benchmarks of community credit needs against which to evaluate the quantitative measures of lending. These quantitative benchmarks were generally indicators of the demand for loans from LMI persons or census tracts, small businesses, or small farms; standards established by other banks; or standards established by the bank being evaluated. The benchmarks included those shown in Table 5.4.

Subjective Standards for Comparing the Quantitative Measures of Bank Lending With the Quantitative Benchmarks of Community Credit Needs

Despite using quantitative measures of bank lending and quantitative benchmarks of community credit needs, the agencies used subjective and imprecise standards to compare the bank's lending with community credit needs and to evaluate the results of the comparisons.[13] The agencies did not define the level of performance necessary to meet a particular standard.[14] Nor was it clear how the agencies distinguished one standard from another. The following is a sample of the standards the agencies used to compare bank lending with community credit needs, arranged roughly in ascending order and grouped according to whether they indicate less than satisfactory, satisfactory, or better than satisfactory performance.

Less than Satisfactory	Satisfactory	Better than Satisfactory
poor	fairly consistent	strong
unreasonable	near	good
significantly lower	approximates	slightly above
substantially smaller	not significantly different	substantial
much lower	adequate	large majority
well below	compares reasonably well	substantial majority
quite low	reasonably	substantial percentage
lower	reasonably compares	significant majority
lacking	reasonably consistent	higher
not satisfactory	very comparable	well above
lagged behind	comparable	exceeded
less than reasonable	meets	significantly higher
did not compare well	reasonable	significantly exceeded
somewhat lower	more than reasonable	greatly exceeded
moderately below	satisfactory	very good
slightly lower	compares favorably	significantly higher
slightly below	substantially equaled	very strong
not a proportionate amount	majority	excellent
relatively weak		
less		

Misleadingly Favorable and Inconsistent Application of Subjective Evaluation Standards

The federal banking agencies applied the subjective standards for evaluating bank lending performance in a misleadingly favorable and inconsistent manner. They frequently found that bank lending that did not meet the relevant community credit needs benchmark nevertheless met satisfactory or higher standards. They also found that similar performances met different standards.

Table 5.5 shows examples of agency application of the subjective standards in a misleadingly favorable way, making it seem the bank's lending was closer to the benchmark than it actually was.[15] The first column of the table shows the standard the agency employed. The second and third columns show the measure of bank lending and the benchmark of community credit needs with which the bank's lending was compared. The fourth column shows the percentage by which the bank's lending was below the benchmark. Comparing the standard the bank met (for example, "adequate") with the percentage the bank's performance was below the benchmark (for example, 67% below) shows the degree to which the agency was misleadingly favorable.

As shown in Table 5.5, the agencies found that bank lending met the standard for "slightly below" when the bank's lending was as much as 38% below the benchmark. They found that bank lending met the standard for "somewhat lower" when the bank's lending was as much as 75% below the relevant benchmark. Finally, the agencies found that bank lending met the standard for "compares favorably" when it was as much as 54% below the relevant benchmark.

Table 5.6 shows examples of the federal banking agencies finding that similar bank performances met different standards. The first column shows the criteria the agency employed, the second column shows the bank performance, and the last column shows the different standards the agency found the banks with similar performances met.

In four instances depicted in Table 5.6, bank performances were identical, yet evaluated differently. The agencies evaluated an improvement of 12% in two banks' LDRs as a "strong positive trend" and an "upward trend," the same 3%/9% ratio of percent CON loans in LI tracts to the percentage of the AA's population in LI tracts as "adequate" and "lower," 70% of SB loans ≤$100G as a "majority" and a "clear majority," and bank LDRs compared with the statewide LDRs of 77%/73% as "excellent" and "satisfactory."

No Weights Assigned to Criteria

Large Retail Banks

The agencies use a large bank's performance on the individual criteria described above to evaluate the bank's performance on the relevant component of the lending test. It is difficult to discern the relative weights, if any, the agencies assigned to the criteria they used to evaluate each component of a large bank's lending under the lending test.[16] Frequently, a bank that performed poorly on one or more evaluative criterion was evaluated favorably on the relevant component of the lending test. While this may be explicable if the bank performed poorly on a criterion that had less weight relative to others on which the bank performed well, it was impossible to discern this because the agencies did not indicate the weight any of the criteria had. Thus, it appears it was entirely within the agencies' discretion to count some criteria highly and to discount or ignore others. The following are examples of banks that performed poorly on one or more evaluative criterion but nevertheless were evaluated as having a satisfactory or better record on the relevant component of the lending test.

Geographic Distribution of Loans

In PE 107 (endnote 5 lists and numbers each PE), the bank made a lower percentage of the dollar volume of its HMDA loans in MI tracts than the percentage of the AA's OOHUs in MI tracts (12/14), but the bank had a "good" geographic distribution of loans. In PEs 102, 109, and 110, the percentages of the banks' HMDA loans in LI tracts were less than the aggregate percentages. Nevertheless, one bank had an "excellent" geographic distribution of loans (PE 110) and the other two had an "adequate" distribution (PEs 102 and 109). In PEs 100, 101, 102, and 109, the banks' percentages of HMDA loans in MI tracts were lower than the aggregate percentages, but all four banks received passing grades on the geographic distribution of loans, including "adequate," "above average," and "excellent."

Distribution of Loans to Borrowers at Different Income Levels

In PE 106, the bank's distribution of loans to borrowers at different income levels was "excellent" even though it made a lower percentage of HMDA loans to LMI persons than the percentage of LMI persons in the AA (27.6/32).

In PEs 100, 102, 104, 105, and 107, despite having lower percentages of HMDA loans to LI families than the percentages of LI families in the AA, the banks' distribution of loans to borrowers at different income levels was at least "marginally acceptable." One bank that made 6% of its HMDA loans to LI persons compared with 21% LI families in the AA had a "good" record (PE 107).

Despite a significantly lower percent dollar volume of HMDA loans to LI persons (5.2) compared with the percentage of LI persons in the AA (20), the bank in PE 10 had a "good" distribution of loans to persons at different income levels.

The banks' percentages of small business loans in amounts less than or equal to $100,000 in PEs 100–103 and 110 were lower than the aggregate percentages, yet each bank's distribution of loans to persons at different income levels was at least "adequate."

Small Retail Banks

It was also difficult to discern the weights, if any, the federal banking agencies assigned to the criteria they used to evaluate the performance of small banks on the lending-related components of the small bank CRA performance evaluation. Small banks that performed poorly on one or more of the components frequently received satisfactory CRA ratings.[17] Banks that outperformed other banks on a particular component of the small bank test also often received a lower CRA rating. This could be understandable if the agencies explicitly assigned weights to the criteria, but they did not, creating the appearance that they could justify a particular rating by manipulating the results.[18]

LDR

Two banks whose LDRs compared poorly with their peers received "substantial non-compliance" CRA ratings: 13.7 compared with 54.6, 66.2, and 72.9 (PE 126) and 45 compared with 56 (PE 136). In contrast, three banks with similarly poor—although in some cases slightly better—LDRs compared with their peer banks received better "needs to improve" CRA ratings: 41.2/101.3; 25/47–87; and 15/68 (PEs 131,134,135). In two PEs, although the banks' LDRs were lower than their peer banks' LDRs, the banks received outstanding CRA ratings: PE 123, 77/79; 77/81; and PE 128, 77/81. On the other hand, four banks whose LDRs were generally equal to or better than most of their peers' LDRs received only satisfactory CRA ratings: PE 121, 98.6/87.6; PE 130, 73/64, 73, and 93; PE 125, 65/62; and PE 132, 60.6/53.3 and 65.4.

In considering a bank's LDR compared with the state average, the federal banking agencies found that identical LDR comparisons of 77/73 for two banks contributed to different CRA ratings: outstanding and needs to improve (PEs 128,132).

AA Lending

One bank that made 3% of its loans in its AA received a substantial noncompliance CRA rating (PE 136). A second bank that made a higher but still very low 7% of its HMDA loans inside its AA received a higher CRA rating—needs to improve (PE 135). A third bank that made a much higher 61% of its loans in its AA than the second bank received a lower rating than the second bank—substantial noncompliance (PE 126). A fourth bank with a lower percentage of loans within its AA (46) than the third bank received a higher CRA rating than the third bank: needs to improve (PE 114). Finally, a fifth bank with 81% of its loans in its AA received an outstanding CRA rating (PE 122), while banks with higher percentages of 85, 86 (HMDA loans), 90.9 (SB loans), 87 (SF loans), and 84.4 (MV loans) received satisfactory CRA ratings (PEs 121,132).

Distribution of Loans to Persons at Different Income Levels

A bank with a mixed record of percentage of loans to LMI persons compared with the percentage of LMI families in the AA—13.4/20, 20.4/21, 23.8/20, and 26.4/21—received an outstanding CRA rating (PE 122). In contrast, in PE 130, the bank made the same percentage of its loans to LMI borrowers (17) as the percentage of LMI persons in the AA (17) but received a lower CRA rating of satisfactory.

In PEs 133, 123, and 124, the banks had poor percentages of loans and dollar volume of loans to businesses with less than $1 million revenue compared with the percentage of such businesses in the AA, yet they received higher CRA ratings than warranted. In PE 133 the bank's ratios were 62/87 and 51/87, and the bank received an outstanding; in PE 123 the bank's ratios were 83/86 and 46/86, and the bank also received an outstanding; and in PE 124 the bank's ratios were 26/86 and 24/86 and the bank received a needs to improve.

Geographic Distribution of Loans

In PEs 123, 128, and 133, the banks received outstanding CRA ratings. In order to merit an outstanding CRA rating, a bank's record should at least top most and equal the remainder of the credit needs benchmarks the agency employs in the PE. However, these banks did not meet most if not all of the benchmarks in their PEs. In PE 133, the bank made 3% of its total number and dollar volume of SB loans to small businesses in LMI tracts compared with 4% of small businesses in such tracts, and 8% of its SB loans and 9% of its dollar volume of SB loans in MI tracts compared with 12% of small businesses in MI tracts. In PE 123, the bank made 3% of its SB loans and 1% of its dollar volume of SB loans in LI tracts compared with 4% of small businesses in LI tracts, and 31% of its SB loans and 53% of its dollar volume of SB loans in MI tracts compared with 56% of small businesses in such tracts. The bank also made 25% of its SF loans and 6% of the dollar volume of its SF loans in LI tracts compared with 4% of small farms in such tracts, and 55% of its loans and 51% of the dollar volume of its loans in MI tracts compared with 71% of small farms in MI tracts. In PE 128, the bank made no SB loans to small businesses in LI tracts compared with 7% of businesses in such tracts; it made 29% of its SB loans and 24% of its dollar volume of SB loans to small businesses in MI tracts compared with 21% of small businesses in such tracts.

Inconsistent and Vague Standards for Evaluating the Retail Lending Component of the Lending Test for Large Retail Banks

The federal banking agencies evaluate five components of the lending activity of large banks to determine whether to give the bank one of five ratings on the lending test component of the overall CRA performance evaluation.[19] The five components of the lending test are the bank's lending activity within its service area, the geographic distribution of the bank's loans, the distribution of the bank's loans to individuals at different income levels, community development lending, and the bank's use of flexible lending criteria. This section examines how the agencies evaluated large bank performance on the first three components of the lending test. It examines the standards the agencies used to evaluate bank performance, whether it was possible to discern the level of performance necessary to meet a particular standard, how the performance of banks who met the same standards compared, and the accuracy of the agencies' evaluations.

The agencies used subjective standards to evaluate bank performance on each of the three components of the lending test under study. The agencies did not define the level of performance necessary to meet a particular standard. It was also impossible to discern the level of performance necessary to meet a particular standard because none of the PEs used the same criteria to evaluate each of the lending test components. This also made it impossible to compare the performances of banks that were evaluated the same or differently on a particular lending test component. When it was possible to make limited comparisons—when different PEs used some criteria in common to evaluate a bank's performance on a particular component of the lending test—occasionally a bank that outperformed another bank on one or more of the common criteria received a lower evaluation on that component of the lending test.[20] This may be explicable, but since the PEs did not use common criteria and since the individual criteria were not weighted, it is not possible to determine whether a lesser evaluation for a bank that outperformed another bank on common criteria was justified. Finally, it also appears that the federal banking agencies frequently overrated bank performance on each of the three components of the lending test under study.[21]

Lending Within the Bank's Service Area

The PEs used seven different standards to evaluate a large bank's lending within its service area. These included "excellent," "strong," "good," "adequate," "marginally adequate," "does not compare well," and "poor." It was not always possible to discern the level of performance necessary to meet a particular standard; sometimes it appeared that a bank with a stronger record than another was evaluated as having a weaker record. For example, one bank whose lending within it service area was "excellent" had an LDR of 93 compared with 87 for its competitors (PE 102). On the other hand, a bank whose LDR compared more favorably with comparable lenders, 98 to 82 (PE 110), was evaluated as having met the apparently weaker standard of "strong" lending within its service area.

Geographic Distribution of Loans

The federal banking agencies used eight different standards to evaluate a large retail bank's geographic distribution of loans. These included "excellent," "good," "above average," "adequate," "marginally acceptable," "did not effectively penetrate," "less than satisfactory," and "poor."

Excellent

In PE 104, the geographic distribution of the bank's HMDA and small business loans was stronger than the community credit needs benchmarks in every comparison the federal banking agency made. In contrast, although the bank in PE 110 met the standards for an "excellent" distribution, its record was not as strong as the bank in PE 104. Its record of lending in LMI neighborhoods compared with wealthier neighborhoods was mixed: the percentages of the bank's HMDA loans in LI and MI neighborhoods were less than the aggregate percentages (2.1/2.8 and 8.5/13); the percentage of the bank's HMDA loans in MI tracts was lower than the aggregate loan percentage in MI tracts of all OTS-regulated banks (8.5/9.7); the percentage of the bank's loans in LI tracts was higher than the percentage in LI tracts by OTS-regulated banks (2.1/1.7); and the percent dollar volume of its HMDA loans in LI and MI tracts was higher than the aggregate percentage (3.7/2.4 and 11.6/10.8).

Good

In PE 106, the bank had a "good" geographic distribution of loans based on a small number of comparisons of the bank's lending with a credit needs benchmark, despite the fact that the bank did not perform well on them. The bank made 2.6% of its HMDA loans in MI tracts compared with 2.9% of the AA's OOHUs in MI tracts and 3% of the AA's families in MI tracts. In PE 112, the bank also had a "good" geographic distribution of loans despite having a mixed record. The percentage of the bank's small business loans in LI tracts (10.2) was lower than the percentage of the AA's small businesses in these tracts (17.3) and the bank's percentage of HMDA loans in LMI tracts (12.2) was lower than the AA's percentage of OOHUs in LMI tracts (18.2). On the other hand, the percentage of the bank's small business loans in MI tracts (12.1) was higher than the percentage of small businesses in these tracts (11.8) and the percentage of HMDA loans in LMI tracts (12.1) was higher than the aggregate percentage (11.9).

In PEs 107 and 103, the banks also had a "good" geographic distribution of loans despite mixed lending records. In PE 107, the bank had a mixed record of HMDA lending by type in LI and MI tracts compared with the percentage of the AA's OOHUs in such tracts, market share of HMDA loans by type in LI and MI tracts compared with its overall market share, small business lending in LI and MI tracts compared with the percentage of the AA's small businesses in such tracts, market share of small business loans in LI and MI census tracts compared with its overall market share, and percentage of consumer loans in LI and MI tracts compared with the percentage of the AA's households living in such tracts. In PE 103, the bank's small business lending was strong in MI tracts; its lending outpaced the aggregate and the percentage of small businesses in MI tracts. Its consumer lending was mixed: its percentage of consumer loans in MI tracts was higher than the percentage of the AA's families living in MI tracts in one comparison and lower in the other. Finally, its home mortgage lending was weak. The percentage of the bank's HMDA loans in MI tracts was lower than the percentage of the AA's OOHUs in MI tracts in both comparisons the agency made.

Above average

In PE 100, the bank's geographic distribution of loans was "above average." While this bank's "above average" classification may or may not be deserved, its performance seemed similar to the performance of the banks that met the standards for a "good" performance. The agency compared the bank's market share of HMDA loans in LMI census tracts with its overall market share of HMDA loans, the percentage of the bank's HMDA loans in LI and MI tracts with the aggregate percentage, and the percentage of the bank's loans in LI and MI tracts with the percentage of the AA's OOHUs in LI and MI tracts. In three comparisons, the bank's percentage of loans in LI or MI tracts was higher; in two, it was lower, but the difference was less than one percentage point. The bank's percentage of small business loans in LI tracts was lower than the aggregate but its percentage in MI and LMI tracts was higher.

Adequate

The federal banking agencies found that five banks had an "adequate" geographic distribution of loans (PEs 101,102,108,109,114). The lending of all five banks did not meet the quantitative community credit needs benchmarks in the majority of comparisons the agencies made, hardly an "adequate" performance.

From "marginally acceptable" to "poor"

The four banks that had less than adequate records all performed poorly on the comparisons between their lending and credit needs benchmarks the relevant agencies made. The agencies could easily have evaluated each of these four banks the same way, but they did not.

> PE 105 ("marginally acceptable"): The percentage of the bank's loans in MI tracts was lower than the percentage of the AA's OOHUs in MI tracts (5/8) and the percentage of the bank's HMDA loans in MI tracts was 5.1, lower than its peers' 7.4.
> PE 111 ("did not effectively penetrate"): The percentage of the bank's HMDA loans in LI census tracts (0.3) and MI census tracts (3) was lower than the percentage of the AA's OOHUs in LI census tracts (1.9) and MI census tracts (7.6). The percentage of the bank's HMDA loans in LI tracts (.4) and MI tracts (2.6) was lower than the aggregate percentage of loans in LI tracts (1.2) and MI tracts (4.6).
> PE 113 ("less than satisfactory"): The bank had "noticeable" lending gaps in its small business and HMDA lending in LMI neighborhoods. The bank made 25% of its HMDA loans and 13% of its small business loans in LMI tracts compared with 58% of the AA's population living in LMI tracts.
> PE 115 ("poor"): The bank was deficient in its three previous CRA evaluations and had done little or no small business lending in LMI neighborhoods.

Distribution of Loans to Persons at Different Income Levels

The federal banking agencies used seven standards to evaluate large retail bank lending to individuals, businesses, and small farms at different income levels. These included "excellent," "good," "adequate," "reasonable," "marginally adequate," "needs to improve," and "poor."

Excellent

The bank in PE 103 had an "excellent" record of making loans to persons at different income levels. The agency did not explain how it concluded the bank had an excellent record; in fact, the bank's record was mixed, making it hard to understand how it met the standards for "excellent." The bank in PE 106 also met the standards for "excellent." The bank's lending performance did not meet the credit needs benchmark the agency used, making it difficult to understand how the bank deserved an "excellent."

Good

The bank in PE 115 had a "good" record of lending to persons at different income levels. The agency did not employ criteria that used a quantitative benchmark of community credit needs against which to measure the bank's lending, so it is difficult to evaluate the agency's rating. The bank in PE 112 also had a "good" distribution of loans to small businesses. The bank's lending record was mixed, so objectively it did not appear to have a "good" record. On the other hand, its record was similar to the bank in PE 103 that was "excellent." The bank in PE 104, which also had a "good" record of lending to persons at different income levels, had a mixed lending record, but no worse than the banks that had excellent distributions of loans to persons of different income and possibly better. In the comparisons of the bank's lending to community credit needs benchmarks the agency made, the bank outperformed the credit needs benchmark four times and did not meet it twice. The bank's market share of HMDA loans to LI or MI persons was greater than its overall market share in five comparisons and was lower in one. The bank's small business lending record was also mixed; it outperformed the relevant credit needs benchmark once and did not reach it once.

The bank's record in PE 107 was somewhat weaker than the bank in PE 104, but it also had a "good" distribution of loans to persons at different income levels. The agency evaluated the same performance criteria relating to loan percentages and market share as in PE 104, but examined two years of data. The bank's percentages of loans to LI and MI persons was lower than the AA's percentages of LI and MI families in eight of twelve comparisons. The bank's market share of HMDA loans by type to LI and MI persons was higher than its overall market share in five comparisons and lower in five. The bank's lending did not meet the small business credit needs benchmarks the agency employed twice and it equaled them twice.

The bank in PE 102 had a "good" distribution of loans to persons at different income levels, once again despite a mixed lending record. The agency made various comparisons relating to the bank's HMDA lending; the bank's HMDA lending surpassed community credit needs four times and was below nine times. The bank's small business lending record was also mixed.

Adequate

Five banks had an "adequate" distribution of loans to persons at different income levels. None of the banks objectively met this standard. In PE 112, the bank's record was weak. Its percentage of HMDA loans to LI and MI borrowers was lower than the aggregate (LI: 9.5/13.1; MI: 20.3/24.5). The bank's percentage of loans to LI persons was lower than the percentage of LI families in the AA (12.5/22.5) while the percentage to MI borrowers was higher (19.6/16.5).

The bank in PE 108 had a mixed record of HMDA, small business, and consumer lending, although no worse than banks that were rated as having a "good" distribution of loans to people at different income levels. The bank's lending exceeded the community credit needs benchmarks the agency employed twice and failed to meet them four times.

In PE 114, the bank's record was mixed. Its lending was greater than the community credit needs benchmark on one comparison and was below on three comparisons.

In PEs 101 and 110, despite meeting the standard for "adequate" performance, the banks' lending did not meet the credit needs benchmark on nearly all the comparisons the agency made.

Reasonable

In PE 100, the bank had a mixed record of HMDA and small business lending. Its lending exceeded the community credit needs benchmark four times and was below the benchmark five times. Its record appears to be stronger than some banks that received an evaluation of "adequate," begging the question: which is better, reasonable or adequate?

Marginally adequate

The bank in PE 105 had a "marginally adequate" record of meeting the credit needs of persons at different income levels. The bank's performance was worse than this; its lending did not meet the credit needs benchmark on any comparisons the agency made.

Needs to improve

The bank in PE 111 received a "needs to improve" record of lending to persons at different income levels. The bank seemed to deserve this classification, but its record was no worse than banks whose records were characterized as "adequate." The percentage of the bank's HMDA loans to LI persons and MI persons increased, from 3.5 to 4.2 (LI) and 15.9 to 17.6 (MI). The percentage of the bank's HMDA loans to LI borrowers was lower than the percentage of LI families in the bank's AA, 4.2 to 15.8. On the other hand, the percent dollar volume of the bank's HMDA loans to MI persons was higher than the percentage of MI families in the bank's AA: 17.6/16.6.

Poor

The bank in PE 109 was evaluated as having a poor record of meeting the credit needs of persons at different income levels. The percentage of the bank's loans to LI and MI persons compared with the percentage of LI and MI families in the bank's AA was lower in all years under comparison (LI: 3/4 and 2/4; MI: 12/13 and 10/13) and the percentages of the bank's loans to LI and MI persons compared with the aggregate percentages were also lower (LI: 3/8; MI: 10/18).

Inconsistent and Inflated CRA Ratings for Small Retail Banks

There are five components of the small bank CRA performance evaluation: the bank's LDR; concentration of loans in its AA; record of lending to borrowers at different income levels, small businesses and small farms; geographic distribution of loans; and responsiveness to complaints from the public. This section seeks to determine the level of performance necessary to earn a particular CRA rating, how the performances of banks with the same and with different CRA ratings compared, and whether the ratings accurately reflected the bank's performance. Based on the analysis of the sixteen small bank PEs under study, it was impossible to determine the level of performance necessary to earn a particular rating because the PEs did not use the same criteria. Even if the PEs used the same criteria, this might not have mattered. According to regression analyses CRA researcher Kenneth Thomas conducted, the small banks' performance on the evaluative criteria was not the most important factor in determining a small bank's CRA rating. The bank's examiner and "all of the subjective, and other qualitative characteristics that go along with the person responsible for assigning ratings" was the most important factor in determining the bank's record, not the evaluative criteria.[22] Thomas found that the agencies frequently overrated small banks by at least one rating level.[23]

Outstanding (PEs 122, 123, 128, 133)

Four banks in the PE sample received a CRA rating of outstanding; their records were mixed at best, hardly deserving an outstanding rating. In PEs 122, 123, and 128, the quantitative measures of the banks' lending were higher than the credit needs benchmarks on some of the comparisons the agencies made but were lower on others. In PE 133, the quantitative measures of the bank's lending record did not meet any of the credit needs benchmarks the agency used.

Satisfactory (PEs 121, 125, 130, 132)

The satisfactory ratings also seemed higher than deserved. The banks' lending records in PEs 125, 130, and 132 compared with the credit needs benchmarks the PEs used were mixed. It is difficult to evaluate the satisfactory rating of the bank in PE 121 because the agency used only one criterion that compared bank lending with community credit needs; the bank's LDR was higher than its peer group: 98.5/87.6.

Needs to Improve (PEs 124, 131, 134, 135)

Three of the four banks that received needs to improve CRA ratings could easily have received substantial noncompliance ratings; their records were similar to the banks that were rated substantial noncompliance. In PE 131, the bank's lending generally did not meet the credit needs benchmarks the agency used. The bank in PE 134 received a needs to improve primarily because it had a low lending volume. Its LDR was 25 compared with LDRs ranging from 47 to 87 for its peers. Its overall loan volume was, with one exception, less than half the volume of comparable banks. It increased its overall loan volume by 49%, not sufficient to increase its CRA rating. Otherwise, the bank performed fairly well compared with the credit needs benchmarks the agency employed, but the agency discounted this performance because the bank's lending volume was very low. In PE 135, the bank's lending volume was also low, and its lending compared with the credit needs benchmarks the agency employed was mixed.

The bank in PE 124 was the one bank whose needs to improve seemed appropriate. The bank's LDR was 77 compared with LDRs ranging from 43 to 82 for its peers. The bank made 46% of its loans in its AA. The percentage of its loans (26) and the dollar volume of its loans (24) to businesses with less than or equal to $1M revenue was less than the percentage of such businesses in its AA (86), and the bank's percentage of such loans ranked fifth of six lenders in the AA.

Substantial Noncompliance (PEs 126, 127, 129, 136)

The four banks with substantial noncompliance ratings deserved them. In PE 126, the bank's LDR was 13.7 and it compared poorly with its peers. The bank made 61% of the number and 35% of the dollar volume of its loans in its AA and its lending levels compared with the credit needs standards the agency employed was mixed. In PE 136, the bank over the course of two years made 3% and 44% of its loans in its AA and 8% and 32% of the dollar volume of its loans in its AA. The bank's lending was poor compared with the credit needs benchmarks the agency employed. In PE 127, the bank's LDR was 2.4 compared with 53.8 for area lenders and 61.7 for its national peer group. While the bank made all its loans in its AA, the agency discounted this because of its low lending volume.

CRA Ratings

During the second CRA enforcement regime, CRA ratings were as shown in Table 5.7. According to the data, during the second CRA enforcement regime, 97.1% to 98.9% of banks annually received CRA ratings of satisfactory or higher. This is higher than during the first CRA enforcement regime, when 89% to 98% of banks annually received CRA ratings of satisfactory or higher.[25] Community groups have complained that these ratings are inflated.[26] Kenneth Thomas, who conducted an extensive survey of small bank CRA ratings during the second CRA enforcement regime, agreed. His research indicated that 47.1% of the small bank CRA ratings and 61% of the large bank CRA ratings were inflated.[27] Daniel Immergluck of the Woodstock Institute conducted a study that found that CRA ratings at the start of the second CRA regime were following a similar pattern as under the first regime.[28] Community advocates believe that ambiguous standards for evaluating CRA compliance contribute to grade inflation; if a bank's performance was borderline, the agency would give the bank the benefit of the doubt and give it a higher rating.[29] Allen Fishbein, then general counsel of the Center for Community Change, concluded that one of the problems with grade inflation and ambiguous standards is that it is difficult to determine whether a bank that received an outstanding rating deserved it.[30]

Decisions on Applications

This section examines decisions the Federal Reserve and the OCC issued on bank expansion applications when the CRA record of the bank was discussed in detail.[31] There are many similarities between how the agencies considered bank lending in expansion applications and PEs. The decisions did not use a fixed set of evaluative criteria and used subjective standards for evaluating bank lending. The decisions generally listed facts about the bank's lending, emphasized strengths and excused weaknesses, and did not disclose the reasoning they employed in reaching their conclusions. In some decisions, the agency acknowledged the accuracy of critical public comments about bank lending, but approved the applications without explaining the reason the criticism was not sufficient to deny the application. Finally, the agencies did not take the opportunity when considering the applications to encourage banks to improve weaknesses in their lending records.

The Board of Governors of the Federal Reserve System

The Board of Governors of the Federal Reserve System (the "Federal Reserve") issued at least sixty-nine orders on bank applications that involved the CRA from July 1, 1997 through September, 2003.[32] The Fed granted all the applications. The Federal Reserve's analysis of the banks' CRA records—and particularly their lending—in these decisions had certain common characteristics. The analysis summarized the findings of the bank's most recent PE, emphasized the strong points of the bank's lending record, and rarely mentioned weaknesses. If the Federal Reserve mentioned a weakness in the bank's lending, it generally excused it. Usually, the weakness was that data about the bank's lending disclosed through HMDA indicated the bank treated white mortgage loan applicants better than minority loan applicants. The Federal Reserve generally expressed concern about this, but indicated that HMDA data did not provide a sufficient basis to draw conclusions about discrimination. In addition, the decisions did not contain traditional legal reasoning, applying the law to facts and reaching a conclusion; generally the Federal Reserve simply listed facts about the bank's CRA record and found that the record was consistent with approving the application. Finally, the decisions did not use a fixed set of criteria for evaluating the bank's lending and used subjective standards for evaluating the bank's lending performance.

The Federal Reserve's analysis of the CRA record of the relevant banks in considering the 2000 application of Wells Fargo & Company to acquire First

Security Corporation is representative of its decisions on bank expansion applications.[33] The Federal Reserve started its analysis by stating that all of the subsidiary banks of Wells Fargo & Company and First Security Corporation had CRA ratings of outstanding or satisfactory. Of particular importance was that Wells Fargo Bank ("Wells Fargo"), which represented 45% of the assets of Wells Fargo & Company, and First Security Bank ("First Security"), which represented 76% of the assets of First Security Corporation, had received outstanding CRA ratings on their most recent CRA PEs. In addition, bank examiners found no evidence of prohibited discrimination or illegal credit practices by the banks. Examiners also determined that the subsidiary banks' CRA lending areas were reasonable and did not arbitrarily exclude LMI areas.

The Federal Reserve noted that Wells Fargo had adopted a business strategy that concentrated on small business lending and deemphasized residential lending, resulting in an increase of $2.7 billion in small business lending and a decrease of $2.2 billion in residential lending. The bank's examiners found that Wells Fargo's gains in small business lending more than offset its losses in residential lending. Wells Fargo made 239,000 small business loans for $9.3 billion during the review period; 26% of the loans were to businesses in LMI neighborhoods. The bank made 36% of its residential loans, totaling $240 million, to LMI borrowers. Wells Fargo's examiners found it exhibited a "strong" level of community development lending, having originated 149 community development loans totaling $651 million in California, Arizona, and Washington. The Federal Reserve did not use credit needs benchmarks to evaluate these data.

The Federal Reserve then described Wells Fargo's performance in several states, including California, Idaho, Montana, Nevada, New Mexico, Oregon, South Dakota, Utah, Washington, and Wisconsin. The Federal Reserve's findings for California and Idaho are illustrative of it methodology. One of the essential characteristics of this methodology is that the Federal Reserve rarely used credit needs benchmarks to evaluate the lending.

California

—"Very strong" lending record based on large volume of CD lending to support LI and very LI housing and large volume of SB loans in LMI areas
—7,000 residential loans totaling $700M
—"Leader" in providing financing for affordable housing
—99 CD loans totaling $469M
—191,000 SB loans totaling $7B

Idaho

—2,164 SB loans totaling $107M
—More than 50% of loans to businesses with less than $1M revenue
—90% of loans in amounts less than $100G
—80% SB loans in LMI neighborhoods cf 17% agg
—"Adequate" penetration of residential loans among borrowers at all income levels
—% loans to LMI borrowers "compared favorably" to % LMI households
—806 residential loans totaling $30M
—3 CD loans totaling $30M

The Federal Reserve then turned to First Security's CRA performance. First Security was rated outstanding on the lending test component of its most recent PE. Its lending record in Utah was outstanding and in Idaho and Oregon was high satisfactory. The bank had a good distribution of home mortgage loans to borrowers of all income levels. First Security had a good record of home purchase lending to LI individuals in Idaho and Oregon, an excellent record of lending to MI individuals, and a "high level" of community development lending.

Finally, the Federal Reserve devoted a separate section of its analysis to Wells Fargo's and First Security's HMDA data. The Federal Reserve stated that Wells Fargo "generally lagged" behind the aggregate percentage of housing loans to LMI individuals and neighborhoods. The percentage of Wells Fargo's housing loans to Native Americans, African-Americans, and Latinos approximated the aggregate percentage but the percentages of such loans by both Wells Fargo and aggregate lenders were less than the percentage of minority individuals in the AA. The Federal Reserve also pointed out that Wells Fargo's minority/white denial rate ratio was higher than the aggregate ratio. In boilerplate language the Federal Reserve used in many decisions, it stated, "The Board is concerned when the record of an institution indicates disparities in lending and believes that all banks are obligated to ensure that their lending practices are based on criteria that ensure not only safe and sound lending, but also equal access to credit by creditworthy applicants regardless of their race or income level."[34] Despite these concerns, the Federal Reserve indicated that HMDA data were insufficient to draw any conclusions, again in boilerplate:

> The Board recognizes, however, that HMDA data alone provide an incomplete measure of an institution's lending in its community because these data cover only a few categories of housing-related lend-

> ing. HMDA data, moreover, provide only limited information about the covered loans. HMDA data, therefore, have limitations that make them an inadequate basis, absent other information, for concluding that an institution has not assisted adequately in meeting its community credit needs or has engaged in illegal lending discrimination.[35]

The problem with the Fed's approach to HMDA data is that the Fed expects too much of the data and does not take advantage of HMDA's usefulness. While it is true that a bank's HMDA data alone do not show that an institution is not meeting community credit needs or engaging in illegal discrimination—HMDA, after all, is only a quantitative measure of bank lending—community credit needs benchmarks are available to compare with the bank's lending. The agencies, including the Fed, use these benchmarks in the PEs and frequently refer to them in their decisions. These benchmarks include aggregate lending levels, the percentage of owner-occupied housing units in the bank's CRA service area, and the percentage of small businesses, small farms, or LMI persons in the bank's service area. The Federal Reserve could have concluded, for example, from comparing the percentage of Wells Fargo's HMDA loans to LMI persons and neighborhoods with the aggregate lending percentage, that Wells Fargo was not meeting community credit needs for housing credit. It simply chose not to do so.

The Office of the Comptroller of the Currency

The Office of the Comptroller of the Currency ("OCC") issued several decisions on bank expansion applications between July 1, 1997 and November 2003 in which it analyzed the CRA record of the banks in detail.[36] Like the Federal Reserve, the OCC in each of its decisions relied on different criteria and subjective standards to evaluate bank lending. The OCC's decisions also frequently emphasized the strong points about the bank's lending record and rarely mentioned weaknesses. If the OCC mentioned a weakness in the bank's lending, it generally excused or ignored it. Frequently, the weakness was that the bank's HMDA data indicated that the bank rejected home mortgage loan applications from minorities at higher rates than from whites. The OCC generally expressed concern about this, but, like the Federal Reserve, stated that HMDA data provided an insufficient basis upon which to draw any conclusions about the bank's lending record. The decisions did not contain legal reasoning; generally, again like the Federal Reserve, the OCC simply listed facts about the bank's record and found the record was consistent with granting the application without further explanation.

The OCC's decision on the application of Bank of America ("BofA") to merge with NationsBank ("NB") is representative of the OCC's mode of analyzing a bank's CRA record when considering an expansion application.[37] The OCC indicated that NB had received an outstanding CRA rating and that banks it subsequently purchased all received satisfactory or better CRA ratings on their most recent CRA examinations. BofA had received an outstanding CRA rating on its most recent CRA examination. The OCC then summarized BofA's and NB's overall lending in 1997: NB and its mortgage subsidiary made 12,920 home mortgage, home improvement, and refinance loans totaling $834 million in LMI areas while BofA made 10,777 such loans totaling $920 million. NB made $3.2 billion in small business loans in 1997, $650 million of which was to small businesses in LMI areas. NB made $276 million in community development loans and $248 million in community development investments while BofA made $467 million in loans and $407 million in investments. The OCC did not use credit needs benchmarks against which to measure this lending.

The OCC addressed specific comments from members of the public criticizing both banks' home mortgage lending in various geographic areas. In responding to the comments, the OCC frequently agreed that the comments were accurate, but the comments apparently had no impact on the OCC's decision, and the OCC did not explain the reason for this. The OCC's responses to comments about Arizona and North Carolina are demonstrative:

Arizona

Comment: BofA's HP lending to LMI borrowers was low compared with the aggregate.
Response: BofA's 23.9% HMDA loans to MI borrowers was comparable to the 25.1% aggregate.

North Carolina

Comment: NB's record of lending to LMI borrowers was weak.
Response: NB's MS of HP and HR loans to LMI borrowers was less than its MS of loans to MIDI/UI borrowers. NB's 21.5% HP loans to LMI borrowers was less than the 29.1% aggregate and its 22.3% of all HMDA loans to LMI borrowers was less than the 28.3% aggregate.

Next, the OCC considered NB's and BofA's home mortgage lending to minorities. According to the OCC, "several commenters" asserted that the banks' "denial rates for home loans to minorities in various locations were disproportionate to that for whites and that lending to minorities was below industry averages."[38] The OCC acknowledged that it did identify "for certain groups in certain locations, higher than average denial rates or lower than average origination rates for" the banks and that the HMDA data "revealed some instances in which the banks' performance was less favorable than peer institutions. . . ."[39] Despite these weaknesses, "the OCC found no information that would be inconsistent with approval of this application."[40] The OCC then used its own boilerplate language about HMDA data:

> HMDA data provide information about a bank's mortgage lending activity that is useful, as preliminary information, to highlight potential lending discrimination problems. However, it is important to note that HMDA data alone are inadequate to provide a basis for concluding that a bank is engaged in lending discrimination or in indicating whether its level of lending is sufficient.[41]

The OCC then responded to specific public comments critical of the banks' lending to minorities in particular states or cities. The OCC acknowledged that virtually all the comments criticizing the bank's lending were correct, but it did not seem to matter to the OCC's decision. The OCC did not give a reason for this other than its boilerplate dismissal of the usefulness of HMDA data. The following are comments members of the public submitted about Arizona, California, and Kentucky, which are representative of comments about other states. They show that BoFA's lending to minorities was lower than the industry average, deserving more than a boilerplate response to explain the reason its lending was sufficient to meet credit needs.

Arizona

Comment: BofA is below the industry averages in home mortgage lending to African-American and Latino borrowers.
Response: BofA made 1% of its HMDA loans to African-Americans compared with the aggregate 1.8% and 9.4% of its HMDA loans to Latinos compared with the 10.4% aggregate.

California

Comment: Same as Arizona.
Response: BofA made 1.6% and 12.1% of its HP loans to African-Americans and Latinos compared with the aggregate 3.8% and 16.9%. It made 2.6% of

its HMDA loans to African-Americans and 11.4 % of such loans to Latinos compared with the aggregate 4% and 14%, respectively.

Kentucky

Comment: NB's application denial rates were higher for African-Americans than whites.
Response: NB's denial rates for HMDA loan applications of 28% for African-Americans and 20% for whites was "comparable" to the industry average of 30% and 23%. NB originated 5% of its HMDA loans to African-Americans, equal to the aggregate.

Finally, some commenters stated that NB had a poor record of small business lending to minorities. The OCC found that NB made 5% of its Small Business Administration loans to African-Americans, 7% to Asians, and 5% to Latinos. It did not employ credit needs benchmarks against which to compare these percentages.

In conclusion, the OCC ruled, "our investigation and analysis of the issues relating to CRA performance indicated no basis for denying or conditioning the approval of this application."[42] The OCC offered no analysis or reasons for its decision.

Compliance Manuals and Other Regulatory Materials

The federal banking agencies have promulgated CRA compliance manuals and other regulatory materials in the second CRA enforcement regime that instruct their examiners how to evaluate bank lending when conducting PEs.[43] The manuals do not require examiners to use a fixed set of evaluative criteria composed of quantitative measures of bank lending, quantitative benchmarks of community credit needs, and objective terms for evaluating bank lending. While many of the criteria the manuals employ contain quantitative measures of bank lending and quantitative benchmarks of community credit needs, the standards for evaluating bank lending are subjective.

Small Retail Banks

The manuals include instructions for conducting the various components of the small bank performance evaluation, including evaluating the bank's

LDR, the bank's lending within its AA, the geographic distribution of its loans, and its lending to borrowers at different income levels.

LDR

The manuals adopt a small bank's LDR as a quantitative measure of lending, peer banks' LDRs as a quantitative benchmark, and "reasonable" as a subjective standard for evaluating the bank's LDR. This subjective standard creates a broad loophole for banks whose LDRs are below their peers' LDRs. The manuals instruct bank examiners to determine whether a small bank's LDR is reasonable considering factors such as "the capacity of other similarly-situated institutions to lend in the assessment area(s)."[44] Specifically, examiners should consider the average LDRs for similarly situated institutions and competitors.[45] The current version of the Interagency Questions and Answers Regarding the CRA (the "CRA Q & A") states, "No specific ratio is reasonable in every circumstance," and each ratio should be evaluated in light of the bank's capacity to lend, demographic and economic factors, and lending opportunities."[46] If the LDR "does not appear reasonable," the examiner is to consider the total number and dollar volume of the loans the bank sold to the secondary market and the innovativeness or complexity of its community development loans.[47] If these are sufficient, the bank's lending performance may be considered satisfactory despite the low LDR.[48]

Credit Extended Inside and Outside the Bank's AA

The manuals employ objective terms for evaluating the percentage of a bank's lending within its AA, but once again, they allow a large loophole for a bank with a poor record. A small bank that did not make a majority of its loans in its AA did not make a satisfactory amount of credit available in its community.[49] When considering the effect that the bank's failure to make at least half its loans in its AA will have on the bank's overall CRA rating, examiners are to consider information such as economic conditions, loan demand, and the institution's size, financial condition, branching network, and business strategies.[50] The CRA Q & A makes clear that a bank may still achieve an overall satisfactory CRA rating depending on these other factors.[51]

Geographic Distribution of Loans

The manuals instruct bank examiners to identify by income category census tracts in which there is "little" loan penetration and to reach a conclusion about the reasons for the low lending levels.[52] The manuals instruct examiners to do this by using two quantitative measures of bank lending: the percentage of the bank's loans and dollar volume of loans originated in LI, MI, MIDI, and UI tracts. The manuals then instruct the examiners to compare these measures with a quantitative benchmark of community credit needs: the percentage of the AA's families residing within each of these categories of tracts.[53] However, the manuals do not provide instructions to examiners about how to define "little" loan penetration or how to compare the bank's percentage of loans to tracts of various incomes with the percentages of families living in the tracts at these income levels.

Lending to Borrowers at Different Income Levels

The FDIC manual instructs examiners to identify categories of borrowers by income or business revenue for which there "is little or no loan penetration" and to form conclusions about the reasons for the low lending levels.[54] The FDIC manual suggests that examiners do this by preparing tables that compare two quantitative measures of bank lending—the percentages of the bank's loans and dollar volume of loans by income level of borrowers, small businesses, or small farms—with a quantitative benchmark of credit needs, specifically the percentage of either persons, small businesses, or small farms in the bank's AA at each income level.[55] The manual also indicates the examiners may compare the bank's lending to borrowers at different income levels with the aggregate.[56] The manual does not offer any guidance about how to evaluate these comparisons.

Large Retail Banks

The manuals and other regulatory materials contain instructions for evaluating bank performance on the lending test and its five components, including the geographic distribution of the bank's loans and lending to borrowers at different income levels.

Geographic Distribution of Loans

The manuals instruct examiners to determine the extent to which the bank is serving census tracts at each income level and to determine whether there are unexplained "conspicuous gaps" in lending.[57] "Conspicuous" is never defined. The manuals instruct examiners to use several quantitative measures of bank lending and to make several comparisons of the lending with quantitative benchmarks of credit needs. These include:

#, $ vol, and % of each type of loan by tract income level;

#, $ vol, and % of each type of loan inside and outside the bank's AA;

# of tracts in which the bank has made a loan at each income level and # of tracts at each income level;

and $ vol of each type of HMDA loan in each tract cf # 1-4 fam OOHUs in each tract;

and $ vol MF housing loans in each tract cf # MF structures in each census tract;

and $ vol SB and SF loans in each tract cf # SB and SF in each tract;

whether there are any gaps for each income category, by identifying groups of contiguous tracts that have no loans or those with low penetration relative to other tracts.[58]

If there are gaps, the examiner may compare the bank's performance with the performance of other banks.[59] The examiner may also consider the bank's share of loans in LI and MI tracts compared with its share in MIDI and UI tracts.[60]

The FDIC manual describes the information the examiner should include in a large bank's PE. Among other information, the PE should include the bank's level of lending in LMI tracts compared with several quantitative benchmarks of credit needs, including the aggregate percentage, the percentages of similarly situated banks, and the percentage of OOHUs in tracts at various income levels.[61] A model PE in the manual includes a table that shows the percentage of the bank's loans in LI, MI, MIDI, and UI tracts compared with the percentage of OOHUs and aggregate lending percentages in each grouping of tracts.[62] The model PE uses subjective and vague standards such as "slightly less" and "reasonably similar" to compare the bank lending percentages with the percentage of OOHUs and the aggregate percentage.[63] The same model PE includes a chart that compares the percentage of the bank's small business loans by census tract income level with the percentage of small businesses and aggregate lending percentage by tract income level.[64] The model PE uses the term "adequate" to describe the bank's performance compared with the aggregate.[65]

The OCC Large Bank CRA Guidance (the "CRA Guidance") attempts to promote consistency in the CRA exams of large banks.[66] It requires OCC CRA examiners to use certain criteria for evaluating bank lending and gives the examiners guidance for evaluating bank performance on the criteria. Interestingly, the CRA Guidance gives specific directions about when to find a bank's CRA performance is from "good" to "excellent," but not when to find that a bank's performance is less than good.

The CRA Guidance comes very close to establishing a fixed set of CRA evaluative criteria composed of quantitative measures of bank lending, quantitative benchmarks of community credit needs, and objective standards for evaluating a bank's record of meeting credit needs. The CRA Guidance requires OCC examiners to make the following comparisons of quantitative measures of bank lending with quantitative benchmarks of credit needs. It requires examiners to use quasi-objective standards to evaluate the comparisons including "exceeds," "near or exceeds," and "substantially meets or exceeds" as follows:[67]

HMDA loans (each loan type separately)

% loans to LI and MI tracts cf % AA's OOHUs in such tracts ["good" to "excellent" performance = % loans in LI and MI tracts "near or exceeds" % OOHUs in such tracts]

MS in LI and MI tracts cf overall MS ["good to excellent" performance = % MS in LI and MI tracts "substantially meets or exceeds" overall MS]

SB loans

% SB loans ≤$1M to bus in LI and MI tracts cf % AA's bus in such tracts ["good to excellent" performance = % SB loans ≤$1M in LI and MI tracts is "near to or exceeds" % bus in such tracts"]

MS SB loans ≤$1M to bus in LI and MI tracts cf overall MS such loans ["good to excellent" performance = MS such loans "substantially meets or exceeds" overall MS]

SF loans

% loans ≤$500G to SF in LI and MI tracts cf % AA's farms in such tracts ["good to excellent" performance = % such loans to farms in LI or MI tracts "is near to or exceeds" % farms in such tracts]

MS loans ≤$500G to SF in LI and MI tracts cf overall MS of such loans ["good to excellent" performance = MS in LI and MI tracts "substantially meets or exceeds" overall MS]

CON loans

% CON loans in LI and MI tracts cf % AA's HH in such tracts ["good to excellent" performance = % loans originated in LI and MI tracts "exceeds" % LI and MI HHs in such tracts]

Despite coming close to adopting evaluative criteria composed of quantitative measures and objective standards, the CRA Guidance falls short of maximizing CRA's influence over bank lending decisions. The standards are only quasi-objective, allowing much room for discretion and loopholes. Additionally, the CRA Guidance does not assign weights to the criteria or give instructions as to how to combine them to derive an evaluation.

Distribution of Loans to Persons at Different Income Levels

The materials once again instruct examiners to compare quantitative measures of bank lending with quantitative benchmarks of community credit needs, but direct examiners to use subjective and vague standards to evaluate the comparisons. The manuals require quantitative measures of bank lending such as the number, dollar volume, and percentage of the bank's loans by type to borrowers at different income levels and a comparison of the percentage of each type of loan to borrowers at different income levels with a quantitative benchmark of community credit needs—the percentage of persons in the AA at each income level.[68] A sample passage from a model PE compares the percentage of the bank's number and dollar volume of loans to LMI persons with the percentage of LMI households in the AA, the percentage for similar banks, and the aggregate percentage, but does not indicate how to evaluate the bank's performance compared with these benchmarks.[69] The model PE also compares the percentage of the number and dollar volume of the bank's small business loans with the aggregate percentage and the percentages of similar banks.[70] The model PE includes a table showing the percentage of the bank's total number and dollar volume of HMDA loans by borrower income level and compares these with the percentage of households in the bank's AA at each income level and the aggregate percentage of loans and dollar volume of loans at each income level.[71] The model PE uses subjective and inexact standards such as "good" and "adequate" to compare the bank's percentage with the percentage of families and the aggregate percentage.[72] Finally, the model PE includes a table comparing the percentage of the bank's small business loans and dollar volume of loans with the percentages of similarly situated banks and the aggregate percentage.[73]

The CRA Guidance requires OCC examiners to consider the following comparisons of quantitative measures of bank lending with quantitative benchmarks of community credit needs. It requires examiners to use quasi-objective standards for making these comparisons about the distribution of a bank's loans according to borrower income and to evaluate it as follows:[74]

HMDA loans (each loan type analyzed separately)

% loans to LI and MI persons cf % AA's such fam [performance in lending to LI persons may be considered "good to excellent" even if % loans to LI persons is lower than % such fam depending on barriers to LI homeownership; performance in lending to MI borrowers is "good to excellent" if % loans to MI persons "is near to or exceeds" % MI fam in AA]

MS loans to LI and MI persons cf overall MS ["good to excellent" performance = MS to LI and MI persons "substantially meets or exceeds" overall MS]

SB loans

% loans to bus w/rev≤$1M cf % AA's such bus ["good to excellent" performance = % loans to such bus "meets or exceeds" demographic data]

MS SB loans to bus w/rev≤$1M cf overall MS such loans ["good to excellent" performance = MS loans to such bus "substantially meets or exceeds" overall MS]

SF loans

loans to farms w/rev≤$1M cf % AA's such farms ["good to excellent" performance = % loans to such farms "substantially meets or exceeds" demographic data]

MS loans to farms w/rev≤$1M cf overall MS such loans ["good to excellent" performance = MS to such farms "substantially meets or exceeds" overall MS]

CON loans

% CON loans to LI and MI persons cf % AA's such HH ["good to excellent" performance = % such loans "exceeds" % AA's such HH]

Revisions to the CRA Regulations?

On July 19, 2001, the federal banking agencies published an advance notice of proposed rulemaking ("ANPR") regarding the CRA regulations.[75] The ANPR sought comment on a number of issues; two are relevant here: whether the regulations strike the appropriate balance between qualitative and quantitative measures of bank lending and whether the lending test effectively assess a bank's record of helping to meet the credit needs of the bank's community.[76] Among the responses the agencies received, three major banking associations, the American Bankers Association, the California Bankers Association, and the Consumer Bankers Association called for more consistency in the CRA exams and ratings.[77] California Federal Bank called for better benchmarks in performance evaluations.[78] Among community advocates, ACORN called on the agencies to upgrade CRA ratings standards to reduce grade inflation.[79] The Delaware County Reinvestment Action Council and the National Community Reinvestment Coalition called for more emphasis on quantitative lending measures.[80]

On February 4, 2004, the federal banking agencies issued proposed changes to the CRA regulations.[81] The proposal contains three main changes. The first would increase the asset threshold of the definition of a small bank from $250 million to $500 million. This would mean that hundreds more banks would be evaluated according to the small bank performance evaluation, which is not as rigorous as the large bank performance evaluation and does not evaluate the bank's community development investments or retail banking services. If adopted, this proposal would undermine the CRA's potential for democratizing capital because it would increase the number of banks subject to this weaker test. (As this book was going to publication, the OTS announced it was increasing the small bank asset threshold to $1 billion and the FDIC announed it was considering doing this. *See supra* ch. 4, note 60.) The second proposal specifies that illegal credit practices, including "predatory lending," could result in a reduced CRA rating.[82] The final proposal requires the federal banking agencies to disclose to the public the total number and dollar amount of a bank's small business and small farm loans by census tract.[83] If adopted, this proposal would make it possible to analyze a bank's small business lending according to the racial composition of the neighborhood in which it makes small business loans. This proposal would expand the data available about bank lending, making it easier to hold banks accountable for a weak lending record.

Conclusion

The federal banking agencies' failure during the second CRA enforcement regime to employ CRA evaluative criteria composed of quantitative measures of bank lending, quantitative benchmarks of community credit needs, and objective standards for evaluating bank lending in PEs, decisions on bank expansion applications, and PE examination manuals undermines the CRA's potential for democratizing capital. According to many of the criteria the agencies used in their decisions on bank expansion applications, the banks were not meeting community credit needs. Commenters even pointed out these gaps and the OCC recognized many of the comments were accurate. Nevertheless, without any explanation or reasoning, the agencies granted the applications. In so doing, the agencies reduced the value of the franchise over lending decisions the CRA extended to community members and discouraged future participation.[84] In addition, had the agencies, in their decisions on expansion applications, adopted quantitative measures and objective standards, this may have resulted in increased lending to redlined neighborhoods, bringing more people into the economic mainstream. If the agencies had, for example, adopted standards under which a bank's lending was not sufficient to meet community credit needs if its percentages of loans to LMI and minority persons and neighborhoods were not at least as high as the aggregate, the agencies might have denied or conditionally approved the applications. This may have resulted in the banks improving their records and lending to more LMI and minority persons.

Table 5.1 Large Bank Evaluative Criteria

Lending Test Component	Evaluative Criterion	# of PEs
Overall lending activity	MS Loans	5
Lending inside/outside AA	% loans in AA	11
	% particular type of loan in AA	13
Geographic distribution of loans	% all or particular type of loans in LMI, LI, or MI tracts cf % AA's fam or pop in such tracts	6
	% all or particular type of HMDA loans in LMI, LI, or MI tracts cf % AA's OOHUs in such tracts	13
	% SB loans in LMI, LI, or MI tracts cf AA's % bus in such tracts	8
	% particular type of loan in LMI, LI, or MI tracts cf agg %	7
Lending to borrowers at different income levels	% particular type of loan to LMI, LI, or MI persons cf % AA's such pop	15
	% $ vol particular type of loan to LMI persons cf % AA's LMI pop	5
	% particular type of loan to LMI, LI, or MI persons cf agg %	6
	% SB loans≤$100G	8
	% SB loans≤$100G cf agg %	5
	% SB loans to bus w/≤$1M rev cf % AAs bus w/rev≤$1M	6
	% SB loans to bus w/≤$1M rev cf agg %	7

Table 5.2 Small Bank Evaluative Criteria

Small Bank Evaluation Component	Evaluative Criterion	# of PEs
LDR	LDR	11
	LDR cf LDR peer group or comparable banks	14
Concentration of loans in AA	% loans in AA	15
	% $ vol loans in AA	14
Lending to borrowers at different income levels	% loans to LMI, LI, or MI persons cf % AA's such tracts	8
	% $ vol loans to LMI, LI, or MI persons cf % AA's such fam	4
Geographic distribution of loans	% SB loans in LI or MI tracts cf % AA's bus in such tracts	4

Table 5.3 Quantitative Measures of Bank Lending

Quantitative Measure	Examples
Percentage of all loans or a particular type of loan in LMI, LI, or MI census tracts, or to LMI persons, small businesses, or small farms	% loans in LMI, LI, or MI tracts % loans to LMI, LI, or MI persons % SB loans≤$100G % SB loans to bus w/rev≤$1M
Percent dollar volume of all loans or a particular type of loan in LMI, LI, or MI census tracts, or to LMI persons, small businesses, or small farms	% $ vol loans in LMI, LI, or MI tracts % $ vol loans to LMI, LI, or MI persons % $ vol SB loans≤$100G % $ vol SB loans to bus w/rev≤$1M
Market share of loans	MS MS percentile MS loans in LMI, LI, or MI tracts MS loans to LMI, LI, or MI persons MS rank loans to LMI persons MS $ vol loans to LMI persons MS SB loans to bus w/rev≤$1M
Loan-to-deposit ratio	
Loan-to-asset ratio	

Table 5.4 Quantitative Benchmarks of Community Credit Needs

Benchmarks	Examples
Indicators of demand for loans	% AA's fam in LMI, LI, or MI tracts % AA's OOHUs in LMI, LI, or MI tracts % AA's bus in LMI, LI, or MI tracts % AA's LMI, LI, or MI persons/families % AA's bus w/rev≤$1M
Standards established by other banks and lenders	National peer banks Primary local competitors OTS-regulated banks Peer banks Agg %
Standards established by the bank being evaluated	MS loans in UI neighborhoods

Table 5.5

Standard(s)	Quantitative Measure of Bank Lending	Quantitative Benchmark of Community Credit Needs	% Bank's Lending Below Benchmark
Adequate	3% CON loan in LI tracts	9% AA's fam in LI tracts	67%
	11% CON loans in MI tracts	13% AA's fam in MI tracts	15%
Slightly below, slightly less, slightly lower	0.8% HMDA loans in LI tracts	2.9% AA's OOHUs in LI tracts	38%
	10% HMDA loans in MI tracts	15.4% AA's OOHUs in MI tracts	35%
	6% HMDA loans in MI tracts	9% AA's OOHUs in MI tracts	33%
	46% loans to bus w/rev≤$1M	54% agg	15%
Somewhat lower, somewhat below	5% $ vol HMDA loans to LI persons	20% AA's LI pop	75%
	72% SB loans≤$100G	84% for competitors	14%
Comparable	8.5% HMDA loans in MI tracts	9.7% for OTS-regulated banks	12%
Very comparable	20% HP loans to MI persons	26% agg	23%
	13.3% $ vol HMDA loans to MI persons	16.7% agg	20%

Table 5.5 (cont.)

Compares reasonably well, compares reasonably, reasonably comparable	7.2% $ vol HP loans to LMI persons	9.2% agg	22%
	82.4% SB loans≤$100G	92% agg	10.4%
	20% $ vol loans to bus w/< $100G rev	29% AA's such bus	34%
	18% $ vol loans to bus w/< $100G rev	29% AA's such bus	31%
	3% SB loans in LI tracts	4% AA's SBs in LI tracts	25%
	3% $ vol loans to SBs in LI tracts	4% AA's SBs in LI tracts	25%
	8% loans to SBs in MI tracts	12% AA's SBs in MI tracts	33%
	9% $ vol loans to SBs in LMI tracts	12% AA's SBs in LI tracts	25%
Near	73% loans to bus w/≤$1M rev	83.3% AA's such bus	12%
	73% loans to bus w/≤$1M rev	85% AA's such bus	14%
Compares favorably	15.6% $ vol HMDA loans to LMI persons	35% AA's LMI fam	54%
	29.2% $ vol MV loans to LMI persons	35% AA's LMI fam	17%
Reasonably consistent	21.8% HMDA loans in LI tracts	24.8% AA's fam in LI tracts	12%
	19.3% $ vol HMDA loans in MI tracts	24.5% AA's in MI tracts	21%

Table 5.6

Criterion	Bank Performance	Standard
LDR	97.6% 98.6%	Excellent Very good
	76% 77% 73%	More than reasonable Good Adequate
LDR improvement	12% 12%	Strong positive trend Upward trend
Bank LDR cf state LDR	77% / 73% 77% / 73%	Excellent Satisfactory
$ vol loans in AA	97% 96%	Significant majority Majority
% CON loans in LI tracts cf AA's % pop in LI tracts	3% / 9% 3% / 9%	Adequate Lower

Table 5.6 (cont.)

Criterion	Bank Performance	Standard
% HMDA loans in LMI tracts cf % AA's OOHUs in LMI tracts	0.8% / 2.9% 0.3% / 1.9%	Slightly below Did not effectively penetrate
% HMDA loans to LI persons cf % AA's LI fam	11% / 20% 8.2% / 15.8%	Somewhat lower Much lower
% HMDA loans to MI persons cf agg %	13% / 16.7% 20.6% / 24%	Very comparable Less
% HMDA loans in LMI tracts cf agg %	0.8% / 2.0% 0.4% / 1.2%	Slightly below Did not compare well
% SB loans≤$100G	70% 70%	Majority Clear majority
% SB loans≤$100G cf agg %	82.4% / 91.3% 81.4% / 90.9%	Reasonably comparable Lower

Table 5.7 Percentages of CRA Ratings, July 1, 1997 – June 30, 2003[24]

Year	Outstanding	Satisfactory	Percentage satisfactory or better	Needs to improve	Substantial non-compliance
7/1/97 to 12/31/97	23	75.2	98.2	1.6	0.2
1998	19.1	78.9	98	1.8	0.3
1999	18.3	79.9	98.2	1.6	0.2
2000	14.8	82.7	97.5	2.2	0.3
2001	10.5	86.6	97.1	2.7	0.2
2002	8.3	90.4	98.7	0.9	0.4
2003	10	88.9	98.9	0.8	0.2

CHAPTER SIX

The CRA's Effect on Democratizing Capital: Progress and Potential

This chapter examines the effect the CRA has had on democratizing capital in both ways this book uses that term: enfranchising disenfranchised communities over decisions about bank lending and bringing excluded people into the economic mainstream by encouraging banks to make loans to them. While the CRA has made progress in democratizing capital, it has the potential to do better. Although billions of dollars of loans have been made that likely would not have been made without the CRA, many communities remain starved for credit and basic banking services, and residents of LMI and predominantly minority neighborhoods receive a disproportionate share of subprime and predatory loans.

There is a great amount of evidence consistent with the proposition that the CRA has influenced banks to lend more money in low- and moderate-income ("LMI") and predominantly minority neighborhoods (collectively "redlined neighborhoods") than they otherwise would have. Lawrence Lindsey, a former governor of the Board of Governors of the Federal Reserve, stated, "[t]housands of loans have been made throughout the country which would not have been made but for the CRA."[1] Federal Reserve Board Governor Edward Gramlich echoed Lindsey, stating that $120 billion in loans were made under the CRA in 1997, although he qualified his assertion by stating that many of the loans might have been made anyway.[2] Banks have made lending agreements and commitments to redlined neighborhoods totaling more than $1 trillion in connection with their expansion applications. They have increased their lending to redlined neighborhoods in anticipation of filing such applications. Motivated at least in part to comply with the CRA and to generate good community relations, they have created special lending programs targeting LMI borrowers. They have also created new and innovative vehicles for meeting the credit needs of LMI communities, including community development investments, public/private partnerships, and loan consortia. Finally, empirical studies show that in recent years, bank lending to LMI and minority neighborhoods and individuals has increased at higher rates than lending to upper-income neighborhoods and individuals.

While there is evidence that the CRA has strongly influenced banks to lend to redlined neighborhoods, the CRA has not allocated credit as that term was used in the CRA's legislative history. The lending agreements and commitments banks have made have been voluntary. Banks are not required to make a lending agreement or commitment as a condition of having an expansion application approved, although they may feel pressure to do so. Most of the agreements and commitments include lending targets with specific dollar amounts, but they are only targets, not quotas. The special loan programs were created and developed by banks, not imposed on them by government agencies.

This chapter examines two significant ways the CRA has influenced banks to lend money to LMI and minority persons and neighborhoods. First, it looks at how community groups have influenced banks to lend in LMI and minority neighborhoods by filing or preparing to file "CRA challenges" to bank expansion applications. Actual or imminent CRA challenges create a motive for banks to enter into lending agreements with community groups or to make unilateral lending commitments. Such agreements and commitments promote regulatory approval of the applications and forestall or settle administrative challenges to the applications. Second, this chapter examines special lending programs and other innovative lending and investment vehicles that banks have created to meet the credit needs of LMI persons and neighborhoods and to satisfy their CRA obligations, even in the absence of a pending expansion application. After reviewing how the CRA has influenced banks to lend to LMI persons and neighborhoods, this chapter presents data that support the proposition that the CRA has influenced banks to lend more in LMI neighborhoods than they otherwise would have. Finally, this chapter demonstrates that the CRA has not yet reached its full potential for democratizing capital.

Expansion Applications and "CRA Challenges"

The CRA's requirement that the federal banking agencies take a bank's CRA record into account in connection with deciding certain expansion applications has had a powerful influence on bank lending to LMI and minority neighborhoods and persons. As described in chapter two, a bank must file an application seeking permission to expand (an "expansion application") from the federal banking agency that regulates it, and one of the factors the agency must take into account when deciding the application is the bank's CRA record.[3] The agency has the power to deny the application if the bank has a poor CRA record. In addition, members of the public can submit written comments on the application—including comments on the bank's CRA record—to the federal banking agency that is considering the application.[4] Commonly known as a "challenge" to or a "protest" of the application, the agency must consider the comments in rendering its decision on the application and may hold a public hearing and receive testimony on the application. The CRA challenge process essentially gives a vote to community groups about bank lending decisions.[5]

The combination of agency review of expansion applications and the opportunity for members of the public to challenge them creates a strong motive for banks to strengthen their CRA records prior to filing an expansion application or while an expansion application is pending.[6] First, there is a chance, although remote, that the agency that regulates the bank will deny the merger application if the bank does not have a strong CRA record.[7] Second, a challenge can delay the regulatory approval process.[8] This delay, in turn, could make the merger less attractive financially and possibly cause the deal to fall through.[9] According to banking attorney Thomas Vartanian, a challenge has force because the price of the merger is based on the value of each bank's stock, and "the more time that passes before closing, the greater the likelihood of changes in stock value that could sour the agreement."[10] Third, it may be costly and time-consuming to fight a challenge.[11] Written comments challenging a bank merger are often detailed and lengthy. Frequently, more than one challenge is filed, and if the banks are large and cover significant territory, dozens of challenges might be submitted. Large mergers may also involve more than one banking agency and a public hearing.[12] Even if the merger is approved, a bank could also find itself in court if a challenger sues the agency to overturn the approval.[13] Finally, publicity frequently surrounds a challenge, and many banks would rather avoid public charges that they are not meeting community credit needs or that they are discriminating against minority applicants or predominantly minority neighborhoods.[14]

One way banks have sought to strengthen their CRA records in connection with their expansion applications is to enter into agreements with community groups that have challenged or threatened to challenge the applications to lend more in LMI or minority neighborhoods.[15] In recent years, in contrast to these negotiated agreements between banks and community groups, many banks have made unilateral lending commitments in connection with their expansion applications. These agreements and commitments are not required by the CRA or by the federal banking agencies as part of the application process, but banks feel that the commitments promote the approval of their applications by showing that the merger will serve the public good.[16] The National Community Reinvestment Coalition ("NCRC") has published a catalogue of CRA agreements and commitments.[17] As of 1999, NCRC had counted more than 360 agreements and commitments totaling over $1 trillion.[18] By 2001, the value of commitments had risen to $1.512 trillion.[19] Included in this latter amount are 707 agreements totaling $3.6 billion in loans disclosed through the CRA Sunshine requirement between 1999 and 2001.[20] In 2004, Bank of America and J.P. Morgan Chase made commitments of $750 billion and $800 billion respectively in connection with their mergers, bringing the total value of commitments to more than $3 trillion.[21]

The CRA Challenge Process

There are many variations of the CRA challenge process, but the basic pattern includes an expansion application filed by a bank, an imminent or actual challenge to the application by one or more community groups, and an agreement or commitment by the bank to lend in LMI and minority neighborhoods.[22] The paradigmatic CRA challenge works something like the following. A bank submits its expansion application to the federal banking agency that regulates it. At approximately the same time, the bank publishes a notice in its local newspaper announcing the application and the opportunity for public comment. Notices are also published in agency bulletins and websites. The notice includes a deadline for filing comments. A community group that believes the bank has a poor record of meeting the credit needs of the community contacts the bank to express its concerns about the bank's CRA record and its plans for the future. The community group makes a proposal for the bank to agree to increase its lending in LMI and minority neighborhoods. The bank and the community group negotiate over the proposal. As the deadline for filing a challenge to the merger approaches, the pressure on the bank to forestall the challenge grows,[23] and the parties may reach a lending agreement.[24] If not, the community group may file a challenge, but the negotiations might continue while the challenge is pending. While the challenge is pending, the federal banking agency considering the application might conduct a private meeting with the parties or conduct a public hearing. If the community group and bank did not reach a lending agreement before the challenge was filed, they could reach an agreement after it was filed but before the agency issues a decision.[25]

Two main variations of this paradigm are the following. The first variation generally involves large bank merger applications that cover large regions of the United States. Several community groups from many localities approach the merging banks to discuss their CRA records and may file challenges. The bank, instead of negotiating with the various groups, issues a unilateral lending commitment hoping to forestall prospective challenges, resolve actual challenges, and ensure regulatory approval of the application.[26] In the second variation, a bank that does not have an expansion application pending, but that may have expansion plans for the future, enters into a lending agreement with a community group or issues a unilateral lending commitment in order to forestall a possible challenge.[27]

Terms of Lending Agreements and Commitments

Many lending agreements and commitments are fairly specific, identifying the total dollars to be loaned, the targeted borrowers and communities, and the loan types. Other commitments and agreements are less specific and focus generally on total dollars. The commitments and agreements do not constitute credit allocation as that term is used in the CRA's legislative history. The government does not impose them on banks, and there are no penalties for failing to comply. The terms of the commitments are agreed to by the banks after negotiations with and input from community groups, presumably based on the bank's resources, specialties, and business plan. Even though these commitments do not allocate credit in the manner the CRA prohibits, they demonstrate how the CRA strongly influences banks to lend in LMI and predominantly minority neighborhoods.

Although the term of all agreements and commitments are different, they have several common characteristics. Four key characteristics include: 1) a commitment to lend a specific dollar amount; 2) of a particular type of loan or loans; 3) with flexible loan terms and eligibility criteria; 4) to redlined communities.[28] Commitments and agreements frequently include provisions committing the bank to make a specific number or dollar amount of loans in a particular time period. Commitments and agreements generally target LMI and minority neighborhoods and individuals. Commitments and agreements also generally include the sorts of loans that are most important to these borrowers, including single-family housing, multi-family housing, small and very small businesses, consumer, and economic development projects. Finally, commitments and agreements frequently contain provisions making it more likely that targeted persons will qualify for the committed loans. These include provisions granting lower interest rates, smaller down-payments, waived or reduced fees and costs, and reduced points. They also include provisions agreeing to modify underwriting criteria for loans, particularly those criteria relating to credit history, employment history, sources of income, obligation ratios, and loan-to-value ratio. Finally, agreements may provide for a second review of rejected loan applications from the targeted communities.

The largest commitment to date came in 2004 when J.P. Morgan Chase, in connection with its proposed merger with Bank One, committed to lend $800 billion comprised of $675 billion for mortgage loans, $90 billion for small business loans, and $35 billion for inner-city affordable-housing and community development projects.[29] Prior to that, Bank of America had committed to lend $750 billion in connection with its merger with Fleet Financial Corp.[30] In 1997, Washington Mutual pledged to lend $375 billion over ten years in connection with its purchase of Dime Bancorp.[31] The commitment included $300 billion in single-family home loans to minority and LMI borrowers and borrowers in LMI census tracts; $48 billion for consumer and small business lending including businesses owned by people of color, women, and people with disabilities; $25 billion for apartments and manufactured home park developments in LMI tracts for LMI families; and $2 billion for community economic development.[32] In 2002, Bank of the West announced a 10 year, $30 billion goal for loans, investments, and contributions to LMI persons, small businesses, and community-based organizations.[33] The goals included:

- $4.5 billion in residential mortgage loans to LMI and minority borrowers and residents of LMI census tracts;
- $13 billion for small business loans, SBA loans, and small farm loans, including $250 million for loans of less than $30,000 each;
- $5 billion in commercial loans to businesses in LMI census tracts;
- $2 billion in community development loans;
- $4.2 billion in consumer loans;
- $1 billion in loans to churches;
- $150 million in community development investments; and
- $40 million in charitable contributions to organizations promoting economic development.[34]

Also in 2002, Citibank made a $120 billion lending commitment to California and Nevada.[35] The commitment included $80 billion in home mortgage lending, $10 billion in small business lending, and $3.5 billion in community development lending and investments.[36]

Four large commitments were made in 1998 in connection with four bank mergers. NationsBank and Bank of America made a ten year, $350 billion commitment in connection with their merger.[37] This included $180 billion in small business lending, $115 billion in affordable housing lending, and $30 billion in consumer lending.[38] Washington Mutual signed a ten year, $120 billion lending commitment with the California Reinvestment Institute, the Greenlining Coalition, the Washington Reinvestment Alliance, and other community groups in connection with its application to purchase H.F. Ahmanson & Co. The agreement committed the bank to make $25 billion in small business loans.[39] Citicorp and Travelers made a ten year, $115 billion commitment, including $30 billion in small business lending, $20 billion in home mortgage loans to LMI borrowers, and $59 billion in student loans, credit cards, and other consumer loans.[40] First Union and CoreStates made a $13 billion commitment, including $10 billion in small business loans, $1.25 billion in LMI consumer lending, $875 million in targeted mortgage lending, $750 million in community development lending, $55 million in low-income housing tax credits, and $45 million in contributions to CRA-related efforts.[41] Another large and innovative agreement came in 1995, when the Chicago CRA Coalition reached a six year, $2 billion agreement with First Chicago and NBD Corp. in connection with their merger.[42] The bank agreed to a 25% increase in the number of loans to LMI borrowers and $2.5 million in loans of $100,000 or less to small businesses in LMI neighborhoods.[43] This commitment would increase the ratio of the bank's market share of loans to small businesses and affordable housing in LMI neighborhoods to its market share of loans in upper income neighborhoods to 1/1.[44]

Several other agreements provide examples of provisions that reduce the cost of loans or adopt criteria for evaluating the creditworthiness of borrowers that will make it easier for LMI persons to qualify for loans.[45] These included agreements to:

- make home mortgage loans at 4% interest;
- make loans with interest rates 1% below market rate;
- waive closing points on home mortgages for families with incomes less than $20,000 per year;
- make home mortgage loans with no private mortgage insurance, debt-to-income ratios as high as 33% and 38%, and in amounts as low as $10,000;
- offer mortgages with no private mortgage insurance and 5% down-payments;

- make loans with a 3% downpayment and no mortgage insurance requirement;
- offer unsecured loans or grants to help cover downpayments;
- consider loan applicants with less than perfect credit if the late payments did not occur in the previous year, the credit problems were due to circumstances beyond the applicant's control, and the credit problem was unlikely to affect loan repayment;
- waive its requirement that the applicant work at the same job for two years if the applicant worked continuously at similar paying jobs for two years;
- accept non-traditional sources of income, including Social Security, unemployment benefits, public assistance, self-employment income, and part-time employment income; and
- use a 33% housing expense-to-income ratio and a 45% debt-to-income ratio in evaluating home mortgage loan applications from LMI persons.

Efforts to Increase Lending Outside of the Bank Expansion or CRA Challenge Process

While a bank has an especially strong motive to improve its CRA record when it is planning to file or has filed an expansion application, a bank is also motivated to maintain a good CRA record even in the absence of pending or expected expansion applications. One powerful motive for a bank to comply with the CRA is publicity. A bank's CRA performance rating is public, as is most of the written CRA evaluation report.[46] In addition, detailed information about the bank's home mortgage lending, including the number of applications it receives from individuals by race and income and the number of loans it makes by race and income is available through the Home Mortgage Disclosure Act ("HMDA").[47] A poor CRA rating could have a negative influence on investors who might feel the bank is less valuable, depositors who might put their money elsewhere as a protest, and loan applicants who might seek loans elsewhere for fear of a negative decision.[48] In addition, banks are generally anxious to maintain a good public image, and a good CRA rating helps.[49] As a result, in addition to making lending agreements and commitments in connection with their expansion applications, banks have developed special CRA lending programs and other loan programs that are designed to increase lending to LMI and minority borrowers regardless of whether the bank has an application pending.

CRA Special Lending Programs

One response by banks to the CRA has been to create special lending programs designed to expand lending to LMI borrowers.[50] These CRA special lending programs share several characteristics with programs that banks have introduced in commitments and agreements they made in connection with their expansion applications, but they generally do not include agreements to lend specific dollar amounts.

Pursuant to the Gramm-Leach-Bliley Act, the Federal Reserve undertook an analysis of the profitability of CRA-related lending (the "Fed CRA Study").[51] The Fed CRA Study examined "CRA special lending programs," which it defined as "any housing-related, small business, consumer or other type of lending program that the institution uses specifically to enhance its CRA performance."[52] One of the program's documented purposes must be to enhance the bank's CRA performance.

The Fed CRA Study sample included 143 banks that responded to the Study survey. Of these banks, 73% had at least one CRA special lending program.[53] The banks that offered at least one program offered an average of six programs.[54] The majority of the programs—72%—involved 1-to-4 family home purchase loans; 8% of the programs focused on small business loans.[55]

The results of the Fed CRA Study are consistent with the proposition that the CRA has influenced banks to lend more in LMI neighborhoods than they otherwise would have. Nearly three-quarters of the banks in the study had created a special CRA lending program, three-quarters of the banks that created programs did so because of the CRA, and nearly all of the programs were created following amendments to the CRA and HMDA in 1989 that strengthened the laws by requiring banks to disclose their CRA ratings and more information about their lending by race.

The four most frequent reasons cited by the banks for establishing a CRA special lending program were, in order, responding to the credit needs of the community, promoting community growth and stability, obtaining a satisfactory or outstanding CRA rating (76%),[56] and improving the bank's public image.[57] Banks reported that the benefits of their CRA special lending programs were the same as the reasons for adopting the programs, in the same order.[58] The Fed CRA Study reported that the proportion of home purchase and refinance loan dollars that were extended pursuant to CRA special lending programs constituted 4% for the average bank and 18% for banks with at least one CRA special lending program.[59] Lending pursuant to special CRA lending programs constituted 21% of the total loan dollars of CRA-related lending by banks that responded to the survey and 3% of all of their home purchase and refinance originations.[60]

The Fed CRA Study reported that 62% of the special CRA loan programs were established after 1995, when the federal banking agencies strengthened the CRA regulations by amending them to rely more heavily on quantitative measures of bank lending, and only 6% were created before 1990, when amendments strengthening the CRA by requiring banks to disclose their CRA ratings and HMDA by making it easier to track home mortgage lending to LMI and minority persons and neighborhoods went into effect.[61]

The Fed CRA Study described three common characteristics of these special lending programs.[62] First, many programs included third parties that engaged in activities that reduced the risk of loan default, including making grants to borrowers to pay for downpayments, offering pre-loan education and counseling, and identifying potential borrowers.[63] Second, banks made loans less expensive by waiving or reducing fees and reducing interest rates. Third, banks took steps to identify new borrowers and make it more likely that they could lend to the new borrowers by instituting special outreach and marketing programs, adopting flexible loan underwriting criteria, and instituting a "second review" of rejected loan applications.[64] Among the flexible underwriting criteria are alternative criteria for evaluating creditworthiness, such as accepting a good history of rent and utility payments in place of a clean credit history as evidence of reliability, requiring lower cash reserves, permitting higher debt-income ratios, and being more flexible in evaluating employment history by, for example, accepting as evidence of steady employment two consecutive years of employment even if not at the same job.

The Fed CRA Study analyzed the performance of the CRA special lending programs and CRA-related lending based on three criteria: delinquencies; chargeoffs; and profitability. According to these criteria, CRA special lending programs and CRA-related lending did not perform as well as all other home mortgage lending. Delinquencies were 1.0% for loans made pursuant to CRA special lending programs, compared with 1.42% for loans not pursuant to special CRA lending programs but for loans that nevertheless helped the bank satisfy its CRA obligations, and 0.78% for all home purchase and refinance loans.[65] As to chargeoffs, 0.19% of loans under CRA special lending programs, 0.23% of all loans not under special CRA lending programs but that nevertheless qualified for CRA credit, and 0.14% of all home mortgage loans were charged off.[66] Finally, based on the banks' subjective evaluation of whether the special CRA lending programs and other CRA lending was profitable, 64% of CRA special lending programs were profitable or marginally profitable and 22% were marginally profitable or unprofitable.[67] Further, 77% of all CRA-related lending was at least marginally profitable.[68] In contrast, 94% of all home mortgage lending was at least marginally profitable.[69]

The relatively weaker performance of CRA special lending and other CRA lending compared with overall home mortgage lending the Fed CRA Study disclosed prompted Senator Phil Gramm to state that the CRA allocates credit. "The study demonstrates that CRA lending as it is now practiced is credit allocation that generates loans with higher delinquency rates and lower profit profiles than loans generated through normal channels."[78] A different perspective is that the CRA has not allocated credit because it has not set quotas. Rather, it has worked as Congress intended: it has strongly influenced banks to make loans to redlined neighborhoods that they might not otherwise have made. A banking consultant expressed this sentiment when he stated that the relatively slightly weaker performance of CRA lending was evidence that the CRA had worked as intended by influencing banks to make loans they otherwise would not have made. "The findings suggest that CRA is performing as its advocates had hoped....It may validate CRA advocates' assertion that without CRA, banks might not have been encouraged to look at the business" of lending to non-traditional customers.[79]

Prior to the Fed CRA Study, several other studies attempted to evaluate the performance of CRA-related lending and they generally found CRA lending performed better than the Fed Study indicated. The Federal Reserve and the Woodstock Institute issued reports in 1993.[70] The Federal Reserve report concluded that evidence on the riskiness of lending in low-income and minority neighborhoods was inconclusive.[71] It found that there was no significant, consistent relationship between the profitability of lending and the racial composition or income level of a neighborhood.[72] The Woodstock report compared the risk of CRA loans with other loans. The report found that CRA single-family home mortgage loans had lower delinquency rates than regular loans and that multi-family CRA loans had higher delinquency rates than other multi-family loans.[73] The report also showed low losses on single-family and multi-family CRA loans.[74] A 1994 study by the Bank Insurance Research Group found that nearly 75% of the banks it surveyed said CRA-related lending was either profitable or they expected to make money or break even.[75] According to a 1997 survey by the Federal Reserve Bank of Kansas City, 98% of banks said CRA lending was profitable and 34% said CRA lending was less profitable than conventional lending.[76]

Following the Fed CRA Study, a 2002 study by the National Community Capital Association studied chargeoffs at community development financial institutions ("CDFIs") and they recorded a different conclusion. Seventy percent of the CDFIs' customers were low-income persons and 47% were minorities. Chargeoffs at CDFIs were 0.5% of loans, compared with 0.9% for commercial banks and 0.5% for commercial banks with less than $100 million in assets.[77]

Community Economic Development Loans and Investments

A second response by banks to the CRA is to invest in and lend to community development projects, which are defined generally as any project that has, as its primary purpose, affordable housing, small business, or other economic development projects that will assist LMI persons and communities by providing jobs, services, infrastructure improvements, or affordable housing.[80] According to a report issued by the Brookings Institution, the CRA has helped "spawn a community development infrastructure within the banking industry, the bank regulatory agencies, the secondary market organizations, and in inner-city communities...."[81] James Carras, president of Carras Community Investments, Inc., suggests that "90 percent of the deals that are done for the purposes of community development are done with CRA as the motivation."[82] As an example of community development lending, between 1990 and 1998, Bank of America made $3.2 billion in community development loans and $650 million in low-income housing tax credit investments.[83] In 1997, recognizing the 20th anniversary of the CRA, Fleet announced a $60-million community economic development initiative, including $50 million to low-income housing tax credit projects.[84]

Lending Consortia

The Brookings Institution also found that the CRA has prompted new lending arrangements such as lending consortia.[85] These consortia are generally small groups of banks, sometimes in partnership with community-based organizations, that seek to pool their resources and information and share any risks of lending to redlined communities. For example, in 1991, several lenders created the New York Mortgage Coalition, a consortium of New York City banks that offered loan counseling and a second review of loan applications other banks in the coalition had rejected.[86] In 1993, the Coalition made 191 loans.[87] In 1995, the eleven banks that comprise the New York Clearing

House Association created a $10 million venture capital fund for businesses in LMI areas or owned by female or minority entrepreneurs.[88] The Charleston Banking Consortium, a group of ten Charleston banks, was formed in 1994 to address the loss of affordable housing in Charleston and respond to the CRA.[89] It made a $7.5 million lending commitment that would support 125 low-interest mortgage loans to LMI borrowers in two years.[90] In 2000, nine Arizona banks seeking to meet their CRA obligations by providing credit to Native Americans formed the Arizona Native American Community Development Corporation.[91]

Public/Private Partnerships

A third response by banks to the CRA is an increase in public/private partnerships that promote lending and investments in underserved neighborhoods.[92] For example, between 1991 and 2001, the City of Cleveland entered into $3.1 billion in lending commitments with banks, "due in large part to [...the City's] use of the Community Reinvestment Act."[93] According to the City of Cleveland's Community Reinvestment Program, from 1991 to 1997, "banks with whom [... it had] agreements have reported lending $471 million in home purchase loans; $106 million in home improvement loans; $918 million in small business loans and $321 million in neighborhood development loans."[94] One such commitment came in 1996 when Charter One agreed to lend $69 million over five years and then renewed its commitment in 2001 for $170 million over five years for residential mortgage, home improvement, and consumer loans.[95] In New York City, a partnership among Roosevelt Savings Bank, the City Department of Housing Preservation and Development, and the U.S. Department of Housing and Urban Development provided financing to rehabilitate 633 housing units in Bedford-Stuyvesant.[96] In New Jersey, the State's thrifts, the Housing and Mortgage Finance Agency, and Fannie Mae partnered in a $10 million program that offered below-market home mortgage loans to LMI borrowers.[97]

Other partnerships have arisen between banks and community groups. According to Jim Bliesner, the director of the San Diego City-County Reinvestment Task Force, "Without CRA, we would not have partnerships with banks that make affordable home loans and small business loans to underserved neighborhoods."[98] The National Community Reinvestment Coalition describes two such partnerships. Eric Weaver of Lenders for Community Development in San Jose works with twenty-three banks, and stated, "My organization exists entirely because of CRA...."[99] His organization has loaned $1.4 million to sixty-six small businesses and $7.5 million for affordable housing and community facilities projects.[100] The Mon Valley Initiative in Pennsylvania has a relationship with eight banks in Mon Valley. The banks have made thirty-five housing loans that have resulted in 145 units of affordable housing.[101]

New Investment Vehicles

Finally, several new financial vehicles have been created in order to bring CRA activities into the financial mainstream.[102] There are several examples: Citibank's $1 million equity investment in the National Community Capital Association to capitalize community development financial initiatives; a $29 million private placement through the Local Initiatives Support Corporation of common stock in a real estate investment trust specializing in affordable housing and community development; a $2 billion secondary market mortgage program for affordable home mortgage loans created by Self-Help, a community group in North Carolina, the Ford Foundation, and Fannie Mae; Bear Stearns' private placement of securities backed by 5,400 First Union CRA loans and guaranteed by Freddie Mac; and Wells Fargo's $5 million equity investment in Silicon Valley Community Ventures Investment Partnership to provide equity capital to finance small businesses in low-income communities.[103]

Studies About the CRA's Impact

There have been several attempts to quantify the influence the CRA has had on bank lending. In 2002, the Joint Center for Housing Studies at Harvard University issued a report (the "Harvard Study") that concluded that the CRA has influenced banks to make more loans than they otherwise would have to LMI persons and neighborhoods and African-Americans and Latinos.[104] Prior to the Harvard Study, several studies reported results that were consistent with the conclusion that the CRA has influenced banks to lend more money in LMI neighborhoods than they otherwise would have, but they all stopped short of asserting they had proven such a link between the CRA and increased lending.[105]

The Harvard Study made several findings that support its conclusion that the CRA caused banks to lend more to LMI and minority individuals and persons than they would have without the CRA. First, it compared the lending records of three groups of lenders: banks covered by the CRA in their CRA assessment areas (i.e. within the geographic areas in which they have CRA obligations); lenders not covered by the CRA; and banks covered by the CRA outside their CRA assessment areas (i.e. geographic areas in which they do not have CRA obligations). The Harvard Study assumed that these three groups are all equally affected by market conditions and thus any lending differences among them could be explained by their differing CRA obligations.[106] The Harvard Study found that the market share of CRA-eligible conventional, conforming prime home purchase loans was higher for CRA-covered lenders (36%) than for non-CRA lenders (28.7%) and for CRA-covered lenders outside of their AAs (29.4%).[107] Similarly, the market share of CRA-eligible conventional prime home mortgage loans to African-Americans was as much as 20% higher for CRA-covered lenders in their assessment areas than for the two other groups of lenders.[108] For Latinos, the difference was 16% higher.[109] Second, the Harvard Study conducted several multivariate regression analyses. The Study made several conclusions based on these analyses:[110]

- CRA lenders made 42,000 more CRA-eligible home purchase loans annually than they would have without the CRA;
- CRA lenders made 29,000 more CRA-eligible home purchase loans in higher-income areas than they would have without the CRA;
- CRA lenders' rejection rate for CRA-eligible home purchase loans was 24% lower than it would have been without the CRA, 20.8% instead of 25.3%; and
- Approximately 53,000 prime loans shifted from non-CRA lenders to CRA lenders each year.

A study by the United States Department of Treasury (the "Treasury Study") in 2002 attempted to evaluate the impact the CRA has had on bank lending to LMI persons and neighborhoods. The Treasury Study concluded that an increase in lending in LMI neighborhoods and to LMI persons "points toward a causal link between the CRA and the recent, substantial increase in mortgage lending…"[111] This conclusion, the Treasury Study found, is consistent with the view that the CRA has encouraged banks to lend to LMI borrowers and areas. The Treasury Study qualified its conclusion by stating that many other factors could have contributed to the increase, and no study had yet controlled for them.[112] The Treasury Study contained several key findings to support its conclusion.

First, the Treasury Study found that home mortgage lending by CRA-covered lenders to LMI persons and neighborhoods outgrew such lending in the market as a whole from 1993 to 1998.[113] The increase in the number of home mortgage loans to LMI persons and neighborhoods was greater than the increase in the number of loans in the entire market, 45% to 27%; the difference in growth in the total dollar volume of loans was 80% to 57%.[114] As a result, the share of total mortgage originations by banks and their affiliates to LMI borrowers and neighborhoods increased from 25% in 1993 to 28% in 1998.[115]

Second, the Treasury Study noted that subprime home mortgage lending—lending to borrowers with less than perfect credit—grew substantially from 1993–98. As a result, lenders not covered by the CRA, many of whom specialize in subprime lending, increased their market share of all home mortgage loans to LMI persons and neighborhoods.[116] However, CRA-covered lenders remained the dominant lenders to LMI persons and neighborhoods as a whole, and in prime lending to LMI persons and neighborhoods.[117] The data show the following:

Percent Share of Home Mortgage Lending to LMI Persons and Neighborhoods

	1993	1998
CRA-covered lenders	65%	63%
All other lenders	35%	37%

Percent Share of Prime Home Mortgage Lending to LMI Persons and Neighborhoods

	1993	1998
CRA-covered lenders	66%	71%
All other lenders	33%	29%

Third, the Treasury Study concluded that the fact that lenders covered and not covered by the CRA increased their home mortgage lending to LMI borrowers and neighborhoods from 1993 to 1998 suggests that factors other than the CRA had an impact on lending.[118] It suggested that these factors may have included a strong economy and moderate interest rates, faster growth in the income of African-Americans relative to whites, enactment of affordable housing finance goals for Fannie Mae and Freddie Mac, tightened enforcement of the fair housing and equal credit laws, disclosure under HMDA of home mortgage loan application rejection rates by race and income, and intensified bank merger activity.[119] The Treasury Study did not attempt to control for these factors, and suggested that other studies be done to control for them.[120]

Other studies have echoed the Treasury Study's findings. For example, Robert Avery, a Federal Reserve economist, found that from 1993 to 1997, the number of home purchase loans to low-income persons increased 36%, compared with a 29% increase for moderate-income persons, a 16% increase for middle-income persons, and an 18% increase for upper-income persons.[121]

Avery found that lending to minority borrowers during this time increased 53% compared with a 13% increase for whites.[122] He attributed the higher increases to low-income and minority persons at least in part to the CRA.[123] Another study found that the market share of conventional home mortgage loans to LMI and minority persons and neighborhoods in the New York City metropolitan area increased significantly between 1993 and 1998, and suggested that expanded HMDA disclosures and tightened CRA and fair lending law enforcement was at least partly responsible.[124] Finally, two researchers found that a 3% drop in the homeownership gap between whites and African-Americans from 1995 to 1997 was not due to changes in demographics or income factors, but was due to 1995 amendments to the CRA regulations that focused the regulations on lending performance and more vigorous CRA enforcement.[125]

Data about individual banks is consistent with the preceding studies. For example, the Financial Services Roundtable, which represents the 100 largest financial institutions, reported that community reinvestment lending among its members increased 15.2%, to $77.3 billion, in 1998.[126] Michael LaCour-Little found in his 1998 study of a bank that $187 million in loans to LMI persons and neighborhoods the bank made would not have been made had the bank not substituted a subjective process for evaluating loan applications for an automated scoring system.[127] The study found that the bank changed its evaluative system in response to the 1995 change in the CRA regulations.[128] Bank of America reported that its CRA-related lending grew 10%, to $5.9 billion, in 1994.[129] The bank reported, "lending in lower-income areas has become one of our fastest growing segments, demonstrating that well-structured programs providing wider access to credit for low-income borrowers can produce significant tangible results."[130]

Several studies attempt to gauge the impact of CRA lending agreements on lending to LMI and minority persons and neighborhoods. The most recent study, by Raphael W. Bostic and Breck L. Robinson, concluded that CRA agreements have been associated with lending increases by the institutions that made them.[131] According to Bostic and Robinson, most lenders increased their lending when the agreement was active compared with the years prior to and after the agreement expired.[132] They concluded that these results are consistent with the proposition that CRA agreements are effective in changing the behavior of the lenders who sign them.[133]

In a second study, Alex Schwartz found that the existence of a CRA agreement between a bank and a community group made a positive difference in the bank's lending to underserved communities.[134] In particular, Schwartz found that nearly 75% of the home mortgage loans approved for African-Americans by banks with CRA agreements were for conventional home mortgage loans compared with less than 60% for banks without agreements; the percentage of mortgage loan approvals for banks with CRA agreements was 20% higher than the average for all banks, while the percentage for banks without agreements was 14% lower than the average for all banks; the market share of mortgage loan approvals for LMI and minority households and neighborhoods for banks with CRA agreements exceeded their overall market share by 12%, while the market share of home mortgage loan approvals for LMI and minority households and neighborhoods for banks without agreements was 18% lower than their overall market share; and banks with agreements denied mortgage applications from African-Americans 2.5 times more frequently than from whites, while banks without CRA agreements denied such applications 3.1 times more frequently.[135] The results of individual bank lending agreements are consistent with Schwartz' findings. In 1996, NationsBank reported that over four years, it made 327,000 CRA-related loans totaling $13.4 billion, more than its ten year goal of $10 billion.[136] Chase Manhattan reported it was ahead of schedule on its CRA commitment, having made $4.8 billion in CRA loans in the first year of a five-year, $18.1 billion CRA commitment.[137] Finally, Boston banks exceeded their $400 million commitment for lending in LMI and minority neighborhoods in Boston, having made $514 million in loans.[138]

Anne Shlay compared CRA lending from 1995 to 1998 in three cities where banks had made CRA agreements with lending in three cities where banks had not made agreements.[139] She made two key findings. First, she found that lending to LMI persons and neighborhoods by all banks in the cities with agreements increased, and the increases were greater for banks with agreements.[140] Second, she found that increases in lending to LMI persons and neighborhoods in cities with agreements were roughly the same as in cities without agreements.[141] Shlay concluded from this that although more extensive CRA organizing in one city compared with another did not predict increased citywide CRA lending, CRA organizing resulted in strengthened CRA enforcement at the federal level, resulting in more CRA lending locally.[142]

Finally, Gregory Squires studied the lending records of several banks that entered into CRA agreements with the Fair Housing Coalition in Milwaukee.[143] He found that the eleven lenders that made agreements increased their home purchase lending to African-Americans, Latinos, and LMI neighborhoods over a seven year period at the same or higher rates than the industry average. The eleven lenders' lending changes compared with other lenders was follows: African-Americans, 1.9%/1.9%; Latinos, 2.5%/0.0%; LMI neighborhoods, 0.7%/0.3%.[144]

Conclusion—The CRA's Unfulfilled Potential

This chapter has described the relationship between the two ways the CRA democratizes capital: extending the franchise over bank lending decisions to communities that have never held it and including more people in the economic mainstream by encouraging banks to make loans to them. The "vote" about the distribution of loans that the CRA has given to members of underserved communities is most clearly expressed in CRA challenges to bank merger applications. There is, in turn, significant evidence that the exercise of the vote has resulted in billions of dollars of loans to people who would not otherwise have received them.

Despite the evidence that the CRA has influenced banks to lend more to LMI and minority persons and neighborhoods than they would have without the CRA, there is also evidence that the CRA has not reached its full potential. Chapter five documents how the federal banking agencies' failure to adopt CRA evaluative criteria that contain quantitative measures and objective standards weakens the franchise over lending decisions by making it more difficult to hold banks accountable for poor lending records. It is also difficult to know what the CRA's potential is for extending loans to everyone who qualifies and wants one in the absence of standards for enforcing the CRA that contain quantitative measures of bank lending, quantitative benchmarks of community credit needs, and objective standards for evaluating whether bank lending meets those benchmarks. Nevertheless, while it is difficult to prove a negative, at least two factors point to the conclusion that the CRA has not reached its potential. First, several million people do not even have a bank account.[145] Having a banking relationship is an important first step in getting a loan, so to the extent that households are "unbanked," they cannot be brought into the economic mainstream.[146] Second, LMI and minority persons and neighborhoods receive a disproportionate share of subprime loans.[147] Many of the recipients of subprime loans were eligible for less expensive prime loans.[148] This means that there are LMI and minority individuals who are eligible for prime loans from banks who are not getting them. Had the CRA reached its full potential, these individuals might have received prime loans.

The experience of one community group from the South Bronx, Inner City Press/Community on the Move ("ICP/COM"), with using the CRA to increase lending in its neighborhood, provides an example of the CRA's progress in and unfulfilled potential for democratizing capital.[149] In 1994, ICP/COM filed five CRA challenges and reached five significant lending agreements. In contrast, it filed several challenges to expansion applications by Chase Manhattan Bank between 1994 and 1996, but it was not able to reach a lending agreement with the bank, ultimately losing its battle against Chase in court.

In 1994, ICP/COM filed challenges against five banks that had expansion applications pending: Marine Midland Bank; Republic National Bank; First Fidelity; NatWest; and Dime. Among the types of allegations ICP/COM made in these challenges was that the bank was excluding all or part of the Bronx from its lending service area even though it included the surrounding wealthier areas in its territory and made some loans to relatively well-off customers in the Bronx.[150] ICP/COM reached lending agreements with these five banks. These agreements included millions of dollars of lending for the Bronx, commitments to open loan production offices and branches, and agreements to include all or part of the Bronx within the banks' service areas.[151] ICP/COM made quite a splash with these successes, prompting one reporter to write, "A small South Bronx community group is winning concessions from regional banks that could change the way lenders approach some of New York's poorest neighborhoods."[152]

Despite ICP/COM's success at using the CRA challenge process to influence lenders to lend more in the Bronx, its success only went so far, at least in part due to the lack of consistent, quantitative, and objective criteria for evaluating CRA performance. Starting in 1994, ICP/COM filed challenges against several applications by Chase Manhattan Bank, including its applications to buy U.S. Trust's securities processing business, to merge with its Connecticut subsidiary, and to merge with Chemical Bank.[153] ICP/COM raised serious charges against Chase, including that it engaged in discriminatory lending practices. This was part of ICP/COM's strategy to "protest every Chase application until the $114 billion institution expands its presence in the Bronx and Upper Manhattan."[154] Despite ICP/COM's efforts and its serious charges against Chase, ICP/COM failed to reach a lending agreement with Chase, lost the challenges, and ultimately lost two court challenges to the regulatory approval of Chase's U.S. Trust and Chemical expansion applications.[155] Had the federal banking agencies adopted CRA standards that included quantitative measures and objective standards, the results of ICP/COM's efforts may have been different. For example, ICP/COM may have been able to develop a stronger case, giving it more leverage in negotiating with Chase, enabling it to reach a lending agreement similar to its earlier agreements with the other five banks. The next two chapters examine whether the CRA can reach its potential for democratizing capital through utilizing CRA evaluative criteria that are composed of quantitative measures and objective standards for evaluating CRA performance that do not allocate credit.

CHAPTER SEVEN

Other Governmental Interventions in the Credit Markets: From Consent Decrees to Loan Disclosure

Introduction

Thus far, this book has reviewed the legislative history of the CRA, the legal structure of the CRA, the first CRA enforcement regime, the process of adopting the second set of CRA regulations and those regulations, the second CRA enforcement regime, and the CRA's impact on bank lending. During the course of this analysis, this book has suggested that the CRA was intended to and does influence banks to lend more in redlined neighborhoods without allocating credit. This book has also shown how the CRA has democratized capital by giving a vote on the distribution of loans to people who previously did not have a vote and by including more people in the economic mainstream by encouraging banks to lend to them. This book has also described how the CRA has not reached its full potential, in part because the federal banking agencies have not adopted CRA performance evaluation criteria that include quantitative measures of bank lending, quantitative benchmarks of community credit needs, and objective standards for evaluating whether a bank has met those needs. One of the main reasons the federal banking agencies have not proposed such criteria is their fear that such criteria would allocate credit. This book is approaching the point of proposing CRA performance evaluation criteria that contain quantitative measures of bank lending, quantitative benchmarks of community credit needs, and objective standards for evaluating a bank's record at meeting community credit needs that strongly influence banks to lend to underserved communities but do not allocate credit. Before doing so, this chapter will examine more carefully the characteristics of a system of government-imposed credit allocation and other governmental interventions in the credit markets intended to distribute loans to underserved communities. This examination will help specify the differences between allocating credit and influencing bank lending decisions.

The first section of this chapter attempts to define credit allocation and a government-imposed system of credit allocation. The two key characteristics of a governmental system of credit allocation are a mandate to apportion a specific amount of credit and sanctions for failing to comply. Anything that does not contain these two characteristics is an effort to influence banks to lend, but is not credit allocation. This chapter then investigates government interventions in the credit markets intended to distribute loans to underserved communities that have characteristics of credit allocation and efforts to influence banks to lend. Examples of government-imposed credit allocation are consent decrees that require banks to make specific dollar amounts of loans to specific neighborhoods or groups of borrowers that the Department of Justice reached with banks in lending discrimination cases. The next examples cover federal legislation establishing loan purchase goals for the Federal National Mortgage Association and the Federal Home Loan Mortgage Corporation and legislation that requires banks with interstate branches to maintain a loan-to-deposit-ratio ("LDR") equal to at least 50% of the LDR for banks in the new state. In contrast to the Department of Justice's consent decrees, these do not allocate credit. Rather, they are attempts to have a strong influence on credit decisions. Both establish lending or loan purchase targets, but the targets are tied to market conditions and the lender's own market shares, the targets are conservative, and the penalties for noncompliance are weak and discretionary. Finally, this chapter examines federal legislation that is intended to influence banks to lend in underserved neighborhoods and is clearly not credit allocation. Rather, the legislation requires banks to disclose information about their lending records, thus influencing them to lend to underserved areas.

The Definition of Credit Allocation

"Allocation" is defined as the act of apportioning "for specific purposes or to particular persons or organizations," as in, for example, a governmental or economic control measure.[1] The operative terms in this definition are "apportion," "specific purpose," and "particular" persons or organizations. Based on this definition, the key characteristics of a system of credit allocation include setting aside a specific amount of credit for a particular purpose, person, or organization. Thus, a bank that allocated credit would set aside a specific amount of credit for a particular person or organization for a particular purpose. Allocating credit is in fact what a bank does. A home mortgage loan or a line of credit is an allocation of credit from a bank to the borrower.

This voluntary allocation of credit from a bank to a borrower is not, however, what Congress had in mind when it stated that the CRA was not intended to allocate credit. What they were talking about was government-imposed credit allocation. In such a system, the government would decide how banks should apportion credit to specific persons or organizations for particular purposes. Such a system could take many forms, encompassing many gradations in the degree of specificity with which the government requires a bank to lend. For example, a mandatory system of credit allocation could specify many terms, including the type of loan, the loan recipients, the interest rate, the number of loans a bank is required to make, and the total dollar amount of loans. Thus, a quota of fifty home mortgage loans per year for three years in a particular neighborhood, at 7% interest, would be a form of mandatory credit allocation. A less specific requirement, such as a mandate to make fifty home mortgage loans per year, without further specification of terms, would also constitute credit allocation.[2]

In addition to apportioning credit for or to specific purposes or individuals, a government-imposed system of credit allocation must be mandatory; that is, it must include sanctions for failing to follow the lending mandate. As the penalty for failing to follow the credit allocation mandate increases, the more likely it will be that the bank will follow the mandate.[3] Thus, for example, a recommendation from a federal banking agency to a bank to make fifty conventional home mortgage loans with thirty-year repayment terms at 5% interest in a low-income neighborhood, totaling $10 million over a three-year period—although specific—would not constitute government-imposed credit allocation if it did not include a sanction for failing to follow it. On the other hand, the same recommendation, if stated in the form of an order accompanied by the risk of injunctive relief or financial penalties for failure to comply, is credit allocation.

The Department of Justice's Lending Discrimination Cases

From 1992 to 1997, the Department of Justice ("DOJ") filed and settled twelve cases under the Fair Housing Act ("FHA")[4] and the Equal Credit Opportunity Act ("ECOA")[5] accusing lenders of home mortgage loan discrimination. The consent decrees contain examples of efforts to influence bank lending decisions and examples of credit allocation. Some provisions influence bank lending decisions by requiring banks to take steps that would likely result in making more loans to minority borrowers and communities; other provisions allocate credit by imposing lending quotas on banks that dictate the dollar volume of loans, the terms and types of loans, and the communities in which the banks were to make the loans, and threaten serious sanctions for failing to comply.[6]

In 1992, the Department of Justice filed *United States v. Decatur Federal Savings and Loan Association*,[7] its first case accusing a bank of engaging in a pattern and practice of home mortgage lending discrimination in the twenty-four years the FHA had given the DOJ the authority to file such cases. Between 1992 and 1997, the DOJ filed eleven more cases alleging a pattern and practice of home mortgage lending discrimination against home mortgage lenders around the country.[8] The cases covered all stages of the real-estate related lending process. They accused lenders of establishing lending territories that excluded predominantly minority communities,[9] failing to advertise in predominantly minority communities,[10] discriminating against borrowers on the basis of race,[11] placing more onerous application burdens on minority loan applicants than white applicants,[12] and charging higher interest rates to minority borrowers.[13]

The DOJ and the lenders settled all these cases. The consent decrees imposed various obligations on the lenders. Some provisions required lenders to take certain steps that would likely result in more loans to predominantly minority neighborhoods but did not allocate credit because they lacked specific lending mandates.[14] Such provisions required banks to:

- add previously excluded areas to the bank's CRA lending area;[15]
- expand marketing and advertising efforts in predominantly minority communities;[16]
- expand efforts to ascertain the credit needs of minority communities;[17]
- adopt branch opening/closing policies that account for the credit needs of minority communities;[18]

- conduct home mortgage seminars in predominantly minority communities;[19]
- recruit and hire more minority employees for positions in the loan solicitation and origination process;[20]
- adopt more stringent fair lending policies;[21]
- participate in government-guaranteed loan programs;[22]
- open one or more branches or loan offices in predominantly African-American neighborhoods;[23]
- offer financial bonuses to loan officers for making loans in low-income areas or on lower-valued homes;[24]
- participate in home mortgage loan programs designed to make loans in low-income neighborhoods;[25] and
- adopt procedures to ensure minorities are treated equally in the loan origination process, including requiring loan processors to complete an information checklist, implementing a second review of all rejected applications, and implementing a customer assistance program.[26]

Other provisions in the consent decrees took the form of government-imposed credit allocation.[27] They required banks to make specific dollar amounts of loans to minority neighborhoods or borrowers and dictated many of the loan terms. Failure could result in judicial intervention to enforce compliance.[28] Several consent decrees provide illustrative examples of credit allocation. These decrees contain specific provisions allocating credit and prescribe clear penalties for failing to comply. One consent decree committed Chevy Chase Federal Savings Bank ("Chevy Chase") to invest $11 million in African-American communities, $7 million in the form of loan subsidies.[29] The loans were to be conventional, fixed-rate mortgages up to $203,150, secured by single-family residences. The interest rate would be, at the borrower's choice, either one percent below market rate or one-half percent below market subsidized by a grant in the amount of two percent of the loan and a waiver of $400 in fees.[30] The loan program would permit the borrower to obtain two percent of the down payment through gifts, waive the requirement that the borrower have reserves equal to two mortgage payments, and allow closing cost flexibility.[31] Each $1 million in subsidies would support $20 million in loans, so Chevy Chase agreed, in effect, to lend a total of $140 million over the five year life of the consent decree, in roughly equal amounts each year.[32] The consent decree required Chevy Chase to lend these amounts "apportioned between the District of Columbia and Prince George's County in relation to the United States' estimate of the manner in which the alleged underlying violation affected each community."[33] The initial estimated annual amounts were $20 million in the District of Columbia and $8 million in Prince George's County.[34] If the bank failed to comply, the United States could bring suit in district court to enforce the decree.[35]

A second example is the consent decree in *United States v. Albank* ("Albank"), which required Albank to lend at least $55 million in home mortgage loans in five years in designated census tracts within previously allegedly redlined minority neighborhoods in Connecticut and Westchester County, New York.[36] The loans were to have an interest rate 1.5 percentage points below market rate, be available to any qualified borrower seeking a mortgage loan up to $214,600, and be secured by a home located in designated census tracts.[37] The consent decree required Albank to make $20 million in loans in Westchester within twenty-six months: at least $10 million in the first fourteen months and $10 million in the next twelve months.[38] The decree also required Albank to make at least $35 million in below-market loans on properties located within designated census tracts in seven allegedly redlined cities in Connecticut: Hartford; New Haven; New Britain; Waterbury; Bridgeport; Stamford; and Norwalk. The loans were to be evenly distributed over a five year period.[39] The decree required Albank to lend 40% of the $35 million in designated census tracts in three of the cities.[40] The total cost to Albank of this subsidized lending program would be $8.2 million.[41] The consent decree provided that if Albank failed to comply with these terms, the United States could file suit in district court to enforce the decree.[42]

The third example of a consent decree that allocated credit is *United States v. First National Bank of Doña Ana*, ("First National") which required First National to create a $750,000 mobile home loan fund through which it would offer below-market mobile home loans and pay $100,000 to provide interest subsidies for the mobile home loan fund.[43] If First National failed to comply, the United States could sue in district court to enforce the decree.[44]

Finally, the consent decree in *United States v. First National Bank of Vicksburg* ("Vicksburg") required the Bank to adopt and offer at least one new lending program for LMI borrowers and to establish a $1 million lending goal pursuant to that program.[45] Vicksburg intended to institute two new loan programs: unsecured home improvement loans with an interest rate of one percent below market rate, a maturity of up to sixty months, and no minimum loan amount; and second mortgage loans that would include an interest rate equal to prime plus one-quarter percent, a maturity of up to fifteen years, and individual loan amounts up to $15,000.[46] The consent decree provided that if

Vicksburg failed to comply, the United States could sue in district court to enforce the decree.[47]

Home Mortgage Loan Purchase Targets for Fannie Mae and Freddie Mac

This section examines federal legislation that establishes annual home mortgage loan purchase goals for the Federal National Mortgage Association ("Fannie Mae") and the Federal Home Loan Mortgage Corporation ("Freddie Mac").[48] The goals require Fannie Mae and Freddie Mac to purchase from lenders a certain percentage of home mortgage loans that the lenders made to LMI families, affordable housing projects, and underserved areas. While the legislation establishes goals, the goals are not quotas, as they are set based on Fannie Mae's and Freddie Mac's overall purchases. There are penalties for failure to comply, but the penalties are weak—relatively small monetary penalties only after other efforts to comply have failed—and do not require Fannie Mae or Freddie Mac to purchase loans. This legislation is thus a strong effort to influence Fannie Mae and Freddie Mac to purchase certain loans but is not credit allocation.

Fannie Mae and Freddie Mac are government-sponsored enterprises ("GSEs") that Congress created to provide a secondary market for home mortgage loans.[49] Congress' goal was to help provide liquidity for the home mortgage market and facilitate the distribution of home mortgage loan credit throughout the country. Congress granted Fannie Mae and Freddie Mac the power to purchase home mortgage loans originated by banks and other lenders and hold them in their portfolios or package and sell them as securities.[50] Congress also specified that Fannie Mae and Freddie Mac have "an affirmative obligation to facilitate the financing of affordable housing for low- and moderate-income families in a manner consistent with their overall public purposes, while maintaining a strong financial condition and a reasonable economic return. . . ."[51] This is reminiscent of the language in the CRA that requires banks to meet the credit needs of the community consistent with safe and sound banking practices.

In 1992, Congress passed the Federal Housing Enterprises Financial Safety and Soundness Act ("FHEFSSA").[52] As part of the FHEFSSA, Congress required the Secretary of the Department of Housing and Development ("HUD") to create annual goals for the GSEs' purchase of home mortgage loans.[53] Congress required HUD to create home mortgage loan purchase goals in three different categories: LMI housing; special affordable housing; and housing in central cities, rural areas, and other underserved areas.[54] The legislation requires HUD to consider several factors in establishing these goals, including national housing needs; economic, housing, and demographic conditions; the GSEs' performance at meeting the goals in previous years; the size of the market in each category compared with the size of the overall conventional mortgage market; the ability of the GSEs to lead the industry in making mortgage credit available in the relevant category; and the GSEs' safety and soundness.[55]

In the FHEFSSA, Congress established interim targets for the LMI housing and underserved areas categories for 1993 and 1994. For LMI home mortgage loan purchases, Congress established an interim target of 30% of the total number of dwelling units financed by each GSE's home mortgage loan purchases.[56] The target for the underserved areas goal was 30% of the total number of dwelling units financed by each GSE's mortgage purchases.[57]

For the special affordable housing goal, Congress required Fannie Mae to purchase no less than $2 billion in such home mortgages, with half of such purchases for multi-family housing and half for single-family housing.[58] Congress required Freddie Mac to purchase $1.5 billion in such mortgages, with half for single-family housing and half for multi-family housing.[59] Congress established specific income requirements for these goals. For the multi-family goal, Congress required that 45% of the purchases be of loans for housing affordable to low-income families and 55% of loans for housing in which at least 20% of the units were affordable to families whose income did not exceed 50% of the area median income and at least 40% of the units were affordable to very low-income families.[60] For single-family housing, Congress required that 45% of the purchases be of mortgages to low-income families who live in low-income census tracts and 55% of the purchases be of mortgages to very low-income families.[61]

Congress gave HUD the authority to monitor and enforce the GSEs' compliance with these goals. These provisions include the authority to require a GSE that has not satisfied one of its goals to submit a housing plan to ensure compliance, issue an order to cease and desist any failure to submit a plan or make a good faith effort comply with such a plan, and assess civil money penalties not exceeding $25,000 per day for failing to submit a housing plan and up to $10,000 per day for failing to make a good faith effort to comply with the plan.

In setting the annual goals, HUD took a number of steps to ensure that the impact on the GSEs would not be too great.[62] First, the goals were conservative and attainable under several economic scenarios. Second, the goal categories were not mutually exclusive. Third, the goals were generally consistent with then-current GSE mortgage purchase activities. Finally, the return on equity of goals-related purchases would be between one and four percent lower than other purchases.[63]

The GSEs have generally met these goals, and their loan purchases in each of the three goal categories have grown moderately. Tables 7.1, 7.2 and 7.3 depict the LMI housing, special affordable housing, and underserved areas housing goals for 1993–2003 and the GSEs' percentage of such purchases in parentheses below the goals.[64] These tables show that both GSEs met the LMI housing goals in each year from 1993–2003. They also met the special affordable housing goals in each year from 1996–2003. Fannie Mae failed to meet the underserved areas goals in 1993, but met them from 1994–2003. Freddie Mac failed to meet the underserved areas goals in 1993 and 1994, but met the goals from 1995–2003.

Overall, the GSEs showed growth in loan purchases in each of the three goals categories. Fannie Mae's performance on the LMI housing goal improved from 1993 to 2003, increasing from 34.2% of all home mortgage loans purchased to 51.8%. Freddie Mac's performance also jumped significantly from 1993 to 2003, going from 29.7% to 51.1%. Under the special affordable housing goal, both GSEs showed slight growth between 1996 and 2003. Fannie Mae's percentage of special affordable housing loans purchased increased from 17.1% to 20.9% while Freddie Mac's increased from 14.2% to 20.2%. Fannie Mae's percentage of underserved areas loans purchased grew from 23.6% in 1993 to 32.0% in 2003. Freddie Mac's percentage of loans purchased increased from 25.2% to 32.3%.

HUD conducted a study of the impact of the GSE goals on GSE performance.[65] According to HUD, shortly after Congress passed the FHEFSSA, Fannie Mae and Freddie Mac changed the underwriting criteria for loans they would purchase. They increased the loan-to-value ratio from 90% to 95%, the housing debt payment/income ratio from 25% to 28%, and the overall debt payment/income ratio from 28% to 36%.[66] As a result, lenders that sell loans to Fannie Mae and Freddie Mac can offer conventional loans with similarly flexible criteria.[67] The HUD study found statistical evidence that the affordable housing goals and the GSEs' resultant change in underwriting criteria were having an effect. For example, the percentage of the GSEs' purchases of loans from below-average income individuals, African-Americans, and Latinos increased between 1993 and 1998, as shown in Table 7.4.[68]

The GSEs' market shares of the total number and dollar volume of all loans and prime loans only to low-income and minority persons increased in the

Table 7.1 LMI Housing

	1993	1994	1995	1996	1997	1998	1999	2000	2001	2002	2003
Fannie Mae	30% (34.2%)	30% (44.8%)	30% (42.3%)	40% (45.1%)	42% (45.5%)	42% (44.1%)	42% (45.9%)	42% (49.5%)	50% (51.5%)	50% (51.8%)	50% (51.8%)
Freddie Mac	28% (29.7%)	30% (37.4%)	30% (38.9%)	40% (41.3%)	42% (42.9%)	42% (42.9%)	42% (46.1%)	42% (49.9%)	50% (53.2%)	50% (51.4%)	50% (51.1%)

Table 7.2 Special Affordable Housing

	1993–94	1995	1996	1997	1998	1999	2000	2001	2002	2003
Fannie Mae	$2 billion (2 yr. goal)	11%	12% (17.1%)	14% (19.1%)	14% (14.3%)	14% (17.6%)	14% (19.2%)	20% (21.6%)	20% (21.3%)	20% (20.9%)
Freddie Mac	$1.5 billion (2 yr. goal)	11%	12% (14.2%)	14% (15.3%)	14% (15.9%)	14% (17.2%)	14% (20.7%)	20% (22.6%)	20% (21.4%)	20% (20.2%)

Table 7.3 Underserved Areas Housing

	1993	1994	1995	1996	1997	1998	1999	2000	2001	2002	2003
Fannie Mae	28% (23.6%)	30% (31.9%)	18% (31.9%)	21% (28.2%)	24% (29%)	24% (27%)	24% (26.8%)	24% (31.0%)	31% (32.5%)	31% (32.7%)	31% (32.0%)
Freddie Mac	26% (25.2%)	30% (26.4%)	18% (26.4%)	21% (25.0%)	24% (26.3%)	24% (26.1%)	24% (27.5%)	24% (29.2%)	31% (31.7%)	31% (31.9%)	31% (32.3%)

Table 7.4

	1993	1998
Income less than 100% MSA median		
Fannie Mae	29%	39%
Freddie Mac	28%	40%
African-Americans		
Fannie Mae	2.7%	3.4%
Freddie Mac	2.0%	3.5%
Latinos		
Fannie Mae	3.8%	6.0%
Freddie Mac	3.1%	5.5%

conventional loan market and in the underserved market increased from 1995–99.[69] Finally, according to HUD, one of the consequences of these increases was growth in homeownership rates for LMI persons and minorities from 1992–98.[70]

Mandatory Loan-to-Deposit Ratios for Banks with Interstate Branches

This section examines an attempt by Congress to ensure that banks chartered in one state that open branches in another state do not use their branches in the new state primarily for accepting deposits. The law requires the interstate branches of a bank to have a loan-to-deposit ratio ("LDR") equal to at least half the average LDR of the new state. The legislation is similar to the GSE legislation in that it establishes lending goals that are not quotas but are tied to market conditions in the new states. Additionally, the requirement is so minimal as to be almost irrelevant, and the penalties for noncompliance are discretionary and weak and do not require a bank to lend or divest deposits.

The Riegle-Neal Interstate Banking and Branching Efficiency Act of 1994 (the "Riegle-Neal Act") permitted banks to establish branches ("interstate branches") in a state other than the state in which the bank is chartered (a "host state").[71] Section 109 of the Riegle-Neal Act prohibits a bank that establishes branches in a host state from using those branches primarily for receiving deposits as opposed to making loans.[72] The Riegle-Neal Act establishes an LDR test, a provision for evaluating whether the bank is meeting the credit needs of its host state, and penalties for a bank that uses its interstate branches primarily to receive deposits.

The Riegle-Neal Act establishes a two-step test for determining whether a bank is using its interstate branches primarily for receiving deposits.[73] The first step of the test is an LDR test. The test is based on the dollar value of the bank's loans in the host state divided by the dollar value of deposits in the bank's branches in the host state (the LDR) compared with the average LDR for all banks that are chartered in the host state.[74] In order to pass the test, within one year of acquiring or establishing interstate branches, the LDR of the bank's interstate branches must equal at least 50% of the average LDR for the branches of all banks chartered in the host state.[75]

The agencies issued the first lists of host state LDRs in 1998, 1999, and 2000.[76] Examining some trends in the host state LDRs helps elucidate how the LDR test works and whether it is difficult for banks to comply. The test is not burdensome. The highest LDR a bank was required to have for its interstate branches was lower than the lowest host state LDR. With only a few exceptions, annual increases in LDRs were small, and the LDRs in several states decreased.

The lowest host state LDR was 62% in Colorado in 1999 and 2000.[77] This means that a bank with interstate branches in Colorado in 1999 or 2000 had to have an LDR in Colorado of at least 31% to pass the LDR test. In contrast, the highest LDR was in Washington, at 115% in 1999 and 2000.[78] The interstate branches of a bank from outside Washington had to have an LDR in Washington of 57.5%. Thus, the highest LDR that a bank was required to have—57.5%—was lower than the lowest host state LDR of 62%.

Annual changes in LDRs were not significant. The host LDR increased by more than ten percentage points in a year on only four occasions: Arizona, 79% to 95% from 1999–2000; District of Columbia, 43% to 71% from 1998–99; North Dakota, 73% to 90% from 1998–99; and Wyoming, 73% to 99% from 1999–2000.[79] Banks with interstate branches in these states on these four occasions had to increase their LDRs in these states by half these increases, or 8, 14, 8.5, and 13 percentage points, respectively. Increases in the LDRs of twenty-two states over three years were less than five percentage points and the ratios declined in twelve states. This means that banks with interstate branches in these states were not required to make significant changes in their LDRs in order to comply with Section 109 of the Riegle-Neal Act.

Trends from 2001 to 2003 were similar to trends from 1998 to 2000. From 2001 to 2002, there were four increases of at least ten percentage points (District of Columbia, 80–90%; Indiana, 106–119%; South Dakota, 120–130%; Wyoming, 56-84%); from 2002–2003 there was one such increase (Georgia, 89–101%). LDRs declined in thirty-one states from 2001 to 2003. Of the twenty increases, nine were fewer than five percentage points.[80] Finally, as illustrated by Table 7.5, the highest required LDRs were slightly higher than the lowest state LDRs.[81]

Table 7.5

	Lowest State LDR	Highest Required LDR
2001	56% (Wyoming)	62.5% (based on Ohio's 123% LDR)
2002	58% (Arizona)	65% (based on South Dakota's 130% LDR)
2003	60% (Arizona, New Jersey)	65.5% (based on 131% LDR in South Dakota)

If a bank fails the LDR test, the next step is for the federal banking agency that regulates the bank to determine whether the bank is reasonably helping to meet the credit needs of the communities the bank serves in the host state.[82] The agency considers six factors, including whether the interstate branches were part of a failed institution; whether the interstate branches were part of another institution that had a low LDR; whether the interstate branches have a high concentration of commercial or credit card lending, trust services, or other specialized activities; the CRA rating of the bank; and the safe and sound operation of the bank.[83] This test should be easy for a bank to satisfy.[84] As demonstrated in chapter five, the agencies tend to apply subjective standards such as these favorably toward banks.[85] In addition, well over 90% of banks receive satisfactory or higher CRA ratings.[86]

If a bank's interstate branches fail to meet the LDR test and are not meeting the credit needs of the communities they serve in the host state, the bank faces penalties. The bank cannot open a new interstate branch in the host state unless the bank provides assurances acceptable to the federal banking agency that regulates it that the branches will serve the credit needs of its communities[87] and, at the agency's discretion, the bank must close its interstate branches unless the bank satisfies the agency that it has an acceptable plan to meet the credit needs of the communities served by the bank in the host state.[88] Given the agencies' weak record of enforcing the CRA described in chapter five, it is likely that the agencies will accept such assurances and not close branches.

Disclosure of Information About Loans[89]

Congress has also attempted to influence lending decisions by requiring lenders to disclose information about their lending through the Home Mortgage Disclosure Act of 1975 ("HMDA").[90] HMDA is a federal home mortgage lending disclosure law that provides a significant amount of the data the federal banking agencies use to evaluate a bank's CRA record. HMDA contains no lending mandate; in fact it explicitly states that Congress did not intend that HMDA allocate credit.[91] Nevertheless, like the CRA's sponsors, HMDA's congressional sponsors did intend that disclosure of lending data would influence lenders to lend more money in LMI and inner-city areas.[92] This is what appears to have happened. Following the disclosure of expanded home mortgage lending data in 1991 that showed that lenders rejected African-American loan applicants at twice the rate of whites, pressure on lenders to improve this record grew, and their lending to LMI and minority persons and neighborhoods grew proportionately faster than their lending to upper-income and white persons and neighborhoods, resulting in an increase in the market share of loans held by LMI and minority individuals and neighborhoods.

Initial Passage and Legislative History of HMDA

As originally enacted, HMDA required banks to disclose the location, by state, county, and census tract, of each residential real estate-related loan they made.[93] The legislative history and purpose of HMDA are similar to the legislative history and the purpose of the CRA. Congress made clear that HMDA was intended to influence banks to lend more in LMI neighborhoods but not to allocate credit. When considering HMDA, Congress heard evidence that banks had redlined older, urban, and racially integrated neighborhoods, contributing to their decline.[94] HMDA states: "Congress finds that some depository institutions have sometimes contributed to the decline of certain geographic areas by their failure pursuant to their chartering responsibilities to provide adequate home financing to qualified applicants on reasonable terms and conditions."[95]

Congress passed HMDA as a way to stop bank redlining.[96] The theory behind HMDA was that disclosure of data about bank lending records would help end redlining.[97] Forcing banks to disclose information about their home mortgage lending records would motivate them to increase their lending in redlined neighborhoods rather than face embarrassing publicity.[98] Disclosure of HMDA data would also assist local community groups and public officials who were seeking to increase lending in their communities.[99] Such information would assist them to identify banks with poor lending records and devise strategies to end redlining and disinvestment.[100] As evidence that disclosure would work, the Senate Report on HMDA cited three examples of lending agreements between LMI communities and banks that followed voluntary disclosure of home mortgage lending records by the banks.[101] An opponent of HMDA agreed that Congress intended HMDA's information disclosures to influence lenders to make more loans to underserved communities. "The theory behind [HMDA] is that once depositors know where their money is being invested, they will make demands upon the savings institutions that that money or a portion of that money be returned to their neighborhood."[102]

Opponents of HMDA argued that it was a step toward credit allocation.[103] HMDA's opponents stated, "We fear that this disclosure is the first step toward a form of credit allocation—the next would be to say that at least *x* percentage of the deposits must be invested in a certain area."[104] HMDA proponents denied this. The statute states explicitly, "Nothing in this chapter is intended to, nor shall it be construed to, encourage unsound lending practices or the allocation of credit."[105] Supporters also stated that HMDA would not require lenders to allocate credit.[106] According to HMDA's supporters, however, HMDA disclosures would influence lenders to make more loans in redlined communities.[107]

In 1989, Congress amended HMDA to expand its disclosure requirements significantly. Starting in 1990, HMDA required depository institutions to disclose additional information about their residential real estate-related loans, including the number of applications they received; the race, income, and gender of each applicant; the census tract in which the property that was the subject of the loan application was located; and the disposition of each application.[108] The goal of these amendments was to influence lenders to do more to meet the credit needs of certain individuals and communities, particularly African-Americans, Latinos, LMI persons, predominantly minority neighborhoods, and LMI neighborhoods.[109]

The Impact of the Disclosure of Expanded HMDA Data

In late 1991, the Federal Reserve released the first set of expanded HMDA data, covering lending in 1990. The data showed that in 1990, lenders across the nation denied conventional home mortgage loan applications from African-Americans more than twice as frequently as from whites and denied conventional home mortgage loan applications from Latinos nearly 1.5 times as frequently.[110] Lenders denied applications for conventional home mortgage loans to purchase property in predominantly minority neighborhoods more than twice as frequently as they denied loans to purchase property in predominantly white neighborhoods.[111]

The disclosure of this data caused controversy around the country.[112] Community leaders called on banks to investigate the reasons for the rejection rate disparities and improve their lending records.[113] Community groups, journalists, and scholars published numerous studies of bank lending records that generally confirmed the national data at the local level.[114]

The federal government strengthened its enforcement of the FHA and ECOA following the disclosure of expanded HMDA data in 1991.[115] The DOJ's efforts beginning in 1992 were described earlier in this chapter. In addition to the DOJ's efforts, the federal banking agencies also tightened their own efforts to enforce the FHA and ECOA. First, upon releasing the expanded HMDA data in October 1991, Federal Reserve Governor John LaWare said the federal banking agencies would use the expanded HMDA data as an additional tool to evaluate bank compliance with the FHA and ECOA.[116] Following this, the OCC targeted for investigation 266 banks whose HMDA data raised questions about whether they were engaging in discriminatory lending practices.[117] Second, the OCC announced that it was beginning to conduct matched-pair tests of the banks it regulated to determine whether they were discriminating in their lending.[118] Third, the federal banking agencies began to use their authority to refer potential lending discrimination cases to the DOJ and HUD for investigation, some of which became the subject of the DOJ complaints and consent decrees described earlier.[119] Prior to 1991, the agencies rarely, if ever, used this authority.[120] Referrals increased from one in 1990 to twelve in 1993 and peaked at twenty-five in 1994.[121] Fourth, the federal banking agencies changed their procedures for examining banks for fair lending compliance, and in doing so adopted a theory of discrimination more likely to uncover violations. Previously, they examined files of individual minority applicants to see if denials were based on credit-related reasons or other illegal reasons. By 1992, they changed their procedures so that they compared the application files of minorities with the files of whites to see if lenders were treating them equally.[122] This was a significant shift because it expanded the pool of victims of discrimination from applicants who met credit standards but did not receive a loan to applicants who did not meet credit standards but were not given exceptions to credit standards that similarly situated white applicants received. Finally, the federal banking agencies also notified banks about their concerns regarding the lending patterns disclosed by HMDA data and urged them to review their own data and their own lending practices for evidence of differential treatment.[123] In March 1992, the federal banking agencies issued a statement suggesting how banks could reduce their rejection rate disparities between whites and minorities, including establishing second review procedures for denied applications, implementing matched-pair testing, offering credit counseling, and examining lending criteria that might have a disparate impact on minority borrowers.[124]

Following the disclosure of the expanded HMDA data, the federal banking agencies strengthened their CRA enforcement efforts. From June 30, 1990 to July 1, 1992, they awarded 89% of banks a CRA rating of satisfactory or higher, down from 98% of all banks prior to June 30, 1990.[125] They also denied bank expansion applications and commenced enforcement proceedings against banks based on CRA, HMDA, and fair lending concerns more frequently than they had prior to 1991.[126]

In 1993, the federal banking agencies announced that they intended to strengthen the CRA regulations to focus more on a bank's lending record. They adopted new regulations, fully effective as of July 1, 1997.[127] The new regulations are more demanding than the previous ones, in that they evaluate a bank's CRA record according to its lending, investing, and providing banking services in low-income communities.[128]

Other federal agencies increased their efforts to enforce the fair lending laws as well. In 1994, a federal interagency task force comprised of nine federal agencies with fair lending law enforcement authority adopted a policy statement on lending discrimination.[129] The statement described practices the agencies believed constituted lending discrimination and the enforcement actions the agencies would take against lenders who violated the law. The statement indicates that both the ECOA and the FHA prohibit lenders from engaging in several forms of discrimination, including, on the basis of race, failing to provide information about credit services, providing different information about credit services, discouraging or selectively encouraging credit applicants, refusing to extend credit, using different standards in determining whether to extend credit, or varying the terms of credit offered.[130] The statement also indicated that the various agencies would take several actions to enforce the law, including commencing administrative and court enforcement proceedings; seeking civil money penalties, damages, and credit extensions for victims; and requesting injunctive relief.[131]

The Secretary of HUD, who has the authority to enforce the FHA on its own initiative by filing an administrative complaint with HUD,[132] used this authority more aggressively to enforce the FHA against non-bank mortgage lenders. In 1994, HUD signed a "best practices" agreement with the Mortgage Bankers Association, the trade organization that represents non-bank mortgage lenders, outlining lending practices they would undertake to prevent or eliminate lending discrimination.[133] By November 1997, HUD had reached best practices agreements with 114 non-bank mortgage lenders.[134] HUD also reached consent decrees with at least seven home mortgage lenders in cases involving allegations of lending discrimination, including at least two agreements to lend more than $1 billion to minority borrowers.[135]

Finally, community group leaders began to use the CRA more aggressively. As described earlier, community groups play an important part in CRA enforcement by challenging bank expansion applications and generating lending agreements or commitments from banks.[136] Of the approximately $1.03 trillion in CRA lending agreements that the National Community Reinvestment Coalition catalogued in 1999, agreements totaling more than $1 trillion came after 1991.[137]

In response to the public controversy, increased activism, and strengthened law enforcement that followed the 1991 HMDA data disclosures, lenders took several steps to increase their conventional home mortgage lending to LMI and minority borrowers and communities.[138] These steps included adopting new lending programs designed to make loans to low-income persons,[139] implementing new lending procedures such as a second review of rejected loan applications,[140] examining and changing loan underwriting criteria,[141] creating lending consortia with other banks,[142] increasing outreach to minority and LMI communities,[143] and working with community groups to design credit counseling programs to assist LMI home buyers to qualify for loans.[144]

Lending Increases Following the Disclosure

Lending nationally to African-Americans, Latinos, LMI persons and neighborhoods, and predominantly minority neighborhoods (the "underserved communities") surged starting in 1992, following the disclosure in 1991 of the first set of expanded HMDA data. Two important indicators show this. The first indicator is the market share of applications submitted by the underserved communities. This is an important indicator of banks' efforts to solicit business in these communities.[145] As demonstrated in Table 7.6,[146] the market share of applications for conventional home mortgage loans from the underserved communities increased significantly from 1991 to 1998.[147]

Table 7.6 Market Share of Applications

	1991	1998	% Increase
African-Americans	4.2	8.3	97.6
Latinos	4.8	5.8	20.8
LMI persons	22.8	31.3	37.3
Predominantly minority neighborhoods	2.3	3.7	60.1
LMI neighborhoods	10.2	14.6	43.1

The second indicator is the market share of conventional home mortgage loan approvals in each underserved community from 1991 to 1998.[148] The market share of approved loans increased nationally in all five underserved communities from 1991–98 (see Table 7.7).

Table 7.7 Market Share of Loan Approvals

	1991	1998	% Increase
African-Americans	3.1	5.2	67.7
Latinos	4.1	4.9	19.5
LMI persons	18.6	25.3	36
Predominantly minority neighborhoods	2.5	2.7	8
LMI neighborhoods	9.2	11.8	28.3

The National Community Reinvestment Coalition found that as of 2001, although loan market shares in these underserved communities had declined from their 1998 levels, they still remained higher than the 1991 levels (see Table 7.8).[149]

Table 7.8 Market Share of Loans

	1991	2000
African-Americans	3.1	4.8
Latinos	4.1	6.2
LMI persons	18.6	24.7
Predominantly minority neighborhoods	2.5	3.5
LMI neighborhoods	9.2	12.2

These statistics do not prove that the disclosure of expanded HMDA data caused the increases in lending. Many other factors could have caused or contributed to these increases, including changes in demographics, property values, or economic conditions. However, the extent and timing of the increases, combined with the evidence of strengthened enforcement of the CRA, increased community activism, and lenders' own acknowledgment of the problem and their efforts to respond, is consistent with the hypothesis that the disclosure of more lending data pursuant to HMDA influenced lenders to make more loans to the subject communities.

CHAPTER EIGHT

Democratizing Capital

Introduction

This chapter proposes criteria for evaluating a bank's CRA performance that are designed to maximize the CRA's potential for democratizing capital. Each proposed criterion is composed of a quantitative measure of bank lending, a quantitative benchmark of community credit needs, and an objective standard for evaluating whether a bank's lending meets credit needs. This chapter also proposes a predictable and consistent method for the federal banking agencies to employ when assigning a CRA rating to a bank and taking account of a bank's CRA record when considering its expansion applications. The proposed criteria will influence banks to lend as Congress intended, but they will not allocate credit. They will maximize the CRA's potential for democratizing capital because they will make it easier to hold a bank accountable for a weak record and they will result in more loans to creditworthy members of underserved communities. Finally, because the criteria are fixed, objective, quantitative, and equally applicable to all banks, they will be easier, cheaper, and less time-consuming to apply than the current criteria. They will inject regularity, consistency, and predictability into the CRA evaluation process.

To put the proposed criteria in context, it is helpful to review several key points. Chapter one reviewed the legislative history of the CRA and showed that Congress passed the CRA to end redlining and increase bank lending in redlined neighborhoods. Congress intended the CRA to influence lenders to make more loans in redlined neighborhoods but not to allocate credit. Since Congress enacted an affirmative obligation on banks to help meet credit needs, the federal banking agencies that enforce the CRA may, consistent with congressional intent, implement a regulatory system that influences banks to lend up to the point of allocating credit. In addition, since Congress did not specifically prohibit credit allocation nor offer a specific definition, the agencies may define credit allocation narrowly. As described in chapter two, the CRA as structured reflects congressional intent. It influences banks to meet the credit needs of the entire community, including LMI neighborhoods, by requiring the federal banking agencies to examine each bank periodically to determine its record of meeting the credit needs of the community, issue a written evaluation report with a rating, and take a bank's record into account when considering its expansion applications. The CRA does not establish loan quotas or mandatory penalties for failure to comply. Several studies described in chapter six conclude that relevant data is consistent with the conclusion that the CRA has influenced banks to lend hundreds of billions of dollars to LMI and other underserved neighborhoods, but that it had nevertheless not met its full potential.

The federal banking agencies have implemented two CRA enforcement regimes. The first, described in chapter three and running from 1978 to mid-1997, was characterized by an emphasis on a bank's efforts to lend over its lending, subjective standards for evaluating bank lending performance, and limited use of enforcement tools. Underlying this approach was the federal banking agencies' selective reading of the CRA's legislative history. They concluded that in order to be faithful to congressional intent that the CRA not allocate credit, the only way they could influence banks to lend in LMI neighborhoods was by correcting an information failure in the market by forcing banks to learn more about lending opportunities in LMI communities. The federal banking agencies' approach to enforcing the CRA led to great dissatisfaction with the first CRA enforcement regime. Neither banks, nor community advocates, nor the federal banking agencies themselves, could discern the standards for a satisfactory CRA rating. Banks complained that the federal banking agencies imposed useless, expensive and burdensome paperwork obligations on them. Community advocates complained that despite lending increases in local communities, they could not effectively hold a bank to its CRA obligations and that the CRA had not reached its full potential.

Responding to these criticisms, the federal banking agencies adopted new CRA regulations. As described in chapter four, the new regulations eliminated all of the efforts-oriented criteria of the first set of regulations and adopted several quantitative criteria for measuring bank lending and community credit needs. However, the federal banking agencies did not adopt objective standards for evaluating whether a bank's lending meets community credit needs. Instead, the new regulations employ subjective standards for evaluating whether a bank's lending meets community credit needs. Proposed versions of the second set of

CRA regulations included objective standards for evaluating a bank's record at meeting community credit needs, such as a market share test for large banks and a loan-to-deposit ratio test for small banks. However, after the banking industry complained that these standards would allocate credit, the federal banking agencies dropped them from the final regulations.

Chapter five examined how the federal banking agencies evaluated bank lending during the second CRA enforcement regime. The agencies did not use a fixed set of criteria for evaluating lending, many of the criteria they used compared a quantitative measure of bank lending with a quantitative measure of community credit needs, the agencies used subjective and imprecise standards to make these comparisons, and the agencies applied the standards inconsistently and in a way that favored banks. Thus, despite the shift in focus from lending efforts to lending results in the second set of CRA regulations, the federal banking agencies continued to enforce the CRA in a way that made it difficult to hold a bank accountable for a weak lending record.

Chapter seven examined more carefully the difference between a system of government-imposed credit allocation and a system designed to influence bank lending decisions. Chapter seven defined a system of government-imposed credit allocation narrowly, as a system in which the government requires banks to lend a specific amount of money or make a specific number of loans to particular recipients or neighborhoods for a specific purpose upon pain of meaningful penalties. For purposes of following Congress' intent in creating a CRA regime that influences banks to lend but does not explicitly define or prohibit credit allocation, anything short of such a system does not constitute credit allocation but is a system designed to influence bank lending decisions. Chapter seven examined four examples of governmental intervention in the credit markets. The Department of Justice's consent decrees in lending discrimination cases demonstrate a system of government-imposed credit allocation because several decrees imposed lending quotas on banks. In contrast, while the second and third examples set purchase and lending targets, the targets are not quotas and do not allocate credit. The second example is federal legislation creating home mortgage loan purchase targets for Fannie Mae and Freddie Mac. The targets, however, are not quotas but are tied to overall investment activities. The targets are conservative and the penalties for not reaching them are weak. The third example is the federal legislation that created loan-to-deposit ratio requirements for the interstate branches of multistate banks. Like the home mortgage loan purchase targets for the GSEs, this legislation establishes lending targets, but the targets are easy to reach, they are tied to the bank's market presence, and the penalties for failing to meet them are weak. Finally, the fourth example, the Home Mortgage Disclosure Act ("HMDA"), is a system intended to influence bank lending decisions. HMDA contains no lending quotas, targets, or goals, but attempts to influence bank lending decisions by requiring banks to disclose information about their home mortgage lending records.

The Proposed Criteria for Evaluating the CRA Performance of a Bank

This section proposes new criteria for evaluating the CRA performance of a bank. Up to this point, this book's analysis has focused on retail lending. The CRA regulations also require the federal banking agencies to consider a large bank's community development loans, investments, grants, and services and retail banking services when they evaluate its CRA performance. There is good reason for this, as community development activities and retail banking services create and support individual credit opportunities. For the same reasons that criteria for evaluating bank lending that are composed of quantitative measures of bank lending, quantitative benchmarks of community credit needs, and objective standards for evaluating lending help maximize the CRA's potential for democratizing capital, such criteria for evaluating a bank's community development activities and retail banking services would help maximize the CRA's democratizing potential as well.[1] The proposed criteria for evaluating the CRA performance of a bank thus include quantitative measures and objective standards for evaluating lending, community development activities, and retail banking services.[2] After describing criteria for evaluating lending, community development, and banking services, this chapter describes methodologies for assigning a CRA rating to a bank and for taking account of the bank's CRA record when evaluating a bank expansion applications.

Criteria for Evaluating Lending

The criteria for evaluating lending contain three main components: three quantitative benchmarks of the credit needs of the community; five quantitative measures of bank lending; and a set of objective standards for comparing the bank's lending with the credit needs of the community.

Quantitative Benchmarks of Community Credit Needs

In order to measure the credit needs of the community, it is first necessary to define "credit" and the "community."

Credit

There are many types of credit. Although Congress passed the CRA with residential real estate lending in mind, the federal banking agencies also consider small business, small farm, and community development lending when considering a bank's CRA record, as well as consumer lending at the bank's option.[3] The proposed measures of credit needs assess these forms of lending as well.[4] Real estate-related lending includes all the loan types covered by HMDA. This includes conventional and federally insured home purchase loans, home refinance loans, home improvement loans, and permanent financing on multi-family housing.[5] Small business loans include small business loans as defined in the CRA regulations, which includes loans to businesses with gross annual revenue of $1 million or less.[6] Community development loans and investments include loans and investments the primary purpose of which is to benefit LMI persons through, for example, the creation of affordable housing or other economic development projects that will create jobs and benefit LMI areas.[7] Consumer lending includes student loans, secured loans, and credit card loans.[8]

Community

The next component of the quantitative benchmarks of community credit needs is the "community." The definition of community has two parts: the geographic area that constitutes the bank's local community, and the populations within that community whose credit needs the bank is required to meet.

Under current CRA regulations, a bank is required to delineate the geographic community in which it has CRA obligations (the "CRA assessment area"), taking into account factors such as the location of its branches, loans, and marketing efforts.[9] The CRA regulations suggest that the boundaries of the CRA assessment area be consistent with political boundaries, and suggest that for large banks, the boundaries of a metropolitan statistical area ("MSA") are appropriate.[10] The proposed definition of the bank's CRA assessment area differs somewhat from the regulations. They define a bank's CRA assessment area as any MSA in which the bank has at least one branch, and each MSA in which the bank's loan market share and total number of loans is sufficient to make a meaningful objective measure and invite CRA scrutiny.[11] This definition of a bank's CRA assessment area might be challenged as unfair to a bank that has only one or a few branches in an MSA, particularly if the branch or branches are in a wealthy neighborhood. However, an MSA is defined as a metropolitan area in which the central city and surrounding suburbs share socioeconomic interdependence.[12] A bank should not be permitted to forsake its CRA obligations to LMI neighborhoods in its MSA simply because it chooses to operate in a wealthy portion of the MSA.

The second part of the definition of community includes the populations within the bank's CRA assessment area whose needs are to be met. The proposed definition of community includes four "subject communities" within the bank's CRA assessment area whose needs are to be met. These are LMI persons, LMI neighborhoods, minority persons,[13] and predominantly minority neighborhoods.[14] Currently, the federal banking agencies evaluate lending to LMI neighborhoods and LMI persons when conducting CRA performance evaluations, but do not evaluate lending to predominantly minority neighborhoods or minority persons.[15] Instead, the agencies consider the results of a separate fair lending examination of a bank to determine whether the bank's CRA rating should be decreased because the bank is engaging in discriminatory lending practices.[16] The banking agencies' justification for not evaluating bank lending to minority individuals or predominantly minority neighborhoods in CRA examinations is that the explicit language of the CRA addresses lending according to income, not race.

The agencies' justification for not considering a bank's record of lending to minorities and in predominantly minority communities when evaluating its CRA record is untenable on a number of grounds. First, the legislative history of the CRA supports the proposition that Congress intended the CRA to promote lending in predominantly minority neighborhoods as well as LMI neighborhoods.[17] When debating the CRA, its supporters identified not only income-based redlining as a harmful practice but racial redlining and inner-city redlining as well.[18] In hearings on the CRA, the Senate Committee on Banking, Housing, and Urban Affairs received evidence of racial redlining as well as income redlining.[19]

Second, it is disingenuous of the federal banking agencies to separate race and income. A disproportionate number of minority persons are low-income, and minorities on average have lower incomes and fewer assets than whites.[20] Focusing on providing more credit to LMI communities is likely to result in more credit to minority persons and neighborhoods.[21]

Third, the federal banking agencies' narrow reading of the CRA regarding race is inconsistent with their reading regarding income. The CRA does not explicitly require banks to meet the credit needs of LMI individuals, but the CRA regulations include bank lending to LMI individuals as part of a bank's CRA performance evaluation.

Fourth, the CRA explicitly requires a bank to meet "the credit needs of its entire community, including low- and moderate-income neighborhoods...."[22] When Congress modified "the entire community" by "including" LMI neighborhoods, it did not exclude other types of communities. LMI communities are not the only beneficiaries of banks' obligation to meet credit needs. The entire community is the beneficiary, and the entire community includes predominantly minority neighborhoods and minority individuals. A bank that is not meeting the credit needs of minorities or predominantly minority neighborhoods can hardly be said to be meeting the credit needs of its entire community.

Fifth, a fair lending examination is not an adequate substitute for a CRA examination because the standards under the fair housing laws and the CRA are different. The fair lending laws are essentially prohibitive: as long as a bank is not treating applicants differently based on race, it is in compliance.[23] The CRA, however, is affirmative. It requires banks to meet community credit needs.[24] To satisfy the CRA, a bank must show that it is meeting credit needs, while to satisfy the fair lending laws, a bank must show it is not discriminating. Because of these different standards, a bank could satisfy its fair lending obligations by not discriminating against minorities or minority neighborhoods, but nevertheless it could be failing to meet their credit needs.

Finally, the federal banking agencies' approach to race in CRA performance evaluations is different from their approach when evaluating expansion applications. The Federal Reserve and the Comptroller of the Currency—the only agencies that consistently issue written decision on expansion applications—regularly consider a bank's lending according to race when evaluating a bank's expansion application.[25] One possible explanation for this differing approach is that the agencies consider lending according to race when evaluating expansion applications pursuant to their independent statutory authority to consider the convenience and needs of the community and not under the CRA. However, this explanation is not sufficient. The CRA states that banks have an obligation to meet the convenience and needs of the community and that convenience and needs includes credit services.[26] If the agencies consider race under the umbrella of "convenience and needs" when considering expansion applications, logically they should do so when conducting CRA performance evaluations.

Quantitative Benchmarks of Community Credit Needs

Because a key characteristic of governmental credit allocation is a predetermined number or dollar amount of loans that a bank must make regardless of the demand for loans, the quantitative benchmarks of credit needs cannot include predetermined numbers of loans. The proposed quantitative benchmarks of community credit needs do not establish loan quotas. Instead, they are based on the market for loans itself. In this way, the market—instead of a predetermined number—measures credit needs.

Specifically, the proposed benchmarks include three measures of the credit needs of each of the four subject communities: loan application percentage; loan origination percentage; and denial rate ratio.[27] The loan application percentage is the percentage of all loan applications from the bank's CRA assessment area that a subject community submits. The loan application percentage is a measure of the demand for loans from each of the four subject communities. For example, if 13% of all loan applications in a bank's CRA assessment area are from residents of LMI neighborhoods, the application percentage for LMI neighborhoods is 13%. If 15% of the loan applications from a bank's CRA assessment area are from LMI persons—regardless of whether they live in an LMI neighborhood—the application percentage for LMI persons is 15%. Under the proposed CRA evaluative criteria, the "credit need" of LMI neighborhoods in terms of the demand for loans is 13% of all loan applications, and the "credit need" of LMI persons is 15% of all applications. The total number of loan applications a community submits has been found to be an important determinant of the number of loans the community receives.[28]

The second quantitative measure of community credit needs, the loan origination percentage, is the percentage of the loans in the bank's CRA assessment area that a particular subject community receives. The loan origination percentage is a measure of what the market determines to be the creditworthy portion of the loan demand from a subject community. For example, if 10% of the loans in the bank's CRA assessment area go to predominantly minority neighborhoods, the loan origination percentage for predominantly minority neighborhoods is 10%. If 23% of all loan originations were made to minority persons—whether they live in predominantly minority neighborhoods or not—the loan origination percentage is 23% for minority persons. Under the proposed CRA evaluative criteria, the demand for market-defined creditworthy loans in predominantly minority neighborhoods is 10% and the demand for market-defined creditworthy loans for minority individuals is 23%.

Finally, the third quantitative measure of community credit needs is the denial rate ratio—the percentage of applications from a subject community that is denied (the "denial rate") divided by the denial rate for the subject community's control community. The control communities share the characteristics of the subject community except for the characteristic under review. The assumption is that the control communities are treated without discrimination. The denial rate ratio is a way to identify the percentage of market-defined creditworthy applicants in each subject community relative to a control community. The denial rate ratio is also an important predictor of lending, since a decrease in the denial rate ratio in a community has been shown to be consistent with increased lending.[29] The particular control community for each subject community is:

1. LMI neighborhoods—upper-income ("UI") neighborhoods;
2. LMI individuals—UI individuals;
3. Predominantly minority neighborhoods—predominantly white neighborhoods; and
4. Minority individuals—white individuals.[30]

For example, if the denial rate for applications from minority individuals is 40% and the denial rate for its control community—white applicants—is 20%, the denial rate ratio for minority individuals is 2 (40/20=2). This means that in the bank's community, according to the market, twice as many white applicants than minority applicants are creditworthy. This, of course, does not account for discrimination in the loan marketplace, which may result in the market overstating the difference in creditworthiness between white and minority applicants.

The benefit of using market-based benchmarks for measuring credit needs comes at a cost. The benefit is that the market establishes a quantitative benchmark of credit needs that is not a quota. The market does not allocate credit; it is what it is. The cost of using market-based standards to measure credit needs, however, is significant. The market very likely underestimates credit needs because there is strong evidence that the market includes discrimination against the subject communities.[31] Thus, the application percentages for the subject communities are probably lower than the actual demand for loans, the loan origination percentages for each subject community probably underestimate the true percentage of creditworthy applicants, and the denial rate ratios are probably higher than they would be if the subject communities were treated equally. Despite this cost, the market is a useful way to measure community credit needs because it is quantitative and does not allocate credit. It does not set a predetermined lending quota. The proposed quantitative market-based measures of community credit needs are thus based on the conclusion that the benefits of using the market as a basis for measuring credit needs outweigh it deficiencies.

Chapter five described several other benchmarks that the federal banking agencies used in the PEs. On their face, these benchmarks appear not to reflect discrimination. These include the percentage of LMI persons in the bank's CRA assessment area and the percentage of owner-occupied housing units. Another possible benchmark is the percentage of minority persons in the bank's CRA assessment area. These benchmarks are not employed in the proposed criteria for two main reasons. First, these benchmarks might actually reflect discrimination as well. For example, the percentage of minority persons in the bank's CRA assessment area might reflect housing discrimination. Second, as demonstrated in the performance evaluations examined in chapter five, it is too easy to excuse poor bank performance compared with these benchmarks, by, for example, stating that housing is too costly for LMI persons to afford. Using the market as a benchmark precludes this excuse because the market controls for affordability.

Quantitative Measures of Bank Lending

The proposed standards employ five quantitative measures of bank lending in each subject community. The first quantitative measure of bank lending is the percentage of the bank's applications from each subject community. Thus, if 15% of the bank's loan applications are from LMI persons, its loan application percentage for LMI persons is 15%. The application percentage is a good indicator of a bank's efforts to solicit business in a particular community or among a particular group of persons.[32] This measure may be reminiscent of the efforts-oriented criteria of the final CRA enforcement regime, but there is a key difference in that this measure is quantitative and measures a meaningful result.

The second quantitative measure of bank lending is the percentage of the bank's loan originations to each subject community. For example, if 20% of the bank's loans are in LMI neighborhoods, the bank's loan origination percentage for LMI neighborhoods is 20%. The loan origination percentage thus measures the bank's record at meeting the demand for loans in the subject communities.

The third quantitative measure of bank lending is the bank's denial rate ratio for each subject community. The denial rate ratio measures the bank's treatment of loan applicants from the subject communities relative to its treatment of loan applicants from the control communities. For example, if the bank's denial rate for minority applicants is 20% and its denial rate for white applicants is 10%, the bank's denial rate ratio for minority applicants is two.

The denial rate ratio is not used to determine whether a bank is engaging in discriminatory lending practices against a subject community. Instead, the denial rate ratio determines how a bank treats members of the subject communities relative to members of the control communities.[33]

The next two quantitative measures of bank lending are the bank's market share of applications from each subject community and the bank's market share of loans in each subject community. These measures are similar to the market share test from the first set of proposed CRA regulations in 1993. They measure the percentage of the bank's applications from and loans to each subject community within the market as a whole. For example, if 1,000 loan applications in the bank's entire community are from minority persons, and a bank received 10 of them, its market share of applications from LMI persons is 1%. If 5,000 loans in the bank's entire community are to LMI neighborhoods and the bank made 500 of them, its market share of loan originations in LMI neighborhoods is 10%.[34]

Objective Standards for Evaluating Bank Lending

The next part of the proposal contains the objective standards for evaluating whether the bank's lending meets the quantitative benchmarks of credit needs of the community. The standards evaluate a bank based on a comparison of the quantitative measures of a bank's lending with the corresponding quantitative benchmark of community credit needs. Thus, the standards evaluate the bank's application percentage for each subject community compared with the overall application percentage for all lenders (the "aggregate") for each subject community in the bank's geographic area, the bank's loan origination percentage for each subject community compared with the aggregate loan origination percentage for each subject community in the bank's geographic community, and the bank's denial rate ratio for each subject community compared with the aggregate denial rate ratio for each subject community in the bank's geographic area. Second, the standards compare the bank's market share of applications and loan originations in each subject community with its market share of applications and loan originations in the corresponding control community. As shown in the list below, there are thus twenty comparisons, all of which are based on straightforward mathematical calculations:[35]

LENDING EVALUATION COMPARISONS

Loan Application Percentage

1. Percentage of applications from minority persons: bank compared with ("cf.") aggregate
2. Percentage of applications from LMI persons: bank cf. aggregate
3. Percentage of applications from predominantly minority neighborhoods: bank cf. aggregate
4. Percentage of applications from LMI neighborhoods: bank cf. aggregate

Loan Origination Percentage

5. Percentage of loan originations to minority persons: bank cf. aggregate
6. Percentage of loan originations to LMI persons: bank cf. aggregate
7. Percentage of loan originations to predominantly minority neighborhoods: bank cf. aggregate
8. Percentage of loan originations to LMI neighborhoods: bank cf. aggregate

Denial Rate Ratio

9. Denial rate ratio—minority applicants/white applicants: bank cf. aggregate
10. Denial rate ratio—LMI applicants/UI applicants: bank cf. aggregate
11. Denial rate ratio—predominantly minority neighborhoods/predominantly white neighborhoods: bank cf. aggregate
12. Denial rate ratio—LMI neighborhoods/UI neighborhoods: bank cf. aggregate

Market Share of Applications

13. Market share of applications from minority applicants cf. market share from white applicants
14. Market share of applications from LMI applicants cf. market share from UI applicants
15. Market share of loan applications from predominantly minority neighborhoods cf. market share from predominantly white neighborhoods
16. Market share of loan applications from LMI neighborhoods cf. market share from UI neighborhoods

Market Share of Loan Originations

17. Market share of loan originations to minority borrowers cf. market share to white borrowers

18. Market share of loan originations to LMI borrowers cf. market share to UI borrowers
19. Market share of loan originations to predominantly minority neighborhoods cf. market share to predominantly white neighborhoods
20. Market share of loan originations to LI neighborhoods cf. market share to UI neighborhoods

The proposed criteria use three objective standards for making these comparisons: higher; equal; and lower. If the bank's percentage on a particular measure is equal to or higher than the aggregate percentage, it is meeting the credit needs of the community on that particular measure. If a bank's percentage is lower than the aggregate, it is not meeting the credit needs of the community on that measure.[36] Thus, for example, if the bank's application percentage for minority individuals is higher than the aggregate application percentage for minority individuals in the bank's CRA assessment area, it is meeting the need to make credit available to minority persons. On the other hand, if a bank's loan origination percentage to LMI neighborhoods is lower than the aggregate loan origination percentage to LMI neighborhoods in the bank's CRA assessment area, it is not meeting the need for loans in LMI neighborhoods. If the bank's denial rate ratio for LMI neighborhoods is lower than the aggregate denial rate ratio in the bank's CRA assessment area, the bank is treating applications from LMI neighborhoods more favorably than the market. If the bank's market share of applications or loan originations is higher in a subject community than in a control community, it is meeting that community's credit needs; if its market share is lower, it is not.

Criteria for Evaluating Community Development Investments, Grants, and Services

The proposal includes four criteria for evaluating a bank's community development loans, investments, grants, and services.[37] The criteria compare the bank's community development loan/asset ratio, community development investment/asset ratio, and community development grant/asset ratio with the aggregate ratios for all banks in the bank's community. The criterion for community development services evaluates whether the bank offers certain community development services commensurate with its size. These services include technical assistance to community development organizations, seminars on topics such as financial literacy, membership on boards of directors of community development organizations, providing credit counseling, and offering individual development accounts.

Criteria for Evaluating Retail Banking Services

The proposal includes several criteria for evaluating a bank's retail banking services.[38]

1. Percentage of the bank's branches in LMI neighborhoods compared with the aggregate percentage of all banks' branches in the bank's CRA assessment area;
2. Percentage of the bank's branches in predominantly minority neighborhoods compared with the aggregate percentage;
3. Percentage of the bank's alternative physical delivery systems (e.g. ATMs or loan production offices) in LMI neighborhoods compared with the aggregate percentage;
4. Percentage of the bank's alternative physical delivery systems in predominantly minority neighborhoods compared with the aggregate percentage;
5. Percentage of usage by LMI persons of non-physical delivery systems (e.g. telephone, internet) compared with the percentage of LMI persons in the bank's CRA assessment area;
6. Percentage of usage by minority persons of non-physical delivery systems compared with the percentage of minority persons in the bank's CRA assessment area;
7. Percentage of LMI bank account holders compared with the percentage of LMI persons in the bank's CRA assessment area;
8. Percentage of minority account holders compared with the percentage of minority persons in the bank's CRA assessment area;
9. Total number of low-cost accounts commensurate with the bank's size and resources; and
10. Provision of other services for LMI persons, including low-cost check cashing and bill payment services, low-cost money orders, and multi-lingual literature.

Applying the Proposed CRA Evaluative Criteria to a Bank

A bank will be evaluated for its CRA performance in each of its CRA assessment areas based on the bank's performance on the thirty-four criteria described above: twenty relating to lending; four related to community development investments and services; and ten related to retail banking services. All the lending and community development criteria and the first two retail banking services criteria have equal weight. The remaining eight retail banking service criteria have one-quarter the weight of the other criteria. The effect of this is that approximately 71% of the criteria on which the bank's CRA rating is based relate to the bank's lending performance, 14.5% relate to community development performance, and 14.5% relate to retail banking services performance.[39] These relative weights reflect two things: on the one hand, community development investments are important for community economic viability and retail banking services are an important entry point into the economic mainstream, but on the other hand increasing lending in redlined neighborhoods is the purpose of the CRA.

Scoring the Bank's Performance on Lending, Community Development, and Retail Banking

Lending

A bank will get one of three scores on each of the twenty lending criteria: +1; -1; or 0.[40] A bank will receive +1 each time its loan application percentage or loan origination percentage for a subject community is higher than the aggregate. For each percentage that is lower, a bank will receive -1. For each percentage that is equal, a bank will receive 0. For denial rate ratios, a bank will receive +1 each time its denial rate ratio for a subject community is lower than the aggregate denial rate ratio, -1 each time its denial rate ratio is higher than the aggregate, and 0 each time it is equal. On the market share comparisons, a bank will receive +1 each time its market share in a subject community is higher than in a control community, -1 each time its market share is lower, and 0 each time it is equal.

A bank's rating on its lending may be adjusted down based on its record of subprime lending. Subprime loans are loans made to a borrower with a weak credit history or repayment capacity. Subprime loans charge higher interest rates than prime loans.[41] If a bank's percentage of applications for subprime loans from and subprime loan originations to a subject community is higher than the industry average, any +1 or 0 score it receives for that subject community will be changed to -1.[42] The reason for the reduction is that if the bank's percentage of subprime loans to a subject community is higher than the industry average, it may be targeting that community for subprime loans or steering community members who may be eligible for prime loans to subprime loans.[43] As a result, borrowers who are eligible for prime loans may be forced to borrow at subprime rates, at greater cost to them.

Community Development Loans, Investments, Grants, and Services

The bank will get +1, -1, or 0 on each of its community development loan/asset ratio, community development investment/asset ratio, and community development grant/asset ratio comparisons. If a ratio is higher than the aggregate, the bank will receive +1, if it is lower it will receive -1, and if it is equal it will receive 0. The bank will receive +1 or -1 on its community development services record; +1 if it offers sufficient services and -1 if it does not.

Retail Banking Services

On the first eight criteria for evaluating a bank's retail services, a bank will receive +1 if its percentage is higher than the relevant benchmark, 0 if its percentage is equal, and -1 if its percentage is lower than the benchmark. On the final two criteria, it will receive +1 if it opens and maintains a sufficient number of low-cost bank accounts and -1 if it does not, and +1 if it offers sufficient other services and -1 if it does not. The bank's overall score on the service test will be derived by adding a bank's scores on the first two standards relating to branches and adding that total to one-fourth the total on the remaining eight criteria.

Example

Tables 8.1, 8.2 and 8.3 show how the hypothetical "X Bank" would be evaluated for CRA performance in "Y CRA Assessment Area."

Assigning a CRA Rating to a Bank

A bank will receive a CRA rating for each of its CRA assessment areas and an overall CRA rating for all its assessment areas combined. Once the bank's score is tabulated for a particular CRA assessment areas, it will receive one of three CRA ratings. If the bank's total score is higher than zero, it will receive a rating of "better than average" record of helping to meet the credit needs of the community. If the bank's score is zero it will receive a rating of "average"

Tables 8.1–8.3: X Bank CRA Performance Evaluation
Y CRA Assessment Area

Table 8.1 Lending

	Bank	Community	+/0/-
	Loan Application Percentage		
1. Minority applicants	29.4	31.0	-1
2. LMI applicants	12.3	11.4	+1
3. Minority neighborhoods	10.8	14.3	-1
4. LMI neighborhoods	10.3	10.9	-1
	Loan Origination Percentage		
5. Minority applicants	26.2	30.0	-1
6. LMI applicants	10.1	9.1	+1
7. Minority neighborhoods	9.4	10.7	-1
8. LMI neighborhoods	9.4	8.5	+1
	Denial Rate Ratio		
9. Minority/white applicants	1.7	1.6	-1
10. LMI/UI applicants	2.0	1.8	-1
11. Minority/white neighborhoods	1.6	1.7	+1
12. LMI/UI neighborhoods	1.1	1.3	+1
	Subject Community	**Control Community**	**+/0/-**
	Market Share-Applications		
13. Applicants-race	1.0	1.2	-1
14. Applicants-income	1.2	1.1	+1
15. Neighborhoods-race	0.8	1.1	-1
16. Neighborhoods-income	1.1	1.2	-1
	Market Share-Originations		
17. Applicants-race	1.1	1.3	-1
18. Applicants-income	1.3	1.2	+1
19. Neighborhoods-race	1.0	1.2	-1
20. Neighborhoods-income	1.3	1.1	+1
Subtotal: Lending			**-4**

Table 8.2 Community Development Investments and Services

	Bank	Community	+/0/-
21. CD Loan/Asset Ratio	.06	.05	+1
22. CD Investment/Asset Ratio	.05	.06	-1
23. CD Grant/Asset Ratio	.01	.03	-1
24. CD Services	Yes	N/A	+1
Subtotal: Community Development			**0**

Table 8.3 Retail Banking Services

	Bank	Community	+/0/-
25. % Branches in LMI n'hoods	0.13	0.11	+1
26. % Branches in min. n'hoods	0.09	0.1	-1
27. % Alternative physical delivery systems in LMI n'hoods	0.8	0.7	+.25
28. % Alternative physical delivery systems in min. n'hoods	0.6	0.7	-0.25
29. % Usage of alternative systems by LMI individuals	0.5	0.6	-0.25
30. % Usage of alternative system by min. individuals	0.4	0.5	-0.25
31. % LMI account holders	0.15	0.14	+1
32. % Min. account holders	0.14	0.20	-1
33. Low-cost accounts	No	N/A	-0.25
34. Other services	Yes	N/A	+0.25
Subtotal: Services			**-0.5**
TOTAL			**-4.5**

record of helping to meet the credit needs of the community. Finally, if the bank's score is less than zero, it will receive a rating of "below average" record of helping to meet community credit needs. There are two adjustment factors. The first involves "predatory" lending. Predatory lending is defined as a set of lending practices that includes making unaffordable loans based on the borrower's assets rather than ability to repay, inducing a borrower to refinance a loan repeatedly in order to charge high points and fees each time the loan is refinanced, or engaging in fraud or deceptive sales tactics.[44] If the bank is engaged in predatory lending practices, its CRA rating will automatically be deemed below average.[45] If the bank has engaged in discriminatory lending practices, its CRA rating will also automatically be reduced to below average.

Because X Bank's overall score in CRA Assessment Area Y was -4.5, its CRA rating for Y CRA Assessment area would be "below average record of meeting community credit needs." X Bank's overall CRA rating would be determined by combining its score for each of its individual CRA assessment areas. For example, assume X Bank received the scores shown in Table 8.4 in each of its CRA assessment areas. With an overall score of -3, X Bank's overall CRA rating would be "below average record of meeting community credit needs."

Table 8.4 X Bank Overall CRA Rating

CRA Assessment Area	Score
Y	-4.5
Z	+1.5
A	+4
B	+1
C	-3
D	-2
Total	-3

Evaluating a Bank Expansion Application

The CRA and its implementing regulations require the appropriate federal banking agency to take account of a bank's CRA rating when considering the bank's application to expand its business.[46] A poor CRA record can result in a denial of the application. This section proposes a methodology for the federal banking agencies to employ when evaluating a bank's CRA record in connection with an expansion application. The methodology is designed to ensure consistent and predictable decisions. The methodology uses the quantitative measures and benchmarks and objective standards of the proposed CRA performance evaluation, but does not apply them mechanistically and thus avoids credit allocation.

The proposed methodology creates two rebuttable presumptions for deciding applications. First, a bank with an overall CRA rating of below average record of meeting the credit needs of the community should have its application for a deposit facility denied absent mitigating factors. Second, a bank with an average or above average CRA rating should have its application granted absent aggravating factors. The federal banking agencies would, in their decisions on applications, using reason and precedent, create a "common law" of mitigating and aggravating factors that could, if of sufficient weight, rebut these presumptions. There are several possible mitigating and aggravating factors. Mitigating factors could include whether the bank improved its performance since it received its CRA rating, whether its score was close to an average rating, whether the bank's quantitative performance measures were close to the corresponding credit needs benchmarks, and whether the bank had an above average rating in the community or communities affected by the merger application. Aggravating factors could include whether the bank's CRA performance deteriorated since it received its CRA rating, whether it had a below average CRA rating in the community or communities affected by the rating, or whether it had a particularly poor score on the lending, community development services, or retail banking services component of the evaluation. If the bank was engaged in discriminatory or predatory lending practices, this would result in denial of the application. The federal banking agencies would also determine, based on reason and precedent, the weight each of these mitigating and aggravating factors should have. For example, if the hypothetical X Bank in the above example submitted an application to merge with a bank in Y CRA Assessment Area, there would be a rebuttable presumption that its application should be denied because its CRA rating is less than average record of meeting the credit needs of the community. Mitigating factors in favor of rebutting this presumption would include that X Bank's score was -3, which is close to the score necessary for an "average rating"; X Bank's scores on the community development activities and retail banking services components in Y Assessment Area were close to the score necessary for an "average rating"; and several of X Bank's below-average quantitative measures were relatively close to the benchmark. For example, the bank's minority loan application percentage was 29.4% compared with the 31.0% benchmark. The ultimate decision on the application would be based on these factors, the existence of other mitigating or aggravating factors, and the weight of these factors based on precedent. Although this methodology for deciding applications has subjective elements, it is based on quantitative measures and benchmarks and objective standards, and can be consistent and predictable if the federal banking agencies establish clear mitigating and aggravating factors and apply them consistently, equally, and based on reason and precedent.

Conclusion

The proposed CRA criteria evaluate lending, community development activities, and retail banking services. The evaluative criteria are composed of quantitative measures of bank lending, quantitative benchmarks of the credit needs of the community, and objective terms for evaluating whether a bank's lending meets community credit needs. The proposed criteria will maximize the CRA's potential for democratizing capital. They create consistent and predictable standards, thus making it easier for both the banking agencies and community groups to hold a bank accountable for a poor lending record. The proposed criteria also will help ensure that all creditworthy individuals who want a loan will get a loan because the objective standards hold a bank to quantitative benchmarks of credit needs and are designed to ensure that a bank is doing at least as well as average.

The proposed criteria democratize capital without allocating credit. The proposed criteria do not establish lending quotas or contain mandatory penalties for failing to comply. Rather than requiring banks to make a predetermined number or dollar amount of loans, the proposed criteria compare a bank's lending record with a benchmark established by the market as a whole. In addition, the proposed criteria consider aspects of a bank's record other than loan originations, including its record of receiving applications and its record of denying applications. Finally, a CRA rating of below average does not automatically lead to a denial of a bank's expansion application, which is the only tangible penalty for a poor CRA record.

Recalling the words of Senator Sarbanes in the debates over the CRA, the CRA is "the best opportunity we have" to provide investment in redlined neighborhoods.[47] The evaluative criteria proposed in this book ensure we will take full advantage of this opportunity.

Endnotes

INTRODUCTION

1. 12 U.S.C. §§2901-2908 (2000).

2. *See* Gregory D. Squires, Capital and Communities in Black and White 69 (1994) ("More importantly, the law created organizing opportunities for community groups to influence mortgage lending policies of private financial institutions."); John Taylor & Josh Silver, *The Essential Role of Activism in Community Reinvestment*, *in* Organizing Access to Capital: Advocacy and the Democratization of Financial Institutions 171, 172 (Gregory D. Squires ed., 2003) (The CRA "has created a democratic dialogue between community groups and banks. It mandates that banks meet the credit needs of all the communities in which they are chartered and from which they take deposits. Ultimately, the only way banks can do this is to listen as communities articulate their credit needs."); Donald A. Lash, *The Community Development Banking Act and the Evaluation of Credit Allocation Policies*, 7 J. Aff. Hous. 385, 398 (1998) (describing the early twentieth-ctury movement to "democratize credit").

3. *See* Taylor, *supra* note 2, at 182 ("The CRA achieves higher loans and investments for traditionally underserved communities through a process of information sharing, evaluation, debate, and compromise.").

4. The CRA has also helped bring people into the economic mainstream by influencing banks to provide retail banking services and invest in community development projects in low-income, inner-city, and predominantly minority neighborhoods. Chapter eight addresses retail banking services and investments.

5. 12 U.S.C. §2901(a)(3)(2000).

6. *Id.* at §2903(a)(1).

7. The four federal banking agencies that enforce the CRA are the Board of Governors of the Federal Reserve System ("Federal Reserve"), the Office of the Comptroller of the Currency ("OCC"), the Federal Deposit Insurance Corporation ("FDIC"), and the Office of Thrift Supervision ("OTS"). *Id.* §2902(1). Each agency regulates a different type of bank and all the agencies have adopted CRA regulations. The agencies, the banks they regulate, and the location of their CRA regulations are shown in Table A below.

8. 12 U.S.C. §§2901(b), 2903(a)(2), and 2906.

Table A

Agency	Jurisdiction	Regulations
OCC	National banks	12 C.F.R. pt. 25 (2003)
Federal Reserve	State-chartered banks that are members of the Federal Reserve System	12 C.F.R. pt. 228 (2003)
FDIC	State-chartered banks that are not members of the Federal Reserve System	12 C.F.R. pt. 345 (2003)
OTS	Savings and loans	12 C.F.R. pt. 563e (2003)

9. *See* Taylor, *supra* note 2, at 171.

10. NATIONAL COMMUNITY REINVESTMENT COALITION, CRA COMMITMENTS 1997-1998.

11. *See* BLACK'S LAW DICTIONARY 1283 (7th ed. 1999) ("[Redlining is] credit discrimination (usually unlawful discrimination) by a financial institution that refuses to make loans on properties in allegedly bad neighborhoods."); GLENN B. CANNER, BOARD OF GOVERNORS OF THE FEDERAL RESERVE SYSTEM, REDLINING: RESEARCH AND FEDERAL LEGISLATIVE RESPONSE 1 & n.2 (1982); Katherine L. Bradbury et al., *Geographic Patterns of Mortgage Lending in Boston, 1982–1987*, NEW ENG. ECON. REV., Sept.–Oct. 1989, at 3.

12. This efforts-oriented approach is not the only approach to correcting an information failure in the market. The agencies could have evaluated whether the banks had corrected this information failure by measuring their outputs in the form of loans. The author thanks Josh Silver, vice president for policy analysis and research of the National Community Reinvestment Coalition, for this point.

13. *Community Reinvestment Act: Hearings Before the Subcomm. on Financial Institutions & Consumer Credit of the House Comm. on Banking and Financial Services*, 104th Cong. 148 (1995) (prepared statement of Eugene A. Ludwig, Comptroller, Office of the Comptroller of the Currency) ("[N]o other set of bank regulations was so universally criticized by bankers and customers than these regulations, criticized precisely because they created needless burdens on the one hand and failed to fulfill the promise of the Community Reinvestment Act on the other."), *reprinted in* OFF. OF THE COMPTROLLER OF THE CURRENCY Q.J., June 1995, at 37; *Existing Efforts to End the Crisis: A Report Card: Hearing Before the Subcomm. on Consumer Credit and Insurance of the House Comm. on Banking, Finance & Urban Affairs*, 103d Cong. 55 (1993) (prepared statement of Lawrence B. Lindsey, governor, Board of Governors of the Federal Reserve System), *reprinted in* 79 FED. RES. BULL. 285 (1993); *Plans and Progress to Date of Interagency CRA Regulatory Reform Effort: Hearing Before the Subcomm. on General Oversight, Investigations, & the*

Resolution of Failed Financial Institutions of the House Comm. on Banking, Finance & Urban Affairs, 103d Cong. 36 (1993) (prepared statement of Eugene A. Ludwig, Comptroller, Office of the Comptroller of the Currency), *reprinted in* OFF. OF THE COMPTROLLER OF THE CURRENCY Q.J., Dec. 1993, at 27; U.S. GEN. ACCOUNTING OFFICE, COMMUNITY REINVESTMENT ACT: CHALLENGES REMAIN TO SUCCESSFULLY IMPLEMENT CRA 5 (1995).

CHAPTER ONE

1. The CRA was passed as Pub. L. No. 95-128, tit. VIII, 91 Stat. 1111, 1147–48 (codified at 12 U.S.C. §§2901–2908 (2000)). The notion that it is possible to discern legislative intent has been the subject of severe criticism. *See, e.g.*, WILLIAM N. ESKRIDGE, JR. ET AL., LEGISLATIVE AND STATUTORY INTERPRETATION 211–47 (2000). Despite these criticisms, discerning legislative intent remains a legitimate, necessary, and possible exercise in a democratic society. *See* M.B.W. Sinclair, *Statutory Reasoning*, 46 DRAKE L. REV. 299 (1997).

2. The four federal agencies responsible for enforcing the CRA are the Board of Governors of the Federal Reserve System, the Office of the Comptroller of the Currency, the Federal Deposit Insurance Corporation, and the Office of Thrift Supervision. 12 U.S.C. §2902(1)(2000). *See supra* Introduction, note 7 for further information about the federal banking agencies.

3. The purpose of this effort to discern Congress' intent in passing the CRA is somewhat different from the purpose which is the subject of the criticism described in ESKRIDGE, JR. ET AL., *supra* note 1. There, the criticism focused on efforts to discern the purpose of a statute in a "hard case," when the language of a statute does not cover a specific fact scenario. Here, the purpose is to determine the potential range of regulations the federal banking agencies could promulgate consistent with Congress' grant of authority to establish regulations enforcing the CRA. *See* Chevron U.S.A., Inc. v. Natural Res. Def. Council, Inc., 467 U.S. 837 (1984). Based on the legislative history, it is within the realm of agency discretion to issue regulations that contain quantitative measures and objective standards as long as they do not allocate credit. *See Chevron*, 467 U.S. at 842–44 (ruling that, in adopting a regulation, a federal agency does not exceed its discretion if the regulation is 1) not contrary to Congress' "directly" expressed intent with respect to the "precise" issue governed by the regulation, and 2) a reasonable construction of the statute that the agency is congressionally-charged with administering). Subsequent chapters will investigate whether such regulations are conceivable.

4. *President Clinton's Community Reinvestment Act Reform Initiative and Enforcement of Federal Fair Lending Laws: Hearing Before the Subcomm. on Consumer Credit and Insurance of the House Comm. on Banking, Finance, and Urban Affairs*, 103d Cong. 130 (1993) (statement of Lawrence B. Lindsey, Governor, Federal Reserve Board), *reprinted in* 79 FED. RES. BULL. 1127, 1128 (1993).

5. *Id.*

6. For a description of redlining and capital export, *see Community Reinvestment Act: Hearings Before the S. Comm. on Banking, Housing, and Urban Affairs*, 100th Cong. 239 (1988) (statement of Robert L. Clarke, Comptroller, Office of the Comptroller of

the Currency), *reprinted in* Off. of the Comptroller of the Currency Q.J. 7-2, June 1988, at 37; 123 Cong. Rec. 17,630 (1977) (statement of Sen. Proxmire).

7. *See supra* ch. 1, n. 11.

8. *See* H.R. Conf. Rep. No. 95-634, at 76 (1977), *reprinted in* 1977 U.S.C.C.A.N. 2,965, 2,995; 123 Cong. Rec. 31, 887 (1977) (statement of Sen. Proxmire).

9. *See* 123 Cong. Rec at 17,630 (statement of Sen. Proxmire); *Community Credit Needs: Hearings on S. 406 Before the S. Comm. on Banking, Hous., and Urban Affairs, 95th Cong.* 41 (1977).

10. *See* 123 Cong. Rec. 17,603, 17,630–31 (statements of Sen. Proxmire), *id.* at 17,625–17,626 (statement of Sen. Morgan); *id.* at 17,632 (statement of Sen. Morgan); *id.* at 1,958 (statement of Sen. Proxmire); *Hearings on S. 406, supra* note 9, at 141–47, 153, 168.

11. *See* 123 Cong. Rec. 17,630 (statement of Sen. Proxmire).

12. *See id.*; *id.* at 1,958 (statement of Sen. Proxmire).

13. *Id.* at 17,630 (statement of Sen. Proxmire).

14. *Id.*

15. *Id.*

16. *Hearings on S. 406, supra* note 9, at 2.

17. *See* 123 Cong. Rec. 17,630, 31,888 (1977) (statements of Sen. Proxmire).

18. *Id.* at 17,630 (1977) (statement of Sen. Proxmire).

19. *Id.*

20. *Id.*

21. *Hearings on S. 406, supra* note 9, at 2 (statement of Sen. Proxmire).

22. 123 Cong. Rec. 17,630 (1977) (statement of Sen. Proxmire).

23. *Hearings on* S. *406, supra* note 9, at 2 (statement of Sen. Proxmire).

24. 123 Cong. Rec. 17,633 (1977) (statement of Sen. Sarbanes).

25. *See* Comm. on Banking, Housing, & Urban Affairs, 102d Cong., Report on the Status of the Community Reinvestment Act: Views and Recommendations 10, 70, 79 (Comm. Print 1992) [hereinafter Views and Recommendations]; 123 Cong. Rec. 17,604 (1977) (statement of Sen. Proxmire); Remarks on Signing H.R. 6655 into Law, 1977 Pub. Papers 1777 (Oct. 12, 1977).

26. 123 Cong. Rec. 17,604 (1977) (statement of Sen. Proxmire).

27. S. Rep. No. 95-175, at 33–35 (1977); *see* 123 Cong. Rec. 1958 (1977) (statement of Sen. Proxmire); Views and Recommendations, *supra* note 20, at 17, 70, 79; Statement of the Federal Financial Supervisory Agencies Regarding the Community Reinvestment Act, 54 Fed. Reg. 13742 (Apr. 5, 1989) ("The agencies believe that the CRA intends financial institutions to help meet the credit needs of their communities in a positive, ongoing way...."); William C. Gruben et al., *Imperfect Information and the Community Reinvestment Act*, Fed. Res. Bank of San Francisco Econ. Rev., Summer 1990, at 27, 36; Eugene A. Ludwig, Equal Credit Opportunity, Remarks Before the National CDFI Institute (Jan. 31, 1994), *reprinted in* Off. of the Comptroller of the Currency Q.J. 13-2, June 1994, at 37, 38.

28. *Hearings on S. 406, supra* note 9, at 154 (statement of Sen. Proxmire).

29. 123 Cong. Rec. 17,630 (1977) (statement of Sen. Proxmire). *See also id.* at 31,887–88 (statement of Sen. Proxmire); S. Rep. No. 90-175, at 33, 35.

30. *Hearings on S. 406*, *supra* note 9, at 2 (statement of Sen. Proxmire).
31. 123 CONG. REC 17,631 (1977) (statement of Sen. Proxmire).
32. *Id.* at 31,887.
33. *See Hearings on S. 406*, *supra* note 9, at 2 (statement of Sen. Proxmire).
34. S. REP. NO. 95-175, at 33.
35. *Hearings on S. 406*, *supra* note 9, at 152–53 (statement of Sen. Tower).
36. 123 CONG. REC. 17,625 (1977) (statement of Sen. Morgan).
37. S. REP. NO. 95-175, at 81. Three heads of federal banking agencies similarly were opposed to the CRA's provisions yet supported its purpose, as reflected in their written comments to Senator Morgan on the legislation. *See* 123 CONG. REC. 17,628 (1977) (letter of Arthur F. Burns, Chairman, Federal Reserve Board (May 23, 1977)); *id.* at 17,628–29 (letter of Garth Marston, Chairman, Federal Home Loan Bank Board (May 18, 1977)); *id.* at 17,629 (letter of Robert Bloom, Acting Comptroller of the Currency, Office of the Comptroller of the Currency (June 2, 1977)).
38. Pub. L. No. 95-128, 91 Stat. 1111 (codified as amended at 12 U.S.C. §§2901–2908 (2000) and 42 U.S.C. §§1490h, 5318 (2000)).
39. H.R. CONF. REP. NO. 95-634, at 76.
40. *Id.*
41. *Hearings on S. 406*, *supra* note 9, at 1 (statement of Sen. Proxmire).
42. 123 CONG. REC. 1958 (1977) (statement of Sen. Proxmire).
43. *Id.* at 17,603; *see Hearings on S. 406*, *supra* note 9, at 323 (statement of Sen. Proxmire).
44. H.R. CONF. REP. NO. 95-634, at 76.
45. 123 CONG. REC. 17,630 (1977) (statement of Sen. Proxmire).
46. *Id.* at 1,958.
47. *Id.*
48. *Id.*; *see Hearings on S. 406*, *supra* note 9, at 1 (statement of Sen. Proxmire).
49. 123 CONG. REC. 1,958 (1977) (statement of Sen. Proxmire).
50. *Id.*
51. *Id.*; *see* 12 C.F.R. pt. 217, 329.2 (2003) (prohibiting payment of interest on demand deposits).
52. *See* 123 CONG. REC. 1,958 (1977) (statement of Sen. Proxmire); *see also, e.g.*, N.Y. BANKING LAW §32 (McKinney 2001) (requiring New York State chartered banks to purchase deposit insurance); S. REP. NO. 94-187, at 11 (1975) ("lending institutions.... are supplied a substantial government benefit from the Federal government in terms of insurance" (quoting Robert Embry, Jr., Baltimore Commissioner of Housing)); 12 U.S.C. §329 (2000); CARL FELSENFELD, BANKING REGULATION IN THE UNITED STATES 71–73 (2001); KENNETH F. HALL, THE COMPLIANCE GUIDE TO UNITED STATES BANKING LAWS AND REGULATIONS 56 (1997).
53. 123 CONG. REC. 1958 (1977) (statement of Sen. Proxmire); *see* 12 U.S.C. §§301, 347–347b, 357 (2000); 12 C.F.R. pt. 201 (2002); HALL, *supra* note 52, at 110. The Federal Home Loan Banking System provides discounted long term loans to its members for their use in making home mortgage loans. 12 U.S.C. §1430(a)(2002).
54. S. 406, 95th Cong. §4(1)(C) (1977), *reprinted in Hearings on S. 406*, *supra* note 9, at 5; *see* 123 CONG. REC. 1958 (1977) (statement of Sen. Proxmire); CONSUMER

Advisory Council of the Board of Governors of the Federal Reserve System, The Federal Reserve's Implementation of The Community Reinvestment Act of 1977 app. B, at 1 (1983) [hereinafter CRA Implementation].

55. *See* CRA Implementation, *supra* note 54, app. B, at 1.

56. *See* S. Rep. No. 95-175, at 34.

57. *See id.*

58. *Id.*

59. *Id.*

60. *Id.*

61. 123 Cong. Rec. 17,630 (1977) (statement of Sen. Proxmire).

62. *See Hearings on S. 406*, *supra* note 9, at 394 (statement of Sen. Proxmire).

63. *See id.*

64. *Id.*

65. *See* 123 Cong. Rec. 17,628 (1977) (letter of Arthur F. Burns, Chairman, Federal Reserve Board, to Sen. Morgan (May 23, 1977)).

66. *See id.*

67. *Hearings on S. 406*, *supra* note 9, at 154 (statement of Sen. Proxmire).

68. *Id.*

69. S. Rep. No. 95-175, at 33; *see id.* at 35; 123 Cong. Rec. 17,631, 31,887 (1977) (statements of Sen. Proxmire).

70. 123 Cong. Rec. 31,887 (1977) (statement of Sen. Proxmire).

71. *Id.* at 32,133 (statement of Rep. Ashley).

72. S. Rep. No. 95-175, at 33–34; 123 Cong. Rec. 31,887 (1977) (statement of Sen. Proxmire).

73. 123 Cong. Rec. 31,888 (1977) (statement of Sen. Proxmire); *see id.* at 17,603. Arthur Burns, Chairman of the Federal Reserve at the time, suggested that this was a weak sanction for violating the law. *Id.* at 17,628 (letter of Arthur F. Burns to Sen. Morgan (May 23, 1977)). Senator Lugar, another opponent of the CRA, agreed. *See id.* at 17,633 (statement of Sen. Lugar).

74. S. Rep. No. 95-175, at 34.

75. 123 Cong. Rec. 17,630 (1977) (statement of Sen. Proxmire).

76. *See* S. Rep. No. 95-175, at 34; 123 Cong. Rec. 17,630–31 (1977) (statement of Sen. Proxmire).

77. S. Rep. No. 95-175, at 34.

78. *Id.*

79. *Id.*

80. 123 Cong. Rec. 17,628–29 (1977) (reprinting letters in opposition to the CRA by the heads of Federal Reserve, the Federal Home Loan Bank Board (now the Office of Thrift Supervision), and the Office of the Comptroller of the Currency).

81. *Hearings on S. 406*, *supra* note 9, at 153 (statement of Sen. Tower).

82. S. Rep. No. 95-175, at 82.

83. 123 Cong. Rec. 17,628 (1977) (statement of Sen. Morgan).

84. *Id.* at 17,633 (statement of Sen. Lugar).

85. *Id.* (statement of Sen. Tower).

86. *Id.* at 17,636 (statement of Sen. Schmitt).

87. S. Rep. No. 95-175, at 82.

88. *Id.*

89. *Id.* at 83.

90. *Id.*; *see* 123 Cong. Rec. 17,629 (1977) (letter of Garth Marston, Chairman, Federal Home Loan Bank Board, to Sen. Morgan (May 18, 1977)) ("[The CRA] reflects a basic misunderstanding as respects the sources of savings and the areas in need of mortgage credit.").

91. S. Rep. No. 95-175, at 82.

92. 123 Cong. Rec. 17,633 (1977) (statement of Sen. Tower).

93. *See id.* at 17,636 (statement of Sen. Schmitt).

94. Pub. L. No. 94-200, at §§ 302–311, 89 Stat. 1124, 1125–28 (codified as amended at 12 U.S.C. §§2801–2810 (2000)).

95. *See* 121 Cong. Rec. 25,163 (1975) (statement of Sen. Garn).

96. *Id.*

97. *See* 123 Cong. Rec. 17,625, 17,627 (1977) (statement of Sen. Morgan); *id.* at 17,629 (letter of Garth Marston, Chairman, Federal Home Loan Bank Board, to Sen. Morgan (May 18, 1977)); *id.* at 17,632–33 (statement of Sen. Lugar).

98. S. Rep. No. 95-175, at 84.

99. 123 Cong. Rec. 17,628 (1977) (letter of Arthur F. Burns, Chairman, Federal Reserve, to Sen. Morgan (May 23, 1977)).

100. *See* S. Rep. No. 95-175, at 84; 123 Cong. Rec. 17,625 (1977) (statement of Sen. Morgan); *id.* at 17,628 (letter of Arthur F. Burns, Chairman, Federal Reserve, to Sen. Morgan (May 23, 1977)); *id.* at 17,636 (statement of Sen. Schmitt).

101. *See* S. Rep. No. 95-175, at 84; 123 Cong. Rec. 17,626 (1977) (statement of Sen. Morgan).

102. *See* S. Rep. No. 95-175, at 81–82; 123 Cong. Rec. 17,626–27 (1977) (statement of Sen. Morgan).

103. *See, e.g.*, 123 Cong. Rec. 17,625 (1977) (statement of Sen. Morgan).

104. S. Rep. No. 95-175, at 81.

105. *See id.* at 83; 123 Cong. Rec. 17,626 (1977) (statement of Sen. Morgan).

106. 123 Cong. Rec. 17,628 (1977) (letter of Arthur F. Burns, Chairman, Federal Reserve, to Sen. Morgan (May 23, 1977)).

107. *Id.* at 17,636 (statement of Sen. Schmitt).

108. *See* S. Rep. No. 95-175, at 84.

109. *Id.* at 35.

110. *Hearings on S. 406*, *supra* note 9, at 2 (statement of Sen. Proxmire).

111. *See* 123 Cong. Rec. 1958 (1977) (statement of Sen. Proxmire).

112. *Id.*; CRA Implementation, *supra* note 54, app B.

113. *See* 123 Cong. Rec. 1,958, 17,630, 17,644 (1977) (statements of Sens. Proxmire and Sarbanes).

114. 123 Cong. Rec. 17,633 (1977) (statement of Sen. Sarbanes).

115. *Id.* at 1959 (statement of Sen. Proxmire).

116. *See* National Bank and Trust Co., 1985 OCC Enf. Dec. LEXIS 20, at *83 (Aug. 15, 1985) (stating that the CRA does not require a bank to lend money in its community without regard for the effect the lending has on the safety and sound-

ness of the bank); *see also* 123 CONG. REC. 17,633 (1977) (statement of Sen. Sarbanes); CRA IMPLEMENTATION, *supra* note 54, app. B; Gruben et al., *supra* note 27, at 36.

117. 123 CONG. REC. 1959 (1977) (statement of Sen. Proxmire).

118. *Id.*

119. *Id.* at 1,958.

120. *Id.* at 17,630.

121. Pub. L. No. 101-73, 103 Stat. 183 (codified as amended in scattered sections of 12, 18, & 31 U.S.C. (West 2001 and Supp. 2003)).

122. *See* Pub. L. No. 101-73, §1212(b), 103 Stat. 183, 527 (codified as amended at 12 U.S.C. §2906 (2000)).

123. H.R. CONF. REP. No. 101-222, at 460 (1989), *reprinted in* 1989 U.S.C.C.A.N. 432, 499; *see* 135 CONG. REC. H2,756 (daily ed. June 15, 1989) (statements of Reps. Kaptur and Vento).

124. VIEWS AND RECOMMENDATIONS, *supra* note 25, at 19 (stating that Congress passed the FIRREA amendment in light of continued evidence of redlining, noted in *id.* at 17–18, and the federal regulatory agencies' failure to enforce the CRA effectively).

125. 135 CONG. REC. H2,756 (daily ed. June 15, 1989) (statement of Rep. Vento).

126. *See* Michael Faber & Robert E. Mannion, *Reinvigorated CRA Requires Greater Attention*, A.B.A. BANK COMPLIANCE, Oct. 1989, at 21, 24.

127. H.R. CONF. REP. No. 101-222, at 461, *reprinted in* 1989 U.S.C.A.A.N. 432, 500.

128. 135 CONG. REC. H4,999 (daily ed. Aug. 3, 1989) (statement of Rep. Pelosi). *See supra* text accompanying notes 121–28 for a discussion of FIRREA's amendments to the CRA.

129. Pub. L. No. 102-242, §222, 105 Stat. 2236, 2306 (codified as amended at 12 U.S.C. §§2906(a)(1), (b)(1)(A)(i)–(ii) (2000)).

130. *See* VIEWS AND RECOMMENDATIONS, *supra* note 25, at 19.

131. VIEWS AND RECOMMENDATIONS, *supra* note 25, at 41 (quoting S. REP. No. 102-67, at 112 (1991)).

132. *Id.*, *quoting* S. Rep. No. 102-67 at 112 (1991).

133. Pub. L. No. 102-233, §402(b), 105 Stat. 1761, 1775 (codified as amended at 12 U.S.C. §2907 (2000)).

134. Pub. L. No. 102-550, §§909–910, 106 Stat. 3672, 3874 (codified at 12 U.S.C. §§2901 note, 2903(a)–(b), and 2907(a) (2000)).

135. §909(1), 106 Stat. at 3874 (codified at 12 U.S.C. §2903(b) (2000)).

136. §402(b), 105 Stat. at 1775. The HCDA amendment amended the RTCA amendment by changing "shall be treated as" to "may be a factor in determining whether the depository institution is." §909(2), 105 Stat. at 3874 (codified at 12 U.S.C. §2907(a) (2000)).

137. Pub. L. No. 103-328, §110(a), 108 Stat. 2338, 2364 (codified at 12 U.S.C. §2906(d)–(e) (2000)).

138. S. REP. No. 103-240, at 18 (1994). The FDICIA, discussed *supra* text accompanying notes 129–32, in one of its earlier versions, would have similarly amended the CRA because of the same concern about siphoning deposits from out of state branches. This provision, however, was stricken from the final bill. *See also* S. REP. No. 102-167, at 73 (1991).

139. *See* 140 Cong. Rec. H1,861 (daily ed. Mar. 22, 1994) (statement of Rep. Neal); *id.* at H6,777 (daily ed. Aug. 4, 1994) (statement of Rep. Roukema); *id.* at S12,771–72 (daily ed. Sept. 13, 1994) (statement of Sen. D'Amato).

140. 140 Cong. Rec. S4,765–66 (daily ed. Apr. 25, 1994) (statement of Sen. Riegle).

141. Pub. L. No. 106-102, §101, 113 Stat. 1338, 1341 (1999) (codified at 12 U.S.C. §§78, 377 (2000)); *see* David L. Glass, *The Gramm-Leach-Bliley Act: An Overview of the Key Provisions,* 17 N.Y.L. Sch. J. Hum. Rts. 1 (2001).

142. §§ 102–103(a), 103(c), 113 Stat. at 1342–49, 1351 (codified at 12 U.S.C. §§ 1841(n), 1841(p)–(q), 1843(c)(8), 1843(k)–(o), 1850, and 1864(f) (2000)).

143. §§ 103(b), 711–712, 714, 113 Stat. at 1350, 1465–70 (codified at 12 U.S.C. §§ 1811 note, 1831y, 2903(c), and 2908 (2000)); *see* Richard D. Marsico, *Foreword: Financial Modernization: The Effect of the Repeal of the Glass-Steagall Act on Consumers and Communities,* 17 N.Y.L. Sch. J. Hum. Rts. iii–iv (2001).

144. *See* §§103(b), 711–712, 113 Stat. at 1350, 1465–69 (codified at 12 U.S.C. §§2903(c), 1831y, 2908 (2000)); Marsico, *supra* note 143, at iii–iv.

145. *See* Dean Anason & Barbara A. Rehm, *Democrats Claim CRA Win, All But Guaranteeing Reform,* Am. Banker, Oct. 26, 1999, at 2.

146. *See* Remarks of Deborah Goldberg, *in* Symposium, *Financial Modernization: The Effect of the Repeal of the Glass Steagall Act on Consumers and Communities,* 17 N.Y.L.Sch. J. Hum. Rts. 67 (2001); Dean Anason, *Activists Plan to Press Full Congress for a Pro-Consumer Reform Bill,* Am. Banker, Mar. 31, 1999, at 3; Leslie Wayne, *A Key Senator Again Blocks the Banking Bill,* N.Y. Times, Oct. 22, 1998, at C8.

147. §103(b), 113 Stat. at 1350 (codified at 12 U.S.C. §2903(c)(1) (2000)).

148. §103(a), 113 Stat. at 1342 (codified at 12 U.S.C. §1843(l)(1)–(2) (2000)).

149. §121(a)(2), 113 Stat. at 1373 (codified at 12 U.S.C. §24a (2000)).

150. *Financial Institutions Bill Criticized by Rubin, CRA Advocates,* [Current Developments] Hous. & Dev. Rep. 668 (Feb. 22, 1999); Richard A. Oppel Jr., *Big Gains by Gramm in Diluting Lending Act,* N.Y. Times, Oct. 23, 1999, at C4.

151. Oppel Jr., *supra* note 146, at C4.

152. *See* Gregory D. Squires, *Introduction: The Road to Reinvestment, in* Organizing Access to Capital: Advocacy and the Democratization of Financial Institutions 18 (Gregory D. Squires ed., 2003)(had Congress extended the CRA to all providers of financial services, this would have resulted in a "level playing field that would not disadvantage the federally regulated depository institutions that are now the focus of the law").

153. Matthew Lee, *Community Reinvestment in a Globalizing World: To Hold Banks Accountable, from The Bronx to Buenos Aires, Beijing, and Basel, in* Organizing Access to Capital: Advocacy and the Democratization of Financial Institutions 146 (Gregory D. Squires ed., 2003).

154. §711, 113 Stat. at 1465 (codified at 12 U.S.C. §1831y(a) (2000)).

155. *See id.* (codified at 12 U.S.C. §1831y(e)(1)(B)(iii) (2000)).

156. *Id.* (codified at 12 U.S.C. §1831y(e)(1)(A)(i) (2000)).

157. *Id.* (codified at 12 U.S.C. §1831y(e)(2)(A)–(B) (2000)).

158. *Id.* (codified at 12 U.S.C. §1831y(b) (2000)).

159. *See id.* (codified at 12 U.S.C. §1831y(g) (2000)).

160. *Id.* (codified at 12 U.S.C. §1831y(c)(1), (3) (2000)).

161. *Id.* (codified at 12 U.S.C. §1831y(f)(1)(A) (2000)).

162. *Id.* (codified at 12 U.S.C. §1831y(f)(1)(B) (2000)).

163. *See* Dean Anason, *Treasury, Regulators Say Bill Would Blunt CRA*, AM. BANKER, Feb. 25, 1999, at 2; Editorial, *Mischief From Mr. Gramm*, N.Y. TIMES, Mar. 17, 1999, at A20; Oppel Jr., *supra* note 150, at C4. *See infra*, ch. 6, text accompanying notes 22 to 27, for more about this.

164. The author thanks Josh Silver, vice-president for policy analysis and research at the National Community Reinvestment Coalition, for these points about the possible effects of the CRA "Sunshine" provision.

165. *See* Anason, *supra* note 163, at 2; Editorial, *supra* note 163, at A20; Oppel Jr., *supra* note 150, at 1.

166. Kathleen McGowan, *Gramm's Fairy Tales*, CITY LIMITS, Nov. 1999, at 11.

167. Pub. L. No. 106-102, §712, 113 Stat. 1338, 1469 (codified at 12 U.S.C. §2908(a)(1)–(2) (2000)). In 2000, the year after the GLBA was enacted, the number of CRA performance evaluations the federal banking agencies completed nationwide dropped 54.4%, from 3,544 to 1,614. *Financial Modernization Law Shrinks CRA Ratings Base*, INSIDE MORTGAGE COMPLIANCE, January 15, 2001, at 45. This reduction was attributed to the reduction in the frequency of CRA exams for small banks with satisfactory or better CRA ratings from every two to three years to every four to five years. *Id.*

168. *CRA, Privacy Groups Spurn Bill's Negotiated Amendments*, INSIDE MORTGAGE COMPLIANCE, Oct. 25, 1990, at 3, 3–4.

CHAPTER TWO

1. There are four federal administrative agencies responsible for enforcing the CRA: the Board of Governors of the Federal Reserve System, Office of the Comptroller of the Currency, Federal Deposit Insurance Corporation, and Office of Thrift Supervision. *See supra* Introduction, note 11 for more about these agencies.

2. 12 U.S.C. §2901(a)(1) (2000). The complete statute appears in Appendix One.

3. *Id.* §2901(a)(2).

4. A "bank" is an institution that takes deposits and makes loans. CARL FELSENFELD, BANKING REGULATION IN THE UNITED STATES 2 (2001). The CRA applies only to banks whose deposits are insured by the Federal Deposit Insurance Corporation, which includes most state and national banks. 12 U.S.C. §2903(2) (2000). Bank charters also generally require banks to satisfy the convenience and needs of the community. FELSENFELD, *supra* at 18.1–18.2.

5. 12 U.S.C. §2903(a)(1).

6. *See* SEN. REP. No. 95-175, at 34 (1977).

7. 12 U.S.C. §2901(b).

8. *See supra* ch.1, text accompanying notes 113–20.

9. 12 C.F.R. §§5.8, 5.10, 225.16, 262.3, 303.7, 303.9 (2002).

10. 12 U.S.C. §2901(b); *see* Hicks v. Resolution Trust Corp., 970 F.2d 378, 382 (7th Cir. 1992).

11. 12 U.S.C. § 2903(a).
12. *Id.* § 2903.
13. *Id.* § 2903(a)(1).
14. *Id.* § 2906(a)(1).
15. *Id.* § 2906(b).
16. *Id.* § 2906(b)(2).
17. *Id.* § 2906(b)(1).
18. *Id.* § 2906(b)(1)(B). A metropolitan area is defined as any primary metropolitan statistical area, metropolitan statistical area, or consolidated metropolitan statistical area, as defined by the director of the Office of Management and Budget, with a population of 250,000 or more, and any other area designated as such by the federal banking agency. *Id.* § 2906(e)(2).
19. *Id.* § 2906(d)(1).
20. *Id.* § 2906(d)(3)(A).
21. *Id.* § 2903(a)(2).
22. *See, e.g., id.* § 36 (opening a new branch–national bank); *id.* § 215(a) (merger of national banks in the same state); *id.* § 215a (merger and consolidation of national banks with state banks or national banks); *id.* §§ 1464(i), (o)–(p) (conversion of federal savings associations to state savings associations and banks and vice versa); *id.* § 1467a(c)(4) (business expansion plans of savings and loan holding companies); *id.* § 1467a(e) (acquisitions by savings & loan holding companies); *id.* § 1816 (application for deposit insurance); *id.* § 1842 (becoming a bank holding company, ("BHC"), acquiring shares of or assets of a bank, merger of BHCs); N.Y. BANKING LAW § 136 (McKinney 2001) (conversion of national bank to state bank); *id.* § 136-a (purchase of assets of national banking association); *id.* § 601-b (merger or acquisition of assets by New York State banks); 12 C.F.R. § 5.24 (2003) (conversion of state bank to national bank); *id.* § 5.26 (national bank to exercise fiduciary powers); *id.* § 5.30 (national bank establishing a branch); *id.* § 5.33 (national bank business combinations); *id.* § 5.34 (new activities for national bank subsidiaries); *id.* § 225.11 (bank holding company's applications to form a bank holding company, acquire a subsidiary bank, merge bank holding companies, and acquire bank assets); *id.* § 500.1(b) (branch openings, mergers, and acquisitions of federal savings associations); *id.* § 545.93 (branching by federal savings associations); *id.* § 546.2 (merger of federal mutual savings association with any depository institution); KENNETH F. HALL, THE COMPLIANCE GUIDE TO UNITED STATES BANKING LAWS AND REGULATIONS 154–55 (1997) (branches in foreign countries).
23. 12 U.S.C. § 2903.
24. *Id.* § 2902(3).
25. *See* 12 C.F.R. §§ 5.13, 25.29(d) (2003) (Office of the Comptroller of the Currency); *id.* § 228.29(d) (Board of Governors of the Federal Reserve System); *id.* § 345.29(d) (Federal Deposit Insurance Corp.); *id.* § 563e.29(d) (Office of Thrift Supervision).
26. *See* Corning Sav. & Loan A'ssn v. Fed. Home Loan Bank Bd., 571 F. Supp. 396, 403 (E.D. Ark. 1983) ("The Court finds that not only has the Board implemented the CRA, but that it has gone beyond the explicit requirements of the CRA

so as to give meaning to the intent of the Act by allowing the Board to, in its discretion, deny an application due to an unsatisfactory CRA evaluation."), *aff'd*, 736 F.2d 479 (8th Cir. 1984).

27. *See supra* ch.1, text accompanying note 73.

28. *See, e.g.*, 12 U.S.C. §1815(a) (2000) (application for deposit insurance); *id.* §1842(a) (application by bank holding company to acquire shares or assets of a regulated financial institution); 12 U.S.C.A §1828(c) (West 2001 & Supp. 2003) (applications to merge, acquire shares, assume the liabilities of another bank, or establish a branch).

29. *See Corning,* 571 F. Supp. at 403 (stating that the Federal Home Loan Bank Board went "beyond the explicit requirements of the CRA so as to give meaning to the intent of the Act by allowing the Board to, in its discretion, deny an application due to an unsatisfactory CRA evaluation").

30. *See, e.g.*, 12 U.S.C. §§1815(b)(6), 1816(6), 1828(c)(5)(B) (2000); 12 U.S.C.A. §§1842(c)(1)(b), (c)(2).

31. 12 U.S.C. §2901(a)(1)–(2).

32. *See* Transfer of Assets Application, 1991 O.T.S. LEXIS 38, at *2 (July 8, 1991) (stating that a bank's CRA performance is an integral part of the analysis of the convenience and needs of the community); U.S. GEN. ACCOUNTING OFFICE, COMMUNITY REINVESTMENT ACT—CHALLENGES REMAIN TO SUCCESSFULLY IMPLEMENT CRA 18 (1995), *available at* http://www.gao.gov.

33. *See* sources noted *supra*, note 9.

34. *See infra* ch. 6, text accompanying notes 22 to 27 for more about this.

35. 12 U.S.C. §§1843 (k)(1), (k)(4), (i)(1)(c).

36. *Id.* §2903(c)(1)(A).

37. *Cf.* Hicks v. Resolution Trust Corp., 736 F. Supp. 812, 817–18 (N.D. Ill.), *judgment vacated*, 738 F. Supp. 279 (N.D. Ill. 1990).

38. *See, e.g.*, Equal Credit Opportunity Act, 15 U.S.C. §§1691–1691f (2000); Fair Housing Act, 42 U.S.C. §§3601–3619 (2000).

39. Lee v. Bd. of Governors of the Fed. Reserve Sys., 118 F.3d 905, 913 (2d Cir. 1997) [hereinafter *Lee I*]; Lee v. Fed. Deposit Ins. Corp., 1997 U.S. Dist. LEXIS 13885, at *24 (S.D.N.Y. Sept. 15, 1997) [hereinafter *Lee II*]; Harambee Uhuru Sch., Inc. v. Kemp, 1992 U.S. Dist. LEXIS 15125, at *17 (S.D. Ohio Sept. 30, 1992).

40. *Costly Timing of CRA Protests Highlighted in Hearing Testimony*, 64 Banking Rep. (BNA) 513 (Mar. 13, 1995). Although there have been several regulatory enforcement actions against banks with poor consumer compliance records, including the CRA, *see* discussion *infra* ch.3, text accompanying notes 165–89, describing several such actions, a subsequent ruling by the Department of Justice found that the federal banking agencies do not have the authority to enforce the CRA through administrative proceedings. *See* Memorandum of Walter Dellinger, Assistant Attorney General, to Eugene A. Ludwig, Comptroller of the Currency (Dec. 15, 1994) (on file with the author).

41. Washington v. Office of the Comptroller of the Currency, 1987 U.S. Dist. LEXIS 11474, at *5 n.1 (S.D. Ga. Nov. 24, 1987), *aff'd*, 856 F.2d 1507 (11th Cir. 1988).

42. *Lee I*, 118 F.3d at 913.

43. The author thanks Josh Silver, vice-president for policy analysis and research at the National Community Reinvestment Coalition, for this point.

44. Of the few reported decisions challenging application approvals on CRA grounds, none have been successful. *See* Inner City Press v. Bd. of Governors of the Fed. Reserve Sys., 130 F.3d 1088 (D.C. Cir. 1997), *cert. denied*, 524 U.S. 937 (1998); *Lee I*, 118 F.3d at 910 (holding that petitioner lacked standing to challenge regulatory approval of bank expansion application, and the court applied substantial evidence and abuse of discretion standards in challenge to regulatory approval of bank expansion applications on the ground that the banks had not complied with the CRA); Kaimowitz v. Bd. of Governors of the Fed. Reserve Sys., 940 F.2d 610, 610-11 (11th Cir. 1991) (holding that petitioner lacked standing to challenge regulatory approval); *Lee II*, 1997 U.S. Dist. LEXIS 13885, at *2-3 (holding that plaintiff lacked standing to challenge regulatory approval of bank expansion applications); Exchange Bank v. Office of Thrift Supervision, 29 F. Supp. 2d 1272 (W.D. Ok. 1998); *Washington*, 1987 U.S. Dist. LEXIS 11474, at *10-12; *Corning*, 571 F. Supp. at 402–4 (applying rational basis test to agency decision upholding bank merger on CRA grounds); Inner City Press/Comm. on the Move v. N.Y. State Banking Bd., N.Y.L.J., July 20, 2001, at 18 (N.Y. Sup. Ct. July 29, 2001); Inner-City Press/Comm. on the Move v. N.Y. State Banking Bd., 657 N.Y.S.2d 275, 282 (Sup. Ct. 1996) (applying rational basis test to challenge to regulatory approval of bank expansion application on the grounds that the bank had not complied with New York State's CRA law).

45. *See* 42 U.S.C. §3613 (2000).

46. *See* 15 U.S.C. §1691e (2000).

47. Administrative Procedures Act, 5 U.S.C. §§701–706 (2000); *see Lee II*, 1997 U.S. Dist. LEXIS 13885, at *1 and n. 1.

48. *See Lee I*, 118 F.3d at 905; *Lee II*, 1997 U.S. Dist. LEXIS 13885.

49. *Lee I*, 118 F.3d at 910–12.

50. *See Kaimowitz*, 940 F.2d at 613–14.

51. *Corning*, 571 F. Supp. at 400.

52. *Washington*, 1987 U.S. Dist. LEXIS 11474, at *5 n.1.

53. *Corning*, 736 F.2d at 480.

54. There could be several other reasons community groups have not challenged mergers in court, among them: the cost; fear of creating bad precedent; and the fast-moving nature of bank mergers.

55. *Lee I*, 118 F.3d at 905.

56. *Id.* at 908.

57. *Id.*

58. *Id.* at 915. The court's discussion of ICP's charges appears *id.* at 915.

59. *See id.*

60. *Id.* The court's description of the Federal Reserve's decision appears *id.* at 915–16.

61. *Id.* at 909–10.

62. *Id.* at 910.

63. *Id.*

64. *Id.*

65. *Id.* at 911.

66. *Id.* The court's discussion of standing appears *id.* at 912–14.

67. *Id.* at 913.

68. *Id.*

69. *Id.* at 914. The court's discussion of the merits appears *id.* at 914–16.
70. *Id.*
71. *Id.*
72. *Id.*
73. *Id.*
74. *Id.*
75. *Id.*
76. *Id.*
77. *Id.*
78. 1997 U.S. Dist. LEXIS 13885 (S.D.N.Y. Sept. 15, 1997).
79. *Id.* at *5–8.
80. *Id.* at *15. The court's discussion of standing appears *id.* at *11–25.
81. *Id.* at *17.
82. *Id.* at *18–19.
83. *See supra* ch.1, text accompanying notes 25 to 34.

CHAPTER THREE

1. Glenn Canner & Joe M. Cleaver, *The Community Reinvestment Act: A Progress Report*, 66 FED. RES. BULL. 87, 87–88 (1980) [hereinafter *CRA Progress Report*]. *See also* JoAnn S. Barefoot, *Looking for Loans in All the Right Places*, A.B.A. BANKING J. 42 (June 1992); GLENN B. CANNER, REDLINING: RESEARCH AND FEDERAL LEGISLATIVE RESPONSE 13 (1982), *summary available in* 68 FED. RES. BULL. 610 (1982) [hereinafter REDLINING]; Philip C. Jackson, Jr., Statement before the Subcomm. on Financial Institution Supervision, Regulation, and Insurance of the House Comm. on Banking, Finance and Urban Affairs (July 26, 1978), *in* 64 FED. RES. BULL. 631, 632 (1978); Manuel H. Johnson, Statement before the S. Comm. on Banking, Hous., and Urban Affairs (Sept. 8, 1988), *in* 74 FED. RES. BULL. 733, 738–39 (1988) [hereinafter Johnson Statement]; Richard Marsico, *A Guide to Enforcing The Community Reinvestment Act*, 20 FORDHAM URB. L. J. 165, 196–97 (1993).

2. Statement of the Federal Financial Supervisory Agencies Regarding the Community Reinvestment Act, 54 Fed. Reg. 13,746 (Apr. 5, 1989) [hereinafter Joint Statement]. *See also* REDLINING, *supra* note 1, at 13; Robert L. Clarke, Statement before the S. Comm. on Banking, Housing and Urban Affairs (Sept. 8, 1988), *in* OFFICE OF THE COMPTROLLER OF THE CURRENCY Q. J. 7-4, Dec. 1988, at 19 (In opposing legislation that would prohibit banks from benefitting from the proposed Glass-Steagall repeal unless they had a satisfactory CRA rating, Comptroller Clarke stated that the legislation would "likely have the effect of changing the purpose of CRA from a law that seeks to balance community credit needs and safety and soundness concerns to one that allocates credit.") [hereinafter Clarke Testimony]; Eugene A. Ludwig, Remarks before Women in Housing and Finance, on Direction of the Banking Industry and Community Reinvestment Act Reform Initiatives (Oct. 21, 1993), *in* OFFICE OF THE COMPTROLLER OF THE CURRENCY Q. J. 13-1, Mar. 1994, at 80; Marsico, *supra* note 1.

3. Lawrence B. Lindsey, Statement before the Subcomm. on Consumer Credit and Insurance of the House Comm. on Banking, Finance, and Urban Affairs (Feb. 18, 1993), *in* 79 FED. RES. BULL. 285, 286 (1993) [hereinafter Lindsey Statement].

4. Glenn Canner, *The Community Reinvestment Act and Credit Allocation*, 68 FED. RES. BULL. 117, 118–19 (1982) (quoting *Community Credit Needs: Hearings on S. 406 Before the Senate Comm. on Banking, Housing, and Urban Affairs*, 95th Cong. 2, 392, and 393 (1977)).

5. Canner, *supra* note 4, at 119. *See supra*, ch. 1, text accompanying notes 54 to 55 for further description of Proxmire's initial proposal.

6. Information Statement Re Community Reinvestment Act, 66 FED. RES. BULL. 30, 30 (1980) [hereinafter Information Statement].

7. Canner, *supra* note 4, at 117–18.

8. Cont'l Bank Corp., 75 FED. RES. BULL. 304 (1989); Banc One Corp., 73 FED. RES. BULL. 124, 126 (1987); Rainier Bancorp., 73 FED. RES. BULL. 55 (1987); Hibernia Corp., 72 FED. RES. BULL. 656, 658 (1986); Manufacturers Hanover Trust Co., 66 FED. RES. BULL. 601, 601–2 (1980); F & M Bancshares, Inc., 66 FED. RES. BULL. 508, 508–9 (1980); Michigan Nat'l Corp., 66 FED. RES. BULL. 247, 249 n.10. (1980); Glenn Canner, *The Community Reinvestment Act: A Second Progress Report*, 67 FED. RES. BULL. 813, 813–15 (1981); Griffith L. Garwood, Statement before the Subcomm. on Consumer and Regulatory Affairs of the S. Comm. on Banking , Hous., and Urban Affairs (July 31, 1989), *in* 75 FED. RES. BULL. 619 (1989)[hereinafter Garwood Statement]; Marsico, *supra* note 1, at 196–97; Martha R. Seger, Statement before the Subcomm. on Consumer and Regulatory Affairs of the S. Comm. on Banking, Hous., and Urban Affairs (June 7, 1989), *in* 75 FED. RES. BULL. 550, 552 (1989)[hereinafter Seger Testimony].

9. NBD Bancorp, Inc., 68 FED. RES. BULL. 306, 308 n.4 (1982); First Nat'l Boston Corp., 67 FED. RES. BULL. 253, 254–55 (1981); Manufacturers Hanover Trust Co., 66 FED. RES. BULL. at 602.

10. Canner, *supra* note 4, at 120.

11. First Nat'l Boston Corp., 67 FED. RES. BULL. at 254–55; Joint Statement, *supra* note 2, at 13,746; Canner, *supra* note 8, at 815; Information Statement, *supra* note 6, at 30, 31; Marsico, *supra* note 1, at 196–97.

12. Lawrence B. Lindsey, Real Progress Without Unintended Consequences: Address to the Federal Reserve Bank of Cleveland's Annual Community Reinvestment Forum (Sept. 24, 1993) *at* http://www.lexis.com (last visited Aug. 22, 2002), at *6 [hereinafter Lindsey Address]. *See also* Lindsey Statement, *supra* note 3, at 285.

13. Eugene A. Ludwig, Remarks before the Subcomm. on Financial Institutions and Consumer Credit of the House Comm. on Banking and Financial Services on the Reform of the CRA (Mar. 8, 1995), *in* OFFICE OF THE COMPTROLLER OF THE CURRENCY Q. J. 14-2, June 1995, at 41 [hereinafter Ludwig Statement].

14. Lindsey Address, *supra* note 12, at *2.

15. Lawrence B. Lindsey, Statement before the Subcomm. on Financial Institutions and Consumer Credit of the House Comm. on Banking and Financial Services (Mar. 8, 1995), *in* 81 FED. RES. BULL. 424, 426 (1995).

16. Canner, *supra* note 4, at 119.

17. Speech by Robert L. Clarke, Comptroller of the Currency, to the Consumer Bankers Association (Dec. 1, 1989) in OFFICE OF THE COMPTROLLER OF THE CURRENCY Q.J. 9-1, Mar. 1990 [hereinafter Clarke Speech].

18. William C. Gruben et al., *Imperfect Information and the Community Reinvestment Act*, FED. RES. BANK OF SAN FRANCISCO ECON. REV., Summer 1990, at 27. *See also* Leonard I. Nakamura, *Information Externalities: Community Lending May Sometimes Need a Jump Start*, FED. RES. BANK OF PHILADELPHIA BUS. REV., Jan–Feb. 1993, at 3 ("Bankers must compete to find and access the good borrowers, and that puts bankers in the information business: the profitable lender is the one who best understands the business that borrowers are engaged in and the value of collateral that borrowers put up to secure loans.").

19. Gruben et al., *supra* note 18, at 29.

20. *Id.*

21. *Id.*

22. *Id.*

23. *Id.* at 28, 29, 31 and 35; Nakamura, *supra* note 18, at 4. Nakamura suggests that this perceived risk may be due to an information externality. For example, bankers need information about the value of property, but if there are few sales in a particular neighborhood, there will not be much information about the value of property, and banks may be unwilling to lend there based on this lack of information. *See also The Economic Growth and Regulatory Paperwork Reduction Act: Hearings on S. 650 Before the S. Comm. on Banking, Hous., and Urban Affairs*, 104th Cong. 419–58 (1995) (statement of Benson F. Roberts, Vice President for Policy, Local Initiatives Support Corporation) [hereinafter *Hearings on S. 650*]. Nakamura suggests that lending decisions come down to judgments about borrowers and neighborhoods, and most of us are more comfortable with what we know than what we do not know.

24. Gruben et al., *supra* note 18, at 28, 19, 31 and 35.

25. *Id.* at 35.

26. *Id.*

27. *Id*; Nakamura, *supra* note 18, at 3 ("In credit markets where information flows are unsteady, private credit institutions may need public assistance or prodding."); *id.* at 7.

28. Gruben et al., *supra* note 18, at 36.

29. *Id.*

30. *Id.*

31. Canner, *supra* note 4, at 2.

32. Lawrence B. Lindsey, Statement before the Subcomm. on Consumer Credit and Insurance of the House Comm. on Banking, Finance, and Urban Affairs (Oct. 21, 1993), *in* 79 FED. RES. BULL. 1127, 1129 (1993) [hereinafter Lindsey Testimony].

33. COMM. ON BANKING, HOUSING, AND URBAN AFFAIRS, 102D CONG., REPORT ON THE STATUS OF THE COMMUNITY REINVESTMENT ACT: VIEWS AND RECOMMENDATIONS (VOL. I) 5 and 61 (Comm. Print 1992) [hereinafter SENATE CRA REPORT]; *id.* at 33 ("The overall performance of an institution, however, is primarily related to its efforts and success in helping to meet the credit needs of its local community."). *See Fed's CRA Ratings Show High Level of Compliance Among 108 Banks Examined,* Fair Housing-Fair Lending Rep. [Prentice-Hall], Dec. 1, 1990, at 7; Jim King, *Key Federal Act Lacks Teeth, Activists*

Charge, THE ATL. J. & CONST., Mar. 22, 1992, at G4; John E. Morris, *Critics: Grade Inflation Plagues Community Lending Ratings*, THE RECORDER, Jan. 21, 1992, at 1.

34. H. Jane Lehman, *Bank Loan Regulators Get a 'D' Grade; Senate Subcommittee Says Agencies Fail on 'Redlining' Tests*, THE WASHINGTON POST, Feb. 6, 1993, at F2.

35. Lindsey Statement, *supra* note 3, at 290.

36. Griffith L. Garwood & Dolores S. Smith, *The Community Reinvestment Act: Evolution and Current Issues*, 79 FED. RES. BULL. 251, 255 (1993) [hereinafter Garwood & Smith]. *See also* Lehman, *supra* note 34.

37. *See* Barry J. Zadworny, *Documentation Can Mean CRA Success*, AM. BANKER, Mar. 4, 1992, at 4.

38. *See* Machelle M. Connally, *The Evolution of the Community Reinvestment Act*, 44 CONSUMER FIN. L. Q. REP. 253 (1990); J. Tol Broome, Jr., *Being Systematic About CRA Can Boost Examiner Ratings (Regulatory/Compliance Report)*, BANK MGMT., Aug. 1, 1992, at 42.

39. *Community Reinvestment Act Enforcement Issues Discussed by Bank Compliance Officers*, Fair Housing-Fair Lending Rep. [Prentice-Hall], Nov. 1, 1989, at 7; *Fed's CRA Ratings Show High Level Compliance*, *supra* note 33.

40. Sandra Jones, *Uptown Bank Sketches Outreach Plan*, CRAIN'S CHI. BUS., May 3, 1993, at 66.

41. Bill Atkinson, *Smallest Banks Seen Least Likely to Make the Grade with CRA Examiners*, AM. BANKER, May 10, 1993, at 6. *See also* Morris, *supra* note 33, at 1.

42. *See* 12 C.F.R. pts. 25 (1992) (Office of the Comptroller of the Currency); 228 (Federal Reserve System), 345 (Federal Deposit Insurance Corporation), and 563 (Former Federal Home Loan Bank Board). For simplicity, all citations to the former regulations will be to the Federal Reserve's regulations.

43. *See* 12 C.F.R. §228.7 (1992); Uniform Interagency Community Reinvestment Act Final Guidelines For Disclosure of Written Evaluations and Revised Assessment Rating System, 55 Fed. Reg. 18,163 (May 1, 1990) [hereinafter Final CRA Guidelines].

44. 12 C.F.R. §228.7(a)–(c).

45. *See* Gore-Bronson Bancorp, Inc., 78 FED. RES. BULL. 784, 785 (1992); Cont'l Bank Corp., 75 FED. RES. BULL. at 304; Canner, *supra* note 8, at 813; *CRA Progress Report*, *supra* note 1, at 91; *Former OCC Official: Some CRA Assessment Categories "More Equal Than Others,"* Fair Housing-Fair Lending Rep. [Prentice-Hall], Jan. 1, 1991, at 1; Garwood Statement, *supra* note 8, at 624; Johnson Statement, *supra* note 1, at 737; Kevin T. Kane, *CRA Getting Good Grades*, MORTGAGE BANKING, June 1992, at 55; Marsico, *supra* note 1, at 200, 203, 208, and text accompanying nn. 95, 113, and 161; Charlotte H. Scott, *CRA Reform Proposal Is a Placebo, Not a Cure*, AM. BANKER, Mar. 25, 1994, at 32.

46. FEDERAL RESERVE SYSTEM COMPLIANCE HANDBOOK II.1.40 (1979) [hereinafter 1979 FRS HANDBOOK]. *See* FEDERAL RESERVE SYSTEM COMPLIANCE HANDBOOK 4.A.4 (1990)[hereinafter 1990 FRS HANDBOOK].

47. Clarke Speech, *supra* note 17.

48. Garwood & Smith, *supra* note 36, at 254.

49. 12 C.F.R. §§228.3, 228.4, 228.5, and 228.6.

50. Joint Statement, *supra* note 2, at 13,743.

51. John P. LaWare, *Getting Serious About the CRA*, NAT'L MORTGAGE NEWS, Nov. 25, 1991, at 3 ("This policy statement does stress process. The major reason is that the agencies simply cannot issue clear guidelines on the specific number, types, and dollar amounts of loans that are expected.").

52. Joint Statement, *supra* note 2, at 13,743.

53. *Id.* at 13,742.

54. *Id.* at 13,743.

55. Clarke Speech, *supra* note 17.

56. Joint Statement, *supra* note 2, at 13,743. *See also* Clarke Speech, *supra* note 17 (the CRA requires management to assess the credit needs of the community, develop plans to meet those needs, and put the plan into effect).

57. Joint Statement, *supra* note 2, at 13,743.

58. Robert L. Clarke, Statement before the S. Comm. on Banking, Housing, and Urban Affairs (Mar. 23, 1988), *in* OFFICE OF THE COMPTROLLER OF THE CURRENCY Q. J. 7-3, June 1988, at 37 [hereinafter Clarke Statement].

59. Joint Statement, *supra* note 2, at 13,745; Clarke Speech, *supra* note 17 ("How can an institution demonstrate that it is complying with the law? The answer: Documentation. Documentation that is required not by specific requirements in law and regulation. Documentation that is required by the CRA management process.").

60. Joint Statement, *supra* note 2, at 13,746.

61. Interagency Policy Statement on the Analysis of Geographic Distribution of Lending for CRA, THRIFT BULL. 47-2, Jan. 10, 1992, at 2-3 [hereinafter Policy Statement].

62. *Id.* at 3.

63. *Former OCC Official, supra* note 45, at 4.

64. Policy Statement, *supra* note 61, at 3.

65. Community Reinvestment Act: Interagency Questions and Answers, 58 Fed. Reg. 9,176 (Feb. 19, 1993) [hereinafter CRA Q & A].

66. *Id.* at 9,180.

67. *Id.*

68. *Id.*

69. *Id.*

70. *Id.*

71. *Id.*

72. COMPTROLLER'S HANDBOOK FOR CONSUMER EXAMINATION 16.1–16.4 (1979)[hereinafter 1979 OCC HANDBOOK]. *See also* 1979 FRS HANDBOOK, *supra* note 46.

73. 1979 FRS HANDBOOK, *supra* note 46, at II.1.48–54; 1979 OCC HANDBOOK, supra note 72, at 60–63.

74. Clarke Testimony, *supra* note 2, at 19.

75. *See* Final CRA Guidelines, *supra* note 43, at 18,167 ("Assessing the CRA performance of an institution is a process that does not rely on absolute standards. Consequently, the rating system purposefully does not preassign any relative weights to individual assessment factors or performance categories.").

76. 12 C.F.R. §228.7(e), (h)–(j) (1992). Assessment criteria (d) and (f) dealt with discriminatory lending practices. These criteria did not measure the extent of a bank's lending, but determined whether the bank's lending was discriminatory.

77. Final CRA Guidelines, *supra* note 43, at 18,173.

78. 1979 OCC HANDBOOK *supra* note 72, at 61; 1979 FRS HANDBOOK, *supra* note 46, at II.1.50–51.

79. COMPTROLLER'S HANDBOOK FOR COMPLIANCE 83 (1991) [hereinafter 1991 COMPTROLLER'S HANDBOOK]; 1990 FRS HANDBOOK, *supra* note 46, at 4.B.3.

80. Final CRA Guidelines, *supra* note 43, at 18,175.

81. 1979 FRS HANDBOOK, supra note 46, at II.1.51–52; 1979 OCC HANDBOOK, supra note 72, at 61.

82. 1991 COMPTROLLER'S HANDBOOK, *supra* note 79, at 83; 1990 FRS HANDBOOK, *supra* note 46, at 4.B.2.

83. Final CRA Guidelines, *supra* note 43, at 18,171–72.

84. 1979 OCC HANDBOOK, *supra* note 72, at 62; 1979 FRS HANDBOOK, *supra* note 46, at II.1.52.

85. 1991 COMPTROLLER'S HANDBOOK, *supra* note 79, at 83; 1990 FRS HANDBOOK, *supra* note 46, at 4.B.

86. Final CRA Guidelines, *supra* note 43, at 18,173.

87. 1979 FRS HANDBOOK, *supra* note 46, at II.1.52; 1979 OCC HANDBOOK, *supra* note 72, at 62.

88. 1990 FRS Handbook, *supra* note 46, at 4.B.3; 1991 COMPTROLLER'S HANDBOOK, *supra* note 79, at 83.

89. *See* Eugene A. Ludwig, Statement before the Subcomm. on General Oversight, Investigations, and the Resolution of Failed Financial Institutions of the House Comm. on Banking, Finance and Urban Affairs, on Improving Implementation of the Community Reinvestment Act (Sept. 17, 1993), *in* OFFICE OF THE COMPTROLLER OF THE CURRENCY Q. J. 12-4, Dec. 1993, at 31 ("The existing CRA examination procedures provide ambiguous guidance to examiners and institutions regarding what constitutes satisfactory CRA performance.") [hereinafter Ludwig CRA Statement]. *See also* U.S. GEN. ACCOUNTING OFFICE, COMMUNITY REINVESTMENT ACT —CHALLENGES REMAIN TO SUCCESSFULLY IMPLEMENT CRA 23 (1995) ("assessing qualitative compliance with the CRA is more difficult and subjective") [hereinafter GAO REPORT].

90. Gruben et al., *supra* note 18, at 36. ("What would make a geographic distribution unwarranted or unattributable to safety and soundness considerations is not stated.").

91. SENATE CRA REPORT, *supra* note 33, at 5, 12, and 47.

92. Debra Cope, *Banks Accused of Waging War on CRA*, AM. BANKER, Sept. 16, 1992, at 14.

93. Clarke Statement, *supra* note 58, at 37.

94. For data about pre-1990 CRA ratings, *see Regulators Find CRA Performance Lacking For One Out of 10 Institutions Examined,* 57 Banking Rep. (BNA), July 22, 1991, at 137. For 1990 to 1992 data, *see* SENATE CRA REPORT, *supra* note 33, at 33–35. For 1993 to 1997, *see* INSIDE FAIR LENDING, Jan. 1996, at 2–4; INSIDE FAIR LENDING, Jan. 1997, at 2–4; INSIDE FAIR LENDING, July 1997, at 2–4; NATIONAL COMMUNITY REINVESTMENT COALITION, CRA RATINGS FROM 1992 TO 2001 (2002).

95. KENNETH H. THOMAS, COMMUNITY REINVESTMENT PERFORMANCE: MAKING CRA WORK FOR BANKS, COMMUNITIES, AND REGULATORS 98 (1994) [hereinafter CRA

PERFORMANCE]. *See also* KENNETH H. THOMAS, CRA'S 25TH ANNIVERSARY: THE PAST, PRESENT, AND FUTURE 8–9 (2002) [hereinafter CRA's 25th].

96. CRA PERFORMANCE, *supra* note 95, at 8–9.

97. *Id.*

98. Thomas hypothesized that because of the degree of subjectivity it was possible for an examiner to move a CRA rating one notch in either direction. *Id.* at 251.

99. *See* SENATE CRA REPORT, *supra* note 33, at 86–144.

100. *Id.* at 49.

101. *Current Status of the Community Reinvestment Act: Hearing Before the Subcomm. on Hous., Banking, and Urban Affairs of the S. Comm. on Banking, Hous., and Urban Affairs*, 102d Cong. 192 (1992) (statement of Deborah Goldberg, Reinvestment Specialist, Center for Community Change) [hereinafter *1992 Hearings*].

102. *Id.*

103. *Id.* at 194.

104. SENATE CRA REPORT, *supra* note 33, at 116–28.

105. *Id.*

106. *Id.* at 135–44.

107. *Id.*

108. *Id.* at 106–12.

109. *Id.*

110. *Id.*

111. *Id.*

112. *Id.* at 112–15.

113. *Id.*

114. *1992 Hearings*, *supra* note 101, at 192 (statement of Deborah Goldberg, Reinvestment Specialist, Center for Community Change); SENATE CRA REPORT, *supra* note 33, at 59–60.

115. SENATE CRA REPORT, *supra* note 33, at 59–60.

116. *Id.* at 60.

117. *1992 Hearings*, *supra* note 101, at 158 (Statement of Calvin Bradford, President, Community Reinvestment Associates); SENATE CRA REPORT, *supra* note 33, at 60.

118. SENATE CRA REPORT, *supra* note 33, at 62.

119. 12 U.S.C. §2902(3).

120. *See* ch. 2, text accompanying notes 26 to 33.

121. *See* Glacier Bancorp, Inc., 78 FED. RES. BULL. 713, 716 (1992); Banc One Corp., 78 FED. RES. BULL. 699, 704 (1992); Comerica, Inc., 78 FED. RES. BULL. 554, 566 (1992); Stichting Prioriteit ABN AMRO Holding, 78 FED. RES. BULL. 296, 299 (1992); First Bancshares of St. Landry, Inc., 78 FED. RES. BULL. 136, 138 (1992); Chemical Banking Corp., 78 FED. RES. BULL. 74, 84 (1992); Apple Merger Corp., 77 FED. RES. BULL. 492, 493 (1991); First Union Corp., 76 FED. RES. BULL. 83, 88 (1990); Comerica, Inc., 74 FED. RES. BULL. 809, 810 and 811 (1988); Somerset Bankshares, Inc., 74 FED. RES. BULL. 619, 621 (1988); Advance Bancorp, Inc., 72 FED. RES. BULL. 834, 835–36 (1986); AmeriTrust Corp., 66 FED. RES. BULL. 238, 242 (1980); The First Nat'l Bank of Coulterville, OFFICE OF THE COMPTROLLER OF THE CURRENCY Q. J. 2-2, June 1982, at 104 (conditionally approved application despite less than satisfactory

CRA record of bank); GAO REPORT, *supra* note 89, at 31; Joint Statement, *supra* note 2, at 13,746; *Community Reinvestment Act*, OFFICE OF THE COMPTROLLER CURRENCY Q. J. 9-1, Mar. 1990, at 55 ("The OCC believes that the use of conditioned approvals is usually more effective than denial of applications in securing such improvement.") [hereinafter Community Reinvestment Act]; Canner, *supra* note 8, at 816; Clarke Statement, *supra* note 58, at 37 ("This low number [of denials on CRA grounds] reflects our view that conditional approvals are more effective than denials in promoting the objectives of the Community Reinvestment Act."); *id.* ("In the final analysis, if the OCC did determine that an unreasonable pattern [of lending] did exist, the corporate application could be denied. However, an approval with conditions might be a more appropriate response."); Garwood Statement, *supra* note 8, at 619, 623–24 (1989).

122. Clarke Statement, *supra* note 58, at 37.

123. *Id.*

124. CRA's 25th, *supra* note 95, at 9.

125. The following description of how the federal banking regulatory agencies applied the four CRA assessment criteria dealing with bank lending when deciding banking applications is based on written decisions by the Board of Governors of the Federal Reserve System and the Office of the Comptroller of the Currency on bank expansion application decisions. The Federal Deposit Insurance Corporation and Office of Thrift Supervision rarely publish written decisions on bank merger applications.

126. Examples of the Federal Reserve's use of these criteria can be found in several decisions, including HSBC Holdings PLC, 83 FED. RES. BULL. 326, 330 (1997); NationsBank Corp., 83 FED. RES. BULL. 148, 152 (1997); Bank of Boston Corp., 82 FED. RES. BULL. 856, 860 & n. 23 (1996); Hibernia Corp., 82 FED. RES. BULL. 838, 841 (1996); First Commerce Banks of Florida, Inc., 82 FED. RES. BULL. 738 (1996); North Fork Bancorp., Inc., 82 FED. RES. BULL. 338, 340 (1996); National City Corp., 82 FED. RES. BULL. 271, 273 (1996); First Citizens Bancshares, Inc., 82 FED. RES. BULL., 232, 233–34 (1996); NationsBank Corp., 82 FED. RES. BULL. 154, 155 (1996); NBD Bancorp, Inc., 82 FED. RES. BULL. 93, 96 (1996); Fleet Fin. Group, Inc., 82 FED. RES. BULL. 50, 59, 61, 65, 67–68 (1996); First Union Corp., 81 FED. RES. BULL. 1143, 1147 (1995); NationsBank Corp., 81 FED. RES. BULL. 1121, 1125 (1995); Marine Midland Banks, Inc., 81 FED. RES. BULL. 1045, 1047 (1995); Manufacturers and Traders Trust Co., 81 FED. RES. BULL. 394, 395 (1995); Firstar Corp., 80 FED. RES. BULL. 1003, 1005–6 (1994); North West Indiana Bancorp, 80 FED. RES. BULL. 824, 825 (1994); First Michigan Bank Corp., 80 FED. RES. BULL. 632, 633 (1994); BankAmerica Corp., 80 FED. RES. BULL. 623, 626–27 n.21 (1994); Marshall & Ilsley Corp., 80 FED. RES. BULL. 556, 559 (1994); Society Corp., 80 FED. RES. BULL. 234, 235 (1994); Fleet Bank of New York, 80 FED. RES. BULL. 170, 172–73 (1994); Banc One Corp., 79 FED. RES. BULL. 1152, 1153 (1993); AmSouth Bancorp., 79 FED. RES. BULL. 951, 953 (1993); Chemical Bank, 79 FED. RES. BULL. 736, 737 (1993); CB Fin. Corp., 79 FED. RES. BULL. 118, 123 (1993); Old Nat'l Bancorp, 79 FED. RES. BULL. 55, 59 (1993); Comerica, Inc., 78 FED. RES. BULL. 554, 560 (1992); Society Corp., 78 FED. RES. BULL. 302, 306 (1992); NCNB Corp., 78 FED. RES. BULL. 141, 151 (1992); Chemical Banking Corp., 78 FED. RES. BULL. 74, 81 (1992); Marsico, *supra* note 1, at 230–32 & n.351.

127. *See* The Chase Manhattan Bank, 82 FED. RES. BULL. 1139, 1141–42 (1996); North Fork Bancorp., 82 FED. RES. BULL. at 340–41; Fleet Fin. Group, 82 FED. RES.

BULL. at 68–69; First Union Corp., 81 FED. RES. BULL. 1143, 1148 (1995); The Chase Manhattan Corp., 81 FED. RES. BULL. 883, 889 (1995); First Nat'l Bank Corp. of Ardmore, Inc., 80 FED. RES. BULL. 1101, 1102 (1994); First Interstate Bank of California, 80 FED. RES. BULL. 168, 169 (1994); Banc One Corp., 79 FED. RES. BULL. 1168, 1170 n. 16 (1993); Chemical Bank, 79 FED. RES. BULL. at 737; Comerica Inc., 79 FED. RES. BULL. 500, 503 (1993); Old Nat'l Bancorp, 79 FED. RES. BULL. at 59; First Bank System, Inc., 78 FED. RES. BULL. 948, 951 (1992); Comerica Inc., 78 FED. RES. BULL. at 564; BankAmerica Corp., 78 FED. RES. BULL. 338, 356 (1992); NCNB Corp., 78 FED. RES. BULL. 141, 156 (1992); Chemical Banking Corp., 78 FED. RES. BULL. at 81, 82; Marsico, *supra* note 1, at 236–39, and cases cited in nn. 239–41, 368–93, 398–412.

128. First Interstate BancSystem of Montana, Inc., 77 FED. RES. BULL. 1007, 1009 (1991).

129. First Colonial Bankshares Corp., 79 FED. RES. BULL. 706, 707 (1993).

130. The First Nat'l Bank of Anchorage, 1993 OCC Ltr. LEXIS 24, at *1 (June 24, 1993).

131. First Interstate Bank of Washington, 1991 OCC Ltr. LEXIS 129, at *2 (June 25, 1991).

132. *See* NationsBank, 83 FED. RES. BULL. at 153; NationsBank Corp., 81 FED. RES. BULL. 1124–25; Northern Trust Corp., 81 FED. RES. BULL. 486, 487 (1995); Chase Manhattan Corp., 81 FED. RES. BULL. 467, 471 (1995); Huntington Bancshares, Inc., 78 FED. RES. BULL. 61, 63 (1992); Marsico, *supra* note 1, at 252 & nn. 495–99.

133. Omni Bank, 1991 OCC Ltr. LEXIS 130, at *1 (July 18, 1991).

134. *Id.*

135. The Nat'l Bank of Corinth, 1993 OCC Ltr. LEXIS 30, at *1 (July 12, 1993).

136. *See* KeyCorp, 81 FED. RES. BULL. 160, 161–62 (1995); First Virginia Bank of Tidewater, 80 FED. RES. BULL. 660, 661 (1994); BankAmerica Corp., 80 FED. RES. BULL. 623, 627 (1994); First Bank System, Inc., 78 FED. RES. BULL. at 951; BankAmerica Corp., 78 FED. RES. BULL. at 349–50; Chemical Banking Corp., 78 FED. RES. BULL. at 80; Huntington Bancshares, Inc., 78 FED. RES. BULL. at 63; Marsico, *supra* note 1, at 212, 216, 219, 221, 222, and nn. 220, 254, 278, 282–88, 315–17.

137. Northern Trust Corp., 81 FED. RES. BULL. at 486; Marsico, *supra* note 1, at 235.

138. First Nat'l Boston Corp., 67 FED. RES. BULL. 253, 255 (1981); Nat'l City Corp., 67 FED. RES. BULL. 52, 54 (1981); AmeriTrust Corp., 66 FED. RES. BULL. 238, 240 (1980); Marsico, *supra* note 1, at 235.

139. *See* AmSouth Bancorp., 76 FED. RES. BULL. 957, 959 & n.11 (1990); First Bank System, Inc., 74 FED. RES. BULL. 824, 826 (1988); Norwest Corp., 74 FED. RES. BULL. 568, 570 (1988); Dominion Bankshares Corp., 72 FED. RES. BULL. 787, 789 (1986); Hutsonville Bank Corp., 67 FED. RES. BULL. 48 (1981); Marsico, *supra* note 1, at 235.

140. Illinois Fin. Services, Inc., 81 FED. RES. BULL. 480, 482 (1995).

141. Irving National Bancshare, Inc., 81 FED. RES. BULL. 484, 486 (1995).

142. *See* Norwest Corp., 77 FED. RES. BULL. 110, 112 & n.12 (1991); Somerset Bankshares, Inc., 74 FED. RES. BULL. 619, 620 (1988); Mellon Nat'l Corp., 69 FED. RES. BULL. 721, 722–23 (1983); Manufacturers Hanover Trust Co., 66 FED. RES. BULL.

601, 602 (1980). *See* also CRA Q & A, *supra* note 65, at 10,901; Final CRA Guidelines, *supra* note 43, at 18,172; Marsico, *supra* note 1, at 212–13.

143. Somerset Bankshares, Inc., 74 FED. RES. BULL. at 620 (a "substantial portion" of bank's loans were outside its community); Manufacturers Hanover Trust Co., 66 FED. RES. BULL. at 602 (The fact that half of the bank's home mortgage loans were made outside its state was not problematic because it was consistent with the record of other similar banks.).

144. Totalbank Corp. of Florida, 81 FED. RES. BULL. 876, 877 (1995); First Colonial Bankshares Corp., 79 FED. RES. BULL. 706, 707 (1993); Gore-Bronson Bancorp, Inc., 78 FED. RES. BULL. 784, 786 (1992); First Interstate BancSystem of Montana, Inc., 77 FED. RES. BULL. at 1009.

145. *See* Chemical Bank FSB, 1996 OCC Ltr. LEXIS 129 (Nov. 1996); Santander Nat'l Bank, 1993 OCC Ltr. LEXIS 5 (Feb. 5, 1993); Grand Nat'l Bank, 1992 OCC Ltr. LEXIS 62 (Apr. 22, 1992); Pacific Nat'l Bank, 1992 OCC Ltr. LEXIS 61 (Apr. 1, 1992); The Nat'l Republic Bank of Chicago, 1992 OCC Ltr. LEXIS 21 (Mar. 4, 1992); Omni Bank, 1991 OCC Ltr. LEXIS 130 (July 18, 1991); First Interstate Bank of Washington, 1991 OCC Ltr. LEXIS 129 (June 25, 1991); Omni Bank, 1991 OCC Ltr. LEXIS 127 (June 24, 1991).

146. American Commerce Nat'l Bank, 1989 OCC Ltr. LEXIS 98, at *1-2 (Dec. 7, 1989).

147. Mayde Creek Bank, 1993 OCC Ltr. LEXIS 77, at *2 (Dec. 9, 1993).

148. *Id.*

149. *See* HSBC Holdings PLC, 83 FED. RES. BULL. 326, 330 (1997); Comerica Inc., 81 FED. RES. BULL. 476, 478 (1995); Rocky Mountain Bank of Billings, 80 FED. RES. BULL. 1030, 1032 (1994); Stichting Prioriteit ABN AMRO Holding, 80 FED. RES. BULL. 652, 654 (1994); NCNB Corp., 78 FED. RES. BULL. 141, 151 (1992); Firstar Corp., 77 FED. RES. BULL. 1005, 1009 (1991); Marsico, *supra* note 1, at 226–27 & nn. 324–25.

150. Omni Bank, 1991 OCC Ltr. LEXIS 127, at *2 (June 24, 1991).

151. *See* Gore-Bronson Bancorp, 78 FED. RES. BULL. at 785–86; First Interstate BancSystem, 77 FED. RES. BULL. at 1008–9; PNC Financial Corp., 75 FED. RES. BULL. 312, 316 (1989); Continental Bank Corp., 75 FED. RES. BULL. 304, 305 (1989); Joint Statement, *supra* note 2, at 13,766; John P. LaWare, Statement Before the S. Comm. on Banking, Finance, and Urban Affairs (Sept. 24, 1991), *in* 77 FED. RES. BULL. 932, 936 (1991); Marsico, *supra* note 1, at 272.

152. *See* TotalBank Corp., 81 FED. RES. BULL. 876; Gore-Bronson Bancorp, 78 FED. RES. BULL. at 785–86; First Interstate BancSystem, 77 FED. RES. BULL. at 1008–9; PNC Fin. Corp., 75 FED. RES. BULL. at 316; Continental Bank Corp., 75 FED. RES. BULL. at 305; Marsico, *supra* note 1, at 272.

153. American Commerce Nat'l Bank, 1989 OCC Ltr. LEXIS 98, at *1-2.

154. *Recent Corporate Decisions*, OFFICE OF THE COMPTROLLER OF THE CURRENCY Q. J. 9-3, Sept. 1990, at 21.

155. Nat'l Bank of Commerce, 1992 OCC Ltr. LEXIS 87, at *1 (Nov. 20, 1992).

156. Mayde Creek Bank, 1993 OCC Ltr. LEXIS 77, at *2.

157. *Id.* at *2-3.

158. Santander Nat'l Bank, 1993 OCC Ltr. LEXIS 5, at *2 (Feb. 5, 1993).

159. *See* First Nat'l Bank in Newton, 1994 OCC Ltr. LEXIS 66 (June 10, 1994); The Nat'l Bank of Corinth, 1993 OCC Ltr. LEXIS 30; The Nat'l Bank of Anchorage, 1993 OCC Ltr. LEXIS 24 (June 24, 1993); Nat'l Commerce Bank, 1993 OCC Ltr. LEXIS 4 (Jan. 7, 1993); First Nat'l Bank of Northwest, 1992 OCC Ltr. LEXIS 87 (Nov. 20, 1992); El Capitan Nat'l Bank, 1992 OCC Ltr. LEXIS 75 (Sept. 4, 1992); The Lake Crystal Nat'l Bank, 1992 OCC Ltr. LEXIS 56 (June 19, 1992); Grand Nat'l Bank, 1992 OCC Ltr. LEXIS 62 (Apr. 22, 1992); Pacific Nat'l Bank, 1992 OCC Ltr. LEXIS 61 (Apr. 1, 1992); Puget Sound Nat'l Bank, 1992 OCC Ltr. LEXIS 13 (Mar. 23, 1992); Puget Sound Nat'l Bank, 1992 OCC Ltr. LEXIS 12 (Mar. 19, 1992); The First Nat'l Bank and Trust Co., 1992 OCC Ltr. LEXIS 11 (Mar. 17, 1992); Nat'l Republic Bank of Chicago, 1992 OCC Ltr. LEXIS 21 (Mar. 4, 1992); Commercebank, 1992 OCC Ltr. LEXIS 58 (Feb. 27, 1992); Commercebank, 1992 OCC Ltr. LEXIS 57 (Feb. 27, 1992); First Interstate Nat'l Bank of Washington, 1991 OCC Ltr. LEXIS 129 (June 25, 1991); First Interstate Nat'l Bank of Washington, 1991 OCC Ltr. LEXIS 128 (June 25, 1991); Mid-City Nat'l Bank of Chicago, 1990 OCC Ltr. LEXIS 28 (June 1, 1990); Firstar Eagan Bank, 1990 OCC Ltr. LEXIS 19 (Apr. 16, 1990); Mercantile Nat'l Bank of Indiana, 1990 OCC Ltr. LEXIS 5 (Feb. 12, 1990); *Recent Decisions*, Office of the Comptroller of the Currency Q. J. 11-2, June 1992, at 11; *Recent Decisions*, Office of the Comptroller of the Currency Q. J. 10-4, Dec. 1991, at 9; *Recent Decisions*, Office of the Comptroller of the Currency Q. J. 10-3, Sept. 1991, at 11; *Recent Decisions*, Office of the Comptroller of the Currency Q. J. 10-2, June 1991, at 25; *Recent Decisions*, Office of the Comptroller of the Currency Q. J. 10-1, Mar. 1991, at 45; *Recent Decisions*, Office of the Comptroller of the Currency Q. J. 9-4, Dec. 1990, at 19.

160. *See* The First Nat'l Bank of Anchorage, 1993 OCC Ltr. LEXIS 24; Nat'l Commerce Bank, 1993 OCC Ltr. LEXIS 4; Grand Nat'l Bank, 1992 OCC Ltr. LEXIS 62; Pacific Nat'l Bank, 1992 OCC Ltr. LEXIS 61; Nat'l Republic Bank of Chicago, 1992 OCC Ltr. LEXIS 21; Omni Bank, 1991 OCC Ltr. LEXIS 130 (July 18, 1991); Omni Bank, 1991 OCC. Ltr. LEXIS 127.

161. *See* Central Fidelity Bank, 1993 OCC Ltr. LEXIS 87 (Dec, 22, 1993); Beneficial Nat'l Bank, 1993 OCC Ltr. LEXIS 40 (Aug. 27, 1993); Citizens Bank of Washington, 1993 OCC Ltr. LEXIS 19 (Feb. 25, 1993); Woodstown Nat'l Bank and Trust Co., 1993 OCC Ltr. LEXIS 18 (Feb. 17, 1993); Santander Nat'l Bank, 1993 OCC Ltr. LEXIS 5; The Liberty Nat'l Bank in Paris, 1992 OCC Ltr. LEXIS 60 (Mar. 16, 1992); Credit Int'l Bank, 1992 OCC Ltr. LEXIS 59 (Mar. 12, 1992); The Nat'l Republic Bank of Chicago, 1992 OCC Ltr. LEXIS 21; Commercebank, 1992 OCC Ltr. LEXIS 58; Commercebank, 1992 OCC Ltr. LEXIS 57; First Interstate Nat'l Bank of Washington, 1991 OCC Ltr. LEXIS 129; First Interstate Nat'l Bank of Washington, 1991 OCC Ltr. LEXIS 128 (June 25, 1991); First Florida Bank, 1990 OCC Ltr. LEXIS 29 (May 23, 1990); First Florida Bank, 1989 OCC Ltr. LEXIS 97 (Nov. 20, 1989); Canner, *supra* note 4, at 55–56; *Recent Decisions*, Office of the Comptroller of the Currency Q. J. 10-4, Dec. 1991, at 9; *Recent Decisions*, Office of the Comptroller of the Currency Q. J. 10-3, Sept. 1991, at 11; *Recent Decisions*, Office of the Comptroller of the Currency Q. J. 10-1, Mar. 1991, at 45; *Recent Decisions*, Office of the Comptroller of the Currency Q. J. 9-4, Dec. 1990, at 19.

162. Omni Bank, 1991 OCC Ltr. LEXIS 127, at *2.

163. Grand Nat'l Bank, 1993 OCC Ltr. LEXIS 5, at *2-4 (Apr. 22, 1992).

164. 12 U.S.C. §1818(b).

165. In 1994, the Office of Legal Counsel of the Department of Justice issued an opinion stating that the agencies do not have the authority to enforce the CRA through administrative enforcement proceedings. *See* Memorandum from Walter Dellinger, Assistant Attorney General, to Eugene A. Ludwig, Comptroller of the Currency (Dec. 15, 1994)(on file with the author).

166. *See In re* Bank of Holland, 1994 FDIC Enf. Dec. LEXIS 215 (July 22, 1994); *In re* First State Bank, 1994 FDIC Enf. Dec. LEXIS 217 (July 12, 1994); *In re* Bank of Coffey, 1994 FDIC Enf. Dec. LEXIS 146 (May 27, 1994); *In re* Buckner State Bank, 1994 FDIC Enf. Dec. LEXIS 127 (April 6, 1994); *In re* Golden Sec. Thrift & Loan, 1993 FDIC Enf. Dec. LEXIS 688 (Sept. 1, 1993); *In re* [Anonymous], 1982 FDIC Enf. Dec. LEXIS 2 (June 14, 1982); *In re* Broadway Nat'l Bank, 1991 OCC Enf. Dec. LEXIS 493 (Sept. 19, 1991); *In re* First Nichols Nat'l Bank, 1991 OCC Enf. Dec. LEXIS 140 (July 25, 1991); *In re* Foxboro Nat'l Bank, 1991 OCC Enf. Dec. LEXIS 115 (July 24, 1991); *In re* Hilton Head Bank & Trust Co., 1991 OCC Enf. Dec. LEXIS 42 (Apr. 30, 1991); *In re* Crown Nat'l Bank, 1991 OCC Enf. Dec. LEXIS 47 (Apr. 29, 1991); *In re* Bank USA, 1991 OCC Enf. Dec. LEXIS 37 (Apr. 25, 1991); *In re* Interstate Nat'l Bank of Dallas, 1991 OCC Enf. Dec. LEXIS 13 (Mar. 26, 1991); *In re* Cont'l Nat'l Bank of Miami, 1991 OCC Enf. Dec. LEXIS 410 (Jan. 9, 1991); *In re* Powell Valley Nat'l Bank, 1990 OCC Enf. Dec. LEXIS 133 (Dec. 13, 1990); *In re* Mid Jersey Nat'l Bank, 1990 OCC Enf. Dec. LEXIS 1 (July 19, 1990); *In re* Proposed Acquisition, 1985 OCC Enf. Dec. LEXIS 20 (Aug. 14, 1985) (bank failed to delineate its local community and revise its CRA statement annually); *In re* [Anonymous] Nat'l Bank, 1982 OCC Enf. Dec. LEXIS 4 (Nov. 8, 1982); Written Agreement between Equitable Bank and Federal Reserve Bank of Atlanta, No. 94-083-WA/RB-SM (Mar. 8, 1995); Written Agreement between First Bank of Berne and Federal Reserve Bank of Chicago, No. 92-110-WA/RB-SM (Dec. 8, 1992); Written Agreement between Columbus Junction State Bank and Federal Reserve Bank of Chicago, No. 92-076-WA/RB-SM (Nov. 30, 1992); Written Agreement between Davis Nat'l Bank of Mullins and the Office of the Comptroller of the Currency, 1993 OCC Enf. Dec. LEXIS 113 (Apr. 21, 1994); *In* re Farmers and Merchants Bank of Long Beach, No. 91-080-B-SM (Board of Governors of the Federal Reserve System Mar, 23, 1992).

167. Formal Agreement Between the Office of the Comptroller of the Currency and First Nat'l Bank of Bar Harbor, 1993 OCC Enf. Dec. LEXIS 285, at *11, *12 (Aug. 6, 1993).

168. Written Agreement between Equitable Bank and Federal Reserve Bank of Atlanta, *supra* note 167. *See also* Rosemary Stewart, Inter-Office Communication to Maryann Kaswell on Inquiry from Representatives St. Germain and Oakan, 1986 FHLBB LEXIS 241 (Apr. 21, 1986). The Federal Home Loan Bank Board, the predecessor of the Office of Thrift Supervision, reached a supervisory agreement with a bank that required it to make a "significant amount of loans" in its CRA lending area. *Id.*

169. Agreement Between South Branch Valley Nat'l Bank and The Office of the Comptroller of the Currency, 1992 OCC Enf. Dec. LEXIS 465 (Oct. 7, 1992).

170. *See* Bill Atkinson, *Regulatory Costs Called Too Burdensome for Smaller Banks,* AM. BANKER, Jan. 27, 1993, at 5; *Compliance Costs: A Big Hole in Banking's Pocket,* A.B.A.

BANKING J., Aug. 1992, at 12; Debra Cope, *Community Bankers Feel Swamped by the Rising Tide of Regulations,* AM. BANKER, Mar. 25, 1992, at 1; Barbara A. Rehm, *Cost of Compliance Equals 59% of Bank Profits,* AM. BANKER, June 18, 1992, at 1; Linda Young, *Bankers Try to Tackle Regulatory Problems at Convention,* MISS. BUS. J. 26 (Nov. 2, 1992). Kenneth Thomas characterized "unnecessary regulatory burden" as the primary argument against the CRA during the first CRA enforcement regime. CRA PERFORMANCE, *supra* note 95, at 327. His study of CRA performance evaluations in the first CRA enforcement regime "documented numerous instances of what appears to be unnecessary and wasteful documentation with little or no direct benefit to the community." *Id.*

171. *See generally, Hearings on S. 650, supra* note 23, at 321–29 (statement of Billy Don Anderson, President & CEO, Valley Federal Savings Bank); *id.* at 315–21 (statement of Richard L. Mount, President & CEO, Saratoga National Bank); FINAL REPORT, NEW YORK STATE SENATE TASK FORCE ON BANKING AND COMMUNITY REINVESTMENT 1–2, 10–11, 13 (1997) [hereinafter NEW YORK STATE SENATE FINAL REPORT]; Community Reinvestment Act Regulations, 60 Fed. Reg. 22,156 (May 4, 1995) [hereinafter CRA Regulations]; GAO REPORT, *supra* note 89, at 5, 31; *Banking Panel Approves Removing Protests To Applications as CRA Enforcement Tool,* 61 Banking Rep. (BNA), July 3, 1993, at 6; *Costly Timing of CRA Protests Highlighted in Hearing Testimony,* Banking Rep. (BNA), Mar. 13, 1995, at 513; *Bankers Endorse CRA Tradeoff of Enforcement for Paperwork,* NAT'L MORTGAGE NEWS, May 17, 1993, at 3; *Banking Execs Cite CRA As #1 Compliance Headache,* CCC's CRA WATCH, Mar. 24, 1995, at 4; Kenneth Cline, *NationsBank Pressing For Change in CRA Enforcement,* AM. BANKER, Mar. 22, 1993, at 2; Debra Cope, *Community Bankers Feel Swamped By Rising Tide of Regulations,* AM. BANKER, Mar. 25, 1992, at 1; *CRA Will Come to Its Own in the 1990's,* AM. BANKER, Dec. 4, 1990, at 4; Olaf de Senerpont Domis, *Bank Panel's Chairman Backs CRA Exemption For Smaller Banks,* AM. BANKER, May 25, 1995, at 2; Olaf de Senerpont Domis, *Bill Would Reduce CRA to a Disclosure Form,* AM. BANKER, June 1, 1995, at 3; Justin Fox, *Regulatory Relief Bill, Cheered by Bankers, Is Put on Fast Track,* AM. BANKER, May 24, 1995, at 2; James Grant, *Beware of Uncle Sam's Quid Pro Quo,* AM. BANKER, June 9, 1992, at 4; William M. Isaac, *It's Hard to Find a Rationale for CRA in Today's Market,* AM. BANKER, May 4, 1995, at 10; Joe Mysak, *Politically Correct Rules Strangle Smaller Banks,* AM. BANKER, Feb. 1, 1993, at 4; Paul S. Nadler, *What Killed the Banks, Daddy?* AM. BANKER, July 12, 1992, at 4; Jaret Seiberg, *20 Years Later, CRA Controversy Going Strong,* AM. BANKER, Oct. 21, 1997; Jaret Seiberg, *275-Page Regulation Sprouts from 2-Page Act,* AM. BANKER, Oct. 22, 1997, at 3; Paulette Thomas, *Bush's Plans to Relax Community Lending Law and Help Inner Cities Are on a Collision Course,* WALL ST. J., July 21, 1992, at A18; Warren W. Traiger, *Examining Agencies Need to Fine-Tune CRA Standards,* AM. BANKER, Oct. 28, 1991, at 8; David Warner, *Banks Seek Change in Lending Law,* NATION'S BUS., Sept. 1991, at 34.

172. CRA Regulations, *supra* note 171, at 22,156.

173. *See* H.R. 317, 104th Cong. (1995) (A bill to amend the Community Reinvestment Act of 1977 to reduce onerous record keeping and reporting requirements for regulated financial institutions, and for other purposes); H.R. 1362, 104th Cong. (1995) (A bill to reduce paperwork and additional regulatory burdens for depository institutions); S. 650, 104th Cong. (1995) (A bill to increase the amount of credit available to fuel local, regional, and national economic growth by reducing the regulatory

burden imposed upon financial institutions, and for other purposes). *See also* New York State Senate Final Report, *supra* note 171; *Costly Timing of CRA Protests Highlighted in Hearing Testimony*, *supra* note 171, at 513; *Attempts to Amend CRA in Senate Banking Committee Unsuccessful*, [Current Developments] Hous. & Dev. Rep. (West) 306 (Sept. 21, 1991); Olaf de Senerpont Domis, *CRA Exemption for Small Banks, Shield for Big Ones in House Bill*, Am. Banker, Jan. 12, 1995, at 2; Robert Garsson, *Dole Seeing Less Regulations*, Am. Banker, June 4, 1992, at 21; Bill McConnell, *Leach Pulling CRA Provisions from Bank Bill*, Am. Banker, Oct. 9, 1995, at 4; Bill McConnell, *Senate Panel Agrees to Reduce Red Tape, Doesn't Touch CRA*, Am. Banker, Sept. 28, 1995, at 2; Barbara A. Rehm, *Activists Warn Banks that Campaign to Ease CRA Rules Might Backfire*, Am. Banker, June 29, 1992, at 1; Thomas, *supra* note 171, at A18; Paulette Thomas, *Minority-Area Lenders Faulted in Acorn Study*, Wall. St. J., June 5, 1992, at A2.

174. *See 1992 Hearings*, *supra* note 101, at 152 (statement of Calvin Bradford, President, Community Reinvestment Associates); *id.* at 314–15 (statement of ACORN); *Hearings on S. 650*, *supra* note 23, at 377–82 (statement of George Butts, Executive Board Member, ACORN); Lindsey Testimony, *supra* note 32, at 1128 ("I am convinced that thousands of loans have been made that would not have been made but for the CRA."); Ludwig Statement, *supra* note 13, at 38; Senate CRA Report, *supra* note 33, at 6; Seiberg, *20 years later*, *supra* note 172; *Rubin Defends CRA But Backs 'Sensible Regulatory Reform*, Am. Banker, May 5, 1995, at 3.

175. *See 1992 Hearings*, *supra* note 101, at 97 (statement of Gilda Haas, Community Organizer, Communities for Accountable Reinvestment); *Hearings on S. 650*, *supra* note 23, at 272, 377–81 (statement of George Butts); GAO Report, *supra* note 89, at 5; Joel Glenn Brenner, *Bush Plan to Change Lending Law Draws Fire*, Washington Post, Sept. 15, 1992, at F1.

176. Wendy Pelle, *CRA, An Effective Program, But Some Questions on Ratings*, Nat'l Mortgage News, Oct. 28, 1991, at 22.

177. *1992 Hearings*, *supra* note 101, at 11–13, 91–92 (statement of Michael Bodaken, Community Reinvestment Coordinator, Office of Mayor Tom Bradley); *id.* at 14–16, 122–25 (statement of Gilda Haas, Community Organizer, Communities for Accountable Reinvestment); *id.* at 28, 198 (statement of Deborah Goldberg, Reinvestment Specialist, Center for Community Change); CRA Regulations, *supra* note 171, at 22,156; King, *supra* note 33, at G4; Pelle, *supra* note 176, at 22.

178. New York State Senate Final Report, *supra* note 171, at 1, 2, 10–11; *Hearings on S. 650*, *supra* note 23, at 387–89 (statement of Gale Cincotta, Executive Director, National Training and Information Center); CRA Regulations, *supra* note 171, at 22,156; GAO Report, *supra* note 89, at 34–35; Allen J. Fishbein, *Satisfying Your Examiner & Satisfying Your Community Are Not Always the Same*, A.B.A. Bank Compliance, Autumn 1990, at 2, 3–4; *Costly Timing of CRA Protests Highlighted in Hearing Testimony*, *supra* note 171, at 513; Lindsey Statement, *supra* note 3, at 290; Thomas, *supra* note 171, at A18; *Fed's CRA Ratings Show High Level of Compliance*, *supra* note 33, at 8; Pelle, *supra* note 176, at 22; Morris, *supra* note 33, at 1.

179. *See 1992 Hearings*, *supra* note 101, at 7 (statement of Sen. Neal); *id.* at 10 (statement of Michelle White, Executive Director, Fair Housing Congress); *id.* at 14–15 (statement of Gilda Haas, Communities for Accountable Reinvestment); *id.* at 35, 154

(statement of Calvin Bradford, President, Community Reinvestment Associates) (Bradford testified, based on his study of CRA evaluation reports, "[L]enders have been able to get the highest rating (outstanding) in spite of serious problems with service to low-income and minority lending needs. For example, in 1990, both Manufacturers Hanover Trust and Chemical Bank made only one loan between them for critically needed multi-family housing in New York City, but each received a CRA rating of outstanding. Columbia National Bank received an outstanding rating despite the fact that it defined its CRA lending area to exclude adjacent Latino and African-American communities, made few loans in minority communities, and the loans it did make in minority communities were to white borrowers for large amounts."); *CRA Regulations, supra* note 171, at 22,156; A STUDY OF THE NATIONAL IMPLICATIONS OF CRA RATINGS AND HMDA DATA (1992); Teresa Carson, *BankAmerica Faces Ordeal: 145 to Testify*, AM. BANKER, Jan. 14, 1993, at 1; Claudia Cummins, *Fed to Review Adequacy of Its CRA Examinations*, AM. BANKER, Feb. 8, 1993, at 1; *Fed Called "Embarrassing Rubber Stamp" on Mergers*, AM. BANKER, Mar. 8, 1996, at 2.

180. Eugene A. Ludwig, Statement before the S. Comm. on Banking, Hous., and Urban Affairs on Community Development and Community Reinvestment (July 15, 1993), *in* OFFICE OF THE COMPTROLLER OF THE CURRENCY Q. J. 12-4, Dec. 1993, at 9.

181. *Id.*

182. *Id.* at 19–20.

183. *Id.* at 19.

184. Ludwig CRA Statement, *supra* note 89, at 31.

185. Lindsey Address, *supra* note 12, at *1.

186. Lindsey Testimony, *supra* note 32, at 1128.

187. SENATE CRA REPORT, *supra* note 33, at 48.

188. Cope, *supra* note 89; at 14.

189. SENATE CRA REPORT, *supra* note 33, at 51.

CHAPTER FOUR

1. *See* Joint Release, Federal Regulators to Hold Hearings in New York on Community Lending by Financial Institutions (Aug. 26, 1993), *in* 1993 OCC CB LEXIS 95, at *2 [hereinafter Joint Release]; Glenn B. Canner & Wayne Passmore, *Home Purchase Lending in Low-Income Neighborhoods and to Low-Income Businesses*, 81 FED. RES. BULL. 71 (1995)(Banks frequently argue that a performance test for lenders that evaluates the quantity of their lending in various neighborhoods constitutes credit allocation.).

2. Community Reinvestment Act Regulations, 60 Fed. Reg. 22,156, 22,157 (Apr. 19, 1995) (codified in 12 C.F.R. pts. 25, 228, 345, and 563e (2002)) [hereinafter Final CRA Regulations]; Joint Release, *supra* note 1, at *2.

3. *See* Proposed Rules, Community Reinvestment Act Regulations, 58 Fed. Reg. 67,466 (proposed Dec. 21, 1993) [hereinafter 1993 Proposal]; Proposed Rules, Community Reinvestment Act Regulations, 59 Fed. Reg. 51,232 (proposed Oct. 7, 1994) [hereinafter 1994 Proposal].

4. *See generally* Final CRA Regulations, *supra* note 2. A copy of the CRA regulations appears in Appendix Two.

5. 12 C.F.R. §25.51(b)(4)(ii) (2002).
6. *See* 1993 Proposal, *supra* note 3, at 67,468.
7. *Id.* at 67,469.
8. *Id.*
9. *Id.*
10. *Id.* at 67,471.
11. *Id.* at 67,482.
12. *Id.* at 67,470–71.
13. *Id.* at 67,481–82.
14. *Id.* at 67,469.
15. *Id.*
16. *Id.*
17. *Id.* at 67,472.
18. *Id.* at 67,470–71.
19. *Id.* at 67,482.
20. *Id.* at 67,470–71, 67,481–82.
21. *Id.* at 67,473.
22. *Id.* at 67,480.
23. *Id.* at 67,471.
24. *Id.* at 67,474.
25. Canner & Passmore, *supra* note 1.
26. 1994 Proposal, *supra* note 3, at 51,237; Jaret Seiberg, *Revamped CRA Rules Shift The Focus to Performance*, AM. BANKER, Apr. 27, 1995, at 1; S. Alvarez et al., Memorandum to the Board of Governors of the Federal Reserve System on CRA Reform (Sept. 22, 1994) (on file with author) [hereinafter CRA Reform Memorandum]. *See also* Canner & Passmore, *supra* note 1.
27. *Community Reinvestment Act: Hearings before the Subcomm. on Financial Institutions and Consumer Credit of the S. Comm. on Banking and Financial Services*, 104th Cong. 348 (1995) (Statement of James M. Culberson, Chairman, First National Bank and Trust Company) [hereinafter *1995 CRA Hearing*]. *See also President Clinton's Community Reinvestment Act Proposal: Hearing before the Subcomm. on Consumer Credit and Insurance of the House Comm. on Banking, Finance, and Urban Affairs,*103rd Cong. 179 (1994) (Statement of James M. Culberson, Jr., American Bankers Association) [hereinafter *President Clinton's CRA Proposal Hearing*]; *Proposed Regulatory Community Reinvestment Act Reform: Hearings before the Subcomm. on General Oversight, Investigations and the Resolution of Failed Financial Institutions of the House Comm. on Banking, Finance, and Urban Affairs*, 103rd Cong. 48 (1994) [hereinafter *CRA Reform Hearing*].
28. William Plasencia, *CRA Jitters Hit Small Banks; Fears of Quotas Widespread*, AM. BANKER, June 1, 1994, at 10. *See also*, Malcolm Bush & Daniel Immergluck, *Research, Advocacy, and Community Reinvestment, in* ORGANIZING ACCESS TO CAPITAL: ADVOCACY AND THE DEMOCRATIZATION OF FINANCIAL INSTITUTIONS 159 (Gregory D. Squires ed., 2003).
29. *1995 CRA Hearing, supra* note 27, at 348; *President Clinton's CRA Proposal Hearing, supra* note 27, at 179; *CRA Reform Hearing, supra* note 27, at 5, 48.
30. *President Clinton's CRA Proposal Hearing, supra* note 27, at 179.

31. 1994 Proposal, *supra* note 3, at 51,237; Claudia Cummins, *CRA Reform Proposal Rated 'Needs to Improve,'* AM. BANKER, Mar. 25, 1994, at 4; CRA Reform Memorandum, *supra* note 26, at 7.

32. *CRA Reform Hearing, supra* note 27, at 170.

33. *1995 CRA Hearing, supra* note 27, at 756–57.

34. *1995 CRA Hearing, supra* note 27, at 348. *See also President Clinton's CRA Proposal Hearing, supra* note 27, at 179.

35. 1994 Proposal, *supra* note 3, at 51,237.

36. *CRA Reform Hearing, supra* note 27, at 170.

37. *Id.* at 178, 185.

38. S. Alvarez et al., Memorandum to Board of Governors of the Federal Reserve System, on Community Reinvestment Act Reform Project: Proposed Amendments to Regulation BB (Dec. 7, 1993) (on file with author).

39. *President Clinton's CRA Proposal Hearing, supra* note 27, at 93.

40. *Id.* at 21, 83.

41. *Id.* at 70.

42. *CRA Reform Hearing, supra* note 27, at 4.

43. *1995 CRA Hearing, supra* note 27, at 297–98.

44. *Id.* at 155.

45. *Id.* at 155–56.

46. 1994 Proposal, *supra* note 3, at 51,234.

47. *Id.*

48. *Id.* at 51,236.

49. *Id.*

50. *Id.* at 51,238.

51. *Id.* at 51,239.

52. *Id.* at 51,241.

53. *Id.*

54. Final CRA Regulations, *supra* note 3, at 22,157.

55. *Id.*

56. 12 C.F.R. § 25.21(b) (2002).

57. *Id.*

58. *Id.*

59. *See id.* §§ 25.21(b)(3)–(4).

60. *Id.* § 25.21(b)(3) and (4). On August 18, 2004, the OTS amended its regulations to define a small bank as having no more than $1 billion in assets. *See* 59 Fed. Reg. 51,155 (Aug. 18, 2004). The FDIC is considering making a similar change in its regulations. *See* 59 Fed. Reg. 51,611 (Aug. 20, 2004).

61. *Id.* § 25.21(b)(2). A wholesale bank is a bank that is not in the business of extending loans to retail customers and has been designated by the agency that regulates it as a wholesale bank. *Id.* § 25.12(w). A limited purpose bank is a bank that offers only a narrow product line and has been designated by the agency that regulates it as a limited purpose bank. *Id.* § 25.12(o).

62. *Id.* § 25.21(a)(3). A small bank is a bank that, as of December 31 of either of the prior two calendar years, had total assets of less than $250 million and was independent

or an affiliate of a holding company that, as of December 31 of either of the prior two calendar years, had total banking and thrift assets of less than $1 billion. *Id.* §25.12 (t).

63. *Id.* §25.12(a)(4).

64. *Id.* §25.22(a)(1). A home mortgage loan is a home improvement or home purchase loan as defined by the Home Mortgage Disclosure Act. *Id.* §25.12(m). A small farm or small business loan is defined in the instructions for the Consolidated Report of Condition and Income that banks are required to compile. *Id.* §25.12(u) and (v); *id* §25.22(b)(3)(ii). A community development loan is a loan that has community development as its primary purpose. *Id.* §25.12(i). Community development means affordable housing for LMI individuals, community services targeted to LMI individuals, activities that promote economic development through small businesses or small farms, and activities that revitalize or stabilize LMI geographies. *Id.* §25.12(h). In addition, the federal banking agencies will consider a bank's consumer lending if consumer lending constitutes a substantial portion of the bank's business. *Id.* §25.22(a)(1).

65. *Id.* §§25.22(b)(1)–(5).

66. *Id.* §25.22(b)(3); pt. 25 App. A(b)(1).

67. *Id.* pt. 25 App. A(b)(1)(i)–(v).

68. *Id.* pt. 25 App. A(b)(2)(i)–(v).

69. 12 C.F.R. §25.23(a); *id.* §§25.23(e)(1)–(4).

70. 12 C.F.R. §25.23(f); *id.* pt. 25 App. A(b)(2)(i)–(v).

71. *Id.* §25.24.

72. Community development banking services include providing technical expertise to not-for-profits involved in economic development, serving on a board of directors of a community development organization, credit counseling, or low cost government check-cashing. Final CRA Regulations, *supra* note 2, at 22,160 & n.2.

73. 12 C.F.R. §§25.24(d)(1)–(4).

74. *Id.* pt. 25 App. A(b)(3).

75. Final CRA Regulations, *supra* note 2, at 22,168–70.

76. *Id.*

77. 12 C.F.R. §25.29(b).

78. *Id.* §§25.26(a)(1)–(5).

79. *Id.* pt. 25 App. A(d)(1).

80. *Id.* pt. 25 App. A(d)(2).

81. *Id.* pt. 25 App. A(d)(3).

82. *Id.* §25.25(a).

83. *Id.* §25.25(c).

84. *Id.* pt. 25 App. A(c).

85. *Id.* §25.27.

86. *Id.* §§25.27(f)(1)–(4).

87. *Id.* §§25.27(a)(1)–(4).

88. *Id.* §§25.27(d)(1) and (2).

89. *Id.* §25.27(c)(1).

90. *Id.* §25.27(f)(1).

91. *Id.* §25.27(f)(2).

92. *Id.* §25.27(f)(3).

93. *Id.* §25.27(f)(4).
94. *Id.* §25.27(g)(3)(i).
95. *Id.* §25.27(g)(3)(ii).
96. *Id.* §25.27(g)(3)(iii).
97. *Id.* pt. 25 App. A(e)(1) and (2).
98. *Id.* pt. 25 App. A(e)(3).
99. *Id.* §25.28(c).
100. *Id.*
101. Final CRA Regulations, *supra* note 2, at 22,158.
102. Memorandum from Walter Dellinger, Assistant Attorney General, to Eugene M. Ludwig, Comptroller of the Currency (Dec. 15, 1994)(on file with the author).
103. 12 C.F.R. §§25.29(a) and (c).
104. *Id.* §§25.29(c) and (d).
105. Final CRA Regulations, *supra* note 2, at 22,170.
106. *Id.* at 22,170–71.
107. 12 C.F.R. §25.41(a).
108. *Id.* §25.41(a).
109. *Id.*
110. *Id.* §25.41(b).
111. *Id.* §25.41(c).
112. *Id.* §25.41(e).
113. *Id.* §25.42.
114. *Id.* §§25.42(b)(2) and (3); *id.* §25.43(a)(4).

CHAPTER FIVE

1. Chapter Five uses the following abbreviations:

#: total number
≤: less than or equal to
<: less than
AA: CRA assessment area (the geographic area in which the bank has CRA obligations)
agg: aggregate
BUS: business or businesses
CD: community development
cf: compared with
CON: consumer
fam: family or families
G: thousand
HI: home improvement
HH: households
HMDA: Home Mortgage Disclosure Act
HP: home purchase
HR: home refinance
LAR: loan-to-asset ratio

LDR: loan-to-deposit ratio
LI: low-income
LMI: low- and moderate-income
M: million
MF: multi-family
MI: moderate-income
MIDI: middle-income
MS: market share
MV: motor vehicle
OOHU(s): owner-occupied housing unit(s)
OTS: Office of Thrift Supervision
PE: CRA performance evaluation
pop: population
rev: gross annual revenue
SB(s): small business(es)
SF(s): small farm(s)
tract(s): census tract(s)
UI: upper-income
vol: volume
w/: with

2. *Cf.* MICHAEL STEGMAN ET AL., TOWARD A MORE PERFORMANCE DRIVEN SERVICE TEST: STRENGTHENING BASIC BANKING SERVICES UNDER THE COMMUNITY REINVESTMENT ACT 4 (Oct. 2001)(The federal banking agencies' analysis of bank services when conducting the service test portion of the CRA performance evaluation is characterized by confusing and inconsistent standards and a lack of quantitative information.).

3. *See supra* ch. 4, text accompanying notes 65 to 66 for more about this.

4. *See supra* ch. 4, text accompanying notes 79 to 82 for more about this.

5. The analysis of the federal banking agencies' practices in evaluating the lending performance of large retail banks is based on an examination of a sample of sixteen CRA performance evaluations ("PEs") the federal banking agencies issued between March 30, 1998 and September 17, 2001. The sample was constructed by selecting the most recent (at the time of selection) large retail bank PE issued by each agency for each of the five possible lending test ratings under the CRA regulations: outstanding; high satisfactory; low satisfactory; needs to improve; and substantial noncompliance. This should have resulted in a total of twenty PEs (four agencies and five ratings). However, none of the four agencies had issued a substantial noncompliance rating on the lending test for a large bank, so there are only sixteen PEs in the sample. The PEs in the sample are (the number following each citation is for subsequent reference): CENTRAL REGION, OFFICE OF THRIFT SUPERVISION, DOCKET # 04474, COMMUNITY REINVESTMENT ACT PERFORMANCE EVALUATION, ANCHORBANK, F.S.B. (2001)(100); DIVISION OF COMPLIANCE AND CONSUMER AFFAIRS, CHICAGO REGIONAL OFFICE, FEDERAL DEPOSIT INSURANCE CORPORATION, COMMUNITY REINVESTMENT ACT PERFORMANCE EVALUATION, AMERICAN CHARTERED BANK (2001)(101); DIVISION OF COMPLIANCE AND CONSUMER AFFAIRS, FEDERAL DEPOSIT INSURANCE CORPORATION, COMMUNITY REINVESTMENT ACT PERFORMANCE EVALUATION,

Central Bank and Trust Company (2001)(102); Federal Deposit Insurance Corporation, Community Reinvestment Act Performance Evaluation, Exchange Bank (2001)(103); Chicago South Field Office, Office of the Comptroller of the Currency, Community Reinvestment Act Performance Evaluation (2001)(104); Central Region, Office of Thrift Supervision, Docket # 03235, Community Reinvestment Act Performance Evaluation, Time Federal Savings Bank (2001)(105); Federal Reserve Bank of Chicago, Community Reinvestment Act Performance Evaluation, UnionBank (2001)(106); Large Bank Supervision Division, Community Reinvestment Act Performance Evaluation, First Massachusetts Bank, N.A. (2001)(107); South Florida Field Office, Office of the Comptroller of the Currency, Community Reinvestment Act Performance Evaluation, First National Bank of South Miami (2001)(108); Federal Deposit Insurance Corporation, Community Reinvestment Act Performance Evaluation, Marquette Savings Bank (2001)(109); Northeast Region, Office of Thrift Supervision, Docket # 04115, Community Reinvestment Act Performance Evaluation, Astoria Federal Savings & Loan Association (2001)(110); Southeast Region, Office of Thrift Supervision, Docket # 02349, Community Reinvestment Act Performance Evaluation, Arundel Federal Savings Bank (2001)(111); Federal Reserve Bank of Atlanta, Community Reinvestment Act Performance Evaluation, Aliant Bank (2001)(112); Federal Reserve Bank of Philadelphia, Community Reinvestment Act Performance Evaluation, First Republic Bank (1999) (113); Southeastern District, Office of the Comptroller of the Currency, Community Reinvestment Act Performance Evaluation, First National Bank of South Miami (1999)(114); Federal Reserve Bank of San Francisco, Community Reinvestment Act Performance Evaluation, California Center Bank (1998)(115).

The analysis of the federal banking agencies' practices in evaluating the lending performance of small retail banks is based on an examination of a sample of sixteen CRA PEs of small retail banks the federal banking agencies issued between September 29, 1997 and September 11, 2001. This sample was constructed by selecting the most recent (at the time of selection) small bank PE issued by each agency for each of the four possible small bank ratings under the CRA regulations: outstanding; satisfactory; needs to improve; and substantial noncompliance. The PEs are (the number following each citation is for subsequent reference): Central Region, Office of Thrift Supervision, Docket # 04059, Community Reinvestment Act Performance Evaluation, The Home Builders Association (2001)(121); Midwest Region, Office of Thrift Supervision, Docket # 07830, Community Reinvestment Act Performance Evaluation, Viking Savings Association, F.A. (2001)(122); Arizona/New Mexico Field Office, Comptroller of the Currency, Community Reinvestment Act Performance Evaluation, Alamosa National Bank (2001)(123); Federal Reserve Bank of San Francisco, Community Reinvestment Act Performance Evaluation, Verdugo National Bank (2001)(124); Southern California Field Office, Office of the Comptroller of the Currency, Community Reinvestment Act Performance Evaluation, Inland Community

BANK, N.A. (2001)(125); FEDERAL DEPOSIT INSURANCE CORPORATION, COMMUNITY REINVESTMENT ACT PERFORMANCE EVALUATION, ODEBOLT STATE BANK (2001)(126); FEDERAL RESERVE BANK OF KANSAS CITY, COMMUNITY REINVESTMENT ACT PERFORMANCE EVALUATION, UNITA COUNTY STATE BANK (2001)(127); FEDERAL RESERVE BANK OF SAN FRANCISCO, COMMUNITY REINVESTMENT ACT PERFORMANCE EVALUATION, DESERT COMMUNITY BANK (2001)(128); MIDWEST REGION, OFFICE OF THRIFT SUPERVISION, DOCKET # 08526, COMMUNITY REINVESTMENT ACT PERFORMANCE EVALUATION, FIRST HEIGHTS BANK (2001)(129); DIVISION OF COMPLIANCE AND COMMUNITY AFFAIRS, FEDERAL DEPOSIT INSURANCE CORPORATION, 1ST CHOICE BANK (2001)(130); CENTRAL REGION, OFFICE OF THRIFT SUPERVISION, DOCKET # 04475, COMMUNITY REINVESTMENT ACT PERFORMANCE EVALUATION, MIDLAND FEDERAL SAVINGS AND LOAN ASSOCIATION (2001)(131); FEDERAL RESERVE BANK OF ST. LOUIS, COMMUNITY REINVESTMENT ACT PERFORMANCE EVALUATION, FIRST STATE BANK OF DEQUEEN (2001)(132); FEDERAL DEPOSIT INSURANCE CORPORATION, COMMUNITY REINVESTMENT ACT PERFORMANCE EVALUATION, BANKWEST OF NEVADA (2000)(133); FEDERAL DEPOSIT INSURANCE CORPORATION, COMMUNITY REINVESTMENT ACT PERFORMANCE EVALUATION, THE BANK OF COMMERCE (2000)(134); DETROIT FIELD OFFICE, COMPTROLLER OF THE CURRENCY, COMMUNITY REINVESTMENT ACT PERFORMANCE EVALUATION, FIRST NATIONAL BANK OF AMERICA (1999)(135); SOUTH FLORIDA OFFICE, OFFICE OF THE COMPTROLLER OF THE CURRENCY, COMMUNITY REINVESTMENT ACT PERFORMANCE EVALUATION, KISLAK NATIONAL BANK (1997)(136).

6. Kenneth Thomas found in his study of PEs issued during the second CRA enforcement regime that there was little consistency among the four federal banking agencies in enforcing the CRA. Jaret Seiberg, *Half of CRA Grades Inflated, Fla. Consultant's Book Claims*, AM. BANKER, May 19, 1998, at 4.

7. *See* KENNETH H. THOMAS, THE CRA HANDBOOK 148 (1998) ("Most subjective examiners inflate CRA ratings by emphasizing positive factors…and ignoring or deemphasizing negative factors."). *See also id.* at 306, 379. Thomas found, for example, that a bank examiner inclined to give a bank a positive CRA rating could manipulate a bank's LDR by emphasizing any positive trends, searching for a peer group whose LDRs would make the banks look good, or compare only current LDRs as opposed to LDRs covering the entire evaluative period. *Id.* at 192. *See also id.* at 266–69. Examiners also could simply not include a poor LDR in the PE. *Id.* at 379. Thomas made similar findings regarding the percentage of the bank's loans in its AA, *id.* at 274–75; percentage of loans to LMI persons, *id.* at 287–89; and percentage of loans in LMI census tracts, *id.* at 295–98.

8. A report issued by the Department of the Treasury's Office of Inspector General concluded that terminology in sixty-three PEs it examined was inconsistent. Jaret Seiberg, *Treasury Watchdog Reports Inconsistent Procedures by CRA Compliance Examiners*, AM. BANKER, June 29, 1998. For example, "reasonable" meant both "exceeds requirements" and "meets requirements." *Id.*

9. The Inspector General's Report also found that banks with similar performances were rated differently. *Inspector General Says OCC Exams Need to Improve*, REINVESTMENT WORKS, Fall 1990, at 16. For example, two banks with similar LDRs received different evaluations on that portion of the exam. *Id.* Bankers also complained that banks received

different ratings despite similar records. Bill McConnell, *Regulators to Review Consistency of Grades Given in CRA Exams*, AM. BANKER, December 17, 1997, at 2.

10. For several reasons, these numbers are only approximations. First, the agencies did not always clearly state in the PEs whether a description of a bank's record was a mere statement of fact or an evaluative criterion. Thus, for example, it was not clear whether recitations of the total number of loans or the total number of loans by type the bank made were meant to profile the bank or evaluate it. For purposes of this chapter, statements of fact about bank lending that appeared to be descriptive are not considered to be evaluative criteria. Second, many of the criteria listed are actually combined versions of several different criteria that contain quantitative measures of bank lending and quantitative benchmarks of community credit needs that are identical in principle but different in manifestation. Thus, for example, a criterion might compare the percentage of a bank's loans in LI census tracts (quantitative measure of bank lending) with the percentage of the population living in those tracts (quantitative benchmark of community credit needs). This measure and benchmark could have several different manifestations, including for example, the percentage of one type of a bank's loans, many different types of loans separately, or all loans combined. For this study, these various manifestations were considered to be only one criterion. Appendix Three lists the criteria the agencies used to evaluate large and small bank lending.

11. Kenneth Thomas found, for example, that only 27% of PEs of small banks reported the number of loans to businesses with $1 million or less annual revenue and only 18% reported similar data for small farms. THOMAS, *supra* note 7, at 276. This was the case even though a higher percentage of banks had a sizeable portion of small business and small farm loans and published OCC guidelines called for inclusion of such data in the PEs. *Id.* He also found that several large bank PEs failed to mention the bank's LDR. *Id.* at 379.

12. The agencies used 43 of the 82 large bank criteria once and 22 of the 45 small bank criteria once.

13. *Cf.* STEGMAN ET AL., *supra* note 2, at 12 (the scoring system for the service test portion of the PE "injects a subjective element into even objective, statistical CRA criteria").

14. For example, Kenneth Thomas found, based on his exhaustive analysis of small bank PEs, that a bank had to make 50% of its loans in its AA to meet the standard for "majority." THOMAS, *supra* note 7, at 270. He found that there was no bright-line test for a "substantial majority" of loans in the AA, but found based on his analysis that 85% seemed to meet the standard for substantial majority, although at least one agency used 80%. *Id.* Thomas found that there was no standard for compliance with the percentage of loans to persons at different income levels for small banks. *Id.* at 286.

15. Kenneth Thomas found similar examples in his study of PEs. *See* THOMAS, *supra* note 7, at 300, 334.

16. *Cf.* Joint Notice of Proposed Rulemaking, 69 Fed. Reg. 5,729, 5,734 (proposed Feb. 6, 2004) [hereinafter 2004 Proposal] (banks and community groups criticized the CRA regulations for not specifying how much weight one activity carries relative to another).

17. For example, Kenneth Thomas identified twenty-seven small banks that received satisfactory CRA ratings even though less than a majority of their loans were

in their AAs. THOMAS, *supra*, note 7, at 273. Thomas also found that sixteen small banks with less than 5% of their loans to LMI persons received at least satisfactory CRA ratings. *Id.* at 286–87. He also found that nineteen small banks with no loans in LMI census tracts had satisfactory or outstanding CRA ratings. *Id.* at 295–96.

18. For example, Kenneth Thomas has suggested that small banks are almost guaranteed to meet the standards for percentage of loans in their AA because the AA is defined as the geographic area in which a bank made the majority of its loans. THOMAS, *supra* note 7, at 269. He suggested, therefore, that the criteria evaluating the percentage of the bank's loan in its AA should have the least weight of all the small bank evaluative criteria. However, since there are no weights, it is possible that a bank's performance on the percentage of loans with in its AA could offset poor performance on other criteria. *Id.*

19. *See supra* ch. 4, text accompanying notes 65–68, for more about this. The five possible ratings are outstanding, high satisfactory, low satisfactory, needs to improve, and substantial non-compliance.

20. *See* THOMAS, *supra* note 7, at 148 ("subjective examiners intent on downgrading a rating overemphasize negative factors...and de-emphasize or leave out positive factors").

21. *Cf.* STEGMAN ET AL., *supra* note 2, at 5 (grade inflation on the service portion of the CRA performance evaluation "may be a problem").

22. Thomas, *supra* note 7, at 353.

23. Kenneth Thomas found in his study of small bank PEs that 36.8% of ratings on the LDR component were inflated. *See* THOMAS, *supra* note 7, at 306–8. He also found that 52% of the ratings of banks' loans to LMI borrowers were inflated. *Id.* at 308. Finally, he found that 36.0% of ratings of the banks' loans to LMI census tracts were inflated. *Id.* at 311–12. Thomas found that 88.6% of outstanding ratings for small banks were inflated, *id.* at 320–21; 32% of satisfactory ratings were inflated, *id.* at 324–25; and 32% of needs-to-improve ratings were inflated. *Id.*

24. The sources of this data are *Slight Rise in 'Outstanding' CRA Ratings Ends Seven-Year Decline*, INSIDE MORTGAGE COMPLIANCE, August 5, 2003, at 6; 1997 *CRA Rating Picture Same as '96: Whopping 98 Percent of Institutions Reviewed Receive High Marks, 2 Percent at Lower End*, INSIDE MORTGAGE COMPLIANCE, January, 1998, at 2; *CRA Ratings for First Half of 1997 Indicate Possible Repeat of Last Year's Record-Breaking CRA Compliance Results*, INSIDE FAIR LENDING, July 1997, at 2.

25. *See supra* ch. 3, text accompanying note 94.

26. DANIEL IMMERGLUCK, IS CRA REFORM FOR REAL? ANALYZING THE RATINGS OF LARGE BANKS OPTING FOR EVALUATION UNDER THE NEW CRA REGULATIONS (1997); *Community Groups Call for Temporary Moratorium on Outstanding CRA Ratings*, [Current Developments] Hous. and Dev. Rep., Sept. 8, 1997, at 266; *Freeze Urged on Assignment of 'Outstanding' CRA Ratings*, INSIDE FAIR LENDING, Sept. 1997, at 8; *Regulators Stand by 'Outstanding Rating,'* AM. BANKER, December 11, 1997, at 2.

27. THOMAS, *supra* note 7, at 316–17, 416–19. *Dr. Thomas' CRA Handbook Finds CRA Exam Deficiencies in All Agencies*, REINVESTMENT WORKS, Fall 1998, at 16. *See* Kenneth H. Thomas, THE CRA'S 25TH ANNIVERSARY: THE PAST, PRESENT, AND FUTURE 15 (2002). In his review of the four lending-related components of small bank PEs,

Thomas found that 36.8% of the ratings of bank LDRs were inflated, THOMAS, *supra* note 7, at 306.

28. IMMERGLUCK, *supra* note 26.

29. Bill McConnell, *Regulators to Review Consistency of Grades Given in CRA Exams*, AM. BANKER, Dec. 15, 1997, at 4.

30. *Id.*

31. This section examines only Federal Reserve and OCC decisions because they are the only federal banking agencies that regularly issue written decisions on bank expansion applications involving the CRA.

32. Despite the fact that the Federal Reserve issued these decisions during the second CRA enforcement regime, not all of the decisions involving the CRA were based on the new CRA regulations. Generally, in evaluating a bank's CRA record in connection with deciding its application, the Federal Reserve relied on the most recent CRA PE. Often, especially in orders prior to 2000, the most recent CRA PE occurred earlier than 1997 and thus the decision was based on the old CRA regulations. The decisions reviewed issued after July 1, 1997 are: Cathay Bancorp, Inc., 89 FED. RES. BULL. 468 (2003); Arvest Bank Group, Inc., 89 FED. RES. BULL. 439 (2003); Bank of Hawaii, 89 FED. RES. BULL. 87 (2003); Cooperative Centrale Raiffeisen-Boerenleenbank B.A., 89 FED. RES. BULL. 81 (2003); Citigroup, Inc., 88 FED. RES. BULL. 485 (2002); Westamerica Bank, 88 FED. RES. BULL. 392 (2002); Royal Bank of Canada, 88 FED. RES. BULL. 385 (2002); JPMorgan Chase Bank, 88 FED. RES. BULL. 325 (2002); Charter One Fin., Inc., 88 FED. RES. BULL. 297 (2002); BNP Paribas, 88 FED. RES. BULL. 221 (2002); The Royal Bank of Scotland Group plc, 88 FED. RES. BULL. 51 (2002); North Fork Bancorp., Inc., 87 FED. RES. BULL. 779 (2001); First Union Corp., 87 FED. RES. BULL. 683 (2001); Canadian Imperial Bank of Commerce, 87 FED. RES. BULL. 678 (2001); The Chase Manhattan Bank, 87 FED. RES. BULL. 626 (2001); Citigroup, Inc., 87 FED. RES. BULL. 613 (2001); Citigroup, Inc., 87 FED. RES. BULL. 600 (2001); Old Kent Bank, N.A., 87 FED. RES. BULL. 471 (2001); Fifth Third Bancorp, 87 FED. RES. BULL. 330 (2001); FleetBoston Fin. Corp., 87 FED. RES. BULL. 252 (2001); Firstar Corp., 87 FED. RES. BULL. 236 (2001); J.P. Morgan & Co., Inc., 87 FED. RES. BULL. 77 (2001); Queens Co. Bancorp, Inc., 87 FED. RES. BULL. 30 (2001); Wells Fargo & Co., 86 FED. RES. BULL. 832 (2000); North Fork Bancorp., Inc., 86 FED. RES. BULL. 767 (2000); FleetBoston Fin. Corp., 86 FED. RES. BULL. 751 (2000); Fleet Fin. Group, Inc., 86 FED. RES. BULL. 747 (2000); Firstar Corp., 86 FED. RES. BULL. 738 (2000); Manufacturers and Traders Trust Co., 86 FED. RES. BULL. 694 (2000); Wells Fargo & Co., 86 FED. RES. BULL. 602 (2000); Nat'l Commerce Bancorp., 86 FED. RES. BULL. 597 (2000); The Charles Schwab Corp., 86 FED. RES. BULL. 494 (2000); Peoples Heritage Fin. Group, Inc., 86 FED. RES. BULL. 425 (2000); Valley View Bancshares, Inc., 86 FED. RES. BULL. 420 (2000); Dime Bancorp, Inc., 86 FED. RES. BULL. 413 (2000); North Fork Bancorp., Inc., 86 FED. RES. BULL. 230 (2000); North Fork Bancorp., 86 FED. RES. BULL. 226 (2000); HSBC Holdings plc, 86 FED. RES. BULL. 140 (2000); First Security Corp., 86 FED. RES. BULL. 122 (2000); AmSouth Bancorp., 85 FED. RES. BULL. 685 (1999); Deutsche Bank AG, 85 FED. RES. BULL. 509 (1999); Chittenden Corp., 85 FED. RES. BULL. 499 (1999); Banco Santander, S.A., 85 FED. RES. BULL. 441 (1999); Valley View Bancshares, Inc., 85 FED. RES. BULL. 64 (1999);

Sesquehanna Bancshares, Inc., 85 FED. RES. BULL. 61 (1999); Peoples Heritage Fin. Group, Inc., 85 FED. RES. BULL. 55 (1999); SunTrust Banks, Inc., 84 FED. RES. BULL. 1115 (1998); Norwest Corp., 84 FED. RES. BULL. 1088 (1998); Firstar Corp., 84 FED. RES. BULL. 1083 (1998); Travelers Group, Inc., 84 FED. RES. BULL. 985 (1998); Banc One Corp., 84 FED. RES. BULL. 961 (1998); NationsBank Corp., 84 FED. RES. BULL. 858 (1998); Royal Bank of Canada, 84 FED. RES. BULL. 855 (1998); Regions Fin. Corp., 84 FED. RES. BULL. 558 (1998); Banc One Corp., 84 FED. RES. BULL. 553 (1998); HUBCO, Inc., 84 FED. RES. BULL. 547 (1998); First Union Corp., 84 FED. RES. BULL. 489 (1998); First Midwest Bancorp, Inc., 84 FED. RES. BULL. 486 (1998); North Fork Bancorp., Inc., 84 FED. RES. BULL. 477 (1998); FirstMerit Corp., 84 FED. RES. BULL. 363 (1988); Regions Fin. Corp., 84 FED. RES. BULL. 354 (1998); Peoples Heritage Fin. Group, Inc., 84 FED. RES. BULL. 351 (1998); North Fork Bancorp., Inc., 84 FED. RES. BULL. 290 (1998); NationsBank Corp., 84 FED. RES. BULL. 129 (1998); Star Banc Corp., 84 FED. RES. BULL. 121 (1998); Centura Bank, 84 FED. RES. BULL. 64 (1998); First Union Corp., 83 FED. RES. BULL. 1012 (1997); The Chase Manhattan Corp., 83 FED. RES. BULL. 905 (1997); Santa Barbara Bancorp, 83 FED. RES. BULL. 833 (1997).

33. Wells Fargo & Co., 86 FED. RES. BULL. 832 (2000). The following analysis of the bank's CRA record appears *id.* at 837–45.

34. *Id.* at 845.

35. *Id.*

36. *See e.g.*, CRA Dec. No. 118, O.C.C. Control No. 2003-ML-02-009, 0010 & 0011 (Nov. 6, 2003); CRA Dec. No. 117, O.C.C. Control No. 2003-ML-02-0008 (Oct. 16, 2003); First Nat'l Bank & Trust Co., O.C.C. CRA Dec. No. 115 (Feb. 11, 2003); Charles Schwab Bank, N.A., O.C.C. Conditional Approval No. 577 (February 4, 2003); CRA Dec. No. 111, O.C.C. Control No. 2002-ML-02-0001 (March 1, 2002); European American Bank, O.C.C. Conditional Approval No. 476, (July 1, 2001); First Bank USA, N.A., O.C.C. Corp. Dec. No. 2001-16 (June 14, 2001); Chase Manhattan Bank, N.A., O.C.C. Corp. Dec. No. 2001-06 (March 13, 2001); Wells Fargo & Co., O.C.C. CRA Dec. No. 108 (Feb.15, 2001); Wells Fargo & Co., O.C.C. CRA Dec. No. 106 (June 23, 2000); Southern Cal. Bank, O.C.C. CRA Dec. No. 101 (Oct. 29, 1999); Provident Bank, O.C.C. CRA Dec. No. 100 (October 14, 1999); Bank of Commerce, O.C.C. CRA Dec. No. 96 (June 30, 1999); Bank of America, O.C.C. CRA Dec. No. 94 (May 20, 1999); Bank of America, O.C.C. CRA Dec. No. 89 (February 19, 1999); Firstar Bank, N.A., CRA Dec. No. 82 (Dec. 23, 1998); Barnett Bank, N.A., O.C.C. Corp. Dec. No. 98-44 (Sept. 18, 1998); Nat'l City Bank, O.C.C. Corp. Dec. No. 98-37 (June 23, 1998); Premierbank & Trust Corp., Dec. No. 98-23 (April 30, 1998); Corestates Bank, N.A., O.C.C. Dec. No. 98-21 (April 15,1998); Boatmen's First Nat'l Bank, O.C.C. Corp. Dec. No. 98-11 (Feb. 3, 1998); Star Bank, N.A., O.C.C. Corp. Dec. No. 98-09 (Jan. 28, 1998); Sun World, N.A., O.C.C. Corp. Dec. No. 98-07 (Jan. 15, 1998); Intercontinental Nat'l Bank, O.C.C. CRA Dec. No. 79 (Dec. 3, 1997); First USA Fed. Savings Bank, O.C.C. Corp. Dec. No. 97-111(Dec 30, 1997) and Huntington Nat'l Bank, O.C.C. Corp. Dec. No. 97-88 (Sept. 15, 1997).

37. Bank of America, O.C.C. CRA Dec. No. 94 (May 20, 1999). The analysis of the bank's CRA record appears *id.* at 13-25.

38. *Id.* at 19.

39. *Id.*

40. *Id.*

41. *Id.* at 20.

42. *Id.* at 25.

43. Comptroller of the Currency, Comptroller's Handbook, Community Reinvestment Act Examination Procedures (Oct. 1997)[hereinafter Comptroller's Handbook]; Comptroller of the Currency, Large Bank CRA Examiner Guidance (Dec. 2002)[hereinafter CRA Guidance]; Federal Deposit Insurance Corporation, Compliance Examination Manual (rev. 3 July 31, 1999)[hereinafter FDIC Manual]; Office of Thrift Supervision, Regulatory Handbook, Compliance Activities[hereinafter OTS Handbook]; Federal Financial Institutions Examination Council, Community Reinvestment Act, Interagency Questions and Answers Regarding the Community Reinvestment Act, 66 Fed. Reg. 36,620 (July 12, 2001)[hereinafter CRA Q & A].

44. FDIC Manual, *supra* note 43, at pt. IV, B1-3. *See also id.* at B2-5; OTS Handbook, *supra* note 42, at 500.7.

45. FDIC Manual, *supra* note 43, at pt. IV, B2-10.

46. CRA Q and A, *supra* note 43, at §.26(a)(1)-2.

47. FDIC Manual, *supra* note 43, at pt. IV, B1-4. *See* OTS Handbook, *supra* note 43, at 500.7.

48. CRA Q and A, *supra* note 43, at §.26(a)(1)-2.

49. FDIC Manual, *supra* note 43, at pt. IV, B1-4; OTS Handbook, *supra* note 43, at 500.7.

50. FDIC Manual, *supra* note 43, at pt. IV, B1-4; OTS Handbook, *supra* note 43, at 500.7.

51. CRA Q and A, *supra* note 43, at §.26(a)(2)-1.

52. FDIC Manual, *supra* note 43, at pt. IV, B1-5; OTS Handbook, *supra* note 43, at 500.8.

53. FDIC Manual, *supra* note 43, at B2-11. *See also id.* at B2-20.

54. *Id.* at B1-5.

55. *Id.* at B2-10. *See id.* at B2-6.

56. *Id.*

57. *Id.* at C-5; OTS Handbook, *supra* note 43, at 500.8; Comptroller's Handbook, *supra* note 43, at 38.

58. FDIC Manual, *supra* note 43, at pt. IV, C-5-6; OTS Handbook, *supra* note 43, at 500.15; Comptroller's Handbook, *supra* note 43, at 38-39.

59. FDIC Manual, *supra* note 43, at pt. IV, C-6; OTS Handbook, *supra* note 43, at 500.15; Comptroller's Handbook, *supra* note 43, at 39.

60. FDIC Manual, *supra* note 43, at pt. IV, C-7; OTS Handbook, *supra* note 43, at 500.15; Comptroller's Handbook, *supra* note 43, at 40.

61. FDIC Manual, *supra* note 43, at pt. IV, C2-11-12.

62. *Id.* at C2-31.

63. *Id.* at C2-30.

64. *Id.* at C2-31.

65. *Id.* at C2-30.

66. CRA Guidance, *supra* note 43, at 1.

67. *Id.* at 21-23.

68. FDIC MANUAL, *supra* note 43, at pt. IV, C-7-8; OTS HANDBOOK, *supra* note 43, at 500.16; COMPTROLLER'S HANDBOOK, *supra* note 43, at 40-41.

69. FDIC MANUAL, *supra* note 43, at pt. IV, C2-15.

70. *Id.*

71. *Id.* at C-32.

72. *Id.*

73. *Id.* at C2-33.

74. CRA GUIDANCE, *supra* note 43, at 23-26.

75. 60 Fed. Reg. 37,602 (2001) [hereinafter 2001 proposal].

76. *Id.* at 37,604.

77. THOMAS, *supra* note 27, at Table 7.

78. *Id.*

79. *Id.* at Table 8.

80. *Id.*

81. *See* 69 Fed. Reg. 5,729 (Feb. 6, 2004).

82. *See infra* ch. 8, text accompanying notes 44 to 45, for more about this.

83. 59 Fed. Reg. at 5,737.

84. Reflecting this concern, the General Accounting Office in a 1997 report suggested to the Fed that it issue public guidelines describing how it takes account of public comments in considering bank merger applications. *Fed to Develop Guidelines Explaining Merger Review*, INSIDE MORTGAGE COMPLIANCE, October 11, 1999, at 8. The report reflected concerns by community advocates that the Fed issued quick decisions on large bank merger application with no explanation of how it took account of public comments. *Id.*

CHAPTER SIX

1. *Revised CRA Rules Unlikely to Have Safe Harbor, Regulators Say,* [Current Developments] Hous. & Dev. Rep. (West), Sept. 27, 1993, at 297.

2. Scott Barancik, *Fed Governor: Study CRA to See If It Works*, AM. BANKER, June 4, 1999, at 2.

3. *See infra* ch.2, text accompanying notes 21–34.

4. *See, e.g.*, 12 C.F.R. §§5.8, 5.10 (OCC) (2002); *id.* §§225.14, 262.3 (Federal Reserve); *id.* §§303.7, 303.9 (FDIC).

5. One CRA researcher has stated, "private community organizations have been the major force for compliance with the nation's fair lending and community reinvestment laws." GREGORY D. SQUIRES, CAPITAL AND COMMUNITIES IN BLACK AND WHITE 67 (1994).

6. *See* Malcolm Bush & Dan Immergluck, *Research, Advocacy, and Community Reinvestment, in* ORGANIZING ACCESS TO CAPITAL: ADVOCACY AND THE DEMOCRATIZATION OF FINANCIAL INSTITUTIONS 156 (Gregory D. Squires ed., 2003); Robert C. Art, *Social Responsibility in Bank Credit Decisions: The Community Reinvestment Act One Decade Later*, 18 PAC. L.J. 1071, 1073–74 & n.10 (1987); Allen J.

Fishbein, *The Community Reinvestment Act After Fifteen Years: It Works, But Strengthened Federal Enforcement is Needed*, 20 FORDHAM URB. L.J. 293, 294–96 (1993).

7. *See also CRA Rating May Hobble WesBanco Deals*, AM. BANKER, Jul. 6, 2001, at 20; Lisa Daigle, *Innovations Seen Outdoing CRA*, AM. BANKER, Oct. 24, 2000, at 6; Paul Sweeney, *War Over CRA*, U.S. BANKER, Aug. 1989, at 22; Warren W. Traiger, *CRA Compliance: A Key Element of Bank Mergers*, BANKER'S MAG., May–June 1996, at 30–31. The odds are 100-1 that an application challenged on CRA grounds will be denied. *See* KENNETH H. THOMAS, THE CRA HANDBOOK 93 (1998). The chances that an application that is not challenged will be denied on CRA grounds are 2,500 to 1. *Id.*

8. *See CRA Trouble for WesBanco Sale*, AM. BANKER, Aug. 7, 2001, at 20; *CRA Plan Keys OTS Approval of Traveler's Thrift Charter Bid, Insurer Commits $430 Million in HELs to Low-Income Groups*, INSIDE FAIR LENDING, Dec. 1997, at 2; *CRA Slowing More Acquisitions*, BANK MERGERS & ACQUISITIONS, Oct. 1992, at 3–4; Olaf de Senerpont Domis, *Bronx Activists Ask Fed to Delay KeyCorp Plans for N.H. Branches*, AM. BANKER, July 3, 1996, at 2; Marianne Lavelle, *Advocates for Poor Pounce When Banks Plan Mergers*, THE NAT'L L.J., Feb. 12, 1996, at B3; Laura Mandaro, *Citi Fast-Track Hopes Fade as Golden Application Lags*, AM. BANKER, Sept. 18, 2002, at 2; Barbara A. Rehm, *How Citi Got Busy to Speed Fed's Merger OK*, AM. BANKER, July 30, 2001, at 1; Barbara A. Rehm, *ACORN Delays Norwest Deal in Arizona*, AM. BANKER, May 10, 1993, at 8; Jaret Seiberg, OTS Orders Dime-Anchor Inquiry After CRA Charge, Am. Banker, Nov. 3, 1994, at 1 [hereinafter *Dime-Anchor*]; Jaret Seiberg, *Amid Protest, Fed Stalls Canadian Bank's Deal and Seeks Detailed CRA Plan*, AM. BANKER, Aug. 23, 1996, at 2; Sweeney, *supra* note 7; Laura K. Thompson, *CRA Victory for WesBanco of W. Va.*, Am. Banker, Nov. 17, 2001, at 7.

9. *See* Sweeney, *supra* note 7; SQUIRES, *supra* note 5, at 6.

10. Lavelle, *supra* note 8.

11. *See CRA Slowing More Acquisitions*, *supra* note 8; Saul Hansell, *Court to Hear A Challenge to Greenpoint*, N.Y. TIMES, Sept. 21, 1995, at D6; Craig Linder, *For Once, Activists are Embracing a Megadeal*, AM. BANKER, Oct. 30, 2003, at 1; Matt Schulz, *Fla. Case Shows Small Banks Not Immune to CRA Protest*, AM. BANKER, June 13, 1996, at 12.

12. *See FUC Pledges $13 Billion to Community Reinvestment*, INSIDE MORTGAGE COMPLIANCE, Mar. 1998, at 11.

13. *See* Lee v. Bd. of Governors of the Fed. Reserve Sys., 118 F.3d 905 (2d Cir. 1997); Lee v. Fed. Deposit Ins. Corp., 95 Civ. 7963, 1997 U.S. Dist. LEXIS 13885 (S.D.N.Y. Sept.12, 1997).

14. *See* Jaret Seiberg, *Activists Fight Long Odds at Fed's Merger Hearings*, AM. BANKER, July 9, 1998, at 1; Memorandum from Gail Hillebrand to Chuck Bell on Work of WCRO Under CRA 4 (Oct. 5, 1989) (on file with author) [hereinafter Hillebrand Memo].

15. *See* Robert B. Avery et al., *Trends in Home Purchase Lending Consolidation and the Community Reinvestment Act*, 85 FED. RES. BULL. 81, 86 (1999); Fishbein, *supra* note 6, at 298–300.

16. *See* Liz Moyer, *Activist Groups Demand $200B CRA Commitment As Part of Citigroup Deal*, AM. BANKER, May 1, 1998, at 22; NATIONAL COMMUNITY REINVESTMENT COALITION, BEGINNER CRA MANUAL, pt. 6, at 1 (2001) [hereafter BEGINNER CRA MANUAL].

17. National Community Reinvestment Coalition, CRA Commitments 1977–1998 [hereafter CRA Commitments].

18. *Id.* at 1.

19. National Community Reinvestment Coalition, CRA Sunshine Reveals Benefits of Bank-Community Group Partnerships 3, 16 (2002) [hereafter CRA Sunshine].

20. *See* CRA Sunshine, *supra* note 19, at 6. *See supra* ch. 1, text accompanying notes 150–62 for more about the CRA Sunshine requirements.

21. Liz Moyer, *JPM Chase Makes CRA Pledge; Faces Merger Scrutiny*, Am. Banker, April 16, 2004, at 18.

22. There are many examples of CRA challenges reported in books, newspapers, magazines, and regulatory decisions on bank expansion applications. For example, *see* Gregory D. Squires & Sally O'Connor, Color and Money: Politics and Prospects for Community Reinvestment in Urban America 166 (2001)(describing five challenges by the Fair Housing Coalition in Milwaukee and subsequent agreements resulting in $160 million in home mortgage and small business loans commitments); Tara Siegel Bernard, *Consumer Advocacy Groups Oppose Citi's Buy of Golden State*, Dow Jones Newswire, June 3, 2002 (challenge by California Reinvestment Committee to Citigroup's proposed purchase of Golden State Bancorp); Brett Chase, *Insurer's Thrift Quest Raises CRA Liability Issues*, Am. Banker, Mar. 16, 1998, at 5 (challenge to State Farm's 1998 application for a savings bank charter by the Woodstock Institute and several other community groups); *CRA Slowing More Acquisitions, supra* note 8, at 3–4 (ACORN challenges 1992 application of United Missouri Bancshares to buy five banks); *Dime-Anchor, supra* note 8; Olaf de Senerpont Domis, *Activists Charge Discrimination, Protest Zions-Sumitomo Merger*, Am. Banker, July 6, 1998, at 7 (1998 protest of Zions Bancorp application to acquire Sumitomo Bank by the Greenlining Institute); Marla Dickerson, *ACORN Banks on Getting Results Through Protests*, The Detroit News, Mar. 12, 1992, at E1 (challenge by ACORN to 1992 merger application of Manufacturers National Corp. and Comerica, Inc.); Carey Gillam, *First Union Says Protests By Community Groups Won't Delay Signet Deal*, Am. Banker, Sept. 9, 1997, at 4 (challenge by Delaware Community Reinvestment Action Council, the Coalition for Non-Profit Housing, and Roanoke Community Reinvestment Coalition to 1997 application by First Union to purchase Signet Bank Corp.); Carey Gillam, *NationsBank's CRA Chief Preparing For a Community Group Onslaught*, Am. Banker, June 29, 1998, at 1; Jacqueline S. Gold, *Local Groups in 5 States Demand Hearings on Fleet-Shawmut Deal*, Am. Banker, June 7, 1995, at 2; *Protests Surge Against BofA, NationsBank Megamerger*, Inside Mortgage Compliance, June 29, 1998, at 2 (protest of 1998 merger of NationsBank and Bank of America by 36 community groups); Rehm, *supra* note 8 (challenge to Norwest's 1993 application to purchase 59 branches from Citibank Arizona); Patrick Reilly, *Citizen Deal Opposed on Bias Grounds*, Am. Banker, Aug. 8, 2001, at 2 (challenge by Delaware Community Reinvestment Action Council and Inner City Public Interest Law Center to proposed acquisition by Citizens Financial Corp. of Mellon Financial Corp.'s retail banking business); Schulz, *supra* note 11, at 12 (1996 challenge by Fair Housing Continuum of Cocoa to merger of First Commerce Bank of Florida and Prime Banks of Central Florida in 1996).

23. Hillebrand Memo, *supra* note 14, at 1.

24. For example, in 1988, California First Bank applied to buy Union Bank. A coalition of several groups in California, including the California Reinvestment Committee and the Greenlining Coalition, contacted the banks to discuss their CRA records. They negotiated over a lending agreement for three weeks, and, due in large part to the impending deadline for filing a challenge, reached a multi-million dollar lending agreement. Hillebrand Memo, *supra* note 14, at 3–4. In 1984, the Chicago Reinvestment Alliance negotiated CRA lending agreements totaling $153 million with First National Bank of Chicago, Harris Trust and Savings Bank, and Northern Trust Co., all of which had applications pending. *See* CALVIN BRADFORD, PARTNERSHIPS FOR REINVESTMENT: AN EVALUATION OF THE CHICAGO NEIGHBORHOOD LENDING PROGRAMS 2 (Sept.1990) *and* Daniel D. Pearlman & Roger L.Q. Nguyen, *The Community Reinvestment Act: 15 Years Later*, 21 HOUSING L. BULL. 124 (Sept.–Oct. 1991). ACORN reached lending agreements in Philadelphia with Fidelcor in 1986 and Mellon Bank in 1990 while they had applications pending. BRADFORD, *supra* at 2. The Woodstock Institute and CANDO, a part of the Chicago CRA Coalition, negotiated a $4.1 billion, six-year lending agreement with First Chicago Bank while it had a merger application pending. BEGINNER CRA MANUAL, *supra* note 16, pt. 6, at 1–2. In 1995, the Pittsburgh Community Reinvestment Group negotiated a CRA lending agreement with Integra Bank in connection with Integra's pending merger with National City of Cleveland. *Id.* at pt. 6, 2–3.

25. For example, in 1992 several community groups filed a challenge to OnBank's application to merge with Merchant's National Bank & Trust Co. Once OnBank reached a lending agreement with the community groups, they dropped their challenge. *See* Fred. R. Bleakley, *How Groups Pressured One Bank to Promise More Inner-City Loans*, WALL ST. J., Sept. 22, 1992, at A1. In 1998, two groups, the Greenlining Institute and the California Reinvestment Committee, dropped their challenge to the merger application of Mafco Holdings and Glendale Federal Bank after they entered a ten year, $25 billion home mortgage lending agreement. *CRA Groups Urge Quick Approval of CalFed Merger*, INSIDE MORTGAGE COMPLIANCE, Aug, 24, 1998, at 10. In 1998, Inner City Press/Community on the Move and the Delaware Community Reinvestment Committee challenged Household International's application to acquire Beneficial Corporation's three banks. They ultimately dropped the challenge upon reaching a three year, $3 billion lending agreement. *ICP and DCRAC Reach Precedent-Setting Agreement with Household International on Fair Pricing and $3 Billion of Lending*, REINVESTMENT WORKS, Fall 1998. In a twist on this, in 1994, Citizen Action of New Jersey reached a $502.5 million affordable housing and small business lending agreement with Fleet after Citizen Action challenged Fleet's application to purchase Nat West, failed to reach an agreement, lost the challenge, but vowed to continue to challenge Fleet's applications. *Fleet to Provide $500 Million in Housing, Small Business Loans Under New Jersey Agreement*, [Current Developments] Hous. & Dev. Rep. (West), Dec. 2, 1995, at 459.

26. Lavelle, *supra* note 8. In 2001, Washington Mutual, after it announced its deal to purchase Dime Bancorp, made a $375 billion commitment to lend in low-income communities and to adopt a best practices list for subprime lending. Erick Bergquist, *Wamu CRA Goal Seen Preemptive Measure*, AM. BANKER, Sept. 6, 2001, at 1. In 1999, HSBC Bank USA agreed to double its CRA activity after buying Republic New York Corp. and Safra Republic Holding S.A. Katharine Fraser, *HSBC Promises to Double Its*

CRA Activity in New York, AM. BANKER, Aug. 23, 1999, at 2. In 1998, First Union made a $13 billion lending commitment in connection with its acquisition of CoreStates Financial Corp. This expanded on a commitment it made when it announced the merger. *FUC Pledges $13 Billion to Community Reinvestment, supra* note 11, at 10–11. In 1998, NationsBank and BankAmerica committed $350 billion in CRA lending in connection with their merger. Jaret Seiberg, *NationsBank and B of A Pledge Record $350B to CRA Lending,* AM. BANKER, May 21, 1998, at 1. In 1997, Travelers Group pledged $430 million in home equity loans to LMI borrowers over three years. The commitment came in response to CRA protests by Inner City Press/Community on the Move and the Delaware Reinvestment Alliance. *CRA Plan Keys OTS Approval of Travelers Thrift Charter Bid, supra* note 8, at 3–4. Also in 1997, First Union committed $2 billion in connection with its proposed merger with Signet Bank in Virginia after a challenge was filed, but the commitment did not resolve the protest. Carey Gillam, *1st Union's $2B CRA Plan Fails to Quell Protest,* AM. BANKER, Nov. 7, 1997, at 4. Other large commitments include: Citibank's $120 billion commitment in connection with its proposed purchase of Golden State Bancorp., Press Release, *Citibank Announces $120 Billion Lending and Investment Commitment to California and Nevada Communities,* July 3, 2002; Wells Fargo's $60 billion lending commitment in connection with its merger with NorWest Corp., *Wells Fargo CRA Pledge Puts NationsBank on the Defensive,* INSIDE MORTGAGE COMPLIANCE, Sept. 7, 1998, at 7; Washington Mutual's $120 billion, ten year CRA lending commitment in 1998 in connection with its proposed acquisition of H.F. Ahmanson & Co., Brett Chase & Jaret Seiberg, *Wamu Expected to Pledge $120B of CRA Lending,* AM. BANKER, May 22, 1998, at 24; Citicorp's and Travelers Group's $115 billion lending commitment in connection with their merger, Liz Moyer, *Citigroup CRA Pledge $115B; Critics Say It's Not Enough,* AM. BANKER, May 5, 1998; Jaret Seiberg, *Chase Makes $4.8B Investment in CRA Push,* AM. BANKER, Mar. 25, 1997 at 2; Chemical Bank's and Chase Manhattan Corp.'s $18.1 billion lending commitment in connection with their 1995 merger, Jaret Seiberg, *Chase and Chemical Commit $18B to Community Lending,* AM. BANKER, Nov. 2, 1995 at 6; UnionBank and Bank of California's $11.25 billion, ten year commitment to lend to LMI housing, small businesses, and community development projects, Barbara A. Rehm, *Calif. Units of Japanese Giants Pledge $11B in CRA Loans,* AM. BANKER, Oct. 19, 1995, at 3; and First Chicago's and NBD Bancorp's $2 billion, six year commitment in connection with their merger, Brett Chase, *First Chicago, NBD Spell Out $6B Plan For Inner-City Loans,* AM. BANKER, Nov. 14, 1995, at 6.

27. For example, in 2002, Union Planters made a $10 million lending commitment to promote lending for home mortgages, small farms, and churches in Central Illinois after meeting with a community group that had criticized its CRA record. David Flaum, *Memphis Tenn.-Based Union Planters Announces Mortgage Lending Plan,* THE COMMERCIAL APPEAL, March 19, 2002. In 2000, First Federal of Michigan committed to $212 million in housing, small business, and consumer loans in Detroit over three years. BEGINNER CRA MANUAL, *supra* note 16, pt. 7 at 17. In 1999, Bank of America and the Neighborhood Assistance Corp. of America agreed on a $3 billion home mortgage loan program for LMI borrowers that required no downpayment, no application fee, and no closing costs. Leslie Miller, *Bank of America Says*

Lending $3 Billion to Poorer Borrowers, Chattanooga Times, Aug. 11, 1999, at C3. In 1998, Star Banc made a three-state, $5 billion lending pledge. Brett Chase, *Star Banc Vows $5 Billion of CRA Lending in 3 States*, Am. Banker, Feb. 26, 1998, at 5. In 1998, PNC Mortgage committed $20 million to increase homeownership for LMI persons in Boston. Beginner CRA Manual, *supra* note 16, pt. 7 at 14. In 1997, the California Reinvestment Committee and First National Bank reached a $14 million multi-family housing lending agreement. *California Reinvestment Committee Signs $14 Million Agreement with First Nationwide Bank*, National Community Reinvestment Coalition, Newsletter, Summer 1997, at 19. In 1996, First Union Bank agreed with Neighborhood Assistance Corp. of America to make $150 million in no-downpayment or no-closing cost loans to LMI consumers. Jaret Seiberg, *First Union Commits $150M to Low-Income Borrowers*, Am. Banker, May 10, 1996, at 3. In 1996, Homeland Bancshares committed $3.75 million for affordable housing to LMI families in Iowa. Beginner CRA Manual, *supra* note 16, pt. 7 at 13. In 1995, NatWest committed $150 million in lending to LMI homeowners, minority-owned small businesses, and housing projects for LMI persons. This commitment grew out of an agreement NatWest reached in 1993 with New Jersey Citizen Action. *Natwest Sets $150M Goal for CRA Lending*, Am. Banker, Mar. 16, 1995, at 5. In 1994, the Massachusetts Affordable Housing Alliance reached a $93 million lending agreement with seven banks to extend an affordable mortgage program that grew out of the Alliance's 1990 challenge of Bay Bank's application to open a branch. Christine Dugas, *Robin Hoods of the '90s*, N.Y. Newsday, Feb. 19, 1995, at 6. In 1988, WRCO approached Bank of America to negotiate a lending agreement even though Bank of America did not have an application pending. The Bank, motivated in part by the expectation of future merger activity, reached an agreement. Hillebrand Memo, *supra* note 14, at 2–3.

28. This analysis is based on CRA Commitments, *supra* note 17, at 1–30, and Richard Marsico, *A Guide to Enforcing the Community Reinvestment Act*, 20 Fordham Urb. L.J. 165, 265–74 (1993). *See also* CRA Sunshine, *supra* note 19, at 11–16. For a more complete description of common provisions of CRA agreements and commitments, *see* Richard Marsico, *Enforcing the Community Reinvestment Act: An Advocate's Guide to Making the CRA Work For Communities*, 17 N.Y.L. Sch. J. Hum. Rts. 129, 194–96 (2001). The rest of this paragraph is drawn, in some instances verbatim, from this article.

29. Liz Moyer, *JPM Chase Makes CRA Pledge; Faces Merger Scrutiny*, Am. Banker, April 16, 2004, at 18.

30. *See Bank of America, FleetBoston Plan to Invest $750 Billion Over 10 Years in Economic Development*, [Current Developments] Hous. & Dev. Rep. (West), Jan. 19, 2004, at 8.

31. *WaMu Shocker: $375 Billion in New CRA Commitments*, Inside Mortgage Compliance, Sept. 10, 2001, at 5.

32. *Washington Mutual's Acquisition of Dime Bancorp Includes $375 Billion CRA Commitment*, [Current Developments] Hous. & Dev. Rep. (West), Jan. 21, 2002, at 593.

33. Press Release, *Bank of the West Sets $30 Billion Goal for Communities*, March 27, 2002.

34. *Id.*

35. Press Release, *Citibank Announces $120 Billion Lending and Investment Commitment to California and Nevada Communities*, July 3, 2002.

36. *Id.*

37. Jaret Seiberg, *NationsBank and B of A Pledge Record $350B to CRA Lending*, AM. BANKER, May 21, 1998, at 1.

38. *Id.*

39. *See* CRA COMMITMENTS, *supra* note 17, at 15, 28.

40. Liz Moyer, *Citigroup CRA Pledge $115B; Critics Say It's Not Enough*, AM. BANKER, May 5, 1998, at 1, 3.

41. *FUC Pledges $13 Billion to Community Reinvestment*, *supra* note 26, at 10–11.

42. Brett Chase, *First Chicago, NBD Spell Out $6B Plan for Inner-City Loans*, AM. BANKER, Nov. 14, 1995.

43. *Id.*

44. *Chicago Coalition Crafts Model Community Reinvestment Agreement*, WOODSTOCK DEVELOPMENTS, Fall 1998, at 1.

45. This paragraph is based on CRA COMMITMENTS, *supra* note 17, at 19–23.

46. Robert B. Avery et al., *CRA Special Lending Programs*, 86 FED. RES. BULL. 711–12 (2000).

47. 12 U.S.C. §§2801–2810 (2000).

48. Avery, *supra* note 46, at 711–12.

49. *Id.* at 712.

50. *Id.* at 711.

51. *Id.* at 713.

52. *Id.* at 714.

53. *Id.* The Consumer Bankers Association conducted a survey in 1999 that showed that 93.1% of its members participated in some form of affordable mortgage program. *See New CRA Survey Highlights Trends In Affordable Lending*, CRA/HMDA UPDATE, Nov. 1993, at 14–15 [hereinafter CRA Survey].

54. Avery, *supra* note 46, at 714.

55. *Id.* at 715.

56. Avery, *supra* note 46, at 716.

57. *Id.*

58. *Id.* at 717. Ninety percent of the banks in a survey by the Federal Reserve Bank of Kansas City reported that CRA lending had non-monetary benefits, including creating a good community image, helping the community grow and prosper, ensuring future profitability by strengthening the community, and developing future customers. *CRA Lending is Profitable, Kansas City Fed Survey Finds*, INSIDE FAIR LENDING, Feb. 1997, at 7, 8.

59. Avery, *supra* note 46, at 715.

60. *Id.*

61. *Id.* at 716.

62. Avery, *supra* note 46, at 717–18. *See also CRA Survey*, *supra* note 53, at 14–15.

63. As an example of such a program, in 1995, NationsBank announced a five year, $500 million, no-downpayment, no-closing cost mortgage program for low-income borrowers. The borrowers would receive pre- and post-mortgage credit counseling from the

Neighborhood Assistance Corp. of America. Jaret Seiberg, *NationsBank Offers No-Down-Payment, No-Closing-Cost Loan*, Am. Banker, Dec. 19, 1995, at 2. *See also* Barton Crockett, *B of A to Put $100M in Low-Income Housing*, Am. Banker, Dec. 4, 1995, at 8.

64. 88.4% of the respondents in the CRA Survey stated that they conducted a second review of rejected applications. *CRA Survey, supra* note 53, at 14.

65. Avery, *supra* note 46, at 720

66. *Id.* at 721 & tbl. 7.

67. *Id.* at 722.

68. *Id.* at 723.

69. *Id.* at 722–23.

70. Board of Directors of the Federal Reserve System, Report to the Congress on Community Development Lending (Oct. 1993) [hereinafter Report to the Congress]; The Woodstock Institute, Sound Loans for Communities: An Analysis of Community Investment Loans (Oct. 1993) [hereinafter Sound Loans].

71. Report to the Congress, *supra* note 70, at 2–3.

72. *Id.* at 49–50.

73. Sound Loans, *supra* note 70, at 15.

74. *Id.*

75. Jaret Seiberg, *CRA Lending is Profitable for Banks, Study Finds*, Am. Banker, Aug. 26, 1994, at 1.

76. *CRA Lending is Less Profitable, Kansas Fed Survey Finds*, Inside Mortgage Lending, Feb. 1997, at 7.

77. *Study: Community Investment Loans Safe*, Am. Banker, Oct. 10, 2002, at 13.

78. Michele Heller, *Capitol Hill Partisans Spin Lessons From CRA Profit, Delinquency Report*, Am. Banker, July 18, 2000, at 1.

79. *Id.*

80. 12 C.F.R. §§25.12(h)–(j), 228.12(h)–(j), 345.12(h)–(j), 563e.12(g)–(i) (2002).

81. Susan White Haag, Community Reinvestment and Cities: A Literature Review of CRA's Impact and Future 2 (2000).

82. Beginner CRA Manual, *supra* note 16, pt. 7 at 11.

83. *Id.* at pt. 7 at 5.

84. *Fleet Pledges $60 Million to Community Development*, Inside Fair Lending, Nov. 1997, at 12.

85. Haag, *supra* note 81, at 2.

86. Richard D. Marsico, *Shedding Some Light on Lending: The Effect of Expanded Disclosure Laws on Home Mortgage Marketing, Lending and Discrimination in the New York Metropolitan Area*, 27 Fordham Urb. L.J. 481, 513 (1999).

87. *Id.*

88. James R. Krause, *N.Y. Banks Start Fund for Minority Ventures*, Am. Banker, Oct. 31, 1995, at 17.

89. *Charleston Banking Consortium Provides $7.5 Million in Loans,* [Current Developments] Hous. & Dev. Rep. (West), Sept. 8, 1997, at 267.

90. *Id.*

91. Beginner CRA Manual, *supra* note 16, pt. 7 at 3.

92. Haag, *supra* note 81, at 2.

93. Beginner CRA Manual, *supra* note 17, pt. 7 at 24.
94. *Id.*
95. CRA Sunshine, *supra* note 19, at 16.
96. Beginner CRA Manual, *supra* note 17, pt. 7 at 20.
97. *N.J. Lending Alliance Offers $10 Million in Pilot Program*, Inside Mortgage Compliance, Sept. 7, 1998, at 9.
98. Beginner CRA Manual, *supra* note 16, pt. 7 at 5.
99. *Id.* at pt. 7 at 6.
100. *Id.*
101. *Id.* at pt. 7 at 26.
102. Haag, *supra* note 81, at 2.
103. *Id.*; Beginner CRA Manual, *supra* note 16, at 7.
104. The Joint Center for Housing Studies, The 25th Anniversary of the Community Reinvestment Act: Access to Capital in an Evolving Financial Services System (2002)[hereinafter Harvard Study].
105. *See, e.g.*, Robert E. Litan et al., The Community Reinvestment Act After Financial Modernization: A Baseline Report, *available at* http://www.ustreas.gov/press/releases/docs/crareport.pdf (2002) (hereinafter Treasury Study); Marsico, *supra* note 86; Alex Schwartz, *Bank Lending to Minority and Low-Income Households and Neighborhoods: Do Community Reinvestment Agreements Make A Difference?*, 20 J. Urb. Aff. 269 (1998); Anne B. Shlay, *Influencing the Agents of Urban Structure: Evaluating the Effects of Community Reinvestment Organizing on Bank Residential Lending Practices*, 35 Urb. Aff. Rev. 247 (1999).
106. Harvard Study, *supra* note 104, at 47–48.
107. *Id.* at 53.
108. *Id.* at iv, 54.
109. *Id.*
110. *Id.* at 59.
111. Treasury Study, *supra* note 106, at 90.
112. *Id.* Among the factors one researcher believes should be controlled for include declining interest and unemployment rates, the shift of assets from bank accounts by wealthy persons, and competition from mortgage companies. Kenneth N. Hylton, Banks and Inner Cities: Market and Regulatory Obstacles to Development Lending 7–8 (Boston Univ. Sch. of L., Working Paper No. 99-15, 1999).
113. Treasury Study, *supra* note 106, at 89–90.
114. *Id.* at 5.
115. *Id.* at 7.
116. *Id.* at 8, 90.
117. *Id.* at 9, 10, 90.
118. *Id.* at 11.
119. *Id.*
120. *Id.* at 13, 80–81.
121. Haag, *supra* note 81, at 9.
122. *Id.*
123. *Id.*

124. Marsico, *supra* note 86.

125. HAAG, *supra* note 81, at 10, 76.

126. *Roundtable: Big-Bank CRA Lending Rose 15% in '98*, AM. BANKER, Jan. 3, 2000, at 2.

127. HAAG, *supra* note 81, at 37.

128. *Id.*

129. *BankAmerica Reports 10% Growth in CRA Loans*, AM. BANKER, Mar. 16, 1995, at 3.

130. *Id.*

131. RAPHAEL W. BOSTIC & BRECK L. ROBINSON, WHAT MAKES CRA AGREEMENTS WORK? A STUDY OF LENDER RESPONSES TO CRA AGREEMENTS 4–5 (2003).

132. *Id.* at 14.

133. *Id.* at 15.

134. TREASURY STUDY, *supra* note 106, at 85.

135. HAAG, *supra* note 81, at 43.

136. *NationsBank Reports $13.4 Billion in CRA Loans,* [Current Developments] Hous. & Dev. Rep. (West), June 3, 1996, at 44, 45.

137. Jaret Seiberg, *Chase Makes $4.8B Investment in CRA Push,* AM. BANKER, Mar. 25, 1997, at 2.

138. Jaret Seiberg, *Mass. Banks Topped Their Own Promises in Low-Income Lending,* AM. BANKER, Aug. 24, 1995, at 2.

139. TREASURY STUDY, *supra* note 106, at 84.

140. HAAG, *supra* note 81, at 43.

141. *Id.*

142. *Id.*

143. SQUIRES, *supra* note 22, at 166.

144. *Id.*

145. MICHAEL A. STEGMAN, ET AL., TOWARD A MORE PERFORMANCE-DRIVEN SERVICE TEST: STRENGTHENING BASIC BANKING SERVICES UNDER THE COMMUNITY REINVESTMENT Act 2-3 (2001); Dory Rand, *Using the Community Reinvestment Act to Promote Checking Accounts for Low-Income People*, CLEARINGHOUSE REV., May–June 1999, at 6. As of 1995, one-third of all LMI families, constituting 13% of all families, had no bank account of any kind. THOMAS, *supra* note 7, at 164.

146. STEGMAN, supra note 145, at 8, 37.

147. *See* PAUL S. CALEM ET AL., THE NEIGHBORHOOD DISTRIBUTION OF SUBPRIME LENDING 10-11 (U. of Pa. L. Sch., Inst. for L. and Econ., Research Paper No. 03-39 2003); JIM CAMPEN, BORROWED TROUBLE? IV: SUBPRIME MORTGAGE REFINANCE LENDING IN GREATER BOSTON, 2000–2002 5 (2004); ALEX SCHWARTZ, THE STATE OF MINORITY ACCESS TO HOME MORTGAGE LENDING: A PROFILE OF THE NEW YORK METROPOLITAN AREA 16–17 (2001); Richard D. Marsico, *Patterns of Lending to Low-Income and Minority Persons and Neighborhoods: The 1999 New York Metropolitan Area Mortgage Lending Scorecard*, N.Y.L. SCH. J. HUM. RTS. 199, 208 (2000).

148. SCHWARTZ, *supra* note 147, at 19 (Freddie Mac found that 10–35 percent of all subprime borrowers could have qualified for prime loans); *Many B & C Borrowers Could Get Prime Loans, GSE Says*, INSIDE B & C LENDING, June 23, 2003 at 5.

149. For a first hand account of these efforts, *see* Matthew Lee, *Community Reinvestment in a Globalizing World: To Hold Banks Accountable, from The Bronx to Buenos Aires, Beijing, and Basel*, *in* ORGANIZING ACCESS TO CAPITAL: ADVOCACY AND THE DEMOCRATIZATION OF FINANCIAL INSTITUTIONS 136–39 (Gregory D. Squires ed., 2003).

150. Jaret Seiberg, *Bronx Community Group Fights Dime-Anchor Deal, Citing CRA*, AM. BANKER, Oct. 26, 1994, at 2; Jaret Seiberg, *Republic National of N.Y. Under Attack By Community Group Over Lending*, AM. BANKER, Oct.13, 1994, at 3; Jaret Seiberg, *Community Group Targets Marine Midland*, AM. BANKER, Sept. 27, 1994, at 4.

151. CRA COMMITMENTS, *supra* note 16, at 10; Jaret Seiberg, *Dime and Anchor Agree to Open Branch and Lend in Poor Areas*, AM. BANKER, Nov. 30, 1994, at 2; Jaret Seiberg, *Marine Midland to Lend $15M in Bronx, Upper Manhattan to Settle CRA Charge*, AM. BANKER, Oct. 20, 1994, at 3; Jaret Seiberg, *Republic New York Agrees to $15 Million Bronx Lending Effort*, AM. BANKER, Oct. 25, 1994, at 3.

152. Miriam Leuchter, *CRA Hammer Forcing Banks to Bend*, CRAIN'S N.Y. BUS., Sept. 12, 1994, at 9.

153. Jaret Seiberg, *N.Y. Activist Changing Strategy to Stay on Course*, AM. BANKER, July, 29, 1997 (merger with Chemical Bank). For a first hand account of these challenges, *see* Lee, *supra* note 149, at 139–41.

154. Jaret Seiberg, *Activist Group Attacks Chase on Two Fronts In Campaign for More Service in the Bronx*, AM. BANKER, May 4, 1995, at 3; Jaret Seiberg, *Dime and Anchor Agree to Open Branch and Lend in Poor Areas*, AM. BANKER, Nov. 30, 1994, at 2. *See also* Justin Fox, *As Regulators Scrutinize Chase, Activists Will Be Watching Closely*, AM. BANKER, Aug. 29, 1995, at 2; Cristina Merrill, *CRA Monkey Wrench Aimed At a U.S. Trust Merger Plan*, AM. BANKER, June 9, 1995, at 10.

155. *See supra* ch. 2, text accompanying notes 55 to 108 for more discussion of these cases.

CHAPTER SEVEN

1. WEBSTER'S THIRD NEW INTERNATIONAL DICTIONARY OF THE ENGLISH LANGUAGE UNABRIDGED 57 (1993).

2. For example, former Federal Reserve Governor Lawrence Lindsey described what credit allocation might look like: "Certainly, it would make everything much easier if we had lists of 'blessed' loans and customers and mathematical ratios of loans by category...." *Existing Efforts to End the Crisis: A Report Card: Hearing Before the Subcomm. on Consumer Credit and Ins. of the House Comm. on Banking, Fin., & Urban Affairs*, 103d Cong. 71 (1993) (prepared statement of Lawrence B. Lindsey, Governor, Board of Governors of the Federal Reserve System), *reprinted in* 79 FED. RES. BULL. 285, 290 (1993).

3. *See* William C. Gruben et al., *Imperfect Information and the Community Reinvestment Act*, ECON. REV. OF THE FED. RES. BANK OF SAN FRANCISCO, Summer 1990, at 27, 38.

4. 42 U.S.C. §§ 3601–3619 (2000). The FHA prohibits discrimination on the basis of race, color, religion, gender, handicap, familial status, and national origin in residential and real estate-related transactions, including loans in connection with such transactions. *See id.* § 3605. The Department of Justice has the authority to institute

a civil action in federal court to challenge a pattern or practice of behavior that violates the FHA. *Id.* § 3614(a). The Secretary of the Department of Housing and Urban Development ("HUD") has the authority to file administrative complaints with HUD alleging FHA violations on its own behalf and to investigate and prosecute administrative complaints filed with HUD by individuals. *See id.* §§ 3610, 3612. Individuals can also commence administrative or court proceedings under the FHA to challenge discriminatory lending practices. *Id.* §§ 3610, 3613.

5. 15 U.S.C. §§ 1691–1691f (2000). The ECOA prohibits discrimination on the basis of race, color, religion, national origin, gender, age, or marital status with respect to any credit transaction. *See id.* § 1691(a). Various federal agencies have the authority to enforce compliance with the ECOA, including the federal banking agencies, the Department of Justice, and the Federal Trade Commission. *See id.* §§ 1691c, 1691e(g). Individuals can also commence court proceedings to challenge ECOA violations. *See id.* § 1691e(f).

6. This assertion that some of the consent decrees allocate credit is not intended as a criticism. Instead, government-imposed credit allocation as a remedy for alleged lending discrimination is appropriate and justified under the FHA and the ECOA. The author thanks Josh Silver, vice-president for policy and research of the National Community Reinvestment Coalition, for this point.

7. Complaint, U.S. v. Decatur Fed. Sav. & Loan Ass'n, 2 Fair Hous.-Fair Lending (P-H) ¶ 19,377 (N.D. Ga. Sept. 17, 1992) (No. 1 92-CV-2198) (filed Sept. 17, 1992), *reprinted in* 2A Fair Hous.-Fair Lending (Aspen L. & Bus.) ¶ 21,056.

8. *See* Complaint, U.S. v. Blackpipe State Bank (D.S.D. Jan. 21, 1994) (No. 93-5115) (filed Nov. 16, 1993); Complaint, U.S. v. Shawmut Mortgage Co., 2 Fair Hous.-Fair Lending (P-H) ¶ 19,383 (D. Conn. Dec. 13, 1993) (No. 3:93 CV-2453 (AVC)) (filed Dec. 13, 1993); Complaint, U.S. v. First Nat'l Bank of Vicksburg, 2 Fair Hous.-Fair Lending (P-H) ¶ 19,384 (S.D. Miss. Jan. 21, 1994) (No. 5:94CV6 (B)(N)) (filed Jan. 21, 1994); Complaint, U.S. v. Chevy Chase Fed. Sav. Bank, 2 Fair Hous.-Fair Lending (Aspen L. & Bus.) ¶ 19,385 (D.D.C. Aug. 22, 1994) (No. 94-1824-JG) (filed Aug. 8, 1994), *reprinted in* 2A Fair Hous.-Fair Lending (Aspen L. & Bus.) ¶ 21,059; Complaint, U.S. v. Northern Trust Co., 2 Fair Hous.-Fair Lending (Aspen L. & Bus.) ¶ 19,388 (N.D. Ill. June 1, 1995) (No. 95-C3239) (filed June 1, 1995), *reprinted in* 2A Fair Hous.-Fair Lending (Aspen L. & Bus.) ¶ 21,062; Complaint, U.S. v. Huntington Mortgage Co., 2 Fair Hous.-Fair Lending (Aspen L. & Bus.) ¶ 19,390 (N.D. Ohio Oct. 18, 1995) (No. 1:95-CV-2211) (filed Oct. 18, 1995), *reprinted in* 2A Fair Hous.-Fair Lending (Aspen L. & Bus.) ¶ 21,063; Complaint, U.S. v. First Nat'l Bank of Gordon, 2 Fair Hous.-Fair Lending (Aspen L. & Bus.) ¶ 19,398 (W.D.S.D. May 7, 1997) (No. 96-5035) (filed Apr. 15, 1996); Complaint, U.S. v. Fleet Mortgage Corp., 2 Fair Hous.-Fair Lending (Aspen L. & Bus.) ¶ 19,391 (E.D.N.Y. May 7, 1996) (No. CV-96-2279) (filed May 7, 1996), *reprinted in* 2A Fair Hous.-Fair Lending (Aspen L. & Bus.) ¶ 21,064; Complaint, U.S. v. Long Beach Mortgage Co., 2 Fair Hous.-Fair Lending (Aspen L. & Bus.) ¶ 19,392 (C.D. Cal. Sept. 5, 1996) (No. CV 96-6159 (CWX)) (filed Sept. 5, 1996); Complaint, U.S. v. First Nat'l Bank of Doña Ana Co., 2 Fair Hous.-Fair Lending (Aspen L. & Bus.) ¶ 19,395 (D.N.M. Jan. 29, 1997) (No. CV97-96HB/JHG) (filed Jan. 29, 1997); Complaint, U.S. v. Albank, 2 Fair Hous.-Fair Lending (Aspen L. & Bus.) ¶ 19,401 (N.D.N.Y. Aug. 13, 1997) (No. 97-CV-1206) (filed Aug. 13, 1997).

9. Complaint para. 14, *Decatur* (No. 1 92-CV-2198); Complaint paras. 7-13, *Blackpipe* (No. 93-5115); Complaint paras. 11, 16, *Chevy Chase* (No. 94-1824-JG); Complaint paras. 8, 14, 16-18, *Albank* (No. 97-CV-1206).

10. Complaint paras. 10, 13, *Decatur* (No. 1 92-CV-2198); Complaint para. 13, *Blackpipe* (No. 93-5115); Complaint paras. 17, 18c, *Chevy Chase* (No. 94-1824-JG).

11. *See* complaint cited *supra* note 8.

12. Complaint para. 17, *Decatur* (No. 1 92-CV-2198); Complaint para. 12, *Blackpipe* (No. 93-5115); Complaint paras. 13-15, *Northern Trust Co.* (No. 95-C3239).

13. Complaint paras. 7–8, *First Nat'l Bank of Gordon* (No. 96-5035); Complaint paras. 6-9, *Huntington Mortgage Co.* (No. 1:95-CV-2211); Complaint paras. 6–7, 9, *Fleet Mortgage Corp.* (No. CV-96-2279).

14. *See, e.g.*, Consent Decree, U.S. v. Decatur Fed. Sav. & Loan Ass'n, 2 Fair Hous.-Fair Lending (P-H) ¶ 19,377, at 19,626, § II(C)(12) (N.D. Ga. Sept. 17, 1992) ("Decatur Federal will follow a home mortgage loan production program... designed to increase its origination of home mortgage loans to black borrowers."); *id.* at 19,630, § III(45) ("The parties anticipate that as a result of the affirmative marketing procedures set forth in this Consent Decree, the volume of black applicants for home mortgage loans may increase significantly.").

15. Consent Decree, U.S. v. Chevy Chase Fed. Sav. Bank, 2 Fair Hous.-Fair Lending (Aspen L. & Bus.) ¶ 19,385, at 19,689-91, §§ III, IV(B) (D.D.C. Aug. 22, 1994); Consent Decree, U.S. v. Blackpipe State Bank, No. 93-5115, at 5, § II(A)(2) (D.S.D. Jan. 21, 1994); Consent Decree, U.S. v. Decatur Fed. Sav. & Loan Ass'n, 2 Fair Hous.-Fair Lending (P-H) ¶ 19,377, at 19,625, § II(A)(2) (N.D. Ga. Sept. 17, 1992).

16. Consent Decree, U.S. v. Albank, 2 Fair Hous.-Fair Lending (Aspen L. & Bus.) ¶ 19,401, at 19,828-29, § III(3)(N.D.N.Y. Aug. 13, 1997); Consent Decree, *Chevy Chase*, 2 Fair Hous.-Fair Lending (Aspen L. & Bus.) at 19,689-93, §§ III, IV(C)(3); Consent Decree, U.S. v. Shawmut Mortgage Co., 2 Fair Hous.-Fair Lending (P-H) ¶ 19,383, at 19,674-75, §II(2)(D. Conn. Dec. 13, 1993); Consent Decree, *Decatur*, 2 Fair Hous.-Fair Lending (P-H) at 19,625-26, § (II)(B)(3)-(6), (9), (C)(13).

17. Consent Decree, *Albank*, 2 Fair Hous.-Fair Lending (Aspen L. & Bus.) at 19,830, § IV(4); Consent Decree, *Chevy Chase*, 2 Fair Hous.-Fair Lending (Aspen L. & Bus.) at 19,693, § IV(C)(4); Consent Decree, *Decatur*, 2 Fair Hous.-Fair Lending (P-H) at 19,627, §(C)(19).

18. Consent Decree, *Chevy Chase*, 2 Fair Hous.-Fair Lending (Aspen L. & Bus.) at 19,692, § IV(C)(2); Consent Decree, *Decatur*, 2 Fair Hous.-Fair Lending (P-H) at 19,627, §(D)(22)-(23).

19. Consent Decree, *Albank*, 2 Fair Hous.-Fair Lending (Aspen L. & Bus.) at 19,828-29, § III(5)-(6); Consent Decree, *Chevy Chase*, 2 Fair Hous.-Fair Lending (Aspen L. & Bus.) at 19,693, § IV(C)(7)(a)-(b); Consent Decree, *Blackpipe*, No. 93-5115, at § II(E)(14).

20. Consent Decree, *Chevy Chase*, 2 Fair Hous.-Fair Lending (Aspen L. & Bus.) at 19,693, § IV(C)(6); Consent Decree, Blackpipe, No. 93-5115, § II(F); Consent Decree, Decatur, 2 Fair Hous.-Fair Lending (P-H) at 19,626, § II(C)(16).

21. Consent Decree, *Chevy Chase*, 2 Fair Hous.-Fair Lending (Aspen L. & Bus.) at 19,693, § IV(C)(6); Consent Decree, *Blackpipe*, No. 93-5115, at 13, § II(F); Consent Decree, *Decatur*, 2 Fair Hous.-Fair Lending (P-H) at 19,626, § II(C)(16).

22. Consent Decree, *Blackpipe*, No. 93-5115, at 11-12, §II(E)(13).

23. Consent Decree, *Chevy Chase*, 2 Fair Hous.-Fair Lending (Aspen L. & Bus.) at 19,686-87, 19,689-90, §§I, III; Consent Decree, *Shawmut*, 2 Fair Hous.-Fair Lending (P-H) at 19,674-75, §II(2); Consent Decree, *Decatur*, 2 Fair Hous.-Fair Lending (P-H) at 19,627, §II(D)(21).

24. Consent Decree, *Chevy Chase*, 2 Fair Hous.-Fair Lending (Aspen L. & Bus.) at 19,689-90, §III; Consent Decree, *Shawmut*, 2 Fair Hous.-Fair Lending (P-H) at 19,674-75, §II(2); Consent Decree, *Decatur*, 2 Fair Hous.-Fair Lending (P-H) at 19,626, §II(C)(14).

25. Consent Decree, *Chevy Chase*, 2 Fair Hous.-Fair Lending (Aspen L. & Bus.) at 19,689-90, §III; Consent Decree, *Decatur*, 2 Fair Hous.-Fair Lending (P-H) at 19,628, §II(F).

26. Consent Decree, *Northern Trust*, 2 Fair Hous.-Fair Lending (Aspen L. & Bus.) at 19,729, §II(2)(A), (C); Consent Decree, *Shawmut*, 2 Fair Hous.-Fair Lending (P-H) at 19,674-76, §II; Consent Decree, *Decatur*, 2 Fair Hous.-Fair Lending (P-H) at 19,627-28, §II(E).

27. Despite the fact that the banks voluntarily entered into these consent decrees, this analysis considers the decrees to be government-imposed because the lenders felt they had little choice but to settle. *See* KENNETH H. THOMAS, THE CRA HANDBOOK 135, 157 (1998). Among the reasons that lenders felt compelled to settle are the time and expense of litigating with the DOJ, the public relations damage such charges create, and the risk that their expansions plans could be delayed or denied while the case was pending. *See id.* at 157–58 (among the reasons for Chevy Chase to settle its lending discrimination case with the DOJ were its expansion plans and the embarrassment of race discrimination charges).

28. *See, e.g.*, Consent Decree, U.S. v. Albank, 2 Fair Hous.-Fair Lending (Aspen L. & Bus.) ¶19,401, at 19,832, §VII(1) (N.D.N.Y. Aug. 13, 1997); Consent Decree, U.S. v. First Nat'l Bank of Doña Ana Co., 2 Fair Hous.-Fair Lending (Aspen L. & Bus.) ¶19,395, at 19,784, §VIII (D.N.M. Jan. 29, 1997); Consent Decree, *Chevy Chase*, 2 Fair Hous.- Fair Lending (Aspen L. & Bus.) at 19,694, §V; Consent Decree, U.S. v. First Nat'l Bank of Vicksburg, 2 Fair Hous.-Fair Lending (P-H) ¶19,384, at 19,685, §VII (S.D. Miss. Jan. 21, 1994).

29. Consent Decree, *Chevy Chase*, 2 Fair Hous.-Fair Lending (Aspen L. & Bus.) at 19,686, 19,694, §§I, V.

30. *Id.* at §V.

31. *Id.*

32. *Id.*

33. *Id.*

34. *Id.*

35. *Id.*

36. Consent Decree, U.S. v. Albank, 2 Fair Hous.-Fair Lending (Aspen L. & Bus.) 19,401, at 19,829, §III(7) (N.D.N.Y. Aug. 13, 1997).

37. *Id.*

38. *Id.* at §III(8).

39. *Id.* at §III(9).

40. *Id.* at 19,829-30, §III(9).
41. *Id.* at 19,830, §III(10).
42. *Id.*
43. Consent Decree, U.S. v. First Nat'l Bank of Doña Ana Co., 2 Fair Hous.-Fair Lending (Aspen L. & Bus.) ¶19,395, at 19,781-84, §§III(8)(b), V(13), (17) (D.N.M. Jan. 29, 1997).
44. *Id.* at 19,784, §VIII.
45. Consent Decree, U.S. v. First Nat'l Bank of Vicksburg, 2 Fair Hous.-Fair Lending (P-H) ¶19,384, at 19,684-85, §VIII (S.D. Miss. Jan. 21, 1994).
46. *Id.* at 19,686, app. 3.
47. *Id.* at 19,685, §XII.
48. For a more complete account of this effort, *see Allen J. Fishbein, Filling the Half-Empty Glass: The Role of Community Advocacy in Redefining the Public Responsibilities of Government-Sponsored Housing Enterprises, in* ORGANIZING ACCESS TO CAPITAL: ADVOCACY AND THE DEMOCRATIZATION OF FINANCIAL INSTITUTIONS 102–17 (Gregory D. Squires ed., 2003).
49. 12 U.S.C. §§1451–1459 (2000) (Freddie Mac); 12 U.S.C.A. §§1716–1723c, 1723i (2001 & Supp. 2003) (Fannie Mae), *amended by* Consolidated Appropriations Act, 2004, Pub. L. No. 108-199, div. A, tit. VII, §774, 118 Stat. 3, 40.
50. *See* 12 U.S.C. §§1454–1455; 12 U.S.C.A. §§1717, 1719.
51. 12 U.S.C. §4501(7) (2000).
52. *Id.* §§4501–4503, 4511–4516, 4541–4548, 4561–4567, 4581–4589, 4601–4603, 4611–4623, 4631–4641.
53. *Id.* §4561.
54. *Id.* §4561(a). The LMI housing goal refers to loans for housing for LMI families. *Id.* §4562(a). "Low-income" is an income not greater than 80% of the area median income, and "moderate-income" is an income not in excess of the area median income. *Id.* §4502(8)–(10). The special affordable housing goal applies to mortgages for housing that meets the "then-existing unaddressed needs of, and affordable to, low-income families in low-income areas and very low-income families." *Id.* §4563(a)–(c). "Low-income" is defined the same way as in the LMI housing goal, *id.* §4502(8)–(9), and "very low-income" is defined as income not in excess of 60% of the area median income. *Id.* §4502(19). Each GSE's investment in special affordable housing may not be less than one percent of the dollar amount of all home mortgage loan purchases by the GSEs in the previous year. *Id.* §4563(a)(1). The "underserved areas goal" refers to mortgages for housing located in central cities, rural areas, and other underserved areas. *Id.* §4564(a). "Central city" means any political subdivision designated as a central city by the Office of Management and Budget. *Id.* §4564(d)(3).
55. *Id.* §§4562(b), 4563(a)(2), 4564(b).
56. *Id.* §4562(d)(1).
57. *Id.* §4564(d)(1). If, as of January 31, 1993, a GSE was not meeting this goal, HUD could set interim annual goals so that the GSE would meet the target at the end of the two-year period. *Id.* at (d)(2).
58. *Id.* §4563(d)(1).
59. *Id.* §4563(d)(2).

60. *Id.* §4563(d)(3)(A).

61. *Id.* §4563(d)(3)(B).

62. Brent W. Ambrose et al., U.S. Dep't of Hous. & Urban Dev., An Analysis of the Effects of the GSE Affordable Goals on Low- and Moderate-Income Families 21 (2002)[hereinafter HUD GSE Analysis].

63. *Id.*

64. The primary sources of information on this chart are Office of Policy Dev. & Research, Dep't of Hous. & Urban Dev., Overview of the GSEs' Housing Goal Performance, 1996–2002 (Aug. 2003) (on file with author); Harold Bruce, Speech Before the HUD Policy Development and Research Information Service (Mar. 7, 2001) (on file with author). *See also* 24 C.F.R. §§81.12(c)(1), 81.13(c)(1), 81.14(c)(1) (2004); Office of Policy Dev. & Research, Dep't of Hous. & Urban Dev., Issue Brief No. V, HUD's Affordable Lending Goals for Fannie Mae and Freddie Mac (2001); Patrick Boxall & Joshua B. Silver, *Performance of the GSEs at the Metropolitan Level*, Cityscape 145 (Vol. 5, No. 3, 2001); *Administration Wants GSEs to Do More for Minorities*, Inside Mortgage Compliance, Feb. 10, 2002, at 8; Joshua Brockman, *Fannie Nearing Midpoint of $1T Affordable Housing Goal*, Am. Banker, Mar. 20, 1998, at 9; *Current Housing Goals Extended for FNMA, FHLMC*, [Current Developments] Hous. & Dev. Rep. (West) 468 (Dec. 5, 1994); *Fannie Mae, Freddie Mac Meet Housing Goals, but Affordable Housing Impact Unclear, GAO Says*, [Current Developments] Hous. & Dev. Rep. (West) 210 (Aug. 10, 1998); *Fannie Mae Reports Success in Meeting 1995 Housing Goals,* [Current Developments] Hous. & Dev. Rep. (West) 626 (Feb.12, 1996); *Fannie Reports 46 Percent of Financing Went to Low-Mods*, Inside Mortgage Compliance, Feb. 21, 2000, at 5; *Fannie Says It Beat HUD Lending Goals*, Am. Banker, Feb. 8, 2000, at 22; *Finally, Freddie Exceeds HUD Affordable Housing Targets*, Inside Fair Lending, Mar. 1997, at 4; *Gains in Targeted Lending, Decline Seen in Other Areas*, Inside Mortgage Compliance, May 1998, at 12; *GSE's 2000 Goal Purchases Hit New Higher 2001 Goals*, Inside Mortgage Compliance, Feb. 12, 2001, at 5; *HUD Finalizes Tough Goals For Fannie And Freddie*, CRA/HMDA Update, Nov. 1993, at 10; *HUD Proposal Would Expand GSE Business in New Niches*, Inside Mortgage Compliance, Feb. 21, 2000, at 4; *HUD Proposes Changes to Spur GSE Purchases of CRA Loans, Guidance Clarifies Treatment of Seasoned Mortgage Purchases*, Inside Mortgage Compliance, Feb. 21, 2000, at 2; *HUD Proposes 50% GSE Affordable Housing Goals*, Inside Mortgage Compliance, Aug. 2, 1999, at 5; *HUD Publishes Affordable Housing Goals for GSEs Fannie Mae and Freddie Mac*, 65 Banking Rep. (BNA) 937 (Dec. 11, 1995) [hereinafter *HUD Publishes Affordable Housing Goals*]; *HUD Releases New Rule for Comment on Affordable Housing Goals for Fannie Mae and Freddie Mac*, NCRC Reinvestment Compendium, Apr.–May 1995, at 1 [hereinafter *HUD Releases New Rule*]; *HUD Ups GSE Housing Goals but Loosens Fair Lending*, CRA/HMDA Update, Dec. 1995, at 3; Edward Kulkosky, *Fannie 'on Course' to $1 Trillion of Lower-Income Loans*, Am. Banker, Mar. 18, 1997, at 11; Snigdha Prakash, *Freddie Mac Misses HUD's 30% Target for Central Cities; Fannie Hits the Mark*, Am. Banker, March 9, 1995, at 15; Snigdha Prakash, *HUD Wants Fannie and Freddie to Boost Lower-Income Lending to 38% This Year*, Am. Banker, Feb. 16, 1995, at 6; Press Release, Freddie Mac, Fannie Mae Exceed HUD Housing Goals for 2003 (Feb. 19, 2004); Press Release, Freddie Mac,

Fannie Mae Helped a Record Number of Families Obtain Low Cost Mortgages and Affordable Housing in 2003 (Feb. 16, 2004); *Strong Refinancing Activity Trips Fannie, Freddie in '98*, Inside Mortgage Compliance, Mar. 1, 1999, at 5.

65. HUD GSE Analysis, *supra* note 62.

66. *Id.* at 22.

67. *Id.* at (ix).

68. *Id.* at 3.

69. *Id.* at 28–33.

70. *Id.* at x. Despite this success, the GSEs still have not met Congress' goal that they lead the lending industry in making credit available to underserved neighborhoods. *See* Boxall & Silver, *supra* note 64.

71. Pub. L. No. 103-28, 108 Stat. 2338 (codified as amended at 12 U.S.C. §§43, 215a-1, 1831u, and 1835a (2000)).

72. §109, 108 Stat. at 2362–64; (codified as amended at 12 U.S.C. §1835a (Supp. 2002)). Section 106 of the Gramm-Leach-Bliley Act amended Section 109 to include any branch of a bank controlled by an out-of-state bank holding company. *See* Pub. L. 106-102, §106, 113 Stat. 1338, 1359 (codified at 12 U.S.C. §1835a(e)(4)). As used hereafter, "interstate branch" means the interstate branches of an out-of-state bank or the branches of a bank controlled by an out-of-state bank holding company.

73. The OCC, the Federal Reserve, and the FDIC have established virtually identical regulations enforcing Section 109 of the Riegle-Neal Act. *See* 12 C.F.R. §§25.61–25.65 (OCC) (2002); *id.* §208.28 (Federal Reserve); *id.* §369.1-369.5 (FDIC).

74. 12 U.S.C. §1835a(c)(1).

75. *Id.*

76. Joint Press Release, Board of Governors of the Federal Reserve System, Federal Deposit Insurance Corporation, Office of the Comptroller of the Currency, Banking Agencies Issue Host State Loan-to-Deposit Ratios (March 23, 2000)[hereinafter 2000 Joint Release]); Joint Press Release, Board of Governors of the Federal Reserve System, Federal Deposit Insurance Corporation, Office of the Comptroller of the Currency, Banking Agencies Issue Host State Loan-to-Deposit Ratios (September 7, 1999)[hereinafter 1999 Joint Release]); Joint Press Release, Board of Governors of the Federal Reserve System, Federal Deposit Insurance Corporation, Office of the Comptroller of the Currency, Banking Agencies Issue Host State Loan-to-Deposit Ratios (August 17, 1998)[hereinafter 1998 Joint Release]).

77. 1999 Joint Release, *supra* note 76; 2000 Joint Release, *supra* note 76.

78. 1999 Joint Release, *supra* note 76; 2000 Joint Release, *supra* note 76.

79. 2000 Joint Release, *supra* note 76; 1999 Joint Release, *supra* note 76; 1998 Joint Release, *supra* note 76.

80. *See* Joint Release, Board of Governors of the Federal Reserve System, Federal Deposit Insurance Corporation, Office of the Comptroller of the Currency, Banking Agencies Issue Host State Loan-to-Deposit Ratios (June 28, 2001), *available at* http://www.fdic.gov/news/news/press/2001/pr4701.html (last visited Apr. 16, 2004); Joint Release, Board of Governors of the Federal Reserve System, Federal Deposit Insurance Corporation, Office of the Comptroller of the Currency, Banking Agencies Issue Host State Loan-to-Deposit Ratios (June 24, 2002), *available at* http://www.fed-

eralreserve.gov/boarddocs/press/bcreg/2002/20020624/default.htm (last visited Apr. 16, 2004); Joint Release, Board of Governors of the Federal Reserve, Federal Deposit Insurance Corporation, Office of the Comptroller of the Currency, Banking Agencies Issue Host State Loan-to-Deposit Ratios (May 22, 2003), *available at* http://www.fdic.gov/news/news/press/2003/pr4903.html (last visited Apr. 16, 2004).

81. See Joint Release, Board of Governors of the Federal Reserve System, Federal Deposit Insurance Corporation, Office of the Comptroller of the Currency, Banking Agencies Issue Host State Loan-to-Deposit Ratios (2001);(http://www.fcid.gov/-news/news/press/2001/pr4701a.html)(last visited Jan. 22, 2004); Joint Release, Board of Governors of the Federal Reserve, Federal Deposit Insurance Corporation, Office of the Comptroller of the Currency, Bank Agencies Issue Host State Loan-to-Deposit Ratios (FDIC-PR-70-2002 June 24, 2002) (on file with the author).

82. 12 U.S.C. §1835a(c)(1).

83. *Id.* §1835a(c)(2).

84. *See* THOMAS, *supra* note 27, at 201.

85. *Id.*

86. *Id.*

87. 12 U.S.C §1835a(c)(1)(B)(ii).

88. *Id.* §1835a(c)(1)(B)(i).

89. This section is adapted from an earlier article by the author, Richard Marsico, *Shedding Some Light on Lending: The Effect of Expanded Home Mortgage Disclosure Laws on Home Mortgage Marketing, Lending, and Discrimination in the New York Metropolitan Area*, 27 FORDHAM URB. L.J. 481 (1999).

90. 12 U.S.C. §§2801–2810 (2000).

91. 12 U.S.C. §2801(c). *See* S. REP. NO. 94-187, at 11 (1975), *reprinted in* 1975 U.S.C.C.A.N. 1135; 121 CONG. REC. 25,161-62 (1975) (statement of Sen. Proxmire).

92. *See* H.R. REP. NO. 94-561, at 14, 20-21 (1975), *reprinted* in 1975 U.S.C.C.A.N. 2,303, 2,315-16, 2,321-22; S. REP. NO. 94-187, at 1-2, 9; 121 CONG. REC. 21,160-62 (1975) (statement of Sen. Proxmire); *id.* at 25,162 (statement of Sen. Brooke).

93. HMDA was originally enacted as Pub. L. No. 94-200, §§301-310, 89 Stat. 1125-1128 (1975). The disclosure provisions were at §304, 89 Stat. 1125-1126. A census tract is a small geographic unit that is designated by the Bureau of the Census for purposes of compiling census data.

94. *See* H.R. REP. NO. 94-561, at 10-13 (1975); S. REP. NO. 94-187, at 2–9; 121 CONG. REC. 25,159-60 (1975) (statement of Sen. Proxmire); *id.* at 34,576 (statement of Rep. Stokes).

95. 12 U.S.C. §2801(a).

96. H.R. REP. NO. 94-561, at 12, 20-21, 40; S. REP. NO. 95-187, at 10; 121 CONG. REC. 25,159 (statement of Sen. Proxmire) (1975); *id.* at 34,576 (statement of Rep. Stokes).

97. *See* GLENN B. CANNER, BOARD OF GOVERNORS OF THE FEDERAL RESERVE SYSTEM, REDLINING: RESEARCH AND FEDERAL LEGISLATIVE RESPONSE 1 (1982), *summarized in* 68 FED. RES. BULL. 610 (1982).

98. 121 CONG. REC. S25,160, S25,161 (1975) (statement of Sen. Proxmire).

99. *See* 12 U.S.C. §2801(b) ("The purpose of this title is to provide the citizens and public officials of the United States with sufficient information to enable them to

determine whether depository institutions are fulfilling their obligations to serve the housing needs of the communities and neighborhoods in which they are located and to assist public officials in the determination of the distribution of public sector investments in a manner to improve the private investment environment."); 121 CONG. REC. 34,576 (1975) (statement of Rep. Stokes).

100. H.R. REP. NO. 94-561, at 14.

101. S. REP. NO. 94-187, at 9.

102. 121 CONG. REC. 27,617 (1975) (statement of Sen. Morgan).

103. *See, e.g.,* H.R. REP. NO. 94-561, at 33 (minority views) (arguing that implicit in HMDA was the notion that local funds should be invested locally); S. REP. NO. 94-187, at 21 (additional views of Sen. Tower and others).

104. S. REP. NO. 94-187, at 21 (additional views of Sen. Tower and others).

105. 12 U.S.C. §2801(c); *see also* S. REP. NO. 94-187, at 11.

106. *See, e.g.,* 121 CONG. REC. 25,160 (1975) (statement of Sen. Proxmire) ("I do not believe that a lender has any obligation to make loans in some pre-determined ratio to the deposits he gets...At the same time, a lender that is chartered to serve a community does have an obligation to give some service to that community. He should not arbitrarily reject loan applications from sound credit risks because he does not like the neighborhood, or because he fears that it may at some future time decline."); *see also* 121 CONG. REC. 27,261 (1975) (statement of Sen. Tunney) ("As important as what this bill does is what it does not do. It does not force the allocation of credit by our Nation's lending institutions, nor does it represent a first step toward credit allocation... [I]t does represent a reasonable, limited and first step in a prudent attempt to deal with an urgent national problem by providing information about this problem."). 121 CONG. REC. 27,622 (1975) (statement of Sen. Brooke) ("[Banks] are supposed to serve the area in which they are located; not only to take deposits but to make loans.").

107. 121 CONG. REC. 25,160-61 (1975) (statement of Sen. Proxmire); *id.* at 25,162 (statement of Sen. Brooke).

108. Financial Institutions Reform, Recovery, and Enforcement Act of 1989, Pub. L. No. 101-73, §1211(a)-(b), (c)(1), (c)(2)(A)–(C), (f), (i), (j), 103 Stat. 524-526 (codified at 12 U.S.C. §2803(a)–(b), (e), and (g)–(i) (2001)); *see* 12 C.F.R. §203.4(a) (2004).

109. *See* H.R. REP. NO. 101-54(i), at 497–99, *reprinted in* 1989 U.S.C.C.A.N. 86; *Id.* at 307, 309, 457. For purposes of HMDA data collection and analysis, a predominantly minority neighborhood has a minority population of 80% or higher. *See, e.g.,* Federal Financial Institutions Examination Council, Applications for One- to Four-Family Home Loans Reported under HMDA, Grouped by Purpose of Loan and Distributed by Characteristic of Applicant and Census Tract, 1998 (1999), *reprinted in* 85 FED. RES. BULL. A65 (Sept. 1999). A predominantly minority neighborhood may include, in its minority population, Native Americans, Asians, African-Americans, and/or Latinos. *Id.* An LMI neighborhood has a median income of less than 80% of the area median income ("AMI"). *See id.* at n.3. An LMI individual has an income less than 80% of the AMI. *See id.*

110. Denial rates were 33.9% for African-Americans, 21.4 % for Latinos, and 14.4% for whites. Glenn B. Canner & Dolores S. Smith, *Home Mortgage Disclosure Act: Expanded Data on Residential Lending*, 77 Fed. Res. Bull. 859, 870, tbl. 5 (1991).

African-Americans were denied 2.4 times as frequently as whites and Latinos were denied 1.4 times as frequently.

111. The denial rate was 24% for predominantly minority neighborhoods and 11.5% for predominantly white neighborhoods. Canner & Smith, *supra* note 110, at 870.

112. *See* Jaret Seiberg, *Banks Making Good Progress in Their Fair-Lending Efforts*, AM. BANKER, Sept. 16, 1996, at 1. ("The first year's [HMDA] data, which covered 1990, focused public attention on disparate rejection rates for whites and minorities. The numbers were publicized on the front pages of newspapers across the country – and inevitably drew charges of bias from activists.").

113. *Id.*; Leslie Wayne, *New Hope in Inner Cities: Banks Offering Mortgages*, N.Y. TIMES, Mar. 14, 1992, at A1.

114. Seiberg, *supra* note 112, at 1. Examples of such studies include: ASSOCIATION OF COMMUNITY ORGANIZATIONS FOR REFORM NOW, TAKE THE MONEY AND RUN: THE SIPHONING OF DEPOSITS FROM MINORITY NEIGHBORHOODS IN 14 CITIES (1992); JONATHAN BROWN, RACIAL REDLINING: A STUDY OF DISCRIMINATION BY BANKS AND MORTGAGE COMPANIES IN THE UNITED STATES (1993); KARL FLAMING & RICHARD ANDERSON, MORTGAGE PRACTICES IN COLORADO (1993); THE GREATER ROCHESTER COMMUNITY REINVESTMENT COALITION, WHERE THE MONEY ISN'T FLOWING, A PRELIMINARY REPORT ON MORTGAGE LENDING IN THE CITY OF ROCHESTER (1994); JOHN E. LIND, EXPANDED METHOD FOR ANALYZING HOME MORTGAGE DISCLOSURE ACT DATA FOR THE EVALUATION OF A LENDER'S COMMUNITY REINVESTMENT PERFORMANCE (1993); NATIONAL COMMUNITY REINVESTMENT COALITION, AMERICA'S WORST LENDERS!: A COMPREHENSIVE ANALYSIS OF MORTGAGE LENDING IN THE NATION'S TOP 20 CITIES (1995); CHARLES SCHUMER, HOME MORTGAGE REDLINING DENIES AMERICAN DREAM TO MINORITIES (1997); PETER SKILLERN & MARGRIT BERGHOLZ, AN ANALYSIS OF 1992 MORTGAGE LENDING ACTIVITY TO AFRICAN-AMERICAN AND LOW INCOME HOUSEHOLDS IN WILMINGTON, NORTH CAROLINA (1994); WASHINGTON LAWYERS' COMMITTEE FOR CIVIL RIGHTS AND URBAN AFFAIRS, RANKING THE LENDERS: INVESTIGATING FOR PATTERNS OF RACIAL DISCRIMINATION IN THE MAKING OF HOME LOANS (1994); Joel Glenn Brenner & Liz Spayd, *A Pattern of Bias in Mortgage Loans*, WASH. POST, June 6 1993, at A1; Ford Fessenden et al., *Race and Mortgages*, NEWSDAY, May 28 – June 1, 1996 (four-part series); Michelle A. Hill & Paul D'Ambrosio, *Race Counts in Home Loans*, ASBURY PARK SUNDAY PRESS, May 22, 1994, at 1; David R. Sands, *D.C. Banks Said to Favor White-Area Investment*, WASH. TIMES, June 5, 1992, at C1; Paulette Thomas, *Minority-Area Lenders Faulted in Acorn Study*, WALL. ST. J., June 5, 1992, at A2; Sean Webby, *Mortgage Discrimination, No Equal Treatment, and Unequal Lending*, GANNETT SUBURBAN NEWSPAPERS, Nov. 25, 1991, at 25, 27.

115. *See* Jo Ann S. Barefoot, *Lending Analysis Must Include Discrimination Check*, A.B.A. BANKING J., Aug. 1992, at 24; Steve Cocheo, *ABA Takes Constructive Tack on HMDA Numbers*, A.B.A. BANKING J., July 1992, at 13; Mary Colby, *Learning to be Colorblind*, BANK MGMT., Jan.1993, at 26; Saul Hansell, *Shamed by Publicity, Banks Stress Minority Mortgages*, N.Y. TIMES, Aug. 30, 1993, at D1; Scott B. Schreiber & Beth S. DeSimone, *Avoiding Liability for Alleged Discriminatory Practices*, BANKING L. REV., Winter 1992, at 3; Warren R. Stern et al., *Meeting the Challenge of Loan Bias Scrutiny*,

AM. BANKER, Aug. 21, 1992, at 4; John R. Wilke, *Home Loans to Blacks, Hispanics Soared in 1994,* WALL ST. J., July 19, 1995, at 2.

116. *See* BOARD OF GOVERNORS OF THE FEDERAL RESERVE SYSTEM, RELEASE OF 1990 HMDA DATA 1 (1991).

117. *See National Banks Need More Work on HMDA*, NAT. MORTGAGE NEWS, June 1, 1992, at 8; Schreiber & DeSimone, *supra* note 115, at 3; Paulette Thomas, *U.S., Some Bankers Sharply Boost Use of 'Testers' to Find Racial Bias in Loans,* WALL ST. J., May 27, 1992, at B6.

118. *OCC Announces Testing Program For Lending Bias,*[4 Transfer Binder] Fair Housing-Fair Lending (P-H) ¶ 12.5 [Aspen L. & Bus.] (June 1, 1993). In a matched-pair test, the testing agency sends pairs of undercover "testers," posing as loan applicants, to apply for a loan. Each member of the pair has identical characteristics except for the characteristic that is the subject of the test.

119. *See* Claudia Cummins, *Fed Using New Statistical Tool to Detect Bias,* AM. BANKER, June 8, 1994, at 3; *O.C.C. Report Lists Lending Discrimination Referrals to HUD, DOJ,* Fair Housing-Fair Lending Rep. ¶ 3.7 [Prentice-Hall] (Mar. 1, 1996).

120. *See Discrimination in Home Mortgage Lending, Hearing before the Subcomm. on Consumer and Regulatory Affairs of the S. Comm. on Banking, Hous., and Urban Affairs,* 101st Cong. 4-139 (1989) (federal banking agencies reported finding few violations of the FHA or ECOA by banks); *Federal Financial Regulators Conducting HMDA Follow-up Study,* 58 Banking Rep. (BNA) 863, 864 (May 18, 1992) (describing study by Representative Kennedy that found one referral in the previous ten years); *HUD to Fund $1 Million Lending Testing Program,* [4 Transfer Binder] Fair Hous.-Fair Lending (P-H) ¶ 1.2 [Aspen L. & Bus.] (July 1, 1992).

121. *See* THOMAS, *supra* note 27, at 106.

122. *See* OFFICE OF THE COMPTROLLER OF THE CURRENCY, INTERIM PROCEDURES FOR EXAMINING FOR RACIAL AND ETHNIC DISCRIMINATION IN RESIDENTIAL LENDING, 1 Fair Hous.-Fair Lending (P-H) ¶ 5247 (Apr. 1993); Stephen R. Steinbrick, Remarks before the Federal Financial Institution Examination Council's Emerging Issues Conference on New Procedures for Examining National Banks for Mortgage Loan Discrimination (Mar. 5, 1993), *in* OFFICE OF THE COMPTROLLER OF THE CURRENCY Q.J., June 1993, at 23; *see also* FEDERAL DEPOSIT INSURANCE CORPORATION, REVISED EXAMINATION PROCEDURES FOR FAIR HOUSING, 1 Fair Hous.-Fair Lending (P-H) ¶ 5287 (Apr. 1993).

123. *See Home Mortgage Disclosure Act: Joint Hearings Before the Subcomm. on Consumers Affairs & Coinage and the Subcomm. on Hous. & Cmty. Dev. of the House Comm. on Banking, Fin. & Urban Affairs,* 102d Cong. 740 (1992) (prepared statement of Susan F. Krause, Senior Deputy Comptroller for Bank Supervision Policy, Office of the Comptroller of the Currency), *reprinted in* OFF. OF THE COMPTROLLER OF THE CURRENCY Q.J., Sept. 1992, at 49.

124. Glenn B. Canner & Dolores S. Smith, *Expanded Data on Residential Lending: One Year Later,* 78 FED. RES. BULL. 801, 813, 815 (1992).

125. STAFF OF THE SENATE COMM. ON BANKING, HOUS., AND URBAN AFFAIRS, 102D CONG., REPORT ON THE STATUS OF THE COMMUNITY REINVESTMENT ACT: VIEWS AND RECOMMENDATIONS 3, 18, 34 (Comm. Print 1992) [hereinafter VIEWS AND RECOMMENDATIONS].

126. Prior to 1991, there are few reported instances of the federal banking agencies denying bank expansion applications on CRA or fair lending grounds or commencing administrative proceedings against banks for violating the fair lending laws. *See* Richard Marsico, *Fighting Poverty Through Community Empowerment and Economic Development: The Role of the Community Reinvestment and Home Mortgage Disclosure Acts*, 12 N.Y.L.SCH. J. HUM. RTS. 281, 295–96 (1995) (observing that between 1977 and 1989, federal banking agencies denied less than 10 of 50,000 banking applications on CRA grounds); Richard Marsico, *A Guide to Enforcing the Community Reinvestment Act*, 20 FORDHAM URB. L.J. 165, 274 (1993) (finding that Federal Reserve denied only one bank expansion application on CRA grounds between 1977 and 1991)[hereinafter Marsico, *A Guide to Enforcing the CRA*].

Starting in late 1991, the federal banking agencies denied bank expansion applications on CRA and fair lending grounds and commenced administrative proceedings against banks to enforce the fair lending laws with greater frequency. Through 1995, the Federal Reserve denied at least seven applications on CRA or fair lending grounds. *See* Totalbank Corp., 81 FED. RES. BULL. 876 (1995); Johnson Int'l, Inc., 81 FED. RES. BULL. 507 (1995); Shawmut Nat'l Corp., 80 FED. RES. BULL. 47 (1994); First Colonial Bankshares Corp., 79 FED. RES. BULL. 706 (1993); Farmers & Merchants Bank of Long Beach, 79 FED. RES. BULL. 165 (1993); Gore-Bronson Bancorp., Inc., 78 FED. RES. BULL. 784 (1992); First Interstate BancSystem of Montana, Inc., 77 FED. RES. BULL. 1007 (1991). The Federal Reserve also reached consent decrees in administrative proceedings with at least four banks requiring them to improve their CRA and fair lending records. *See Written Agreement by and between Equitable Bank and Federal Reserve Bank of Atlanta*, Docket No. 94-083-WA/RB-SM (Mar. 8, 1995), *in* 81 FED. RES. BULL. 523 (1995); *Written Agreement by and between First Bank of Berne and Federal Reserve Bank of Chicago*, Docket No. 92-110-WA/RB-SM (Dec. 8, 1992); *Written Agreement by and between Columbus Junction State Bank and Federal Reserve Bank of Chicago*, Docket No. 92-076-WA/RB-SM (Nov. 30. 1992), in 79 FED. RES. BULL. 75 (1993); *Farmers and Merchants Bank of Long Beach Cease and Desist Order*, Docket No. 91-080-B-SM, *in* 78 FED. RES. BULL. 384 (1992).

The OCC denied at least three applications on CRA grounds. *See* Mayde Creek Bank, 1993 OCC Ltr. LEXIS 69 (Dec. 9, 1993); Nat'l Bank of Commerce, 1992 OCC Ltr. LEXIS 87 (Nov. 20, 1992); First Commerce Nat'l Bank, 1992 OCC Ltr. LEXIS 86 (Nov. 20, 1992). The OCC also brought several enforcement proceedings. *See In re* First Nat'l Bank of Vicksburg, 1994 OCC Enf. Dec. LEXIS 94-271 (Jan. 21, 1994); *In re* Davis Nat'l Bank of Mullins, 1993 OCC Enf. Dec. LEXIS 113 (Apr. 21, 1994); *In re* First Nat'l Bank of Bar Harbor, 1993 OCC Enf. Dec. LEXIS 285 (Aug. 6, 1993); *In re* Lake Area Nat'l Bank, 1993 OCC Enf. Dec. LEXIS 241 (June 21, 1993); *In re* Ka Wah Bank, Ltd., 1993 OCC Enf. Dec. LEXIS 141 (Apr. 29, 1993); *In re* Metrobank of Philadelphia, 1993 OCC Enf. Dec. LEXIS 169 (Mar. 18, 1993); In re Metrobank of Philadelphia, 1993 OCC Enf. Dec. LEXIS 120 (Mar. 18, 1993); *In re* First Nat'l Bank of Downsville, 1993 OCC Enf. Dec. LEXIS 117 (Mar. 22, 1993); *In re* First Nat'l Bank of Polk County, 1993 OCC Enf. Dec. LEXIS 73 (Feb. 25, 1993); *In re* First United Nat'l Bank, 1993 OCC Enf. Dec. LEXIS 11 (Jan. 19, 1993); *In re* City Nat'l Bank, 1992 OCC Enf. Dec. LEXIS 480 (Nov. 18, 1992); *In re* Continental Nat'l Bank of Miami, 1992 OCC Enf. Dec. LEXIS 490 (Nov. 10, 1992); *In re*

Consumer Nat'l Bank, 1992 OCC Enf. Dec. LEXIS 492 (Oct. 28, 1992); In re First Philson Bank, OCC Enf. Dec. LEXIS 464 (Oct. 13, 1992); *In re* South Branch Valley Nat'l Bank, 1992 OCC Enf. Dec. LEXIS 465 (Oct. 7, 1992); *In re* Nat'l Republic Bank of Chicago, 1992 OCC Enf. Dec. LEXIS 180 (Sept. 22, 1992); *In re* Superior Nat'l Bank, 1992 OCC Enf. Dec. LEXIS 182 (Sept. 3, 1992); *In re* Addison Nat'l Bank, 1992 OCC Enf. Dec. LEXIS 121 (Aug. 27, 1992); *In re* First Nat'l Bank of Brooksville, 1992 OCC Enf. Dec. LEXIS 115 (July 15, 1992); *In re* First Nat'l Bank of Logan, 1992 OCC Enf. Dec. LEXIS 114 (July 7, 1992); *In re* Downington Nat'l Bank, 1992 OCC Enf. Dec. LEXIS 210 (May 6, 1992); *In re* Tupper Lake Nat'l Bank, OCC EA No. 92-848, *terminated by* OCC EA No. 93-319, 1992 OCC Enf. Dec. LEXIS 569 (Apr. 29, 1992); *In re* Palmer Nat'l Bank, 1992 OCC Enf. Dec. LEXIS 38 (Mar. 11, 1992); *In re* Vinings Bank and Trust, 1992 OCC Enf. Dec. LEXIS 19 (Jan. 8, 1992).

The FDIC also brought several enforcement proceedings against banks with poor CRA or fair lending records. *See In re* New England Sav. Bank, 1995 FDIC Enf. Dec. LEXIS 368 (July 14, 1995); *In re* Bank of Hollandale, 1995 FDIC Enf. Dec. LEXIS 155 (May 11, 1995); *In re* Sunniland Bank, 1995 FDIC Enf. Dec. LEXIS 1 (Jan. 30, 1995); *In re* Pine Banking Corp., 1994 FDIC Enf. Dec. LEXIS 371 (Nov. 18, 1994); *In re* Bank of Pullman, 1994 FDIC Enf. Dec. LEXIS 399 (Nov. 7, 1994); *In re* First Scotland Bank, 1994 FDIC Enf. Dec. LEXIS 277 (Aug. 29, 1994); *In re* American State Bank, 1994 FDIC Enf. Dec. LEXIS 281 (Aug. 26, 1994); *In re* First State Bank, 1994 FDIC Enf. Dec. LEXIS 217 (July 12, 1994); *In re* Bank of Coffey, 1994 FDIC Enf. Dec. LEXIS 146 (May 27, 1993); *In re* Buckner State Bank, 1994 FDIC Enf. Dec. LEXIS 127 (Apr. 6, 1994); *In re* Golden Security Thrift and Loan, 1993 FDIC Enf. Dec. LEXIS 688 (Sept. 7, 1993). *See also Louisiana Bank Ordered to Reimburse Minority Borrowers,* Fair Housing-Fair Lending Rep. ¶3.2 [Prentice-Hall] (Mar.1, 1995). The FDIC also penalized eight banks for failing to file timely HMDA reports. *See* Fair Housing-Fair Lending Rep. ¶16.15 [Prentice-Hall] (Oct.1, 1994).

127. 60 Fed. Reg. 22,156 (May 4, 1995).

128. *See supra,* ch. 4.

129. *See* Policy Statement on Discrimination in Lending, 59 Fed. Reg. 18,266 (Apr. 15, 1994). The task force was composed of representatives of HUD, the DOJ, the OCC, the OTS, the Federal Reserve, the FDIC, the Federal Housing Finance Board, the Federal Trade Commission, and the National Credit Union Administration.

130. *Id.* at 18,268.

131. *Id.* at 18,267, 18,272-73.

132. 42 U.S.C. §§3602(a), 3610, 3612 (2000).

133. Mortgage Bankers Ass'n of Am. and the U.S. Dept. of Hous. & Urban Dev., Fair Lending-Best Practices Master Agreement, Sept. 14, 1994; *MBA, HUD Reach New Agreement On New 'Best Practices' Pact,* Inside Fair Lending, Nov. 1997, at 3.

134. *MBA, HUD New Agreement on "Best Practices" Pact,* Inside Fair Lending, Jan. 1998, at 13.

135. *See* Michael Janofsky, *Texas Lenders Pledge $1.4 billion in Housing Case,* N.Y. Times, Mar. 10, 1998, at A13; Snigdha Prakash, *Accubank in $2B Settlement of Fair Lending Charges,* Am. Banker, Apr. 6, 1998, at 2; Jaret Seiberg, *Lender Assails*

Implication it Broke Bias Law, AM. BANKER, Jan. 20, 1999, at 1; Warren W. Traiger, *New Fair Lending Initiatives*, REV. BANKING AND FIN. SERV., Mar. 4, 1998.

136. *See supra* ch. 5.

137. *See* NATIONAL COMMUNITY REINVESTMENT COALITION, CRA COMMITMENTS (1999).

138. *See* Canner & Smith, *supra* note 124, at 817–18; J. Linn Allen, *Banks, Activists Tailor Loans to Communities*, CHI. TRIB., Sept. 1, 1992, at 1; Bill Atkinson, *ABA Admits Bias by Home Lenders*, AM. BANKER, May 22, 1992, at 1; Andree Brooks, *Mortgage Outreach Efforts*, N.Y. TIMES, Oct. 30, 1994, sec. 9, at 5; Andree Brooks, *Removing Barriers to Loans*, N.Y. TIMES, Apr. 5, 1992, sec. 10, at 5 [hereinafter *Removing Barriers*]; Claudia Cummins, *Riegle: Congress Will Crack Down On Loan Bias if Regulators Don't*, AM. BANKER, Oct. 29. 1992, at 1; Charles H. Grice, *The Challenge of Lending Disparities*, AM. BANKER , Oct. 24, 1991, at 1; Steve Cocheo, *ABA Takes Constructive Tack on HMDA Numbers*, A.B.A. BANKING J., July 1992, at 13; Timothy R. Dougherty, *Closing the Gap: Stung by Charges of Bias Against Minorities, Lenders are Trying to do Right Thing*, NEWSDAY, Jan. 20, 1993, at 30; Joanne Johnson, *Mortgage Lenders Re-Examining Their Methods*, HARTFORD COURANT, Nov. 17, 1991, at C1; Albert R. Karr, *Loan-Denial Rate is Still High for Blacks*, WALL ST. J., Nov. 11, 1993, at A2; Edward Kulkosky, *Low-Income Lending Tips: Use Local Groups*, AM. BANKER, Feb. 22, 1995, at 11; Paulette Thomas, *Blacks Can Face a Host of Trying Conditions in Getting Mortgages*, WALL ST. J., Nov. 30, 1992, at A1; Heather Timmons, *Improving Minority Lending a Hands-On Proposition*, AM. BANKER, Sept. 17, 1996, at 1; Wilke, *supra* note 115.

139. *See* Glenn B. Canner, Wayne Passmore, & Dolores S. Smith, *Residential Lending to Low-Income and Minority Families: Evidence from the 1992 HMDA Data*, 80 FED. RES. BULL. 79, 87 (1994); Allen, *supra* note 138; Keith Bradsher, *Minority Home Loans Rise, But Many Are Still Rejected*, N.Y. TIMES, Oct. 27, 1994, at D1; Brooks, *Removing Barriers to Loans, supra* note 138; Cummins, *supra* note 138; John R. Wilke, *Giving Credit*, WALL ST. J., Feb. 13, 1996, at A1. For example, in 1990, only 70 lenders nationwide participated in Fannie Mae's Community Homebuyer's Program, which provides loans with flexible terms to low-income borrowers. By 1992, 700 lenders participated, and lending increased from $130 million to $3.5 billion. *See* Dougherty, *supra* note 138.

140. Karr, *supra* note 138; Jaret Seiberg, *Greenspan Says Banks Reaching Out to Minorities*, AM. BANKER, July 20, 1995, at 1.

141. Canner, Passmore & Smith, *supra* note 139, at 79, 88; Karr, *supra* note 138. For example, some banks changed their underwriting criteria relating to employment and credit history, the definition of family members, and the percentage of a downpayment that could be from gifts. *See Brooks, Removing Barriers, supra* note 138.

142. Canner & Smith, *supra* note 124, at 817–18; Press Release, *New York Banks Form Mortgage Coalition*, (May 11, 1992)(on file with author).

143. *See* Canner & Smith, *supra* note 124, at 817–18; Dougherty, *supra* note 138; Seiberg, *supra* note 140.

144. Canner & Smith, *supra* note 124, at 817–18; *Brooks, Removing Barriers, supra* note 138; Dougherty, *supra* note 138; Karr, *supra* note 138; Timmons, *supra* note 138.

145. For studies that use the market share of applications to examine the lending record of individual banks, *see* FLAMING & ANDERSON, *supra* note 114; SAMUEL L.

MYERS, JR. & BILL MILCZARSKI, APPROPRIATE USES OF HMDA DATA IN MEASURING AND DETERMINING DISCRIMINATION IN LOCAL MARKETS: THE CASE OF CHICAGO (1997); NATIONAL COMMUNITY REINVESTMENT COALITION, AMERICA'S BEST AND WORST LENDERS (1998); NATIONAL COMMUNITY REINVESTMENT COALITION, WHO'S FINANCING THE AMERICAN DREAM (1998); NATIONAL COMMUNITY REINVESTMENT COALITION, *supra* note 114; WASHINGTON LAWYERS' COMMITTEE FOR CIVIL RIGHTS AND URBAN AFFAIRS, *supra* note 114.

146. The sources for the information in the following tables are: Canner & Smith, *supra* note 124, at 869, 870, 874; and the Internet URL of the Federal Financial Institutions Examination Council, *at* http://www.ffiec.gov (last visited Nov. 19, 2002).

147. 1991 is the baseline for measuring change because the first set of expanded HMDA data—covering 1990—was disclosed in late 1991, so the first year that the disclosure of expanded HMDA data could have had an impact on lenders' behavior was 1992. The market share of applications and loans approvals is depicted instead of total applications and loan approvals because the total numbers of applications and loan approvals fluctuate from year to year, distorting the meaning of the raw numbers. Relying on relative market share controls for these fluctuations.

148. For a discussion of this methodology and examples of studies that use the market share of loans to evaluate the lending record of individual lenders and overall lending in a community, *see* BROWN, *supra* note 114; JIM CAMPEN, CHANGING PATTERNS IV: MORTGAGE LENDING TO TRADITIONALLY UNDERSERVED BORROWERS & NEIGHBORHOODS IN BOSTON, 1990–1996 (1997); MYERS & MILCZARKSI, *supra* note 145; FAIR LENDING ANALYSIS: A COMPENDIUM OF ESSAYS ON THE USE OF STATISTICS (Anthony M. Yezer ed. 1995); NATIONAL COMMUNITY REINVESTMENT COALITION, AMERICA'S BEST AND WORST LENDERS (1998); NATIONAL COMMUNITY REINVESTMENT COALITION, WHO'S FINANCING THE AMERICAN DREAM (1998); SKILLERN & BERGHOLZ, *supra* note 114; Robert B. Avery et al., *Trends in Home Purchase Lending: Consolidation and the Community Reinvestment Act,* 85 FED. RES. BULL. 81, 93 (1999); Katherine L. Bradbury et al., *Geographic Patterns of Mortgage Lending in Boston, 1982–1987,* NEW ENG. ECON. REV., Sept.–Oct. 1989, at 3;

CHAPTER EIGHT

1. For the view that more quantitative and rigorous service and investment tests for banks would be unduly burdensome, *see* KENNETH H. THOMAS, OPTIMAL CRA REFORM 18, The Levy Econ. Inst., Public Policy Brief No. 68, 2002. [hereinafter CRA REFORM].

2. In contrast, *see* KENNETH H. THOMAS, CRA'S 25TH ANNIVERSARY: THE PAST, PRESENT, AND FUTURE 35 (2002) (proposing to eliminate the investment and service tests as separate tests and to make them part of the lending test) [hereinafter CRA'S 25TH ANNIVERSARY]; CRA REFORM, *supra* note 1, at 17–21.

3. *See, e.g.,* 12 C.F.R. §25.22(a)(1)(2004).

4. Currently, there is sufficient public data available about only one of these five types of lending—real estate-related lending—to develop quantitative benchmarks of community credit needs necessary for the proposed CRA evaluative criteria. There is some data about the other types of loans, but it is not sufficient to develop the necessary benchmarks. The CRA regulations require banks to collect information about the

location of their small business and small farm loans, the dollar value of each loan, and the gross annual revenue of the small business or small farm that received each loan. *See, e.g.*, 12 C.F.R. §25.42(a)–(b). It is currently unlawful under the Equal Credit Opportunity Act regulations to collect data about the race of small business borrowers. 12 C.F.R. §202.5(b)(2004). The Federal Reserve considered amending its regulations to permit the collection of such data but decided not to. *See* Jaret Seiberg, *Banks Hit Plan to Let them Collect Small-Business Race and Sex Data*, AM. BANKER, Aug. 23, 1995, at 4; Jaret Seiberg, *The Fed Scuttles Plan to Record Race, Sex Data*, AM. BANKER, Dec. 23, 1996, at 1. The Community Reinvestment Modernization Act of 2001 would have required lenders to disclose the race of small business and small farm loan applicants and the specific census tract of the farm or business. *See* H.R. 865, 107th Cong. §102(b)(2001). The CRA regulations require the federal banking agencies to report the total number and dollar volume of each bank's community development loans. *See, e.g.*, 12 C.F.R. §25.42(h)(4). Finally, the CRA regulations provide that banks may collect information about the total number, dollar amount, and location of their consumer loans, and the income of the borrowers. *See, e.g.*, 12 C.F.R. §25.42(c). Thus, the proposal in this chapter cannot be fully implemented without changes in the law and regulations that would impose HMDA-like reporting requirements on small business, consumer, and community development lending.

5. *See* 12 C.F.R. §§203.2(e)(1)(iii), 203.2(h), and 203.4(a); pt. 203, App. A, (i)(A)(4) (codes 1 and 3), and 5 (code 3).

6. *See, e.g.*, 12 C.F.R. §§25.12(u); 25.22 (b)(3)(ii).

7. *See, e.g.*, 12 C.F.R. §25.12(h)–(j).

8. *See, e.g.*, *id.* §§25.12(k).

9. *See, e.g.*, *id.* §25.41.

10. *See, e.g. id.*, §25.41(c)(1).

11. *See* CRA REFORM, *supra* note 1, at 28. *Compare* The Community Reinvestment Modernization Act of 2001, H.R. 865, 107th Cong. §102(a) (proposing a .5% market share as a threshold market share to include an MSA within a bank's CRA service area) *with* CRA'S 25TH ANNIVERSARY, *supra* note 2, at 49 ("Assuming this was a reasonable approach, the relevant cutoff would have to be significantly higher, perhaps 5–10% or more, before the subject bank's relative performance might have a meaningful impact on the local credit markets."). *See also* CRA REFORM, *supra* note 1, at 28.

12. *See* Standards for Defining Metropolitan and Micropolitan Statistical Areas, 65 Fed. Reg. 82,228, 82,235-38 (Dec. 27, 2000).

13. *But see* CRA'S 25TH ANNIVERSARY *supra* note 2, at 45 ("Community groups are flat out wrong by asking that CRA become race-based, something that could jeopardize the future of this needs-based law. Nothing could be more damaging to CRA than to change or even redirect its primary focus away from LMI lending.").

14. A minority person is a Native American, Asian/Pacific Islander, African-American, or Latino person, as under HMDA. A predominantly minority neighborhood has a minority population of 80 percent or higher. An LMI person has an income of less than 80 percent of the area median income ("AMI"), also as under HMDA. An LMI neighborhood has a median income of less than 80 percent of the AMI. *See, e.g.*, Federal Financial Institutions Examination Council, Applications for One- to Four-Family Home

Loans Reported under HMDA, Grouped by Purpose of Loan and Distributed by Characteristic of Applicant and Census Tract, 1998 (1999), *reprinted in* 85 Fed. Res. Bull. A65 (1999); *Financial and Business Statistics,* 85 Fed. Res. Bull. A65, tbl. 4.37 (1999).

15. The Community Reinvestment Modernization Act of 2001 would have amended the CRA to require CRA performance evaluations to include an analysis of lending by the racial composition of a neighborhood as well as its income level. *See* H.R. 865, 107th Cong. § 102(6).

16. *See, e.g.,* 12 C.F.R. § 25.28(c).

17. *But see* CRA Reform, *supra* note 1, at 24 ("Even some respected researchers have apparently confused the Act's statutory intent by frequently mentioning "minority" communities alongside "lower income" ones in their discussions of CRA.").

18. *See, e.g.,* 123 Cong. Rec. 17,630 (1977)(statement of Sen. Proxmire).

19. *See Community Credit Needs: Hearings on S. 406 Before the S. Comm. on Banking, Hous., and Urban Affairs,* 95th Cong. 30, 42, 48–49, 52–53, 56, 64, 74–76, 90–91, 96–99, 149, 345, 347 (1977).

20. *See* Dedrick Muhammad et al. , United for a Fair Economy, The State of the Dream 2004: Enduring Disparities in Black and White 6–11 (2004), *available at* http://www.FairEconomy.org; Robert Pear, *Number of People Living in Poverty Increases in U.S.,* N.Y. Times, Sept. 25, 2002, at A1; Theodore M. Shaw, Editorial, *Race Still Matters,* Wash. Post, Mar. 1, 2003, at A19.

21. Glenn B. Canner & Wayne Passmore, *Home Purchase Lending in Low-Income Neighborhoods and to Low-Income Borrowers,* 81 Fed. Res. Bull. 71, 80 (1995).

22. 12 U.S.C. §§ 2903, 2906 (2000).

23. *See, e.g.,* Equal Credit Opportunity Act, 15 U.S.C. §§ 1691–1691(f)(2000).

24. *See supra* ch. 2, text accompanying notes 13 to 14.

25. *See, e.g., Fifth Third Bancorp,* 87 Fed. Res. Bull. 330 (2001); *Bank of Commerce,* CRA Dec. No. 96, Office of the Comptroller of the Currency (Jul. 1999).

26. 12 U.S.C. § 2901(c)(1)–(2) (2000).

27. *See* Gregory Squires, Color and Money: Politics and Prospects for Community Revitalization in Urban America 77 (using three indicators: loan origination percentage; application percentage; and denial rate ratio).

28. Richard D. Marsico, *Shedding Some Light on Lending: The Effect of Expanded Disclosure Laws on Home Mortgage Marketing, Lending, and Discrimination in the New York Metropolitan Area,* 27 Ford. Urb. L. J. 481, 524–26 (1999).

29. *Id.*

30. As used in this proposal, a predominantly white neighborhood has a white population greater than 80 percent, a UI person has an income of 120 percent or higher of the AMI, and a UI neighborhood has a median income of 120 percent or higher of the AMI.

31. *See* Squires, *supra* note 27, at 165. *See* also Kenneth H. Thomas, The CRA Handbook 212 (1998) ("Users of aggregate HMDA benchmarks in evaluating banks must realize that such data merely shows what all covered institutions *supply* in the way of housing credit, and this may be below *demand*.").

32. *See* Squires, *supra* note 27, at 77; Marsico, *supra* note 28, at 524–26.

33. *See* Squires, *supra* note 27, at 77.

34. *See* Malcolm Bush & Daniel Immergluck, *Research, Advocacy, and Community Reinvestment*, *in* ORGANIZING ACCESS TO CAPITAL: ADVOCACY AND THE DEMOCRATIZATION OF FINANCIAL INSTITUTIONS (Gregory D. Squires, ed., 2003) 159 ("...if a bank's market share in low- and moderate-income neighborhoods was equal to the bank's market share in middle- and upper-income neighborhoods, it was likely that the bank was making at least an equal effort in the lower-income communities.").

35. CRA'S 25TH ANNIVERSARY, *supra* note 2, at 43, proposes ten criteria to evaluate CRA performance, including investment and service criteria.

36. Gregory Squires notes that, given the evidence of lending discrimination, this constitutes a conservative approach. SQUIRES, *supra* note 27, at 165.

37. *See supra*, text accompanying note 7, for a description of community development.

38. These standards are derived from three sources. The first two are publications: MICHAEL A. STEGMAN ET AL., TOWARD A MORE PERFORMANCE-DRIVEN SERVICE TEST: STRENGTHENING BASIC BANKING SERVICES UNDER THE COMMUNITY REINVESTMENT ACT 33-37 (rev. ed. 2001); Dory Rand, Using the Community Reinvestment Act to Promote Checking Accounts for Low-Income People, CLEARINGHOUSE REV., May–June 1999, at 66, 72. The third is methodology employed by the National Community Reinvestment Coalition.

39. This difference in the weight ascribed to each component of the overall CRA rating is based on the relative importance of lending under the terms of the CRA compared with community development activities and retail banking services. It differs from the current regulations, which weigh lending at least twice as high as investments and retail banking services individually and equally to their combined weight. *See* Community Reinvestment Act Regulation, 60 Fed. Reg. 22,156, 22,168-70 (Apr. 19, 1995). *See* CRA REFORM, *supra* note 1, at 18 (stating that the community development and service tests currently constitute a "morbidly obese" fifty percent of the full rating).

40. For similar approaches, *see* THOMAS, *supra* note 31, at 261; Richard D. Marsico, *Patterns of Lending to Low-Income and Minority Persons and Neighborhoods: The 1999 New York Metropolitan Area Mortgage Lending Scorecard*, 17 N.Y.L. SCH. L. REV. 239-251 (2000); Richard D. Marsico, *New York Metropolitan Area Lending Scorecard*: 1998, 16 N.Y.L.SCH. L. REV. 769, 791–804 (2000).

41. *See* Expanded Guidance for Subprime Lending Programs, 6 Fed. Banking L. Rep. (CCH) ¶63-792, at 73,299-33 (Feb. 9, 2001).

42. The author acknowledges Matthew Lee, director of Inner City Press/Community on the Move, for this approach. In contrast, the author earlier proposed a different way to evaluate subprime lending. *See* Richard D. Marsico, *Subprime Lending, Predatory Lending, and the Community Reinvestment Act Obligations of Banks*, 22 N.Y.L. SCH. L. REV. 735-744 (2003)(using a market share ratio comparison to evaluate the extent of a bank's subprime lending).

43. Another approach to this could be simply to eliminate subprime loans from the calculus. *See* Bush & Immergluck, *supra* note 34, at 160. This proposal does not adopt this approach because subprime loans are not necessarily harmful. Also, if a bank is targeting communities with subprime loans, excluding subprime loans from its calculus is not a sufficient penalty.

44. Expanded Guidance for Subprime Lending, *supra* note 41, at 73,299-37 to 73,299-38.

45. *See* H.R. 865, 107th Cong. § 103 (penalizing a bank that engages in predatory lending by reducing its CRA rating); CRA REFORM, *supra* note 1, at 21, 27 (proposing considering predatory or other adverse credit factors as part of qualitative analysis of a bank's LMI lending).

46. *See supra* ch. 2, text accompanying notes 21–34 for more about this.

47. 127 Cong. Rec. 17,631 (1977)(statement of Sen. Sarbanes).

APPENDIX ONE

The Community Reinvestment Act

Sec. 2901. Congressional findings and statement of purpose

(a) The Congress finds that—

(1) regulated financial institutions are required by law to demonstrate that their deposit facilities serve the convenience and needs of the communities in which they are chartered to do business;

(2) the convenience and needs of communities include the need for credit services as well as deposit services; and

(3) regulated financial institutions have continuing and affirmative obligation to help meet the credit needs of the local communities in which they are chartered.

(b) It is the purpose of this chapter to require each appropriate Federal financial supervisory agency to use its authority when examining financial institutions, to encourage such institutions to help meet the credit needs of the local communities in which they are chartered consistent with the safe and sound operation of such institutions.

Sec. 2902. Definitions

For the purposes of this chapter—

(1) the term "appropriate Federal financial supervisory agency" means—

(A) the Comptroller of the Currency with respect to national banks;

(B) the Board of Governors of the Federal Reserve System with respect to State chartered banks which are members of the Federal Reserve System and bank holding companies;

(C) the Federal Deposit Insurance Corporation with respect to State chartered banks and savings banks which are not members of the Federal Reserve System and the deposits of which are insured by the

Corporation; and (2) section 1818 of this title, by the Director of the Office of Thrift Supervision, in the case of a savings association (the deposits of which are insured by the Federal Deposit Insurance Corporation) and a savings and loan holding company;

(2) the term "regulated financial institution" means an insured depository institution (as defined in section 1813 of this title); and

(3) the term "application for a deposit facility" means an application to the appropriate Federal financial supervisory agency otherwise required under Federal law or regulations thereunder for—

(A) a charter for a national bank or Federal savings and loan association;

(B) deposit insurance in connection with a newly chartered State bank, savings bank, savings and loan association or similar institution;

(C) the establishment of a domestic branch or other facility with the ability to accept deposits of a regulated financial institution;

(D) the relocation of the home office or a branch office of a regulated financial institution;

(E) the merger or consolidation with, or the acquisition of the assets, or the assumption of the liabilities of a regulated financial institution requiring approval under section 1828(c) of this title or under regulations issued under the authority of title IV of the National Housing Act [12 U.S.C. 1724 et seq.]; or

(F) the acquisition of shares in, or the assets of, a regulated financial institution requiring approval under section 1842 of this title or section 408(e) of the National Housing Act [12 U.S.C. 1730a(e)].

(4) A financial institution whose business predominately consists of serving the needs of military personnel who are not located within a defined geographic area may define its "entire community" to include its entire deposit customer base without regard to geographic proximity.

Sec. 2903. Financial institutions; evaluation

(a) In general

In connection with its examination of a financial institution, the appropriate Federal financial supervisory agency shall—

(1) assess the institution's record of meeting the credit needs of its entire community, including low- and moderate-income neighborhoods, consistent with the safe and sound operation of such institution; and

(2) take such record into account in its evaluation of an application for a deposit facility by such institution.

(b) Majority-owned institutions

In assessing and taking into account, under subsection (a) of this section, the record of a nonminority-owned and nonwomen-owned financial institution, the appropriate Federal financial supervisory agency may consider as a factor capital investment, loan participation, and other ventures undertaken by the institution in cooperation with minority- and women-owned financial institutions and low-income credit unions provided that these activities help meet the credit needs of local communities in which such institutions and credit unions are chartered.

(c) Financial holding company requirement

(1) In general

An election by a bank holding company to become a financial holding company under section 1843 of this title shall not be effective if—

(A) the Board finds that, as of the date the declaration of such election and the certification is filed by such holding company under section1843(l)(1)(C) of this title, not all of the subsidiary insured depository institutions of the bank holding company had achieved a rating of "satisfactory record of meeting community credit needs", or better, at the most recent examination of each such institution; and

(B) the Board notifies the company of such finding before the end of the 30-day period beginning on such date.

(2) Limited exclusions for newly acquired insured depository institutions

Any insured depository institution acquired by a bank holding company during the 12-month period preceding the date of the submission to the Board of the declaration and certification under section 1843(l)(1)(C) of this title may be excluded for purposes of paragraph (1) during the 12-month period beginning on the date of such acquisition if—

(A) the bank holding company has submitted an affirmative plan to the appropriate Federal financial supervisory agency to take such action as may be necessary in order for such institution to achieve a rating of "satisfactory record of meeting community credit needs", or better, at the next examination of the institution; and

(B) the plan has been accepted by such agency.

(3) Definitions

For purposes of this subsection, the following definitions shall apply:

(A) Bank holding company; financial holding company

The terms "bank holding company" and "financial holding company" have the meanings given those terms in section 1841 of this title.

(B) Board
The term "Board" means the Board of Governors of the Federal Reserve System.

(C) Insured depository institution
The term "insured depository institution" has the meaning given the term in section 1813(c) of this title.

Sec. 2904. Report to Congress

Each appropriate Federal financial supervisory agency shall include in its annual report to the Congress a section outlining the actions it has taken to carry out its responsibilities under this chapter.

Sec. 2905. Regulations

Regulations to carry out the purposes of this chapter shall be published by each appropriate Federal financial supervisory agency, and shall take effect no later than 390 days after October 12, 1977.

Sec. 2906. Written evaluations

(a) Required

(1) In general
Upon the conclusion of each examination of an insured depository institution under section 2903 of this title, the appropriate Federal financial supervisory agency shall prepare a written Evaluation of the institution's record of meeting the credit needs of its entire community, including low- and moderate-income neighborhoods.

(2) Public and confidential sections
Each written evaluation required under paragraph (1) shall have a public section and a confidential section.

(b) Public section of report

(1) Findings and conclusions

(A) Contents of written evaluation
The public section of the written evaluation shall—

(i) state the appropriate Federal financial supervisory agency's conclusions for each assessment factor identified in the regulations prescribed by the Federal financial supervisory agencies to implement this chapter;

(ii) discuss the facts and data supporting such conclusions; and

(iii) contain the institution's rating and a statement describing the basis for the rating.

(B) Metropolitan area distinctions

The information required by clauses (i) and (ii) of subparagraph (A) shall be presented separately for each metropolitan area in which a regulated depository institution maintains one or more domestic branch offices.

(2) Assigned rating

The institution's rating referred to in paragraph (1)(C) shall be 1 of the following:

(A) "Outstanding record of meeting community credit needs".

(B) "Satisfactory record of meeting community credit needs".

(C) "Needs to improve record of meeting community credit needs".

(D) "Substantial noncompliance in meeting community credit needs".

Such ratings shall be disclosed to the public on and after July 1, 1990.

(C) Confidential section of report

(1) Privacy of named individuals

The confidential section of the written evaluation shall contain all references that identify any customer of the institution, any employee or officer of the institution, or any person or organization that has provided information in confidence to a Federal or State financial supervisory agency.

(2) Topics not suitable for disclosure

The confidential section shall also contain any statements obtained or made by the appropriate Federal financial supervisory agency in the course of an examination which, in the judgment of the agency, are too sensitive or speculative in nature to disclose to the institution or the public.

(3) Disclosure to depository institution

The confidential section may be disclosed, in whole or part, to the institution, if the appropriate Federal financial supervisory agency determines that such disclosure will promote the objectives of this chapter. However, disclosure under this paragraph shall not identify a person or organization that has provided information in confidence to a Federal or State financial supervisory agency.

(d) Institutions with interstate branches

(1) State-by-State evaluation

In the case of a regulated financial institution that maintains domestic branches in 2 or more States, the appropriate Federal financial supervisory agency shall prepare—

(A) a written evaluation of the entire institution's record of performance under this chapter, as required by subsections (a), (b), and (c) of this section; and

(B) for each State in which the institution maintains 1 or more domestic branches, a separate written evaluation of the institution's record of performance within such State under this chapter, as required by subsections (a), (b), and (c) of this section.

(2) Multistate metropolitan areas

In the case of a regulated financial institution that maintains domestic branches in 2 or more States within a multistate metropolitan area, the appropriate Federal financial supervisory agency shall prepare a separate written evaluation of the institution's record of performance within such metropolitan area under this chapter, as required by subsections (a), (b), and (c) of this section. If the agency prepares a written evaluation pursuant to this paragraph, the scope of the written evaluation required under paragraph (1)(B) shall be adjusted accordingly.

(3) Content of State level evaluation

A written evaluation prepared pursuant to paragraph (1)(B) shall—

(A) present the information required by subparagraphs (A) and (B) of subsection (b)(1) of this section separately for each metropolitan area in which the institution maintains 1 or more domestic branch offices and separately for the remainder of the nonmetropolitan area of the State if the institution maintains 1or more domestic branch offices in such nonmetropolitan area; and

(B) describe how the Federal financial supervisory agency has performed the examination of the institution, including a list of the individual branches examined.

(e) Definitions

For purposes of this section the following definitions shall apply:

(1) Domestic branch

The term "domestic branch" means any branch office or other facility of a regulated financial institution that accepts deposits, located in any State.

(2) Metropolitan area

The term "metropolitan area" means any primary metropolitan statistical area, metropolitan statistical area, or consolidated metropolitan statistical area, as defined by the Director of the Office of Management and Budget, with a population of 250,000 or more, and any other area designated as such by the appropriate Federal financial supervisory agency.

(3) State

The term "State" has the same meaning as in section 1813 of this title.

Sec. 2907. Operation of branch facilities by minorities and women

(a) In general

In the case of any depository institution which donates, sells on favorable terms (as determined by the appropriate Federal financial supervisory agency), or makes available on a rent-free basis any branch of such institution which is located in any predominantly minority neighborhood to any minority depository institution or women's depository institution, the amount of the contribution or the amount of the loss incurred in connection with such activity may be a factor in determining whether the depository institution is meeting the credit needs of the institution's community for purposes of this chapter.

(b) Definitions

For purposes of this section—

(1) Minority depository institution

The term "minority institution" means a depository institution (as defined in section 1813(c) of this title)—

(A) more than 50 percent of the ownership or control of which is held by 1 or more minority individuals; and

(B) more than 50 percent of the net profit or loss of which accrues to 1 or more minority individuals.

(2) Women's depository institution

The term "women's depository institution" means a depository institution (as defined in section 1813(c) of this title)—

(A) more than 50 percent of the ownership or control of which is held by 1 or more women;

(B) more than 50 percent of the net profit or loss of which accrues to 1 or more women; and

(C) a significant percentage of senior management positions of which are held by women.

(3) Minority

The term "minority" has the meaning given to such term by section 1204(c)(3) of the Financial Institutions Reform, Recovery and Enforcement Act of 1989.

Sec. 2908. Small bank regulatory relief

(a) In general

Except as provided in subsections (b) and (c) of this section, any regulated financial institution with aggregate assets of not more than $250,000,000 shall be subject to routine examination under this chapter—

(1) not more than once every 60 months for an institution that has achieved a rating of "outstanding record of meeting community credit needs" at its most recent examination under section 2903 of this title;
(2) not more than once every 48 months for an institution that has received a rating of "satisfactory record of meeting community credit needs" at its most recent examination under section 2903 of this title; and
(3) as deemed necessary by the appropriate Federal financial supervisory agency, for an institution that has received a rating of less than "satisfactory record of meeting community credit needs" at its most recent examination under section 2903 of this title.

(b) No exception from CRA examinations in connection with applications for deposit facilities

A regulated financial institution described in subsection (a) of this section shall remain subject to examination under this chapter in connection with an application for a deposit facility.

(c) Discretion

A regulated financial institution described in subsection (a) of this section may be subject to more frequent or less frequent examinations for reasonable cause under such circumstances as may be determined by the appropriate Federal financial supervisory agency.

APPENDIX TWO

Community Reinvestment Act Regulations[1]

Sec. 25.11 Authority, purposes, and scope.

(a) Authority and OMB control number—

(1) Authority. The authority for subparts A, B, C, D, and E is 12 U.S.C. 21, 22, 26, 27, 30, 36, 93a, 161, 215, 215a, 481, 1814, 1816, 1828(c), 1835a, 2901 through 2907, and 3101 through 3111.

(2) OMB control number. The information collection requirements contained in this part were approved by the Office of Management and Budget under the provisions of 44 U.S.C. 3501 et seq. and have been assigned OMB control number 1557-0160.

(b) Purposes. In enacting the Community Reinvestment Act (CRA), the Congress required each appropriate Federal financial supervisory agency to assess an institution's record of helping to meet the credit needs of the local communities in which the institution is chartered, consistent with the safe and sound operation of the institution, and to take this record into account in the agency's evaluation of an application for a deposit facility by the institution. This part is intended to carry out the purposes of the CRA by:

(1) Establishing the framework and criteria by which the Office of the Comptroller of the Currency (OCC) assesses a bank's record of helping to meet the credit needs of its entire community, including low- and moderate-income neighborhoods, consistent with the safe and sound operation of the bank; and

(2) Providing that the OCC takes that record into account in considering certain applications.

---

1. These are the CRA regulations promulgated by the Office of the Comptroller of the Currency. With one exception, described *infra*, n. 2, they are substantially equivalent to the regulations of the other federal banking agencies.

(c) Scope—

(1) General. This part applies to all banks except as provided in paragraphs (c)(2) and (c)(3) of this section.

(2) Federal branches and agencies.

(i) This part applies to all insured Federal branches and to any Federal branch that is uninsured that results from an acquisition described in section 5(a)(8) of the International Banking Act of 1978 (12 U.S.C. 3103(a)(8)).

(ii) Except as provided in paragraph (c)(2)(i) of this section, this part does not apply to Federal branches that are uninsured, limited Federal branches, or Federal agencies, as those terms are defined in part 28 of this chapter.

(3) Certain special purpose banks. This part does not apply to special purpose banks that do not perform commercial or retail banking services by granting credit to the public in the ordinary course of business, other than as incident to their specialized operations. These banks include banker's banks, as defined in 12 U.S.C. 24 (Seventh), and banks that engage only in one or more of the following activities: providing cash management controlled disbursement services or serving as correspondent banks, trust companies, or clearing agents.

Sec. 25.12 Definitions.

For purposes of this part, the following definitions apply:

(a) Affiliate means any company that controls, is controlled by, or is under common control with another company. The term "control" has the meaning given to that term in 12 U.S.C. 1841(a)(2), and a company is under common control with another company if both companies are directly or indirectly controlled by the same company.

(b) Area median income means:

(1) The median family income for the MSA, if a person or geography is located in an MSA; or

(2) The statewide nonmetropolitan median family income, if a person or geography is located outside an MSA.

(c) Assessment area means a geographic area delineated in accordance with Sec. 25.41.

(d) Automated teller machine (ATM) means an automated, unstaffed banking facility owned or operated by, or operated exclusively for, the bank at which deposits are received, cash dispersed, or money lent.

(e) Bank means a national bank (including a Federal branch as defined in part 28 of this chapter) with Federally insured deposits, except as provided in Sec. 25.11(c).

(f) Branch means a staffed banking facility authorized as a branch, whether shared or unshared, including, for example, a mini-branch in a grocery store or a branch operated in conjunction with any other local business or nonprofit organization.

(g) CMSA means a consolidated metropolitan statistical area as defined by the Director of the Office of Management and Budget.

(h) Community development means:

- (1) Affordable housing (including multifamily rental housing) for low- or moderate-income individuals;
- (2) Community services targeted to low- or moderate-income individuals;
- (3) Activities that promote economic development by financing businesses or farms that meet the size eligibility standards of the Small Business Administration's Development Company or Small Business Investment Company programs (13 CFR 121.301) or have gross annual revenues of $1 million or less; or
- (4) Activities that revitalize or stabilize low- or moderate-income geographies.
  - (I) Community development loan means a loan that:
    - (1) Has as its primary purpose community development; and
    - (2) Except in the case of a wholesale or limited purpose bank:
      - (i) Has not been reported or collected by the bank or an affiliate for consideration in the bank's assessment as a home mortgage, small business, small farm, or consumer loan, unless it is a multifamily dwelling loan (as described in appendix A to part 203 of this title); and
      - (ii) Benefits the bank's assessment area(s) or a broader statewide or regional area that includes the bank's assessment area(s).

(j) Community development service means a service that:

- (1) Has as its primary purpose community development;
- (2) Is related to the provision of financial services; and
- (3) Has not been considered in the evaluation of the bank's retail banking services under Sec. 25.24(d).

(k) Consumer loan means a loan to one or more individuals for household, family, or other personal expenditures. A consumer loan does not include a home mortgage, small business, or small farm loan. Consumer loans include the following categories of loans:

(1) Motor vehicle loan, which is a consumer loan extended for the purchase of and secured by a motor vehicle;
(2) Credit card loan, which is a line of credit for household, family, or other personal expenditures that is accessed by a borrower's use of a "credit card," as this term is defined in Sec. 226.2 of this title;
(3) Home equity loan, which is a consumer loan secured by a residence of the borrower;
(4) Other secured consumer loan, which is a secured consumer loan that is not included in one of the other categories of consumer loans; and
(5) Other unsecured consumer loan, which is an unsecured consumer loan that is not included in one of the other categories of consumer loans.

(l) Geography means a census tract or a block numbering area delineated by the United States Bureau of the Census in the most recent decennial census.

(m) Home mortgage loan means a "home improvement loan" or a "home purchase loan" as defined in Sec. 203.2 of this title.

(n) Income level includes:
(1) Low-income, which means an individual income that is less than 50 percent of the area median income, or a median family income that is less than 50 percent, in the case of a geography.
(2) Moderate-income, which means an individual income that is at least 50 percent and less than 80 percent of the area median income, or a median family income that is at least 50 and less than 80 percent, in the case of a geography.
(3) Middle-income, which means an individual income that is at least 80 percent and less than 120 percent of the area median income, or a median family income that is at least 80 and less than 120 percent, in the case of a geography.
(4) Upper-income, which means an individual income that is 120 percent or more of the area median income, or a median family income that is 120 percent or more, in the case of a geography.

(o) Limited purpose bank means a bank that offers only a narrow product line (such as credit card or motor vehicle loans) to a regional or broader market and for which a designation as a limited purpose bank is in effect, in accordance with Sec. 25.25(b).

(p) Loan location. A loan is located as follows:
(1) A consumer loan is located in the geography where the borrower resides;
(2) A home mortgage loan is located in the geography where the property to which the loan relates is located; and

(3) A small business or small farm loan is located in the geography where the main business facility or farm is located or where the loan proceeds otherwise will be applied, as indicated by the borrower.

(q) Loan production office means a staffed facility, other than a branch, that is open to the public and that provides lending-related services, such as loan information and applications.

(r) MSA means a metropolitan statistical area or a primary metropolitan statistical area as defined by the Director of the Office of Management and Budget.

(s) Qualified investment means a lawful investment, deposit, membership share, or grant that has as its primary purpose community development.

(t) Small bank means a bank that, as of December 31 of either of the prior two calendar years, had total assets of less than $250 million and was independent or an affiliate of a holding company that, as of December 31 of either of the prior two calendar years, had total banking and thrift assets of less than $1 billion.[2]

(u) Small business loan means a loan included in "loans to small businesses" as defined in the instructions for preparation of the Consolidated Report of Condition and Income.

(v) Small farm loan means a loan included in "loans to small farms" as defined in the instructions for preparation of the Consolidated Report of Condition and Income.

(w) Wholesale bank means a bank that is not in the business of extending home mortgage, small business, small farm, or consumer loans to retail customers, and for which a designation as a wholesale bank is in effect, in accordance with Sec. 25.25(b).

Sec. 25.21 Performance tests, standards, and ratings, in general.

(a) Performance tests and standards. The OCC assesses the CRA performance of a bank in an examination as follows:

(1) Lending, investment, and service tests. The OCC applies the lending, investment, and service tests, as provided in... [§§] 25.22 through 25.24, in evaluating the performance of a bank, except as provided in paragraphs (a)(2), (a)(3), and (a)(4) of this section.

---

2. On August 18, 2004, the OTS amended its regulations to define a small bank as having no more than $1 billion in assets. *See* 59 Fed. Reg. 51,155 (Aug. 18, 2004).

(2) Community development test for wholesale or limited purpose banks. The OCC applies the community development test for a wholesale or limited purpose bank, as provided in Sec. 25.25, except as provided in paragraph (a)(4) of this section.

(3) Small bank performance standards. The OCC applies the small bank performance standards as provided in Sec. 25.26 in evaluating the performance of a small bank or a bank that was a small bank during the prior calendar year, unless the bank elects to be assessed as provided in paragraphs (a)(1), (a)(2), or (a)(4) of this section. The bank may elect to be assessed as provided in paragraph (a)(1) of this section only if it collects and reports the data required for other banks under Sec. 25.42.

(4) Strategic plan. The OCC evaluates the performance of a bank under a strategic plan if the bank submits, and the OCC approves, a strategic plan as provided in Sec. 25.27.

(b) Performance context. The OCC applies the tests and standards in paragraph (a) of this section and also considers whether to approve a proposed strategic plan in the context of:

(1) Demographic data on median income levels, distribution of household income, nature of housing stock, housing costs, and other relevant data pertaining to a bank's assessment area(s);

(2) Any information about lending, investment, and service opportunities in the bank's assessment area(s) maintained by the bank or obtained from community organizations, state, local, and tribal governments, economic development agencies, or other sources;

(3) The bank's product offerings and business strategy as determined from data provided by the bank;

(4) Institutional capacity and constraints, including the size and financial condition of the bank, the economic climate (national, regional, and local), safety and soundness limitations, and any other factors that significantly affect the bank's ability to provide lending, investments, or services in its assessment area(s);

(5) The bank's past performance and the performance of similarly situated lenders;

(6) The bank's public file, as described in Sec. 25.43, and any written comments about the bank's CRA performance submitted to the bank or the OCC; and

(7) Any other information deemed relevant by the OCC.

(c) Assigned ratings. The OCC assigns to a bank one of the following four ratings pursuant to Sec. 25.28 and appendix A of this part: "outstanding"; "satisfactory"; "needs to improve"; or "substantial noncompliance" as provided in 12 U.S.C. 2906(b)(2). The rating assigned by the OCC reflects the bank's record of helping to meet the credit needs of its entire community, including low- and moderate-income neighborhoods, consistent with the safe and sound operation of the bank.

(**d**) Safe and sound operations. This part and the CRA do not require a bank to make loans or investments or to provide services that are inconsistent with safe and sound operations. To the contrary, the OCC anticipates banks can meet the standards of this part with safe and sound loans, investments, and services on which the banks expect to make a profit. Banks are permitted and encouraged to develop and apply flexible underwriting standards for loans that benefit low- or moderate-income geographies or individuals, only if consistent with safe and sound operations.

Sec. 25.22 Lending test.

(**a**) Scope of test.

(**1**) The lending test evaluates a bank's record of helping to meet the credit needs of its assessment area(s) through its lending activities by considering a bank's home mortgage, small business, small farm, and community development lending. If consumer lending constitutes a substantial majority of a bank's business, the OCC will evaluate the bank's consumer lending in one or more of the following categories: motor vehicle, credit card, home equity, other secured, and other unsecured loans. In addition, at a bank's option, the OCC will evaluate one or more categories of consumer lending, if the bank has collected and maintained, as required in Sec. 25.42(c)(1), the data for each category that the bank elects to have the OCC evaluate.

(**2**) The OCC considers originations and purchases of loans. The OCC will also consider any other loan data the bank may choose to provide, including data on loans outstanding, commitments and letters of credit.

(**3**) A bank may ask the OCC to consider loans originated or purchased by consortia in which the bank participates or by third parties in which the bank has invested only if the loans meet the definition of community development loans and only in accordance with paragraph (d) of this section. The OCC will not consider these loans under any criterion of the lending test except the community development lending criterion.

(**b**) Performance criteria. The OCC evaluates a bank's lending performance pursuant to the following criteria:

(1) Lending activity. The number and amount of the bank's home mortgage, small business, small farm, and consumer loans, if applicable, in the bank's assessment area(s);

(2) Geographic distribution. The geographic distribution of the bank's home mortgage, small business, small farm, and consumer loans, if applicable, based on the loan location, including:

(i) The proportion of the bank's lending in the bank's assessment area(s);

(ii) The dispersion of lending in the bank's assessment area(s); and

(iii) The number and amount of loans in low-, moderate-, middle-, and upper-income geographies in the bank's assessment area(s);

(3) Borrower characteristics. The distribution, particularly in the bank's assessment area(s), of the bank's home mortgage, small business, small farm, and consumer loans, if applicable, based on borrower characteristics, including the number and amount of:

(i) Home mortgage loans to low-, moderate-, middle-, and upper-income individuals;

(ii) Small business and small farm loans to businesses and farms with gross annual revenues of $1 million or less;

(iii) Small business and small farm loans by loan amount at origination; and

(iv) Consumer loans, if applicable, to low-, moderate-, middle-, and upper-income individuals;

(4) Community development lending. The bank's community development lending, including the number and amount of community development loans, and their complexity and innovativeness; and

(5) Innovative or flexible lending practices. The bank's use of innovative or flexible lending practices in a safe and sound manner to address the credit needs of low- or moderate-income individuals or geographies.

(c) Affiliate lending.

(1) At a bank's option, the OCC will consider loans by an affiliate of the bank, if the bank provides data on the affiliate's loans pursuant to Sec. 25.42.

(2) The OCC considers affiliate lending subject to the following constraints:

(i) No affiliate may claim a loan origination or loan purchase if another institution claims the same loan origination or purchase; and

(ii) If a bank elects to have the OCC consider loans within a particular lending category made by one or more of the bank's affiliates in a particular assessment area, the bank shall elect to have the OCC consider, in accordance with paragraph (c)(1) of this section, all the loans within that lending category in that particular assessment area made by all of the bank's affiliates.

(3) The OCC does not consider affiliate lending in assessing a bank's performance under paragraph (b)(2)(I) of this section.

(d) Lending by a consortium or a third party. Community development loans originated or purchased by a consortium in which the bank participates or by a third party in which the bank has invested:

(1) Will be considered, at the bank's option, if the bank reports the data pertaining to these loans under Sec. 25.42(b)(2); and

(2) May be allocated among participants or investors, as they choose, for purposes of the lending test, except that no participant or investor:

(i) May claim a loan origination or loan purchase if another participant or investor claims the same loan origination or purchase; or

(ii) May claim loans accounting for more than its percentage share (based on the level of its participation or investment) of the total loans originated by the consortium or third party.

(e) Lending performance rating. The OCC rates a bank's lending performance as provided in appendix A of this part.

Sec. 25.23 Investment test.

(a) Scope of test. The investment test evaluates a bank's record of helping to meet the credit needs of its assessment area(s) through qualified investments that benefit its assessment area(s) or a broader statewide or regional area that includes the bank's assessment area(s).

(b) Exclusion. Activities considered under the lending or service tests may not be considered under the investment test.

(c) Affiliate investment. At a bank's option, the OCC will consider, in its assessment of a bank's investment performance, a qualified investment made by an affiliate of the bank, if the qualified investment is not claimed by any other institution.

(d) Disposition of branch premises. Donating, selling on favorable terms, or making available on a rent-free basis a branch of the bank that is located in a predominantly minority neighborhood to a minority depository institution or women's depository institution (as these terms are defined in 12 U.S.C. 2907(b)) will be considered as a qualified investment.

(e) Performance criteria. The OCC evaluates the investment performance of a bank pursuant to the following criteria:

(1) The dollar amount of qualified investments;

(2) The innovativeness or complexity of qualified investments;

(3) The responsiveness of qualified investments to credit and community development needs; and

(4) The degree to which the qualified investments are not routinely provided by private investors.

(f) Investment performance rating. The OCC rates a bank's investment performance as provided in appendix A of this part.

Sec. 25.24 Service test.

(a) Scope of test. The service test evaluates a bank's record of helping to meet the credit needs of its assessment area(s) by analyzing both the availability and effectiveness of a bank's systems for delivering retail banking services and the extent and innovativeness of its community development services.

(b) Area(s) benefitted. Community development services must benefit a bank's assessment area(s) or a broader statewide or regional area that includes the bank's assessment area(s).

(c) Affiliate service. At a bank's option, the OCC will consider, in its assessment of a bank's service performance, a community development service provided by an affiliate of the bank, if the community development service is not claimed by any other institution.

(d) Performance criteria—retail banking services. The OCC evaluates the availability and effectiveness of a bank's systems for delivering retail banking services, pursuant to the following criteria:

(1) The current distribution of the bank's branches among low-, moderate-, middle-, and upper-income geographies;

(2) In the context of its current distribution of the bank's branches, the bank's record of opening and closing branches, particularly branches located in low- or moderate-income geographies or primarily serving low- or moderate-income individuals;

(3) The availability and effectiveness of alternative systems for delivering retail banking services (e.g., ATMs, ATMs not owned or operated by or exclusively for the bank, banking by telephone or computer, loan production offices, and bank-at-work or bank-by-mail programs) in low- and moderate-income geographies and to low- and moderate-income individuals; and

(4) The range of services provided in low-, moderate-, middle-, and upper-income geographies and the degree to which the services are tailored to meet the needs of those geographies.

(e) Performance criteria—community development services. The OCC evaluates community development services pursuant to the following criteria:

(1) The extent to which the bank provides community development services; and

(2) The innovativeness and responsiveness of community development services.

(f) Service performance rating. The OCC rates a bank's service performance as provided in appendix A of this part.

Sec. 25.25 Community development test for wholesale or limited purpose banks.

(a) Scope of test. The OCC assesses a wholesale or limited purpose bank's record of helping to meet the credit needs of its assessment area(s) under the community development test through its community development lending, qualified investments, or community development services.

(b) Designation as a wholesale or limited purpose bank. In order to receive a designation as a wholesale or limited purpose bank, a bank shall file a request, in writing, with the OCC, at least three months prior to the proposed effective date of the designation. If the OCC approves the designation, it remains in effect until the bank requests revocation of the designation or until one year after the OCC notifies the bank that the OCC has revoked the designation on its own initiative.

(c) Performance criteria. The OCC evaluates the community development performance of a wholesale or limited purpose bank pursuant to the following criteria:

(1) The number and amount of community development loans (including originations and purchases of loans and other community development loan data provided by the bank, such as data on loans outstanding, commitments, and letters of credit), qualified investments, or community development services;

(2) The use of innovative or complex qualified investments, community development loans, or community development services and the extent to which the investments are not routinely provided by private investors; and

(3) The bank's responsiveness to credit and community development needs.

(d) Indirect activities. At a bank's option, the OCC will consider in its community development performance assessment:

(1) Qualified investments or community development services provided by an affiliate of the bank, if the investments or services are not claimed by any other institution; and
(2) Community development lending by affiliates, consortia and third parties, subject to the requirements and limitations in Sec. 25.22(c) and (d).

(e) Benefit to assessment area(s)—
(1) Benefit inside assessment area(s). The OCC considers all qualified investments, community development loans, and community development services that benefit areas within the bank's assessment area(s) or a broader statewide or regional area that includes the bank's assessment area(s).
(2) Benefit outside assessment area(s). The OCC considers the qualified investments, community development loans, and community development services that benefit areas outside the bank's assessment area(s), if the bank has adequately addressed the needs of its assessment area(s).

(f) Community development performance rating. The OCC rates a bank's community development performance as provided in appendix A of this part.

Sec. 25.26 Small bank performance standards.

(a) Performance criteria. The OCC evaluates the record of a small bank, or a bank that was a small bank during the prior calendar year, of helping to meet the credit needs of its assessment area(s) pursuant to the following criteria:
(1) The bank's loan-to-deposit ratio, adjusted for seasonal variation and, as appropriate, other lending-related activities, such as loan originations for sale to the secondary markets, community development loans, or qualified investments;
(2) The percentage of loans and, as appropriate, other lending-related activities located in the bank's assessment area(s);
(3) The bank's record of lending to and, as appropriate, engaging in other lending-related activities for borrowers of different income levels and businesses and farms of different sizes;
(4) The geographic distribution of the bank's loans; and
(5) The bank's record of taking action, if warranted, in response to written complaints about its performance in helping to meet credit needs in its assessment area(s).

(b) Small bank performance rating. The OCC rates the performance of a bank evaluated under this section as provided in appendix A of this part.

25.27 Strategic plan.

(a) Alternative election. The OCC will assess a bank's record of helping to meet the credit needs of its assessment area(s) under a strategic plan if:

(1) The bank has submitted the plan to the OCC as provided for in this section;

(2) The OCC has approved the plan;

(3) The plan is in effect; and

(4) The bank has been operating under an approved plan for at least one year.

(b) Data reporting. The OCC's approval of a plan does not affect the bank's obligation, if any, to report data as required by Sec. 25.42.

(c) Plans in general—

(1) Term. A plan may have a term of no more than five years, and any multi-year plan must include annual interim measurable goals under which the OCC will evaluate the bank's performance.

(2) Multiple assessment areas. A bank with more than one assessment area may prepare a single plan for all of its assessment areas or one or more plans for one or more of its assessment areas.

(3) Treatment of affiliates. Affiliated institutions may prepare a joint plan if the plan provides measurable goals for each institution. Activities may be allocated among institutions at the institutions' option, provided that the same activities are not considered for more than one institution.

(d) Public participation in plan development. Before submitting a plan to the OCC for approval, a bank shall:

(1) Informally seek suggestions from members of the public in its assessment area(s) covered by the plan while developing the plan;

(2) Once the bank has developed a plan, formally solicit public comment on the plan for at least 30 days by publishing notice in at least one newspaper of general circulation in each assessment area covered by the plan; and

(3) During the period of formal public comment, make copies of the plan available for review by the public at no cost at all offices of the bank in any assessment area covered by the plan and provide copies of the plan upon request for a reasonable fee to cover copying and mailing, if applicable.

(e) Submission of plan. The bank shall submit its plan to the OCC at least three months prior to the proposed effective date of the plan. The bank shall also submit with its plan a description of its informal efforts to seek suggestions from members of the public, any written public comment received, and, if the plan was revised in light of the comment received, the initial plan as released for public comment.

(f) Plan content—

(1) Measurable goals.

(i) A bank shall specify in its plan measurable goals for helping to meet the credit needs of each assessment area covered by the plan, particularly the needs of low- and moderate-income geographies and low- and moderate-income individuals, through lending, investment, and services, as appropriate.

(ii) A bank shall address in its plan all three performance categories and, unless the bank has been designated as a wholesale or limited purpose bank, shall emphasize lending and lending-related activities. Nevertheless, a different emphasis, including a focus on one or more performance categories, may be appropriate if responsive to the characteristics and credit needs of its assessment area(s), considering public comment and the bank's capacity and constraints, product offerings, and business strategy.

(2) Confidential information. A bank may submit additional information to the OCC on a confidential basis, but the goals stated in the plan must be sufficiently specific to enable the public and the OCC to judge the merits of the plan.

(3) Satisfactory and outstanding goals. A bank shall specify in its plan measurable goals that constitute "satisfactory" performance. A plan may specify measurable goals that constitute "outstanding" performance. If a bank submits, and the OCC approves, both "satisfactory" and "outstanding" performance goals, the OCC will consider the bank eligible for an "outstanding" performance rating.

(4) Election if satisfactory goals not substantially met. A bank may elect in its plan that, if the bank fails to meet substantially its plan goals for a satisfactory rating, the OCC will evaluate the bank's performance under the lending, investment, and service tests, the community development test, or the small bank performance standards, as appropriate.

(g) Plan approval—

(1) Timing. The OCC will act upon a plan within 60 calendar days after the OCC receives the complete plan and other material required under paragraph (d) of this section. If the OCC fails to act within this time period, the plan shall be deemed approved unless the OCC extends the review period for good cause.

(2) Public participation. In evaluating the plan's goals, the OCC considers the public's involvement in formulating the plan, written public com-

ment on the plan, and any response by the bank to public comment on the plan.

(3) Criteria for evaluating plan. The OCC evaluates a plan's measurable goals using the following criteria, as appropriate:

(i) The extent and breadth of lending or lending-related activities, including, as appropriate, the distribution of loans among different geographies, businesses and farms of different sizes, and individuals of different income levels, the extent of community development lending, and the use of innovative or flexible lending practices to address credit needs;

(ii) The amount and innovativeness, complexity, and responsiveness of the bank's qualified investments; and

(iii) The availability and effectiveness of the bank's systems for delivering retail banking services and the extent and innovativeness of the bank's community development services.

(h) Plan amendment. During the term of a plan, a bank may request the OCC to approve an amendment to the plan on grounds that there has been a material change in circumstances. The bank shall develop an amendment to a previously approved plan in accordance with the public participation requirements of paragraph (d) of this section.

(i) Plan assessment. The OCC approves the goals and assesses performance under a plan as provided for in appendix A of this part.

Sec. 25.28 Assigned ratings.

(a) Ratings in general. Subject to paragraphs (b) and (c) of this section, the OCC assigns to a bank a rating of "outstanding," "satisfactory," "needs to improve," or "substantial noncompliance" based on the bank's performance under the lending, investment and service tests, the community development test, the small bank performance standards, or an approved strategic plan, as applicable.

(b) Lending, investment, and service tests. The OCC assigns a rating for a bank assessed under the lending, investment, and service tests in accordance with the following principles:

(1) A bank that receives an "outstanding" rating on the lending test receives an assigned rating of at least "satisfactory";

(2) A bank that receives an "outstanding" rating on both the service test and the investment test and a rating of at least "high satisfactory" on the lending test receives an assigned rating of "outstanding"; and

(3) No bank may receive an assigned rating of "satisfactory" or higher unless it receives a rating of at least "low satisfactory" on the lending test.

(c) Effect of evidence of discriminatory or other illegal credit practices. Evidence of discriminatory or other illegal credit practices adversely affects the OCC's evaluation of a bank's performance. In determining the effect on the bank's assigned rating, the OCC considers the nature and extent of the evidence, the policies and procedures that the bank has in place to prevent discriminatory or other illegal credit practices, any corrective action that the bank has taken or has committed to take, particularly voluntary corrective action resulting from self-assessment, and other relevant information.

Sec. 25.29 Effect of CRA performance on applications.

(a) CRA performance. Among other factors, the OCC takes into account the record of performance under the CRA of each applicant bank in considering an application for:

(1) The establishment of a domestic branch;
(2) The relocation of the main office or a branch;
(3) Under the Bank Merger Act (12 U.S.C. 1828(c)), the merger or consolidation with or the acquisition of assets or assumption of liabilities of an insured depository institution; and
(4) The conversion of an insured depository institution to a national bank charter.

(b) Charter application. An applicant (other than an insured depository institution) for a national bank charter shall submit with its application a description of how it will meet its CRA objectives. The OCC takes the description into account in considering the application and may deny or condition approval on that basis.

(c) Interested parties. The OCC takes into account any views expressed by interested parties that are submitted in accordance with the OCC's procedures set forth in part 5 of this chapter in considering CRA performance in an application listed in paragraphs (a) and (b) of this section.

(d) Denial or conditional approval of application. A bank's record of performance may be the basis for denying or conditioning approval of an application listed in paragraph (a) of this section.

(e) Insured depository institution. For purposes of this section, the term "insured depository institution" has the meaning given to that term in 12 U.S.C. 1813.

Sec. 25.41 Assessment area delineation.

(a) In general. A bank shall delineate one or more assessment areas within which the OCC evaluates the bank's record of helping to meet the credit needs of its community. The OCC does not evaluate the bank's delineation of its assessment area(s) as a separate performance criterion, but the OCC reviews the delineation for compliance with the requirements of this section.

(b) Geographic area(s) for wholesale or limited purpose banks. The assessment area(s) for a wholesale or limited purpose bank must consist generally of one or more MSAs (using the MSA boundaries that were in effect as of January 1 of the calendar year in which the delineation is made) or one or more contiguous political subdivisions, such as counties, cities, or towns, in which the bank has its main office, branches, and deposit-taking ATMs.

(c) Geographic area(s) for other banks. The assessment area(s) for a bank other than a wholesale or limited purpose bank must:

(1) Consist generally of one or more MSAs (using the MSA boundaries that were in effect as of January 1 of the calendar year in which the delineation is made) or one or more contiguous political subdivisions, such as counties, cities, or towns; and

(2) Include the geographies in which the bank has its main office, its branches, and its deposit-taking ATMs, as well as the surrounding geographies in which the bank has originated or purchased a substantial portion of its loans (including home mortgage loans, small business and small farm loans, and any other loans the bank chooses, such as those consumer loans on which the bank elects to have its performance assessed).

(d) Adjustments to geographic area(s). A bank may adjust the boundaries of its assessment area(s) to include only the portion of a political subdivision that it reasonably can be expected to serve. An adjustment is particularly appropriate in the case of an assessment area that otherwise would be extremely large, of unusual configuration, or divided by significant geographic barriers.

(e) Limitations on the delineation of an assessment area. Each bank's assessment area(s):

(1) Must consist only of whole geographies;

(2) May not reflect illegal discrimination;

(3) May not arbitrarily exclude low- or moderate-income geographies, taking into account the bank's size and financial condition; and

(4) May not extend substantially beyond a CMSA boundary or beyond a state boundary unless the assessment area is located in a multistate MSA. If a bank serves a geographic area that extends substantially beyond a state boundary, the bank shall delineate separate assessment

areas for the areas in each state. If a bank serves a geographic area that extends substantially beyond a CMSA boundary, the bank shall delineate separate assessment areas for the areas inside and outside the CMSA.

(f) Banks serving military personnel. Notwithstanding the requirements of this section, a bank whose business predominantly consists of serving the needs of military personnel or their dependents who are not located within a defined geographic area may delineate its entire deposit customer base as its assessment area.

(g) Use of assessment area(s). The OCC uses the assessment area(s) delineated by a bank in its evaluation of the bank's CRA performance unless the OCC determines that the assessment area(s) do not comply with the requirements of this section.

Sec. 25.42 Data collection, reporting, and disclosure.

(a) Loan information required to be collected and maintained. A bank, except a small bank, shall collect, and maintain in machine readable form (as prescribed by the OCC) until the completion of its next CRA examination, the following data for each small business or small farm loan originated or purchased by the bank:

(1) A unique number or alpha-numeric symbol that can be used to identify the relevant loan file;

(2) The loan amount at origination;

(3) The loan location; and

(4) An indicator whether the loan was to a business or farm with gross annual revenues of $1 million or less.

(b) Loan information required to be reported. A bank, except a small bank or a bank that was a small bank during the prior calendar year, shall report annually by March 1 to the OCC in machine readable form (as prescribed by the OCC) the following data for the prior calendar year:

(1) Small business and small farm loan data. For each geography in which the bank originated or purchased a small business or small farm loan, the aggregate number and amount of loans:

(i) With an amount at origination of $100,000 or less;

(ii) With amount at origination of more than $100,000 but less than or equal to $250,000;

(iii) With an amount at origination of more than $250,000; and

(iv) To businesses and farms with gross annual revenues of $1 million or less (using the revenues that the bank considered in making its credit decision);

(2) Community development loan data. The aggregate number and aggregate amount of community development loans originated or purchased; and

(3) Home mortgage loans. If the bank is subject to reporting under part 203 of this title, the location of each home mortgage loan application, origination, or purchase outside the MSAs in which the bank has a home or branch office (or outside any MSA) in accordance with the requirements of part 203 of this title.

(c) Optional data collection and maintenance—

(1) Consumer loans. A bank may collect and maintain in machine readable form (as prescribed by the OCC) data for consumer loans originated or purchased by the bank for consideration under the lending test. A bank may maintain data for one or more of the following categories of consumer loans: motor vehicle, credit card, home equity, other secured, and other unsecured. If the bank maintains data for loans in a certain category, it shall maintain data for all loans originated or purchased within that category. The bank shall maintain data separately for each category, including for each loan:

(i) A unique number or alpha-numeric symbol that can be used to identify the relevant loan file;

(ii) The loan amount at origination or purchase;

(iii) The loan location; and

(iv) The gross annual income of the borrower that the bank considered in making its credit decision.

(2) Other loan data. At its option, a bank may provide other information concerning its lending performance, including additional loan distribution data.

(d) Data on affiliate lending. A bank that elects to have the OCC consider loans by an affiliate, for purposes of the lending or community development test or an approved strategic plan, shall collect, maintain, and report for those loans the data that the bank would have collected, maintained, and reported pursuant to paragraphs (a), (b), and (c) of this section had the loans been originated or purchased by the bank. For home mortgage loans, the bank shall also be prepared to identify the home mortgage loans reported under part 203 of this title by the affiliate.

(e) Data on lending by a consortium or a third party. A bank that elects to have the OCC consider community development loans by a consortium or third party, for purposes of the lending or community development tests or an approved strategic plan, shall report for those loans the data that the bank would have reported under paragraph (b)(2) of this section had the loans been originated or purchased by the bank.

(f) Small banks electing evaluation under the lending, investment, and service tests. A bank that qualifies for evaluation under the small bank performance standards but elects evaluation under the lending, investment, and service tests shall collect, maintain, and report the data required for other banks pursuant to paragraphs (a) and (b) of this section.

(g) Assessment area data. A bank, except a small bank or a bank that was a small bank during the prior calendar year, shall collect and report to the OCC by March 1 of each year a list for each assessment area showing the geographies within the area.

(h) CRA Disclosure Statement. The OCC prepares annually for each bank that reports data pursuant to this section a CRA Disclosure Statement that contains, on a state-by-state basis:

(1) For each county (and for each assessment area smaller than a county) with a population of 500,000 persons or fewer in which the bank reported a small business or small farm loan:

(i) The number and amount of small business and small farm loans reported as originated or purchased located in low-, moderate-, middle-, and upper-income geographies;

(ii) A list grouping each geography according to whether the geography is low-, moderate-, middle-, or upper-income;

(iii) A list showing each geography in which the bank reported a small business or small farm loan; and

(iv) The number and amount of small business and small farm loans to businesses and farms with gross annual revenues of $1 million or less;

(2) For each county (and for each assessment area smaller than a county) with a population in excess of 500,000 persons in which the bank reported a small business or small farm loan:

(i) The number and amount of small business and small farm loans reported as originated or purchased located in geographies with median income relative to the area median income of less than 10 percent, 10 or more but less than 20 percent, 20 or more but less than 30 percent, 30 or more but less than 40 percent, 40 or more but less than 50 percent, 50 or more but less than 60 percent, 60 or more but less than 70 percent, 70 or more but less than 80 percent, 80 or more but less than 90 percent, 90 or more but less than 100 percent, 100 or more but less than 110 percent, 110 or more but less than 120 percent, and 120 percent or more;

(ii) A list grouping each geography in the county or assessment area according to whether the median income in the geography relative to the area median income is less than 10 percent, 10 or more but less than 20 percent, 20 or more but less than 30 percent, 30 or more but less than 40 percent, 40 or more but less than 50 percent, 50 or more but less than 60 percent, 60 or more but less than 70 percent, 70 or more but less than 80 percent, 80 or more but less than 90 percent, 90 or more but less than 100 percent, 100 or more but less than 110 percent, 110 or more but less than 120 percent, and 120 percent or more;

(iii) A list showing each geography in which the bank reported a small business or small farm loan; and

(iv) The number and amount of small business and small farm loans to businesses and farms with gross annual revenues of $1 million or less;

(3) The number and amount of small business and small farm loans located inside each assessment area reported by the bank and the number and amount of small business and small farm loans located outside the assessment area(s) reported by the bank; and

(4) The number and amount of community development loans reported as originated or purchased.

(i) Aggregate disclosure statements. The OCC, in conjunction with the Board of Governors of the Federal Reserve System, the Federal Deposit Insurance Corporation, and the Office of Thrift Supervision, prepares annually, for each MSA (including an MSA that crosses a state boundary) and the non-MSA portion of each state, an aggregate disclosure statement of small business and small farm lending by all institutions subject to reporting under this part or parts 228, 345, or 563e of this title. These disclosure statements indicate, for each geography, the number and amount of all small business and small farm loans originated or purchased by reporting institutions, except that the OCC may adjust the form of the disclosure if necessary, because of special circumstances, to protect the privacy of a borrower or the competitive position of an institution.

(j) Central data depositories. The OCC makes the aggregate disclosure statements, described in paragraph (i) of this section, and the individual bank CRA Disclosure Statements, described in paragraph (h) of this section, available to the public at central data depositories. The OCC publishes a list of the depositories at which the statements are available.

Sec. 25.43 Content and availability of public file.

(a) Information available to the public. A bank shall maintain a public file that includes the following information:

(1) All written comments received from the public for the current year and each of the prior two calendar years that specifically relate to the bank's performance in helping to meet community credit needs, and any response to the comments by the bank, if neither the comments nor the responses contain statements that reflect adversely on the good name or reputation of any persons other than the bank or publication of which would violate specific provisions of law;

(2) A copy of the public section of the bank's most recent CRA Performance Evaluation prepared by the OCC. The bank shall place this copy in the public file within 30 business days after its receipt from the OCC;

(3) A list of the bank's branches, their street addresses, and geographies;

(4) A list of branches opened or closed by the bank during the current year and each of the prior two calendar years, their street addresses, and geographies;

(5) A list of services (including hours of operation, available loan and deposit products, and transaction fees) generally offered at the bank's branches and descriptions of material differences in the availability or cost of services at particular branches, if any. At its option, a bank may include information regarding the availability of alternative systems for delivering retail banking services (e.g., ATMs, ATMs not owned or operated by or exclusively for the bank, banking by telephone or computer, loan production offices, and bank-at-work or bank-by-mail programs);

(6) A map of each assessment area showing the boundaries of the area and identifying the geographies contained within the area, either on the map or in a separate list; and

(7) Any other information the bank chooses.

(b) Additional information available to the public—

(1) Banks other than small banks. A bank, except a small bank or a bank that was a small bank during the prior calendar year, shall include in its public file the following information pertaining to the bank and its affiliates, if applicable, for each of the prior two calendar years:

(i) If the bank has elected to have one or more categories of its consumer loans considered under the lending test, for each of these categories, the number and amount of loans:

(A) To low-, moderate-, middle-, and upper-income individuals;

(B) Located in low-, moderate-, middle-, and upper-income census tracts; and
(C) Located inside the bank's assessment area(s) and outside the bank's assessment area(s); and

(ii) The bank's CRA Disclosure Statement. The bank shall place the statement in the public file within three business days of its receipt from the OCC.

(2) Banks required to report Home Mortgage Disclosure Act (HMDA) data. A bank required to report home mortgage loan data pursuant part 203 of this title shall include in its public file a copy of the HMDA Disclosure Statement provided by the Federal Financial Institutions Examination Council pertaining to the bank for each of the prior two calendar years. In addition, a bank that elected to have the OCC consider the mortgage lending of an affiliate for any of these years shall include in its public file the affiliate's HMDA Disclosure Statement for those years. The bank shall place the statement(s) in the public file within three business days after its receipt.

(3) Small banks. A small bank or a bank that was a small bank during the prior calendar year shall include in its public file:

(i) The bank's loan-to-deposit ratio for each quarter of the prior calendar year and, at its option, additional data on its loan-to-deposit ratio; and
(ii) The information required for other banks by paragraph (b)(1) of this section, if the bank has elected to be evaluated under the lending, investment, and service tests.

(4) Banks with strategic plans. A bank that has been approved to be assessed under a strategic plan shall include in its public file a copy of that plan. A bank need not include information submitted to the OCC on a confidential basis in conjunction with the plan.

(5) Banks with less than satisfactory ratings. A bank that received a less than satisfactory rating during its most recent examination shall include in its public file a description of its current efforts to improve its performance in helping to meet the credit needs of its entire community. The bank shall update the description quarterly.

(c) Location of public information. A bank shall make available to the public for inspection upon request and at no cost the information required in this section as follows:

(1) At the main office and, if an interstate bank, at one branch office in each state, all information in the public file; and
(2) At each branch:

(i) A copy of the public section of the bank's most recent CRA Performance Evaluation and a list of services provided by the branch; and

(ii) Within five calendar days of the request, all the information in the public file relating to the assessment area in which the branch is located.

(d) Copies. Upon request, a bank shall provide copies, either on paper or in another form acceptable to the person making the request, of the information in its public file. The bank may charge a reasonable fee not to exceed the cost of copying and mailing (if applicable).

(e) Updating. Except as otherwise provided in this section, a bank shall ensure that the information required by this section is current as of April 1 of each year.

Sec. 25.44 Public notice by banks.

A bank shall provide in the public lobby of its main office and each of its branches the appropriate public notice set forth in appendix B of this part. Only a branch of a bank having more than one assessment area shall include the bracketed material in the notice for branch offices. Only a bank that is an affiliate of a holding company shall include the next to the last sentence of the notices. A bank shall include the last sentence of the notices only if it is an affiliate of a holding company that is not prevented by statute from acquiring additional banks.

Sec. 25.45 Publication of planned examination schedule.

The OCC publishes at least 30 days in advance of the beginning of each calendar quarter a list of banks scheduled for CRA examinations in that quarter.

APPENDIX THREE[1]

Criteria that the Federal Banking Agencies Used to Evaluate CRA Performance

The Lending Test for Large Retail Banks

Overall Lending Activity

1. Loan portfolio by % type of loan cf peer loan portfolio by % type of loan (106)
2. LDR (103,115)
3. LDR cf national peer bank LDR (106)
4. LDR cf primary local competitors' LDR (102,106,114,115)
5. LDR cf OTS-regulated banks' LDR (110)
6. Change in LDR (102,115)
7. LAR cf peer banks (101,105,111,114)
8. Loan MS (100,101,105,107,109)
9. Loan MS rank (101,105,107,109)
10. Increase in loan MS rank (102)
11. Loan MS rank among competitor banks (107)
12. Loan MS percentile cf deposit MS percentile (104)

---

1. See *supra* ch. 5, note 1 for a list of the abbreviations used in this Appendix.

13. Loan MS cf deposit MS (100,108,114)
14. Loan MS rank cf deposit MS rank (105)
15. Loan MS/deposit MS ratio (105)
16. # loans rank (100)
17. # loans cf other lenders (102)
18. % increase # loans (102,106,110)
19. $ vol loans/Tier 1 capital ratio (107)
20. % increase $ vol loans (110,114)

Lending Inside/Outside AA

21. % loans in AA (101-103,106-110,112,114-115)
22. Change in % loans in AA (111,115)
23. % HMDA loans in AA/asset ratio (111)
24. % HMDA, SB, CON, or SF loans in AA (100,102-109,111,113-115)
25. % increase HMDA loans in AA (113)
26. % $ vol all, HMDA, CON, or SB loans in AA (102,103,109,113)
27. % change $ vol loans in AA (115)

Geographic Distribution of Loans

28. % all, HMDA, SB, or CON loans in LMI, LI, or MI tracts cf % AA's fam or pop in such tracts (103,106,107,108,113,114)
29. % $ vol HMDA or SB loans in LMI tracts cf % AA's fam or pop in LMI tracts (113)
30. % all HMDA, HP, HR, or HI loans in LMI, LI, or MI tracts cf %AA's OOHUs in such tracts (100-109,111,112,114)
31. % SB loans in LMI, LI, or MI tracts cf % AA's bus in such tracts (101-104,107-108,112,114)
32. % HMDA or SB loans in LMI, LI, or MI tracts cf agg % (100-103,109-112)
33. % HMDA loans in LI or MI tracts cf OTS-regulated bank % in such tracts (110)
34. % HMDA loans in MI tracts cf peer bank % in MI tracts (105)

35. % $ vol HMDA loans in LMI, LI, or MI tracts cf agg % (110,111)
36. % all, HMDA, or SF loans in LMI or MI tracts cf % such loans in MIDI or UI tracts (106,112)
37. MS HMDA, HP, HR, HI, or SB loans in LMI, LI, or MI tracts cf overall MS of such loans in LMI, LI, or MI tracts (100,104,107,108)
38. % decrease HMDA loans in LMI tracts cf peer bank % decrease (100)
39. % increase HMDA loans in LMI tracts cf % increase in all income level tracts (110)
40. % increase $ vol HMDA loans in LMI tracts cf % increase in all income level tracts (110)
41. Ratio LMI tracts/LMI tracts that received a loan cf such ratios for MIDI and UI tracts (115)
42. % SB loans in LI or MI tracts cf % AA's LI or MI tracts (110)

Lending According to Borrower Income

43. % HMDA, HP, HR, HI, CON, or MV loans to LMI, LI, or MI persons or fam cf % AA's LMI, LI, or MI persons or fam (100-11,113-15)
44. % $ vol HMDA, CON, or MV loans to LI or MI persons cf % AA's LI or MI pop (100,102,111-112,115)
45. % HMDA, HP, HR, or HI loans to LMI, LI, or MI persons cf agg % (100-102,109-111)
46. % HMDA, HP loans to LMI, LI, or MI persons cf % HP loans to LMI, LI, or MI persons by OTS-regulated banks (101,103,110)
47. % HMDA loans to LI or MI persons cf % HMDA loans to LI or MI persons by peer banks (105)
48. % $ vol HMDA or HP loans to LMI, LI, or MI persons cf agg % (100-102,110)
49. % $ vol HMDA or HP loans to LMI, LI or MI persons cf % OTS-regulated banks (110)
50. % $ vol HMDA loans to LMI persons cf % HMDA loans to LMI persons (101)
51. % MV loans to LMI persons cf % MV loans to persons at other income levels (115)

52. MS HMDA loans to LMI persons (100,110)
53. MS HMDA loans to LMI persons among OTS-regulated banks (110)
54. MS rank HMDA loans to LMI persons (100,110)
55. MS rank HMDA loans among OTS-regulated banks (110)
56. MS $ vol HMDA loans to LMI persons (110)
57. MS HMDA loans to LMI persons cf deposit MS (100)
58. MS HP, HR, or HI loans to LI or MI persons cf overall MS HP, HR, or HI loans (104,107)
59. % SB loans ≤$100G (100,102-103,106-108,112,115)
60. % SB loans ≤$100G cf agg % (100-103,110)
61. % $ vol SB loans ≤$100G cf agg % (110)
62. % $ vol SB loans ≤$100G cf % primary competitors (101)
63. % change SB loans ≤$100G (100,106)
64. % increase $ vol SB loans ≤$100G (106)
65. % SB loans to bus w/rev≤$1M (100,102,113,115)
66. % SB loans to bus w/rev≤$1M cf % AA's bus w/rev≤$1M (101-102,104,107-108,114)
67. % SB loans to bus w/rev≤$1M cf agg % (100-101,103,107,110,112,114)
68. % SF loans ≤$100G (106)
69. % $ vol SB loans to bus w/rev≤$1M (106,110)
70. % $ vol SF loans to SF w/rev≤$1M (106)
71. % $ vol CON loans to LMI persons cf % $ vol CON loans to persons at other income levels (115)
72. % increase HMDA loans to LMI persons (100,110)
73. % increase $ vol HMDA loans to LMI persons (110)
74. % increase HMDA loans to LI persons (105,111)
75. % increase HMDA loans to MI persons (105,111)
76. % increase HMDA loans to LMI persons cf % increase HMDA loans (110)
77. % increase $ vol HMDA loans to LMI persons cf % increase $ vol HMDA loans (110)
78. MS SB loans to bus w/rev≤$1M cf overall MS loans to bus (104,107,108)
79. Decrease # SF loans (106)

80. % $ vol SB loans to bus w/rev≤$1M cf % total loans to such bus (101)
81. % $ vol SF loans to SF w/rev≤ $1M (106)
82. MS rank $ vol HMDA loans to LMI persons (110)

The CRA Performance Test for Small Retail Banks

LDR

1. LDR (121-123,125-128,130,132-133,136)
2. LDR cf LDR peer group or comparable banks (121-128,130-132,134-136)
3. LDR cf state LDR (128,133)
4. LDR cf national LDR (128,132)
5. LDR improvement (121,131)

AA Concentration

6. % loans in AA (121-128,130-136)
7. % $ vol loans in AA (121-123,125-128,130-136)
8. # loans in AA (132)

Lending to Borrowers of Different Incomes

9. % loans to LMI, LI, or MI persons cf agg % (122,128,131)
10. % $ vol loans to LI or MI persons cf agg % (131)
11. % loans to LI, MI, or LMI persons cf % AA's LMI, LI, or MI fam (122-123,126,130-132,134-135)
12. % $ vol loans to LMI, LI, or MI persons cf % AA's LMI, LI, or MI fam (122,123,132,134)
13. % SB loans to bus w/rev<$100G cf % AA's such bus (126,133)
14. % $ vol SB loans to bus w/rev<$100G cf % AA's such bus (133)
15. % SB loans to bus w/rev≤$1M cf % AA's such bus (123,133)
16. % $ vol SB loans to bus w/rev≤$1M cf % AA's such bus (123,124,133)
17. % SB loans to bus w/rev≤$1M cf agg % (124,128)

18. % $ vol SB loans to bus w/rev≤$1M cf agg % (124,128)
19. % SF loans to farms w/rev≤$1M cf % AA's such farms (123)
20. % $ vol SF loans to farms w/rev≤$1M cf % AA's such farms (123)
21. % HMDA or MV loans to LI or MI persons (121,131)
22. % $ vol HMDA or MV loans to LI or MI persons (121)
23. % SB loans ≤$100G (121,132)
24. % SB loans to bus w/rev≤$1M (125)
25. % $ vol SB loans to bus w/rev≤$1M (125)
26. % SF loans≤$100G (121)
27. % SF loans to farms w/rev≤$100G cf % AA's such farms (134)
28. % $ vol SF loans to farms w/rev≤$100G cf % AA's such farms (134)
29. % SF loans to farms w/rev≤$250G cf % AA's such farms (126)
30. % $ vol SF loans to farms w/rev≤$250G cf % AA's such farms (126)

Geographic Distribution of Lending

31. % SB loans in LI or MI tracts cf % AA's bus in LI or MI tracts (123,125,128,133)
32. % $ vol SB loans in LI or MI tracts cf % AA's bus in LI or MI tracts (123,128,133)
33. % SF loans in LI or MI tracts cf % AA's farms in LI or MI tracts (123)
34. % $ vol SF loans in LI or MI tracts cf % AA's farms in LI or MI tracts (123)
35. % HMDA loans in LMI, LI, or MI tracts cf agg % (128,131)
36. % HMDA loans in MI tracts (121)
37. % $ vol HMDA loans in MI tracts (121)
38. % HMDA or CON loans in LI or MI tracts cf % AA's fam in LI or MI tracts (130,135)
39. % $ vol HMDA or CON loans in LI or MI tracts cf % AA's fam in LI or MI tracts (130,135)
40. % loans in LMI, LI, or MI tracts cf % AA's OOHUs in LMI, LI, or MI tracts (131,135)
41. % $ vol loans in LI or MI tracts cf % AA's OOHUs in LI or MI tracts (135)

42. Improvement in % HMDA loans to LI tracts (131)
43. % tracts that received a loan (131)
44. % loans in LI tracts cf % AA's LI tracts (136)
45. % loans in MI tracts cf % AA's MI tracts (136)

Table of Cases

Table of Authorities

Index